Grimm Fairy Tales
MYTHS & LEGENDS

D1199502

zenescope

DISCARD
WIN. RETURN
MOOSE JAW PUBLIC LIBRARY

Grimm Fairy Tales
MYTHS & LEGENDS

CREATED AND STORY BY
RAVEN GREGORY
JOE BRUSHA
RALPH TEDESCO
TROY BROWNFIELD

TRADE DESIGN BY
CHRISTOPHER COTE
KATIE HIDALGO

TRADE EDITED BY
RALPH TEDESCO
MATT ROGERS

THIS VOLUME REPRINTS THE COMIC
SERIES GRIMM FAIRY TALES MYTHS &
LEGENDS ISSUES #18-21 AND GRIMM
FAIRY TALES ISSUE #3 PUBLISHED BY
ZENESCOPE ENTERTAINMENT.

WWW.ZENESCOPE.COM

FIRST EDITION, NOVEMBER 2012
ISBN: 978-1-937068-64-6

WWW.ZENESCOPE.COM
FACEBOOK.COM/ZENESCOPE

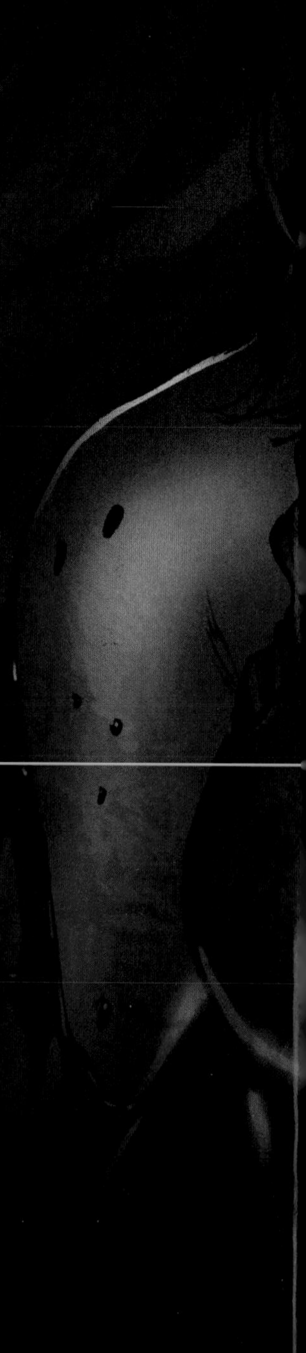

ZENESCOPE ENTERTAINMENT, INC.
Joe Brusha • President & Chief Creative Officer
Ralph Tedesco • Editor-in-Chief
Jennifer Bermel • Director of Licensing & Business Development
Raven Gregory • Executive Editor
Anthony Spay • Art Director
Christopher Cote • Production Manager
Dave Franchini • Direct Market Sales & Customer Service
Stephen Haberman • Marketing Manager

Grimm Fairy Tales Myths & Legends Trade Paperback Vol.
4, November, 2012. First Printing. Published by Zenescope
Entertainment Inc., 433 Caredean Drive, Ste. C, Horsham,
Pennsylvania 19044. Zenescope and its logos are ® and
© 2012 Zenescope Entertainment Inc. all rights reserved.
Grimm Fairy Tales Myths & Legends, its logo and all
characters and their likeness are © and ™ 2012 Zenescope
Entertainment. Any similarities to persons (living or dead),
events, institutions, or locales are purely coincidental. No
portion of this publication may be reproduced or transmitted,
in any form or by any means, without the express written
permission of Zenescope Entertainment Inc. except for
artwork used for review purposes. Printed in Canada.

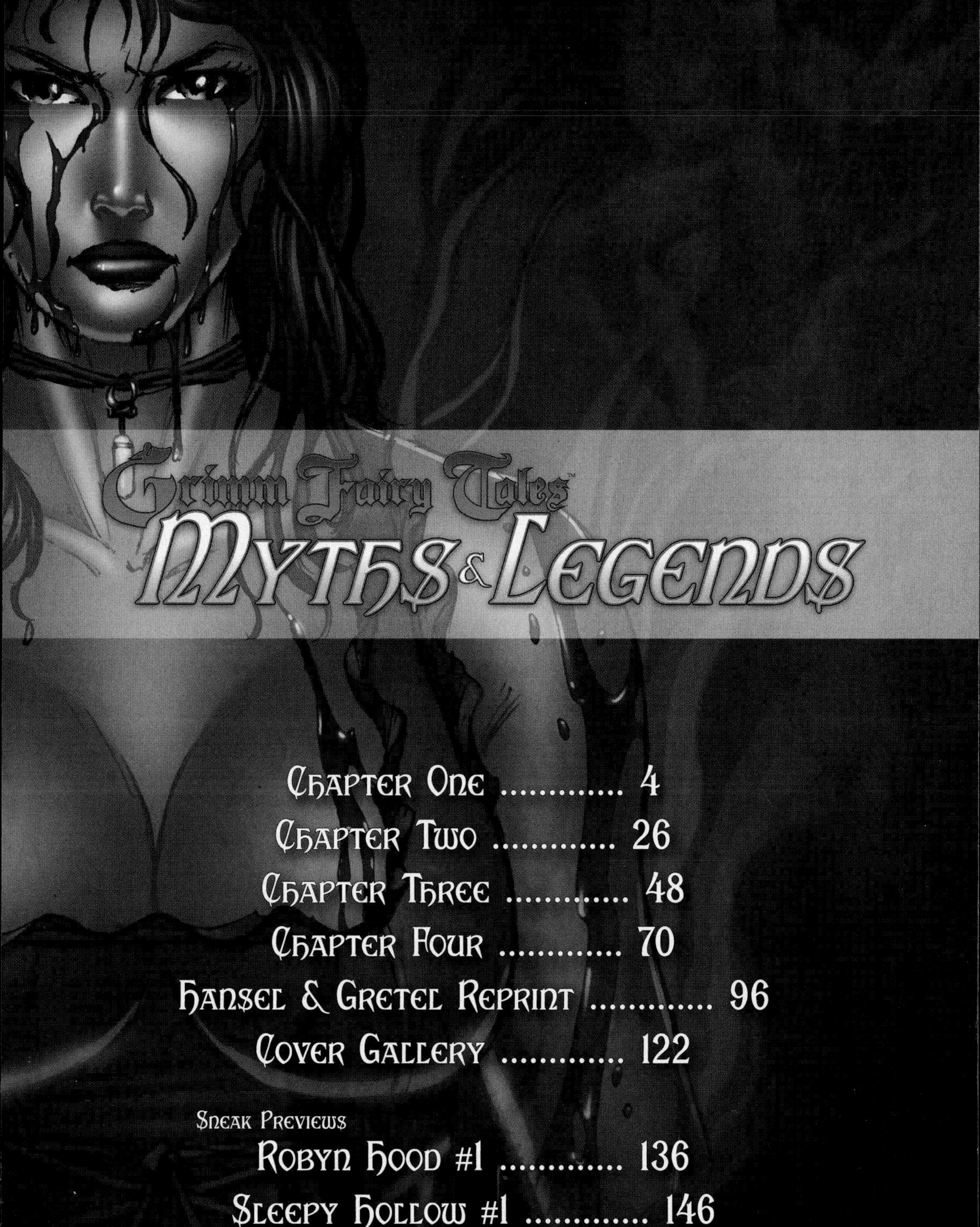
Grimm Fairy Tales™
Myths & Legends

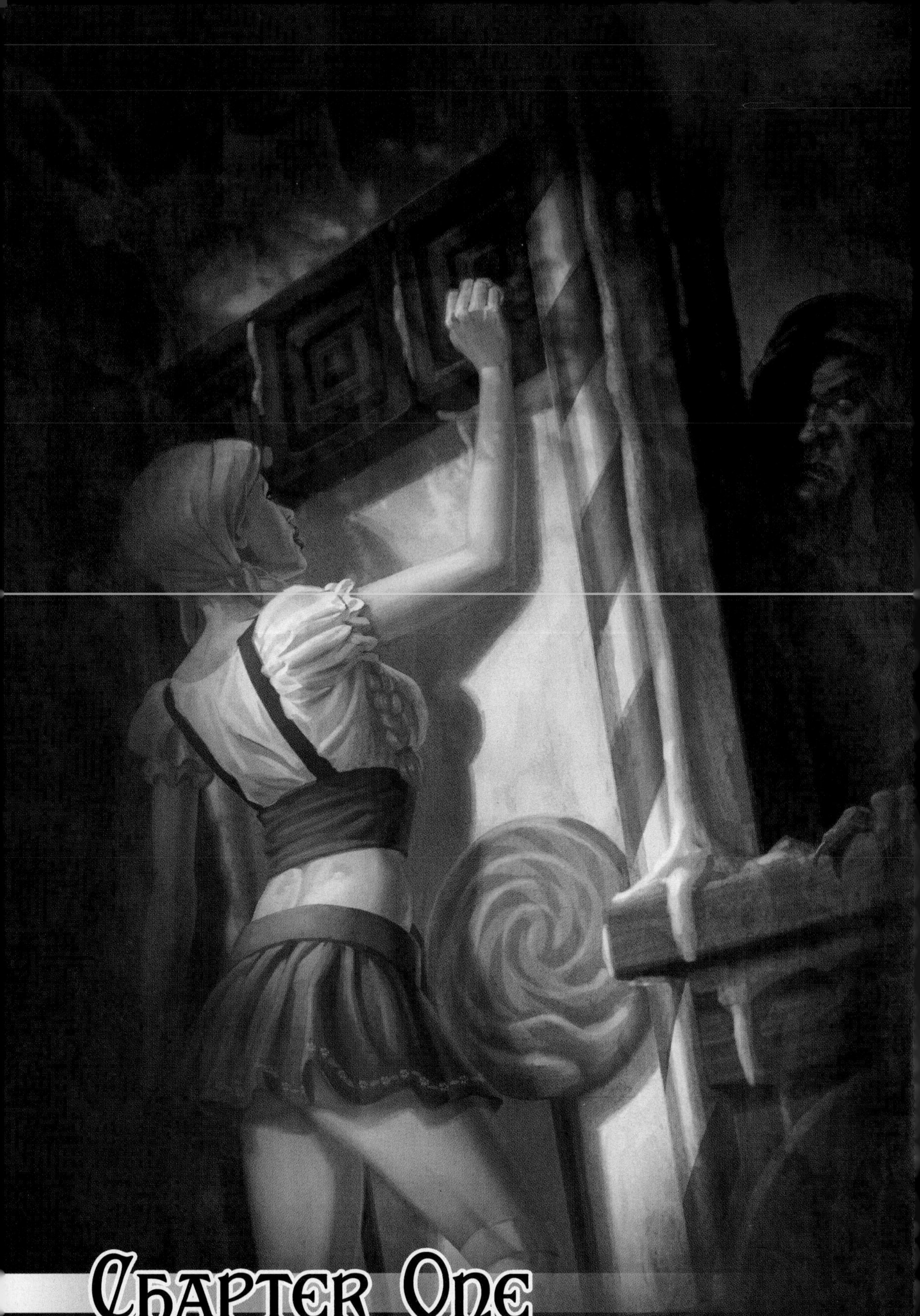

Chapter One

Story by Raven Gregory, Joe Brusha, Ralph Tedesco and Troy Brownfield

Written by Troy Brownfield • Art by Josh Hood

Colors by Roland Pilcz • Letters by Jim Campbell

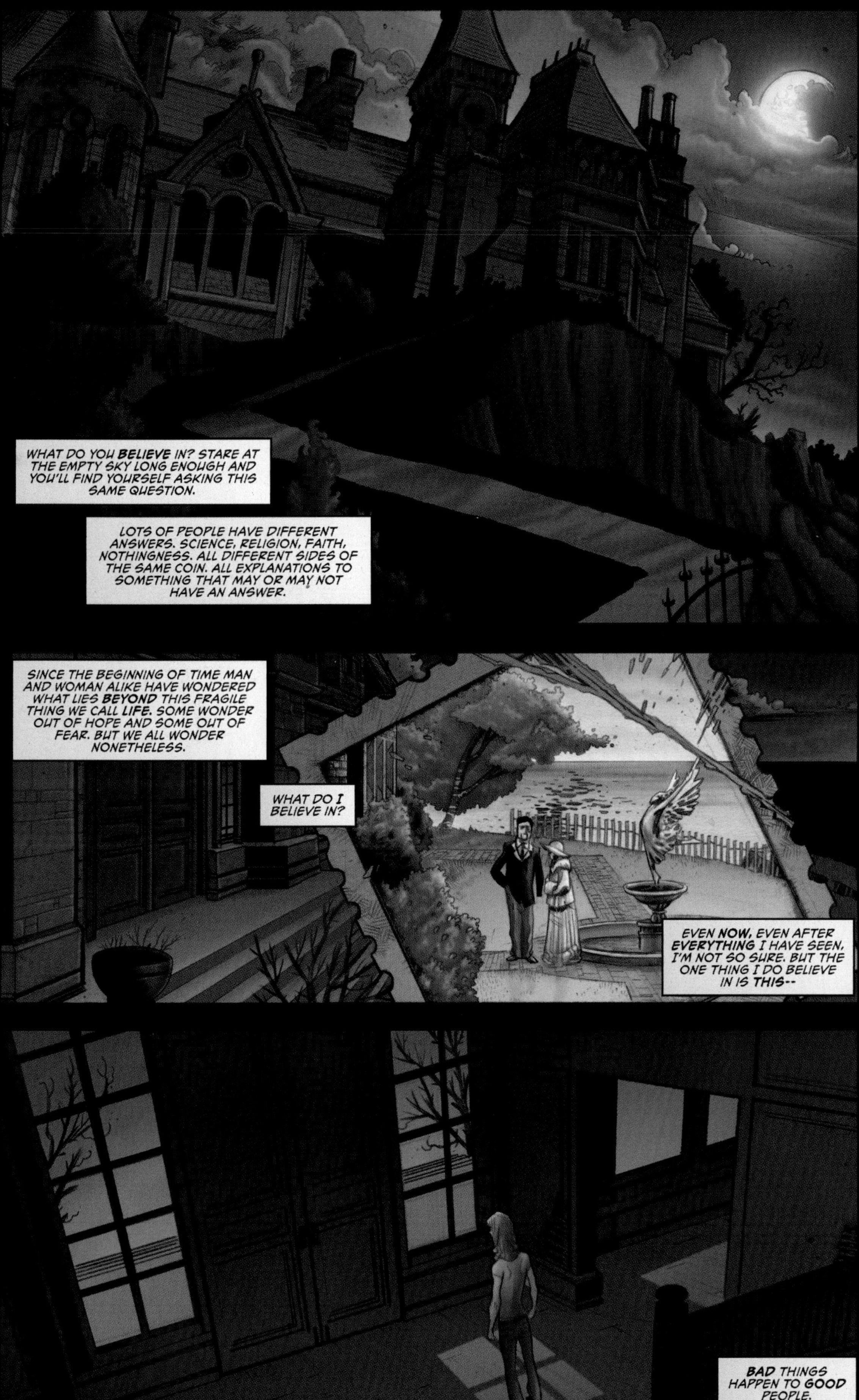
WHAT DO YOU **BELIEVE** IN? STARE AT THE EMPTY SKY LONG ENOUGH AND YOU'LL FIND YOURSELF ASKING THIS SAME QUESTION.
LOTS OF PEOPLE HAVE DIFFERENT ANSWERS. SCIENCE, RELIGION, FAITH, NOTHINGNESS. ALL DIFFERENT SIDES OF THE SAME COIN. ALL EXPLANATIONS TO SOMETHING THAT MAY OR MAY NOT HAVE AN ANSWER.
SINCE THE BEGINNING OF TIME MAN AND WOMAN ALIKE HAVE WONDERED WHAT LIES **BEYOND** THIS FRAGILE THING WE CALL **LIFE**. SOME WONDER OUT OF HOPE AND SOME OUT OF FEAR. BUT WE ALL WONDER NONETHELESS.
WHAT DO **I** BELIEVE IN?
EVEN **NOW**, EVEN AFTER **EVERYTHING** I HAVE SEEN, I'M NOT SO SURE. BUT THE ONE THING I DO BELIEVE IN IS **THIS**--
BAD THINGS HAPPEN TO **GOOD** PEOPLE.

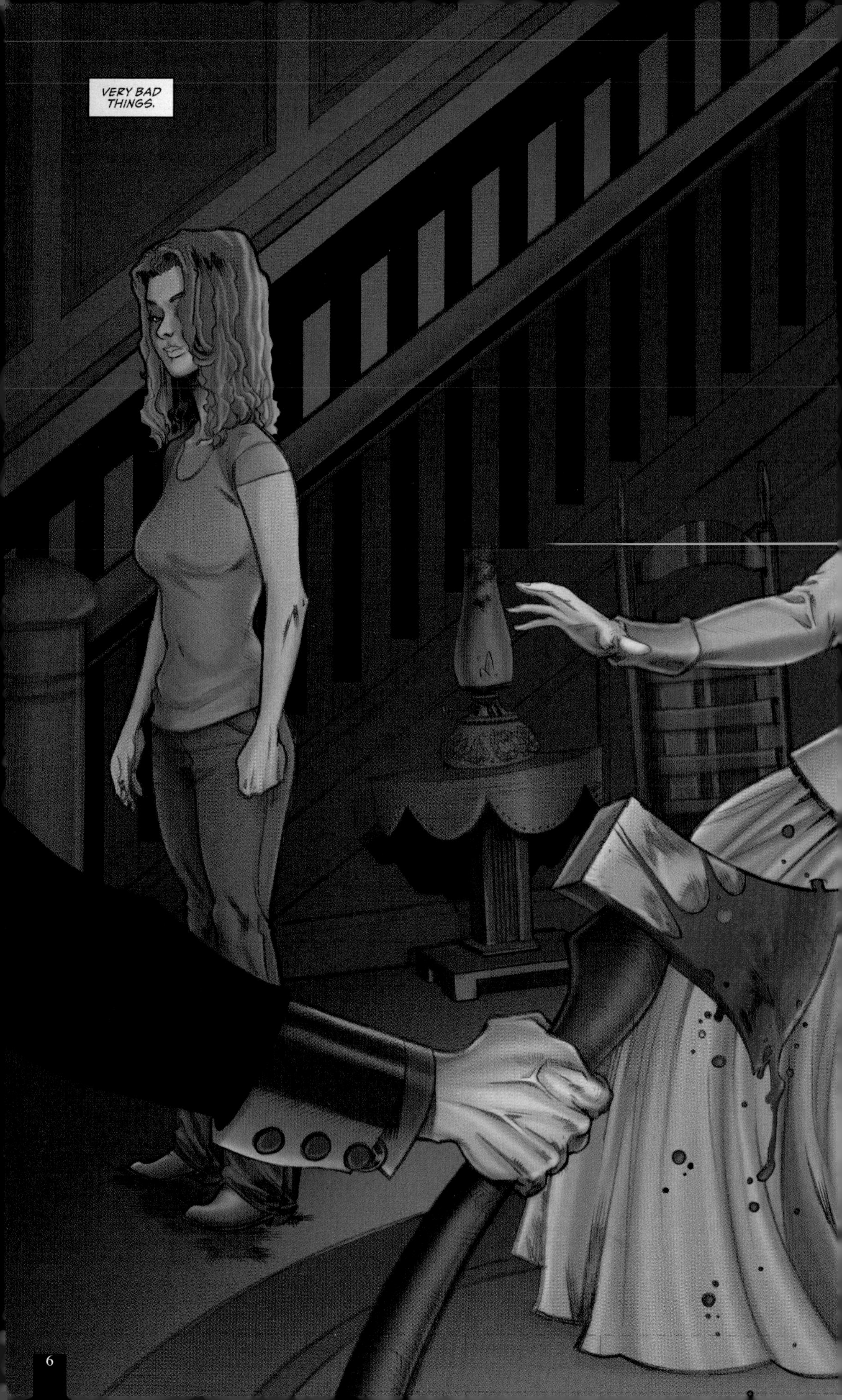
VERY BAD THINGS.

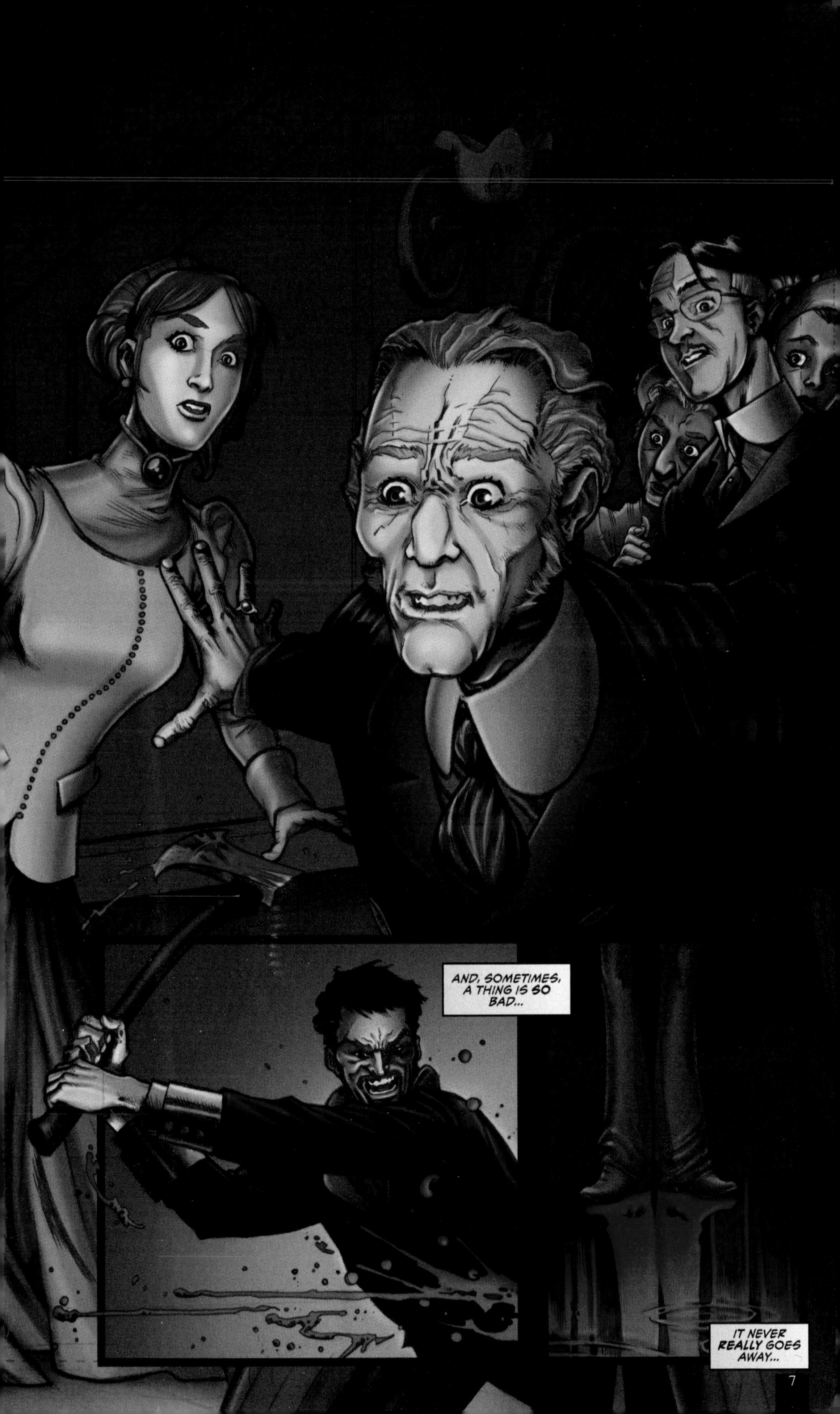
AND, SOMETIMES, A THING IS SO BAD...
IT NEVER REALLY GOES AWAY...

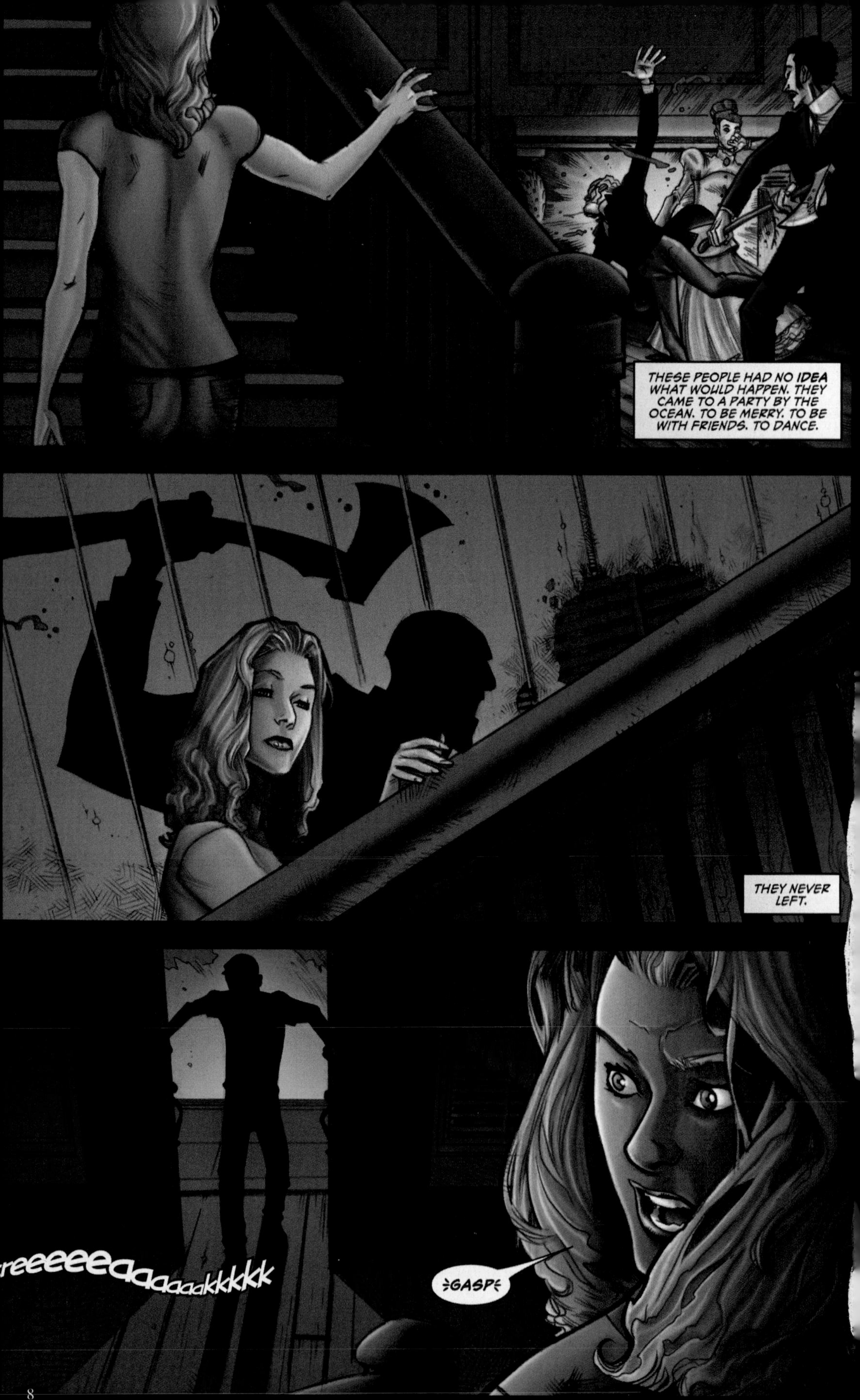
THESE PEOPLE HAD NO IDEA WHAT WOULD HAPPEN. THEY CAME TO A PARTY BY THE OCEAN. TO BE MERRY. TO BE WITH FRIENDS. TO DANCE.
THEY NEVER LEFT.
creeeeeeaaaaaakkkkk
GASP

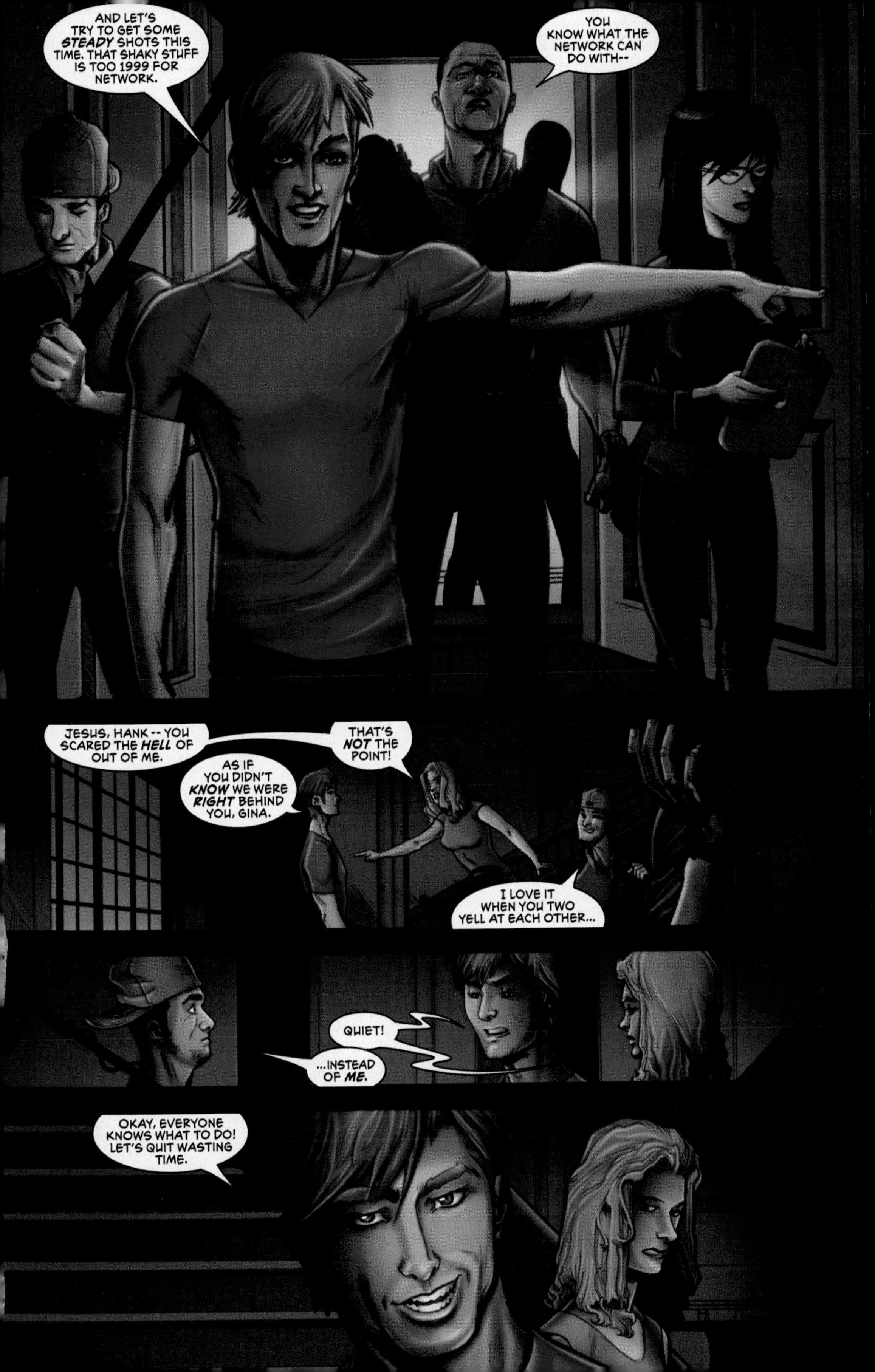
AND LET'S TRY TO GET SOME STEADY SHOTS THIS TIME. THAT SHAKY STUFF IS TOO 1999 FOR NETWORK.
YOU KNOW WHAT THE NETWORK CAN DO WITH--
JESUS, HANK -- YOU SCARED THE HELL OF OUT OF ME.
THAT'S NOT THE POINT!
AS IF YOU DIDN'T KNOW WE WERE RIGHT BEHIND YOU, GINA.
I LOVE IT WHEN YOU TWO YELL AT EACH OTHER...
QUIET!
...INSTEAD OF ME.
OKAY, EVERYONE KNOWS WHAT TO DO! LET'S QUIT WASTING TIME.

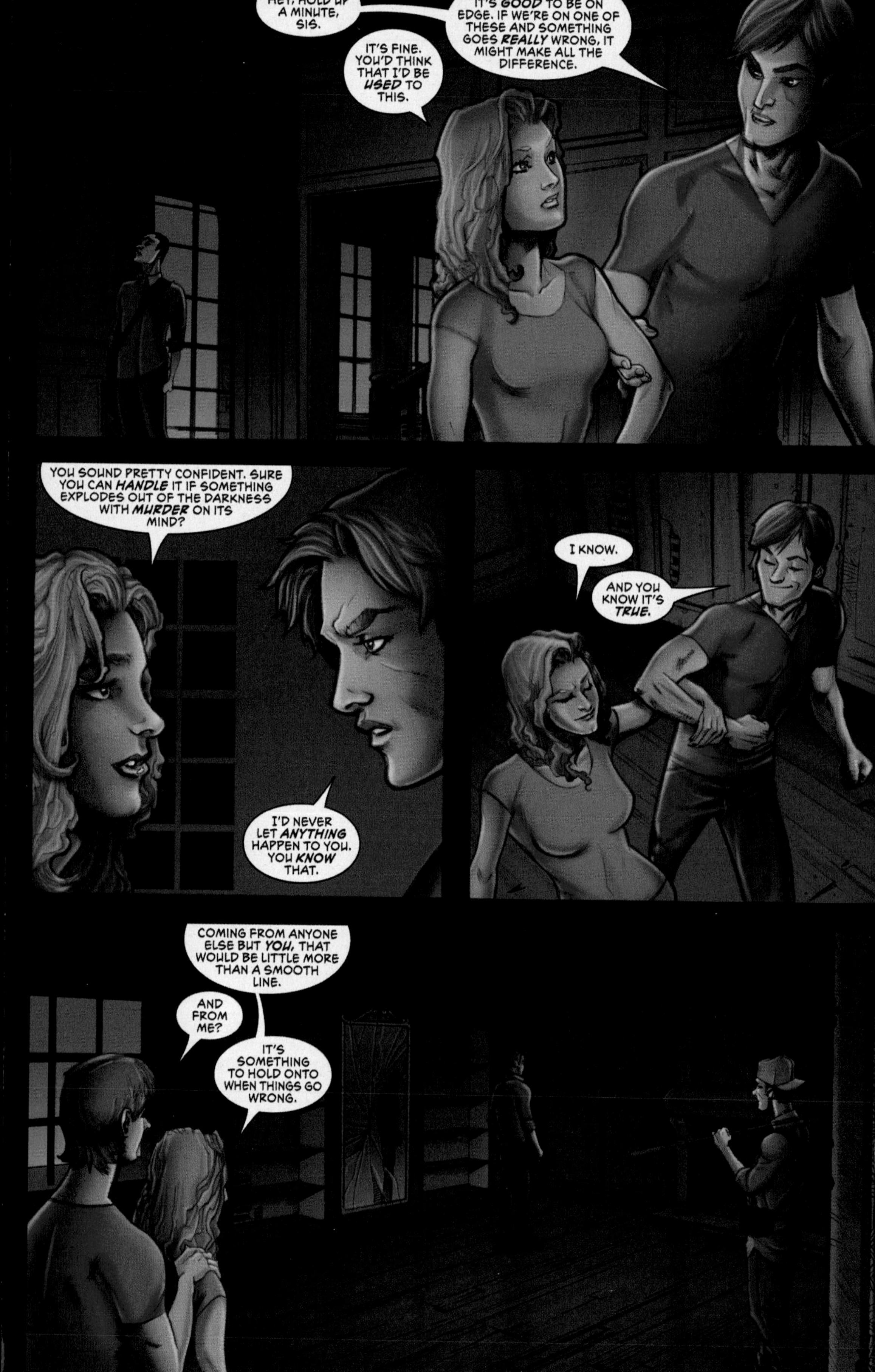

HEY, HOLD UP A MINUTE, SIS.
IT'S GOOD TO BE ON EDGE. IF WE'RE ON ONE OF THESE AND SOMETHING GOES REALLY WRONG, IT MIGHT MAKE ALL THE DIFFERENCE.
IT'S FINE. YOU'D THINK THAT I'D BE USED TO THIS.
YOU SOUND PRETTY CONFIDENT. SURE YOU CAN HANDLE IT IF SOMETHING EXPLODES OUT OF THE DARKNESS WITH MURDER ON ITS MIND?
I'D NEVER LET ANYTHING HAPPEN TO YOU. YOU KNOW THAT.
I KNOW.
AND YOU KNOW IT'S TRUE.
COMING FROM ANYONE ELSE BUT YOU, THAT WOULD BE LITTLE MORE THAN A SMOOTH LINE.
AND FROM ME?
IT'S SOMETHING TO HOLD ONTO WHEN THINGS GO WRONG.

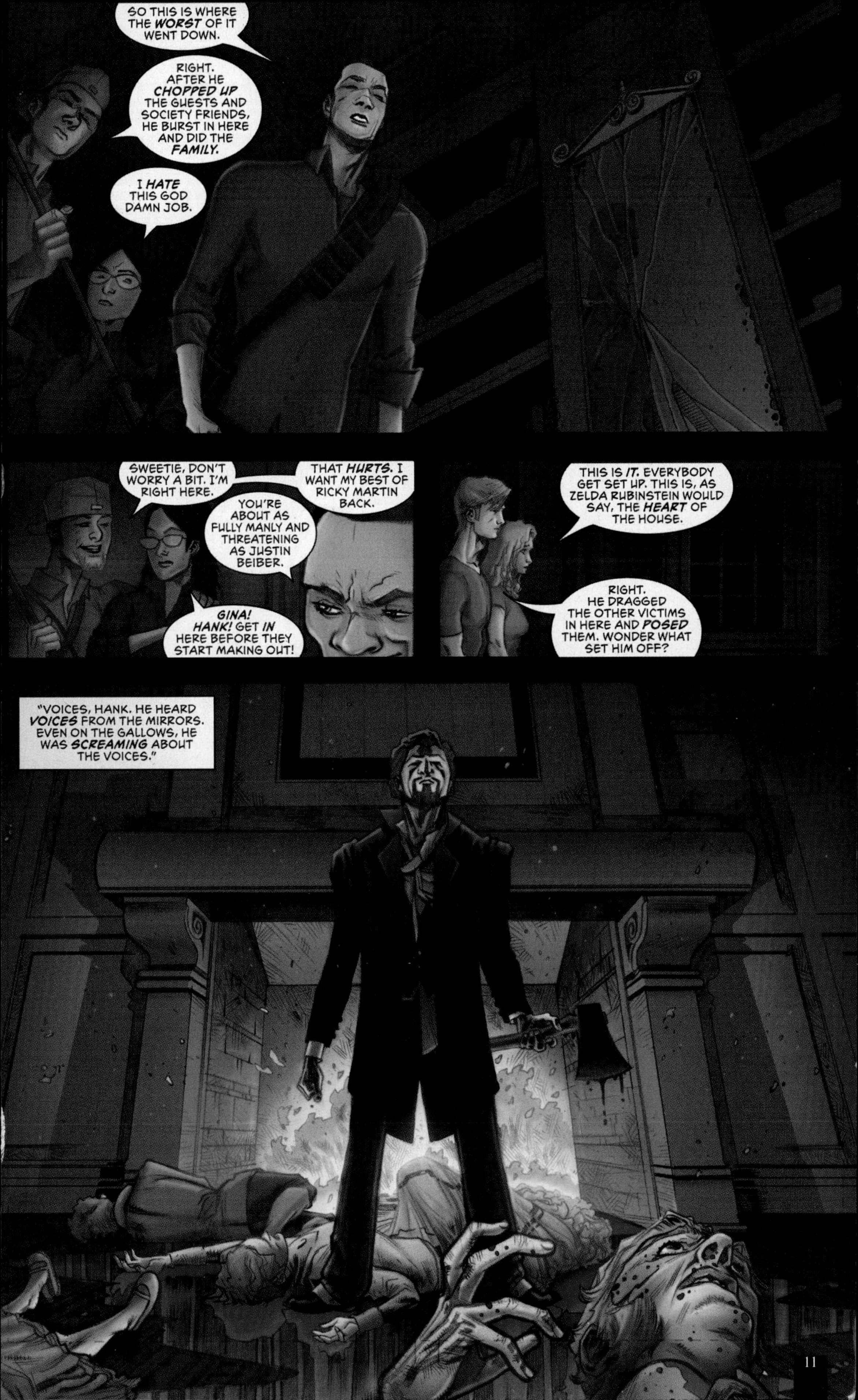

SO THIS IS WHERE THE WORST OF IT WENT DOWN.
RIGHT. AFTER HE CHOPPED UP THE GUESTS AND SOCIETY FRIENDS, HE BURST IN HERE AND DID THE FAMILY.
I HATE THIS GOD DAMN JOB.
SWEETIE, DON'T WORRY A BIT. I'M RIGHT HERE.
THAT HURTS. I WANT MY BEST OF RICKY MARTIN BACK.
YOU'RE ABOUT AS FULLY MANLY AND THREATENING AS JUSTIN BEIBER.
GINA! HANK! GET IN HERE BEFORE THEY START MAKING OUT!
THIS IS IT. EVERYBODY GET SET UP. THIS IS, AS ZELDA RUBINSTEIN WOULD SAY, THE HEART OF THE HOUSE.
RIGHT. HE DRAGGED THE OTHER VICTIMS IN HERE AND POSED THEM. WONDER WHAT SET HIM OFF?
"VOICES, HANK. HE HEARD VOICES FROM THE MIRRORS. EVEN ON THE GALLOWS, HE WAS SCREAMING ABOUT THE VOICES."

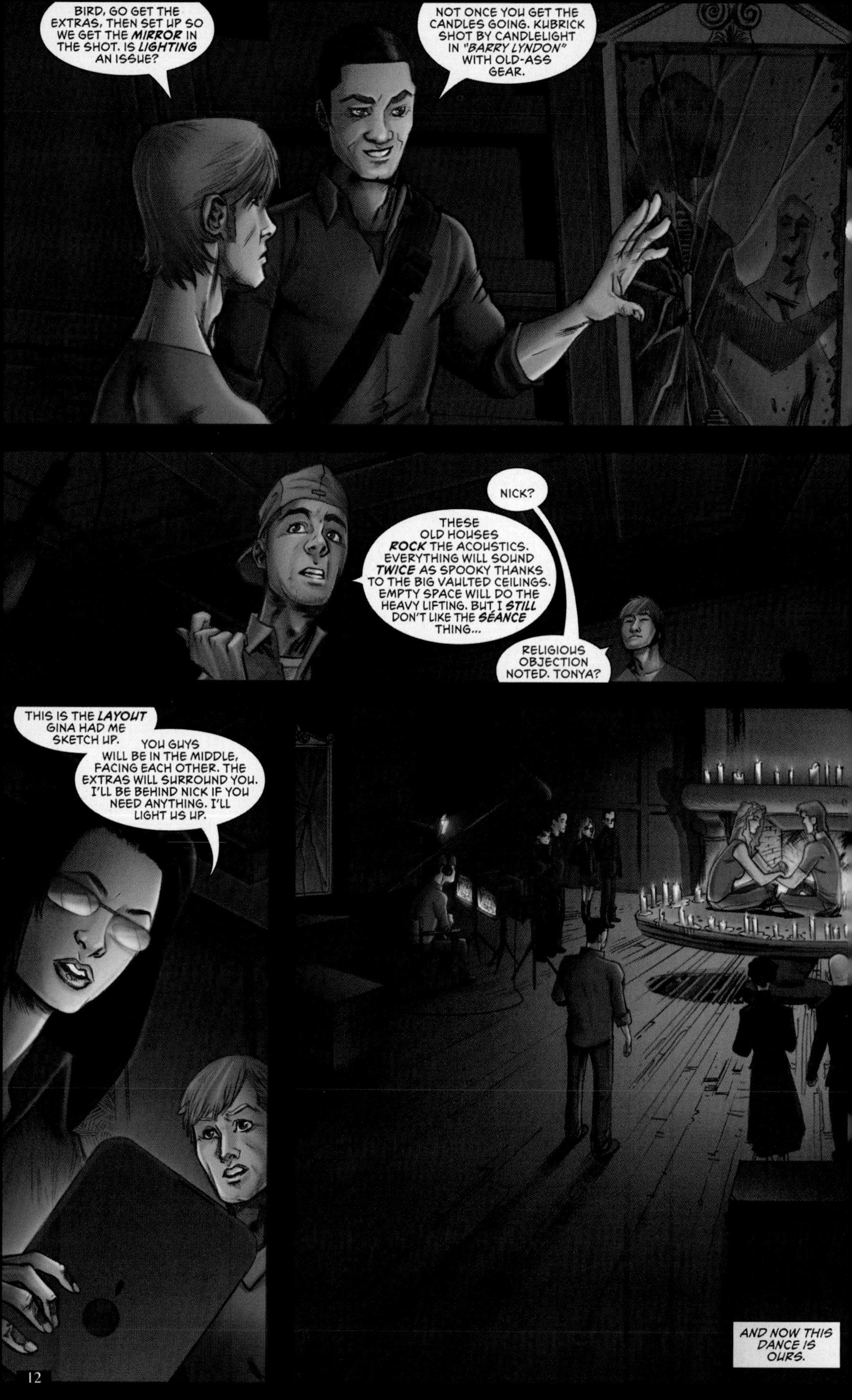

BIRD, GO GET THE EXTRAS, THEN SET UP SO WE GET THE *MIRROR* IN THE SHOT. IS *LIGHTING* AN ISSUE?
NOT ONCE YOU GET THE CANDLES GOING. KUBRICK SHOT BY CANDLELIGHT IN *"BARRY LYNDON"* WITH OLD-ASS GEAR.
NICK?
THESE OLD HOUSES *ROCK* THE ACOUSTICS. EVERYTHING WILL SOUND *TWICE* AS SPOOKY THANKS TO THE BIG VAULTED CEILINGS. EMPTY SPACE WILL DO THE HEAVY LIFTING. BUT I *STILL* DON'T LIKE THE *SÉANCE* THING...
RELIGIOUS OBJECTION NOTED. TONYA?
THIS IS THE *LAYOUT* GINA HAD ME SKETCH UP.
YOU GUYS WILL BE IN THE MIDDLE, FACING EACH OTHER. THE EXTRAS WILL SURROUND YOU. I'LL BE BEHIND NICK IF YOU NEED ANYTHING. I'LL LIGHT US UP.
AND NOW THIS DANCE IS OURS.

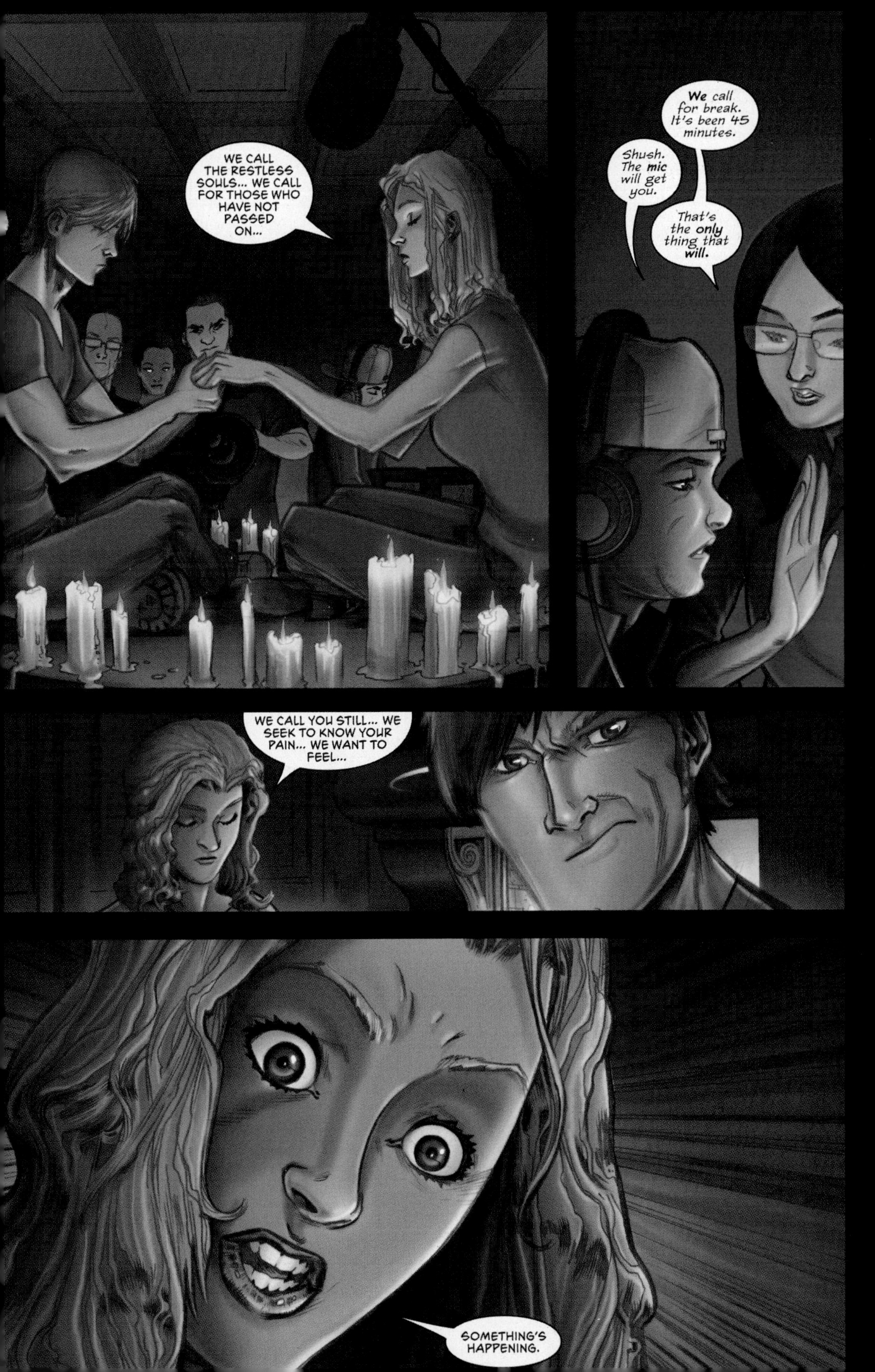

WE CALL THE RESTLESS SOULS... WE CALL FOR THOSE WHO HAVE NOT PASSED ON...
We call for break. It's been 45 minutes.
Shush. The mic will get you.
That's the only thing that will.
WE CALL YOU STILL... WE SEEK TO KNOW YOUR PAIN... WE WANT TO FEEL...
SOMETHING'S HAPPENING.

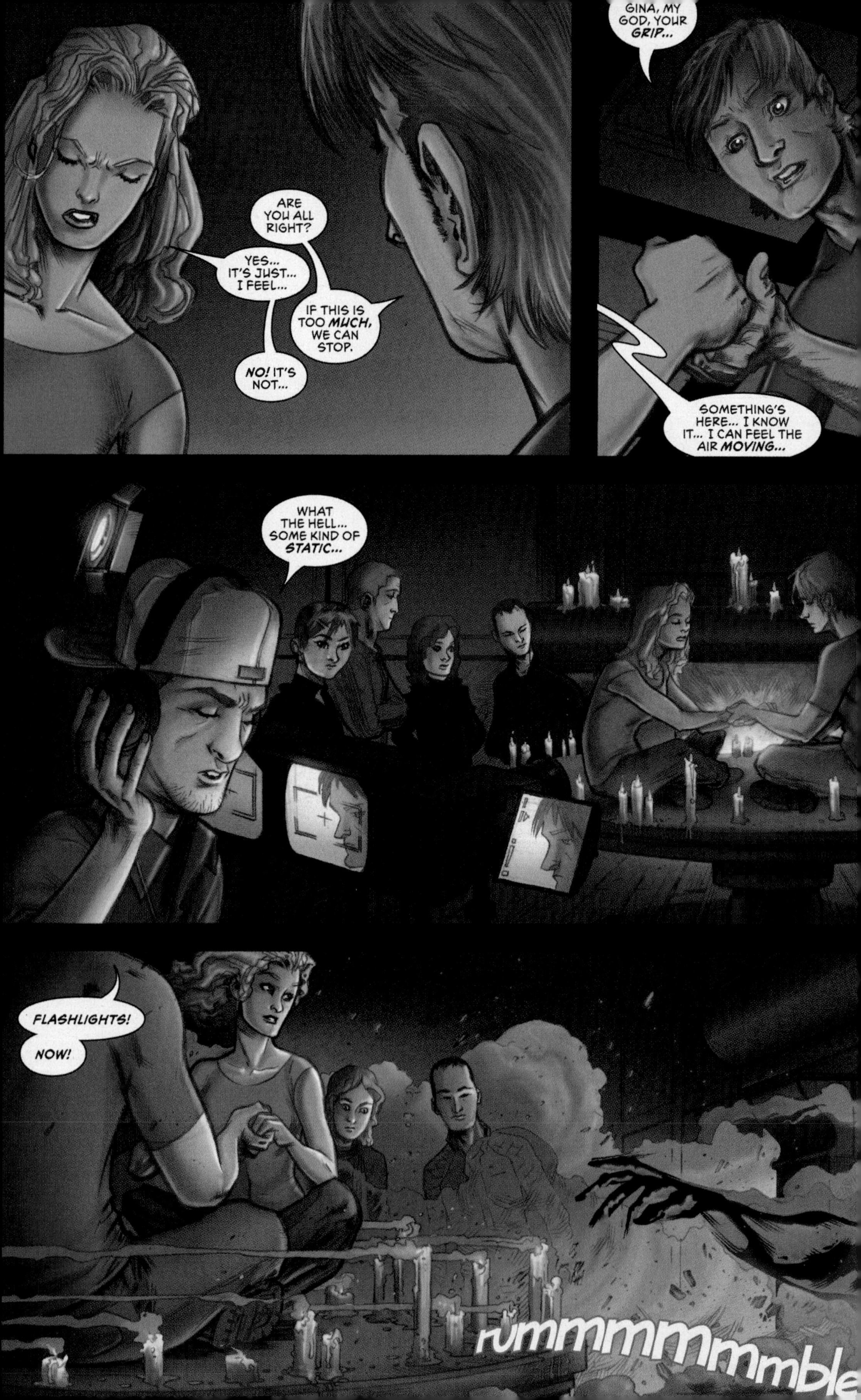
ARE YOU ALL RIGHT?
YES... IT'S JUST... I FEEL...
IF THIS IS TOO MUCH, WE CAN STOP.
NO! IT'S NOT...
GINA, MY GOD, YOUR GRIP...
SOMETHING'S HERE... I KNOW IT... I CAN FEEL THE AIR MOVING...
WHAT THE HELL... SOME KIND OF STATIC...
FLASHLIGHTS!
NOW!
rummmmmmmble

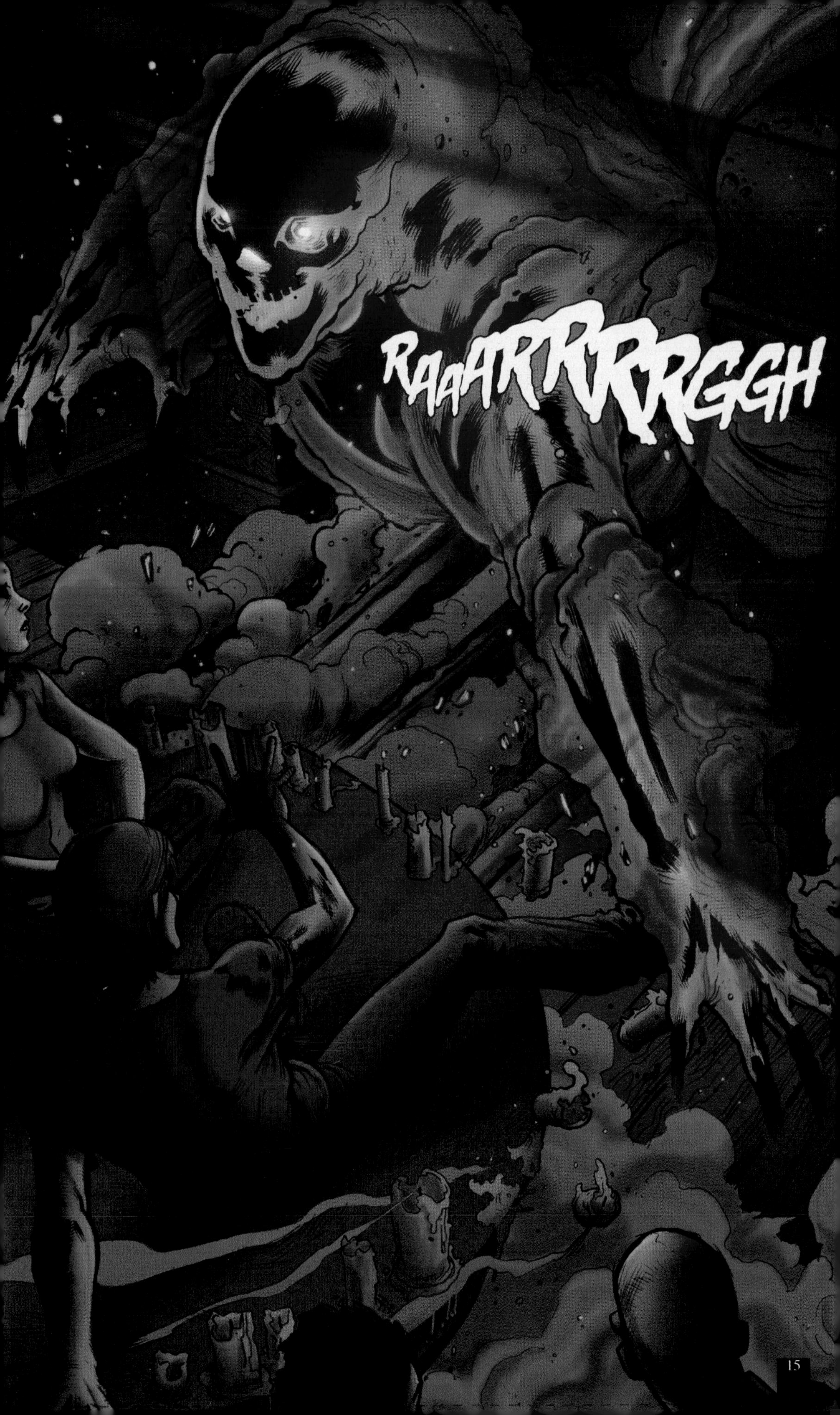
RAAARRRRGGH

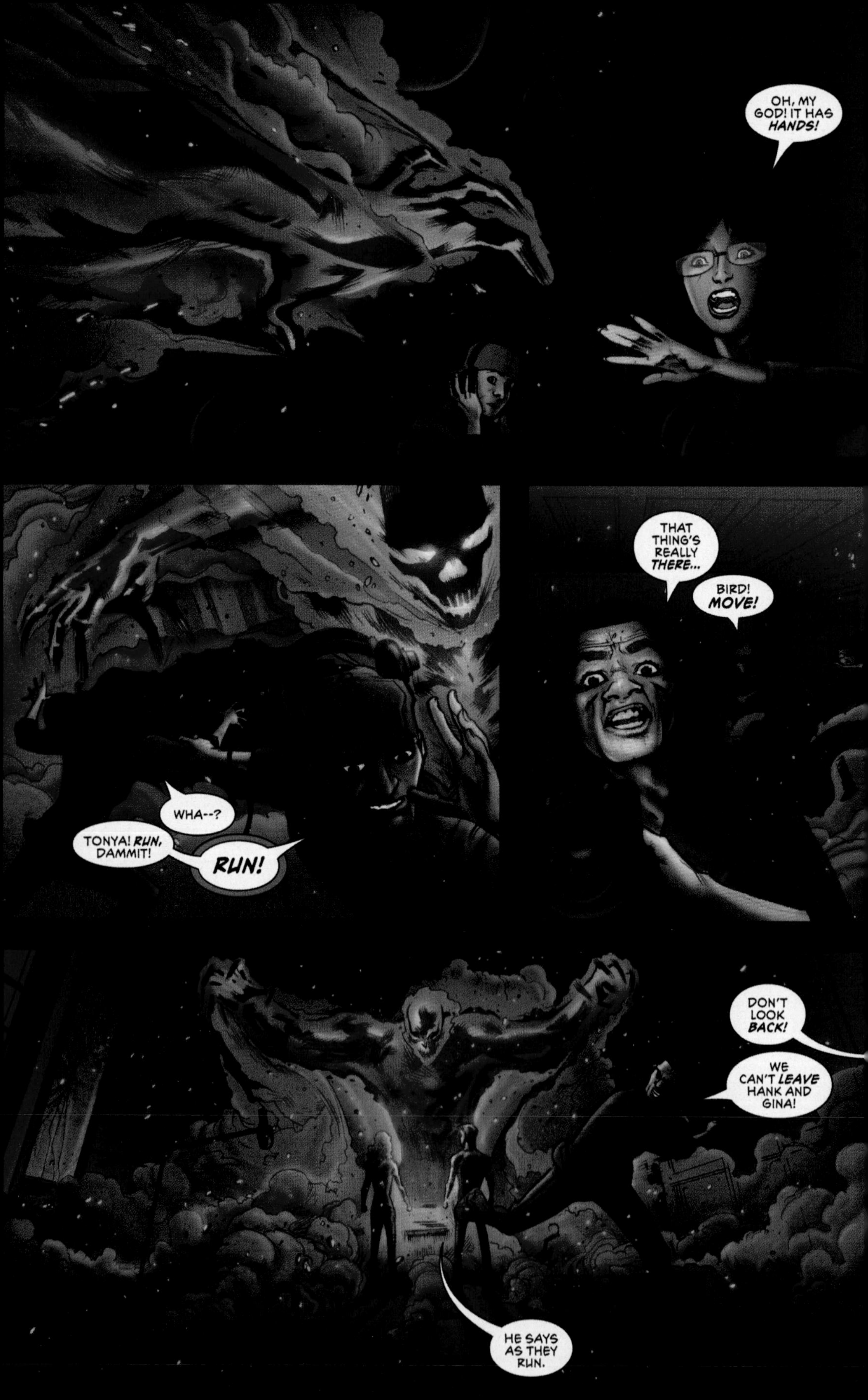
OH, MY GOD! IT HAS HANDS!
THAT THING'S REALLY THERE...
BIRD! MOVE!
WHA--?
TONYA! RUN, DAMMIT!
RUN!
DON'T LOOK BACK!
WE CAN'T LEAVE HANK AND GINA!
HE SAYS AS THEY RUN.

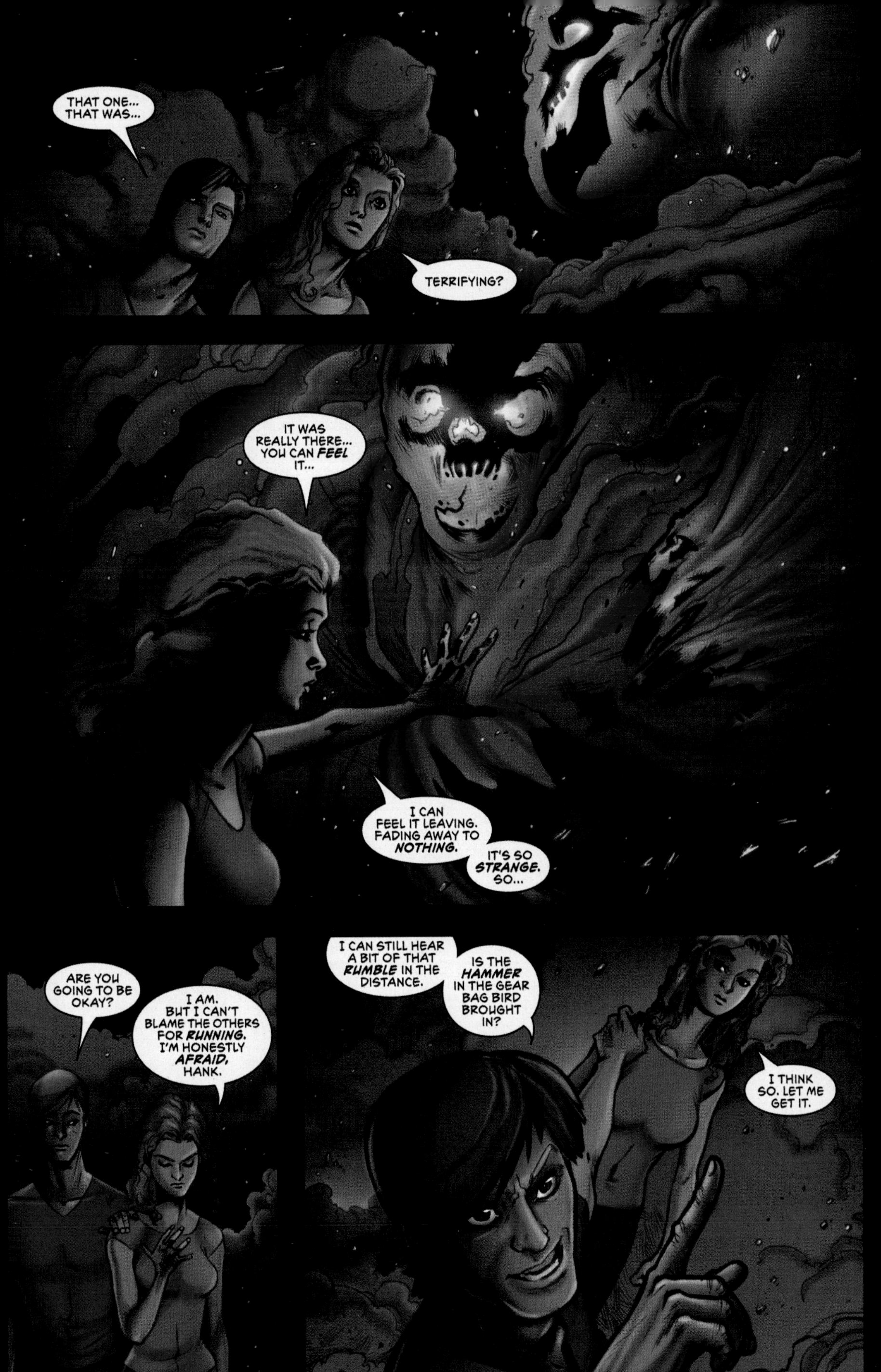
THAT ONE... THAT WAS...
TERRIFYING?
IT WAS REALLY THERE... YOU CAN FEEL IT...
I CAN FEEL IT LEAVING. FADING AWAY TO NOTHING.
IT'S SO STRANGE. SO...
ARE YOU GOING TO BE OKAY?
I AM. BUT I CAN'T BLAME THE OTHERS FOR RUNNING. I'M HONESTLY AFRAID, HANK.
I CAN STILL HEAR A BIT OF THAT RUMBLE IN THE DISTANCE.
IS THE HAMMER IN THE GEAR BAG BIRD BROUGHT IN?
I THINK SO. LET ME GET IT.

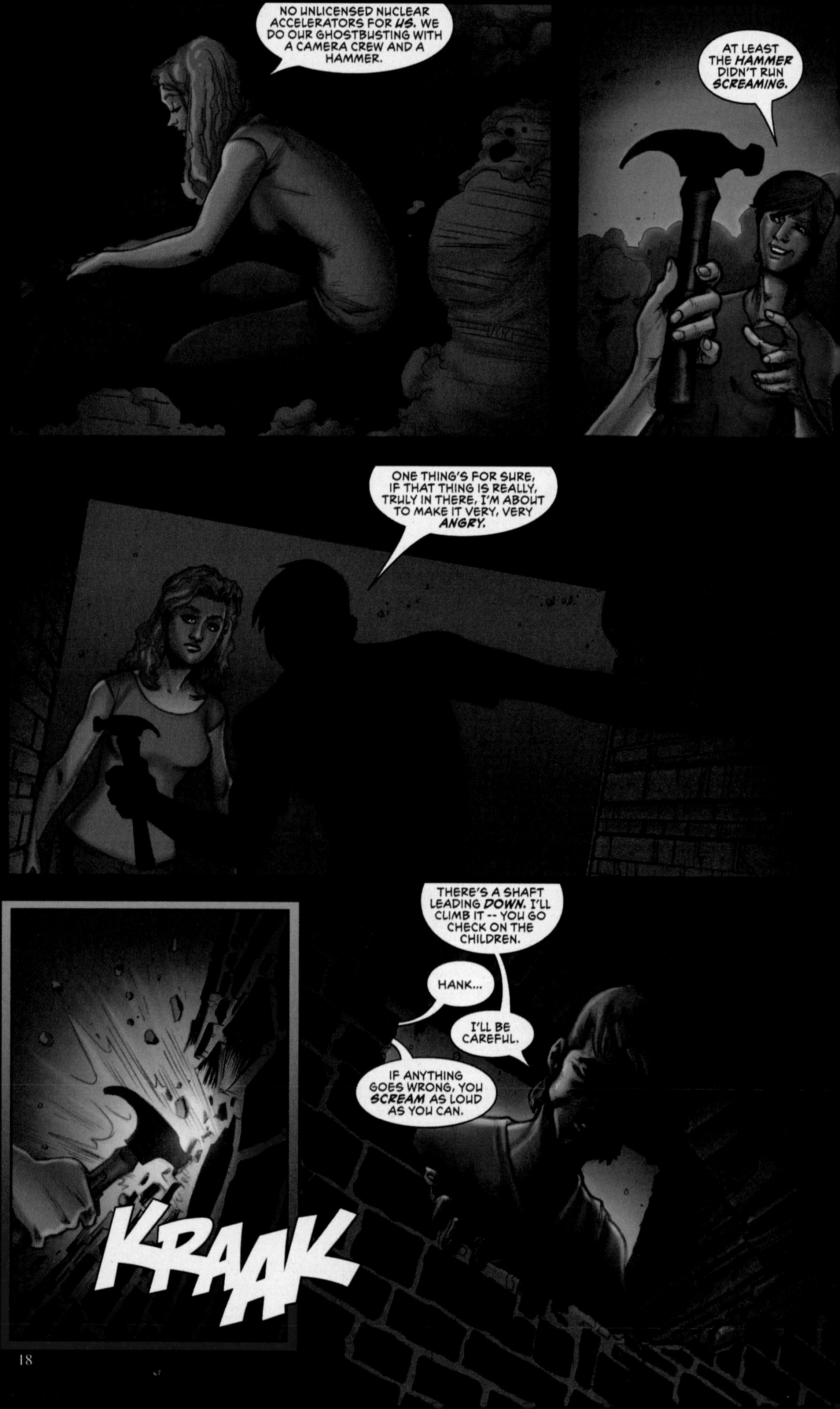
NO UNLICENSED NUCLEAR ACCELERATORS FOR *US*. WE DO OUR GHOSTBUSTING WITH A CAMERA CREW AND A HAMMER.
AT LEAST THE *HAMMER* DIDN'T RUN *SCREAMING*.
ONE THING'S FOR SURE, IF THAT THING IS REALLY, TRULY IN THERE, I'M ABOUT TO MAKE IT VERY, VERY *ANGRY*.
KRAAK
THERE'S A SHAFT LEADING *DOWN*. I'LL CLIMB IT -- YOU GO CHECK ON THE CHILDREN.
HANK...
I'LL BE CAREFUL.
IF ANYTHING GOES WRONG, YOU *SCREAM* AS LOUD AS YOU CAN.

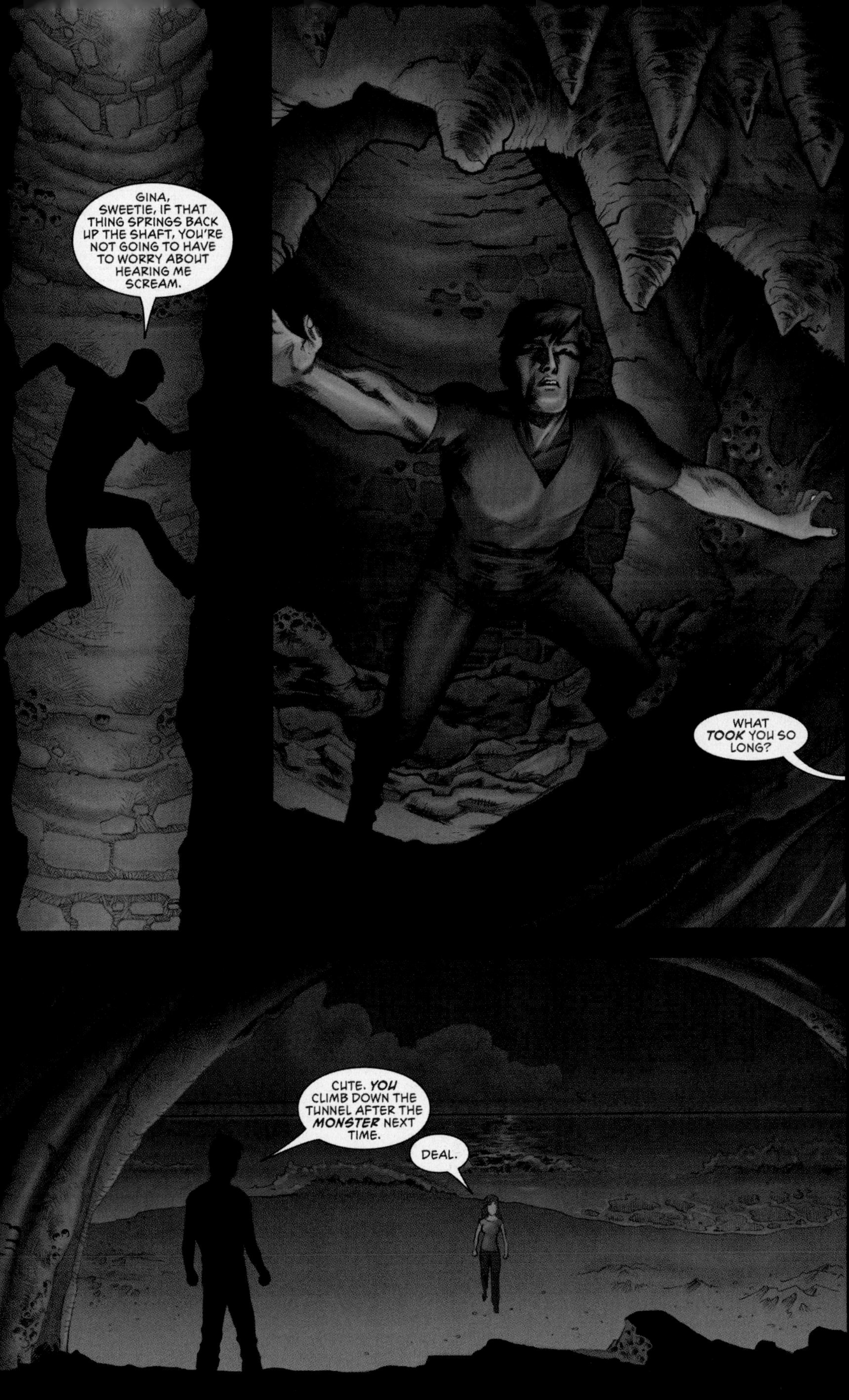
GINA, SWEETIE, IF THAT THING SPRINGS BACK UP THE SHAFT, YOU'RE NOT GOING TO HAVE TO WORRY ABOUT HEARING ME SCREAM.
WHAT TOOK YOU SO LONG?
CUTE. YOU CLIMB DOWN THE TUNNEL AFTER THE MONSTER NEXT TIME.
DEAL.

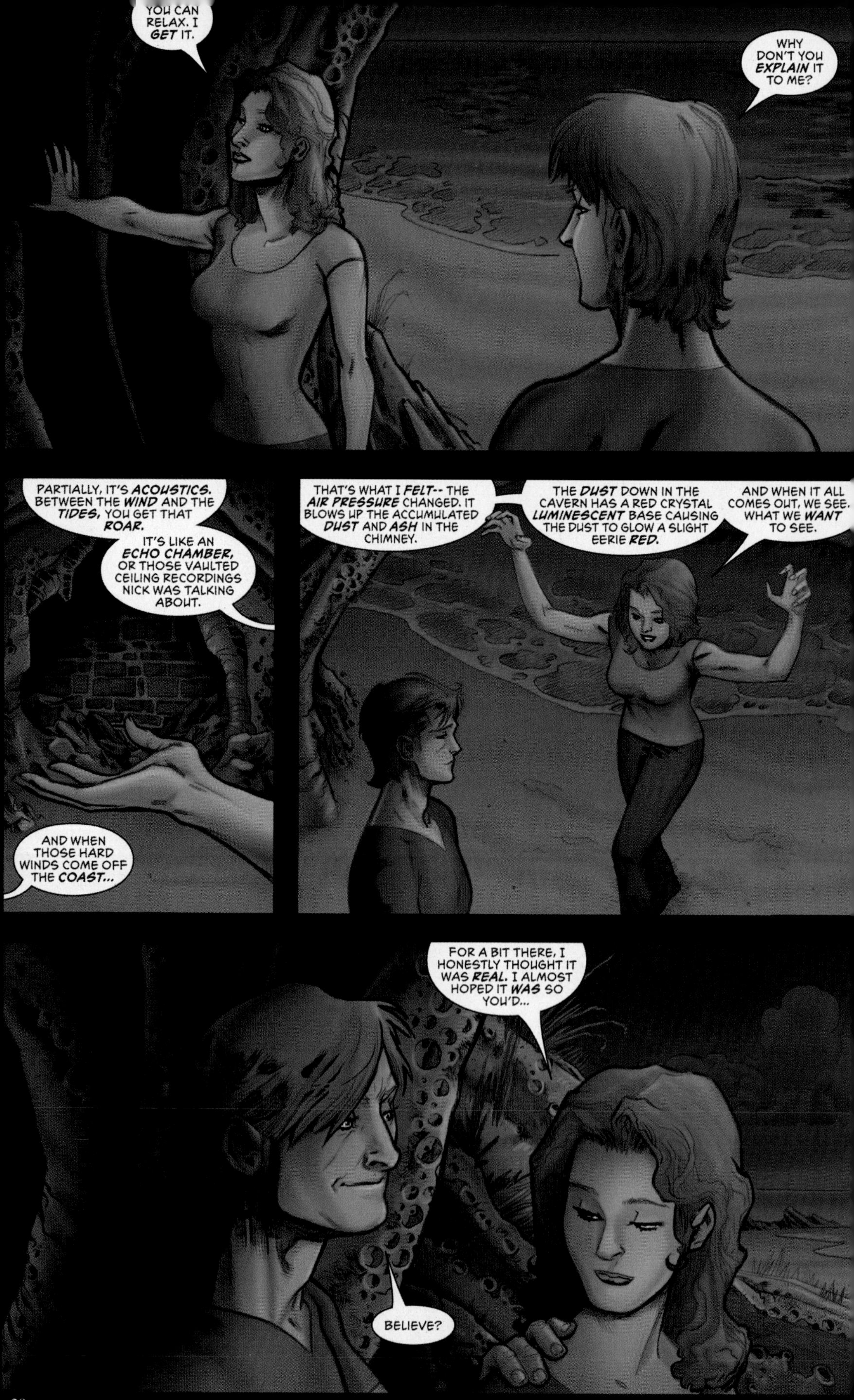
YOU CAN RELAX. I GET IT.
WHY DON'T YOU EXPLAIN IT TO ME?
PARTIALLY, IT'S ACOUSTICS. BETWEEN THE WIND AND THE TIDES, YOU GET THAT ROAR.
IT'S LIKE AN ECHO CHAMBER, OR THOSE VAULTED CEILING RECORDINGS NICK WAS TALKING ABOUT.
AND WHEN THOSE HARD WINDS COME OFF THE COAST...
THAT'S WHAT I FELT-- THE AIR PRESSURE CHANGED. IT BLOWS UP THE ACCUMULATED DUST AND ASH IN THE CHIMNEY.
THE DUST DOWN IN THE CAVERN HAS A RED CRYSTAL LUMINESCENT BASE CAUSING THE DUST TO GLOW A SLIGHT EERIE RED.
AND WHEN IT ALL COMES OUT, WE SEE. WHAT WE WANT TO SEE.
FOR A BIT THERE, I HONESTLY THOUGHT IT WAS REAL. I ALMOST HOPED IT WAS SO YOU'D...
BELIEVE?

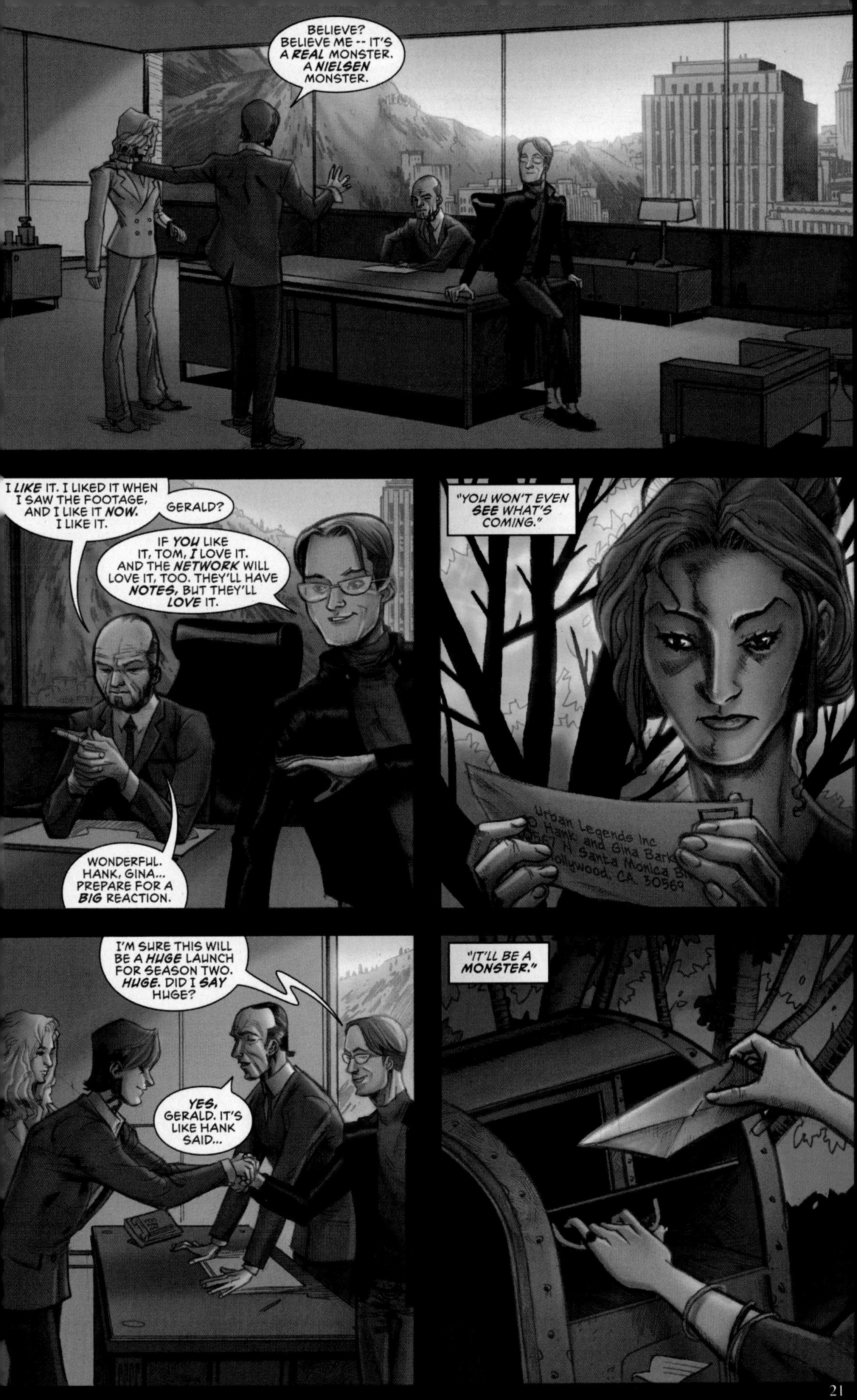
BELIEVE? BELIEVE ME -- IT'S A REAL MONSTER. A NIELSEN MONSTER.
I LIKE IT. I LIKED IT WHEN I SAW THE FOOTAGE, AND I LIKE IT NOW. I LIKE IT.
GERALD?
IF YOU LIKE IT, TOM, I LOVE IT. AND THE NETWORK WILL LOVE IT, TOO. THEY'LL HAVE NOTES, BUT THEY'LL LOVE IT.
WONDERFUL. HANK, GINA... PREPARE FOR A BIG REACTION.
"YOU WON'T EVEN SEE WHAT'S COMING."
Urban Legends Inc
I'M SURE THIS WILL BE A HUGE LAUNCH FOR SEASON TWO. HUGE. DID I SAY HUGE?
YES, GERALD. IT'S LIKE HANK SAID...
"IT'LL BE A MONSTER."

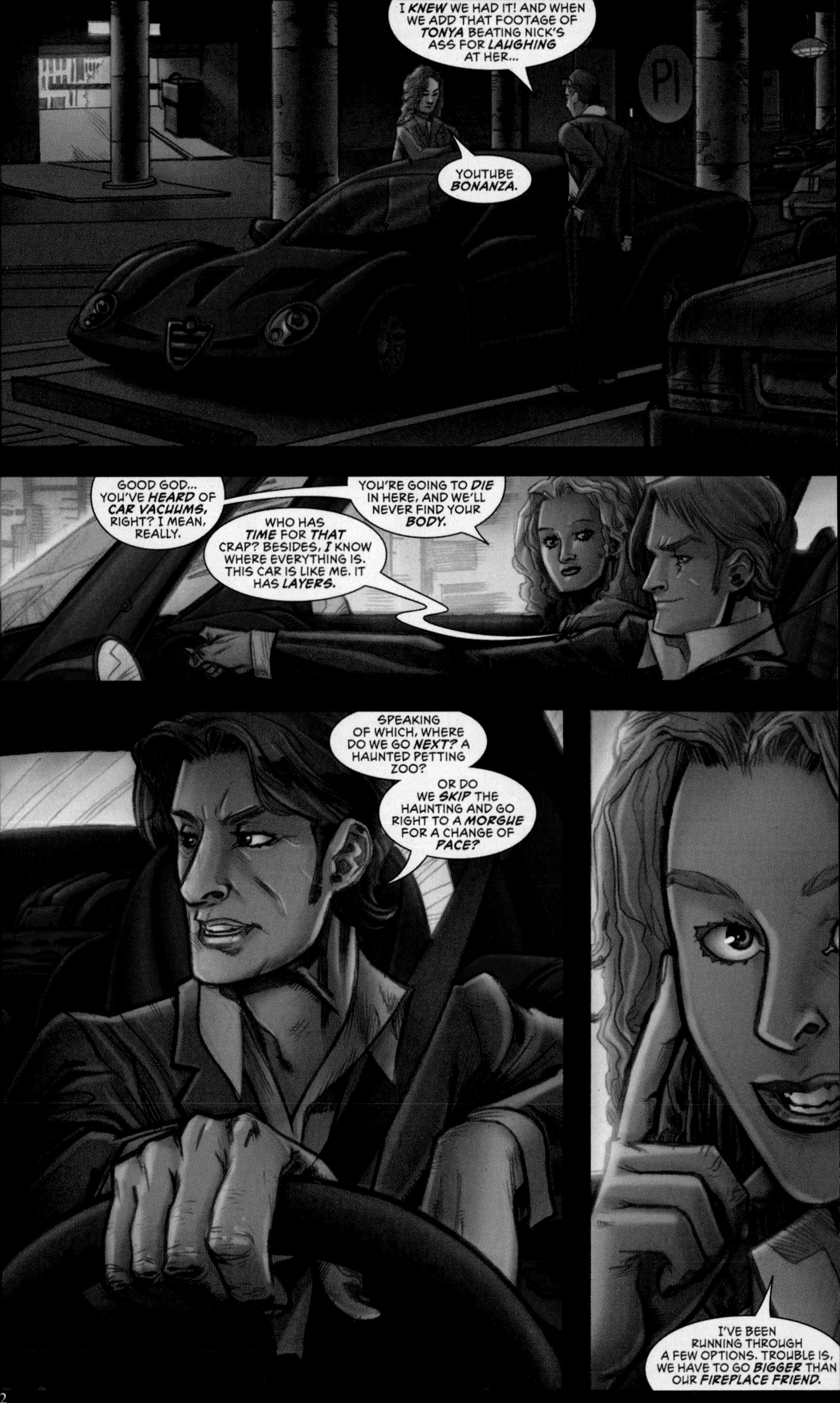
I KNEW WE HAD IT! AND WHEN WE ADD THAT FOOTAGE OF TONYA BEATING NICK'S ASS FOR LAUGHING AT HER...
YOUTUBE BONANZA.
GOOD GOD... YOU'VE HEARD OF CAR VACUUMS, RIGHT? I MEAN, REALLY.
WHO HAS TIME FOR THAT CRAP? BESIDES, I KNOW WHERE EVERYTHING IS. THIS CAR IS LIKE ME. IT HAS LAYERS.
YOU'RE GOING TO DIE IN HERE, AND WE'LL NEVER FIND YOUR BODY.
SPEAKING OF WHICH, WHERE DO WE GO NEXT? A HAUNTED PETTING ZOO?
OR DO WE SKIP THE HAUNTING AND GO RIGHT TO A MORGUE FOR A CHANGE OF PACE?
I'VE BEEN RUNNING THROUGH A FEW OPTIONS. TROUBLE IS, WE HAVE TO GO BIGGER THAN OUR FIREPLACE FRIEND.

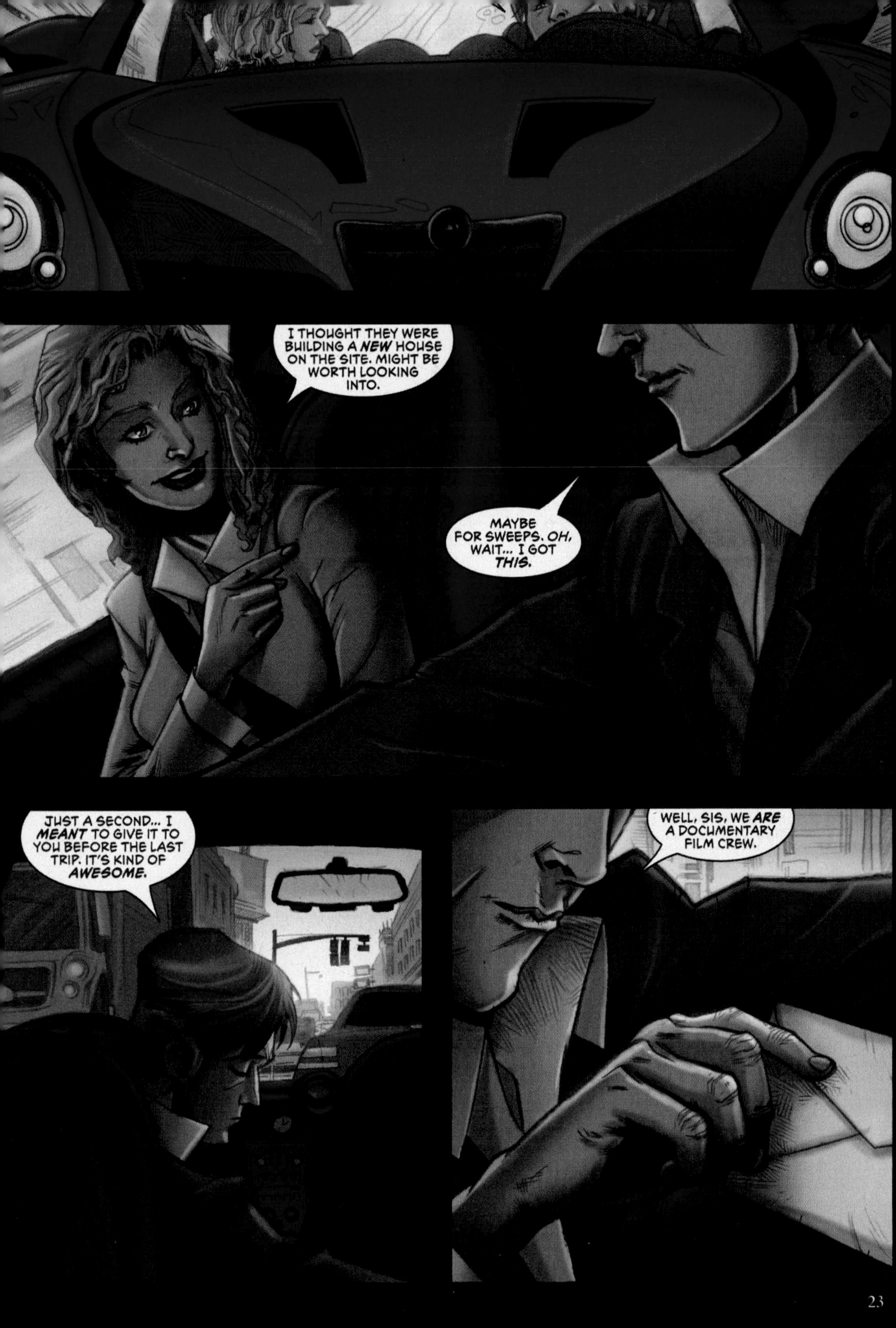
I THOUGHT THEY WERE BUILDING A *NEW* HOUSE ON THE SITE. MIGHT BE WORTH LOOKING INTO.
MAYBE FOR SWEEPS. *OH, WAIT...* I GOT *THIS.*
JUST A SECOND... I *MEANT* TO GIVE IT TO YOU BEFORE THE LAST TRIP. IT'S KIND OF *AWESOME.*
WELL, SIS, WE *ARE* A DOCUMENTARY FILM CREW.

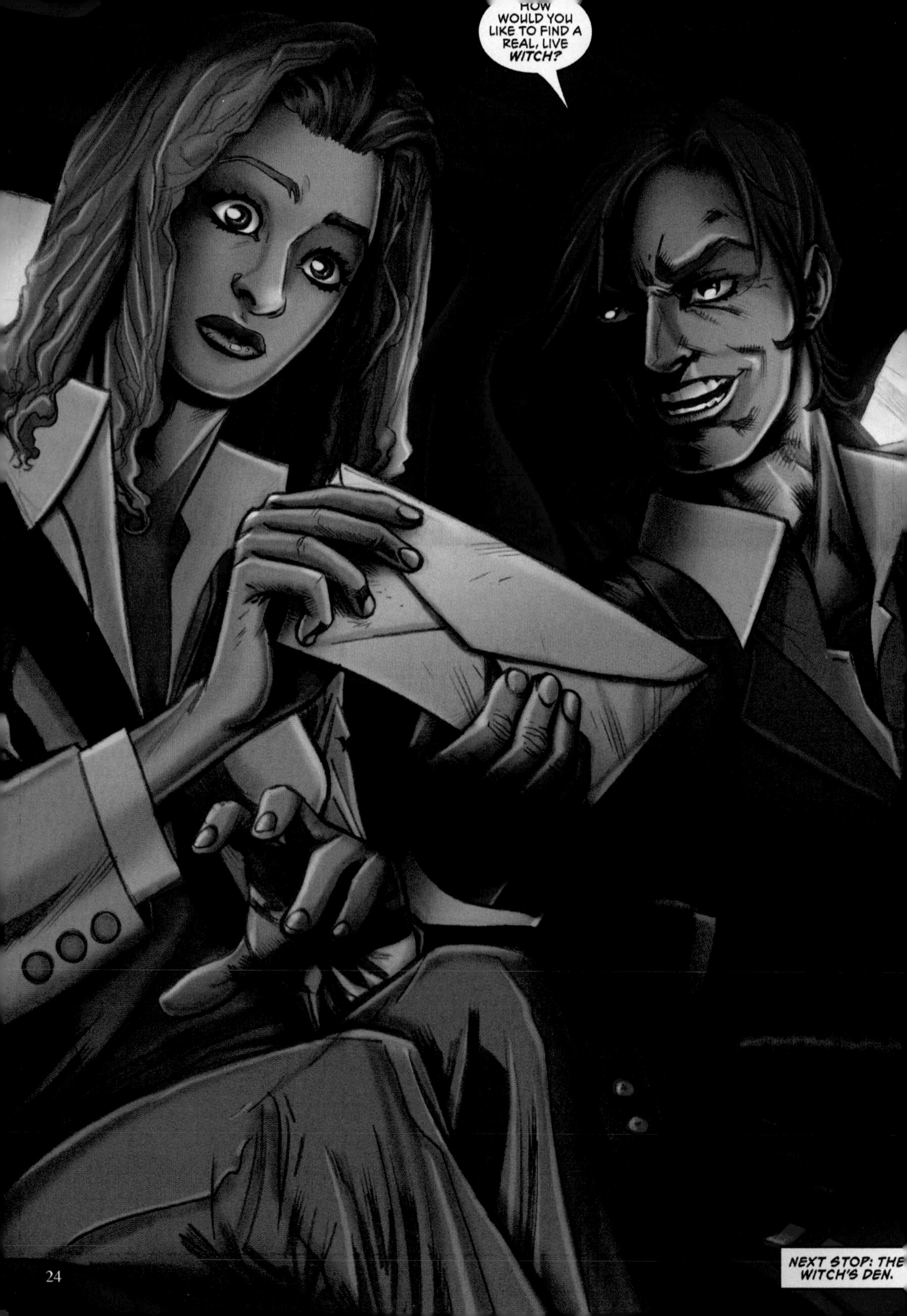
HOW WOULD YOU LIKE TO FIND A REAL, LIVE *WITCH?*
NEXT STOP: THE WITCH'S DEN.

Grimm Fairy Tales
MYTHS & LEGENDS

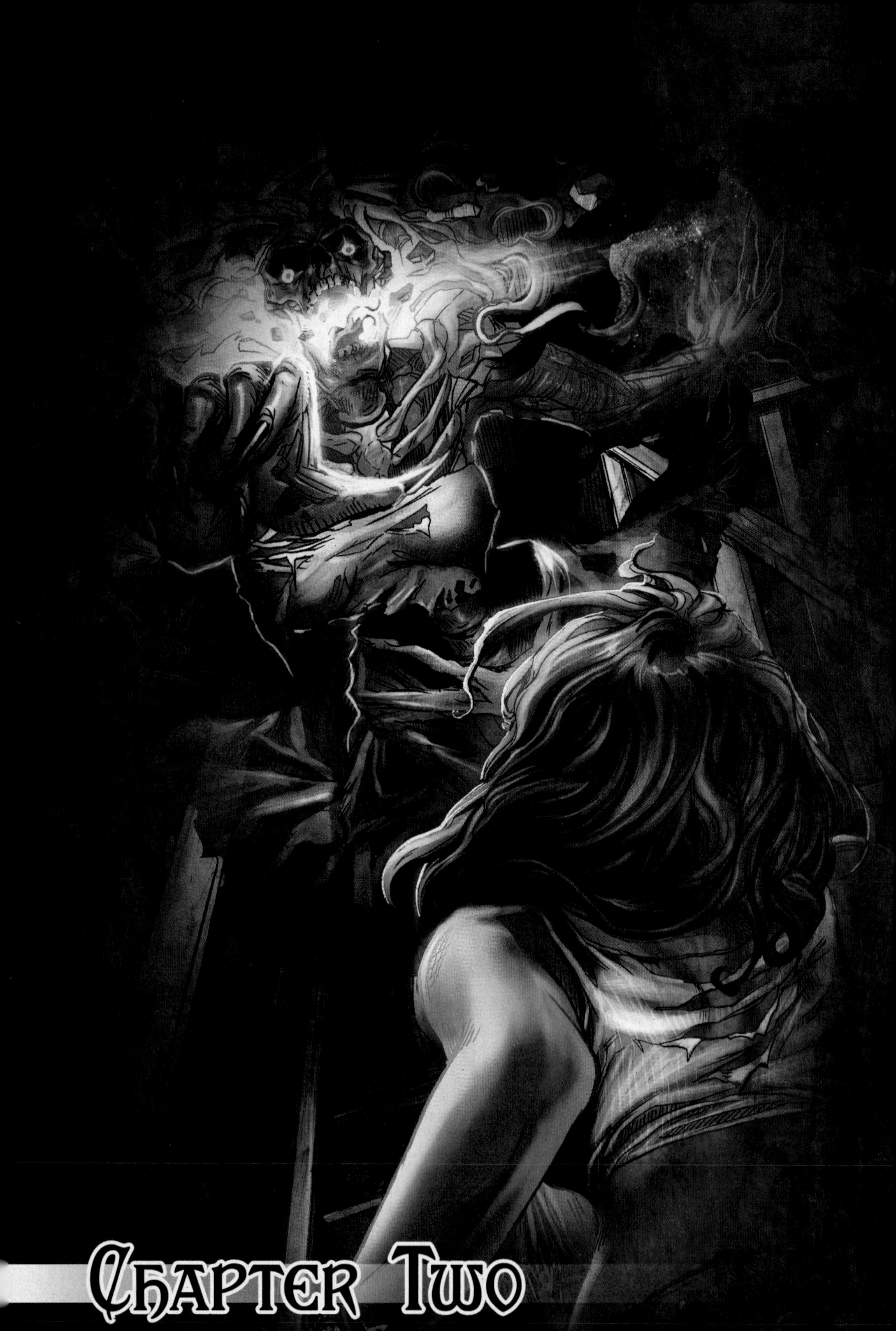

Chapter Two

Story by Raven Gregory, Joe Brusha, Ralph Tedesco and Troy Brownfield

Written by Troy Brownfield • Art by Joyce Maureira

Colors by Ramon Ignacio Bunge • Letters by Jim Campbell

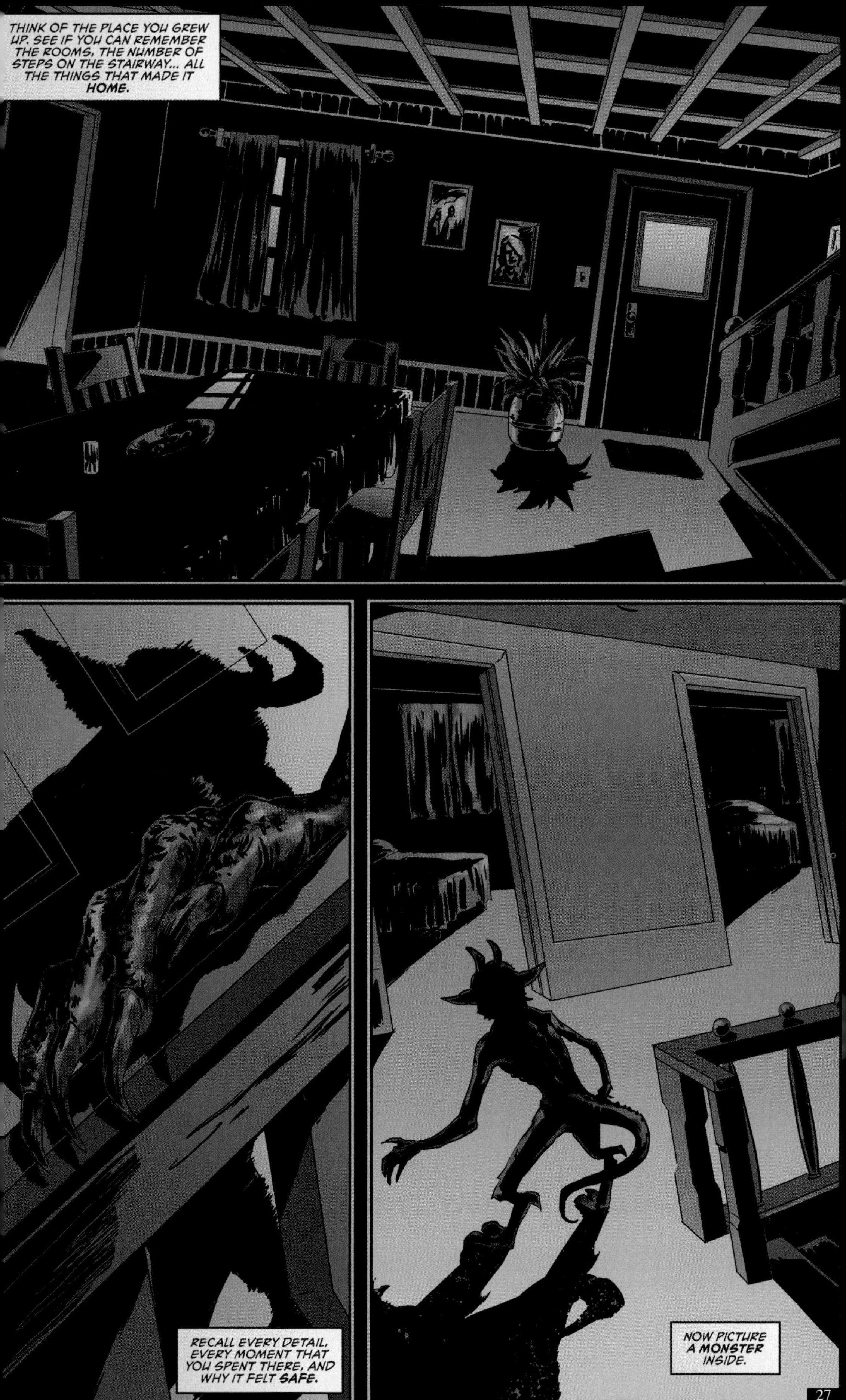
THINK OF THE PLACE YOU GREW UP. SEE IF YOU CAN REMEMBER THE ROOMS, THE NUMBER OF STEPS ON THE STAIRWAY... ALL THE THINGS THAT MADE IT HOME.
RECALL EVERY DETAIL, EVERY MOMENT THAT YOU SPENT THERE, AND WHY IT FELT SAFE.
NOW PICTURE A MONSTER INSIDE.

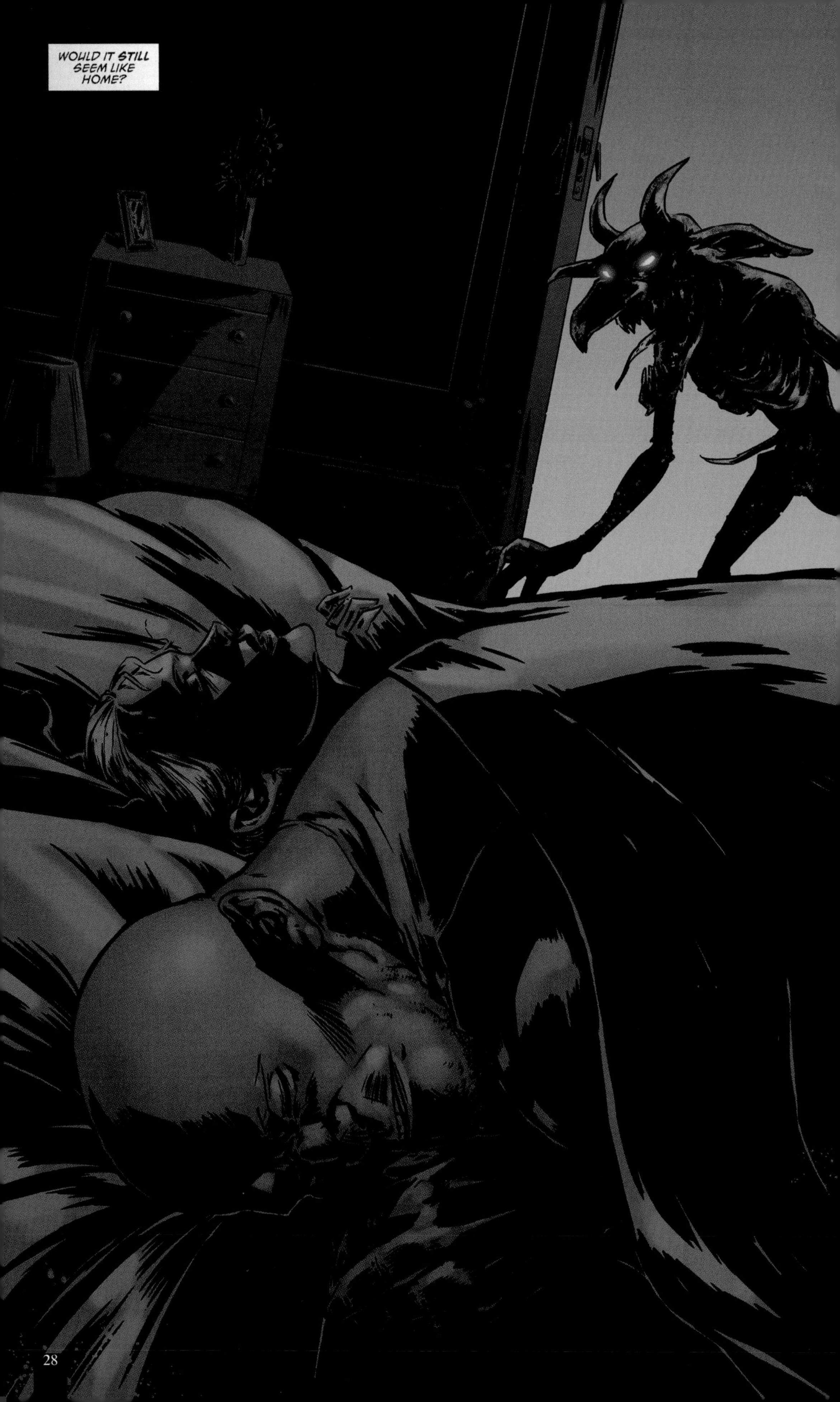
WOULD IT STILL SEEM LIKE HOME?

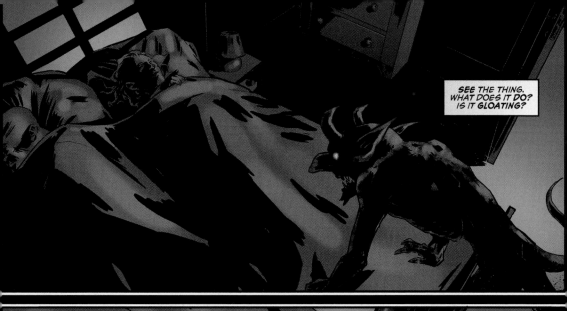

SEE THE THING. WHAT DOES IT DO? IS IT GLOATING?

IS IT SAVORING THE IDEA OF WHAT IT'S ABOUT TO DO? THAT MOMENT WHEN EVERYTHING THAT YOU'VE EVER KNOWN ABOUT YOUR LIFE...

PAM!

...GOES UP IN FLAMES.

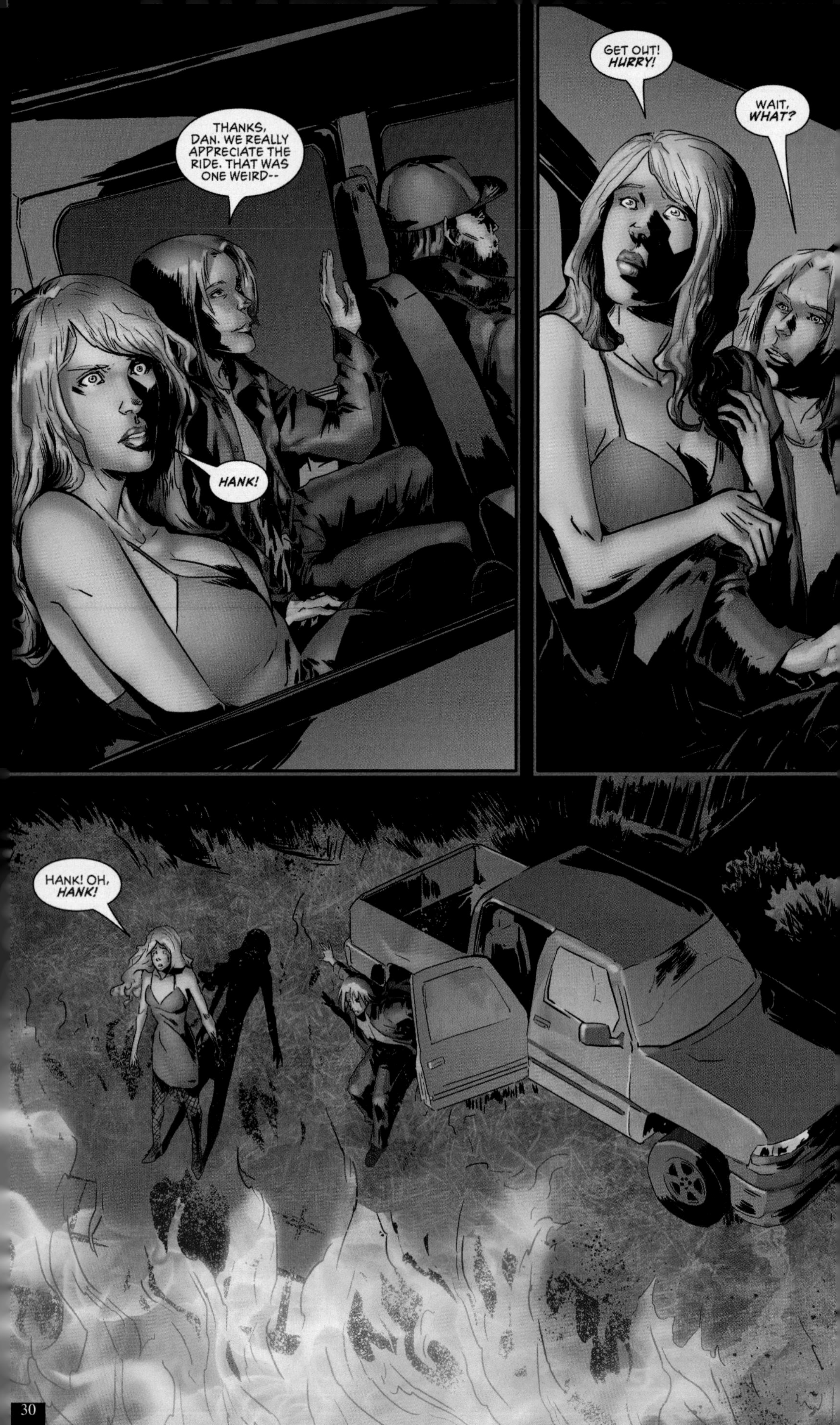
THANKS, DAN. WE REALLY APPRECIATE THE RIDE. THAT WAS ONE WEIRD--
HANK!
GET OUT! *HURRY!*
WAIT, *WHAT?*
HANK! OH, *HANK!*

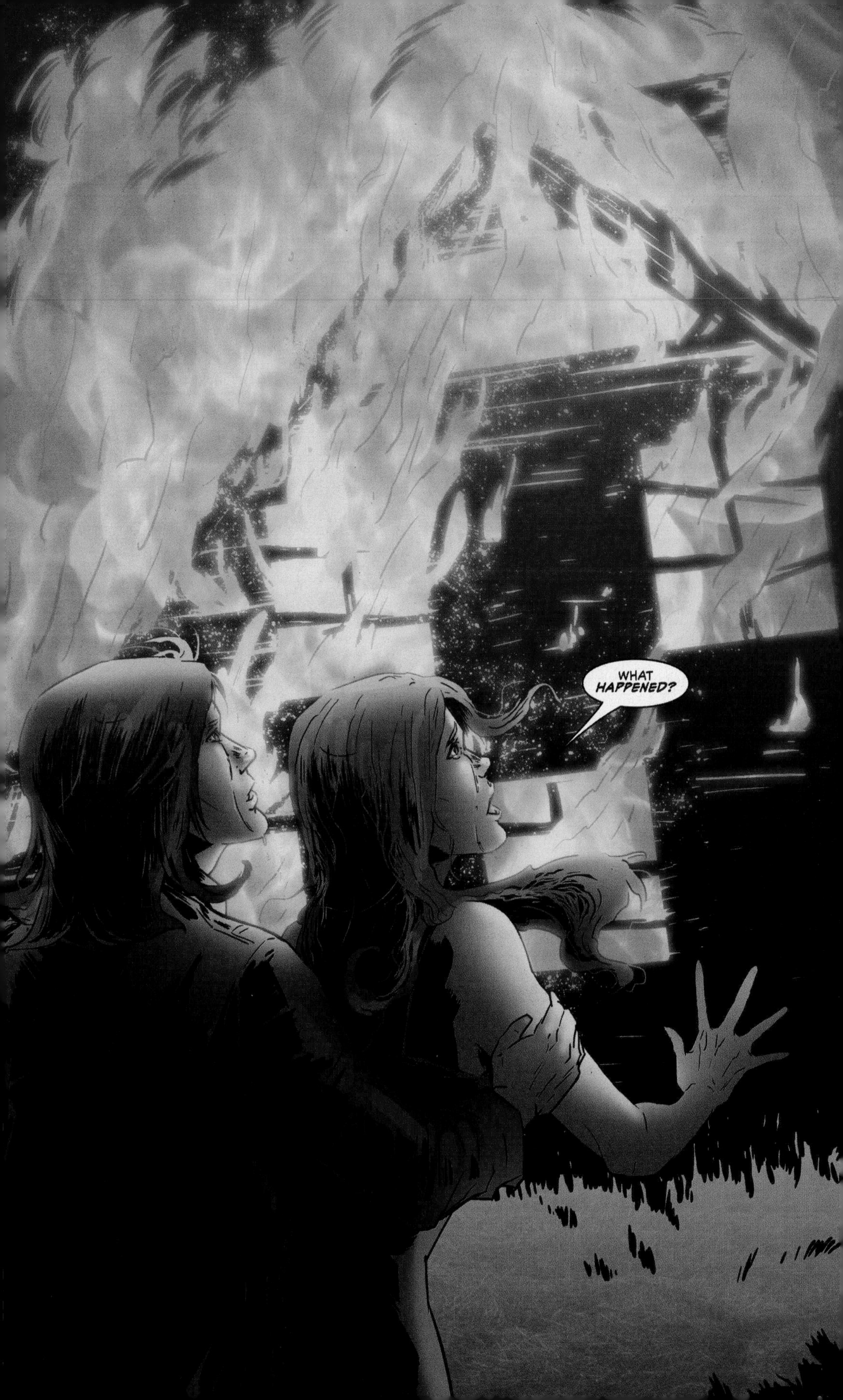
WHAT HAPPENED?

STAY HERE! I HAVE TO SEE IF I CAN GET TO MOM AND DAD!

HANK! YOU CAN'T! IT'S TOO LATE, MAN!

NO! LET ME GO!

HANK! IT'S TOO LATE! DON'T YOU SEE?

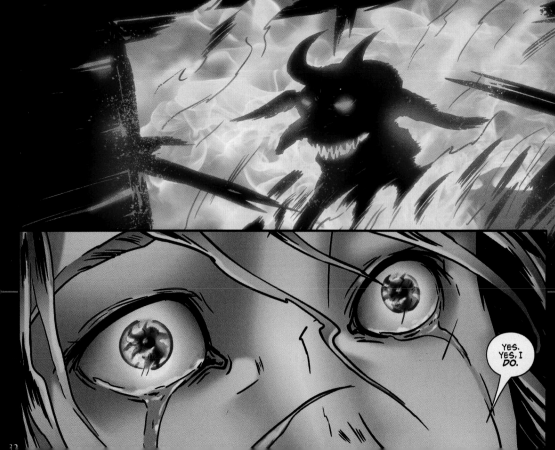

YES. YES, I DO.

THIS IS THE *LAST* OF IT. I COULDN'T FIND MUCH *ELSE*.

HANK...

LOOK AT *THIS*.

WHAT ARE THOSE... *ANIMAL* TRACKS?

NO. IT WAS... SOME *THING*... SOME KIND OF CREATURE THAT I'VE NEVER *SEEN* BEFORE. SOMETHING *EVIL*.

GINA, IT WAS DARK AND YOU WERE PRACTICALLY IN *SHOCK*. YOUR EYES MUST HAVE BEEN PLAYING--

THERE... THERE *HAS* TO BE SOME *OTHER* EXPLANATION FOR WHAT YOU SAW.

I *KNOW* WHAT I *SAW*, HANK!

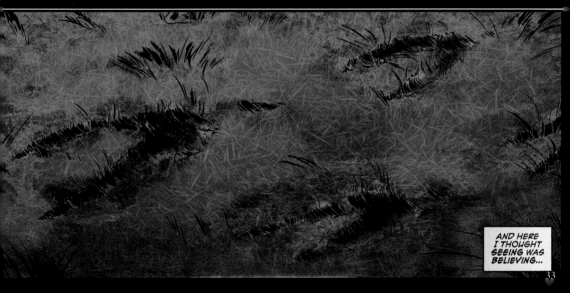

AND HERE I THOUGHT *SEEING* WAS *BELIEVING*...

33

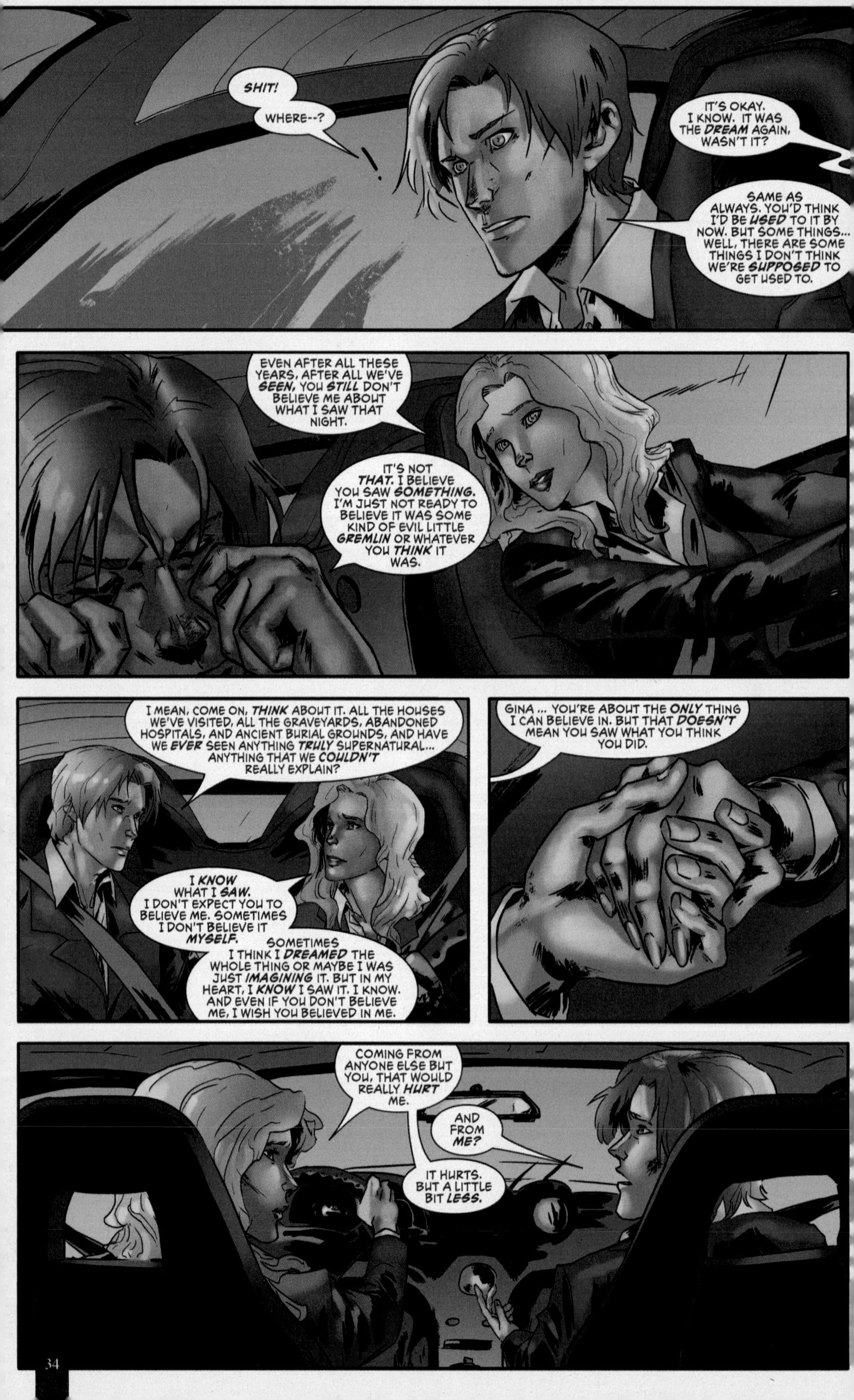

SHIT!
WHERE--?
IT'S OKAY. I KNOW. IT WAS THE DREAM AGAIN, WASN'T IT?
SAME AS ALWAYS. YOU'D THINK I'D BE USED TO IT BY NOW. BUT SOME THINGS... WELL, THERE ARE SOME THINGS I DON'T THINK WE'RE SUPPOSED TO GET USED TO.
EVEN AFTER ALL THESE YEARS, AFTER ALL WE'VE SEEN, YOU STILL DON'T BELIEVE ME ABOUT WHAT I SAW THAT NIGHT.
IT'S NOT THAT. I BELIEVE YOU SAW SOMETHING. I'M JUST NOT READY TO BELIEVE IT WAS SOME KIND OF EVIL LITTLE GREMLIN OR WHATEVER YOU THINK IT WAS.
I MEAN, COME ON, THINK ABOUT IT. ALL THE HOUSES WE'VE VISITED, ALL THE GRAVEYARDS, ABANDONED HOSPITALS, AND ANCIENT BURIAL GROUNDS, AND HAVE WE EVER SEEN ANYTHING TRULY SUPERNATURAL... ANYTHING THAT WE COULDN'T REALLY EXPLAIN?
I KNOW WHAT I SAW. I DON'T EXPECT YOU TO BELIEVE ME. SOMETIMES I DON'T BELIEVE IT MYSELF.
SOMETIMES I THINK I DREAMED THE WHOLE THING OR MAYBE I WAS JUST IMAGINING IT. BUT IN MY HEART, I KNOW I SAW IT. I KNOW. AND EVEN IF YOU DON'T BELIEVE ME, I WISH YOU BELIEVED IN ME.
GINA ... YOU'RE ABOUT THE ONLY THING I CAN BELIEVE IN. BUT THAT DOESN'T MEAN YOU SAW WHAT YOU THINK YOU DID.
COMING FROM ANYONE ELSE BUT YOU, THAT WOULD REALLY HURT ME.
AND FROM ME?
IT HURTS. BUT A LITTLE BIT LESS.

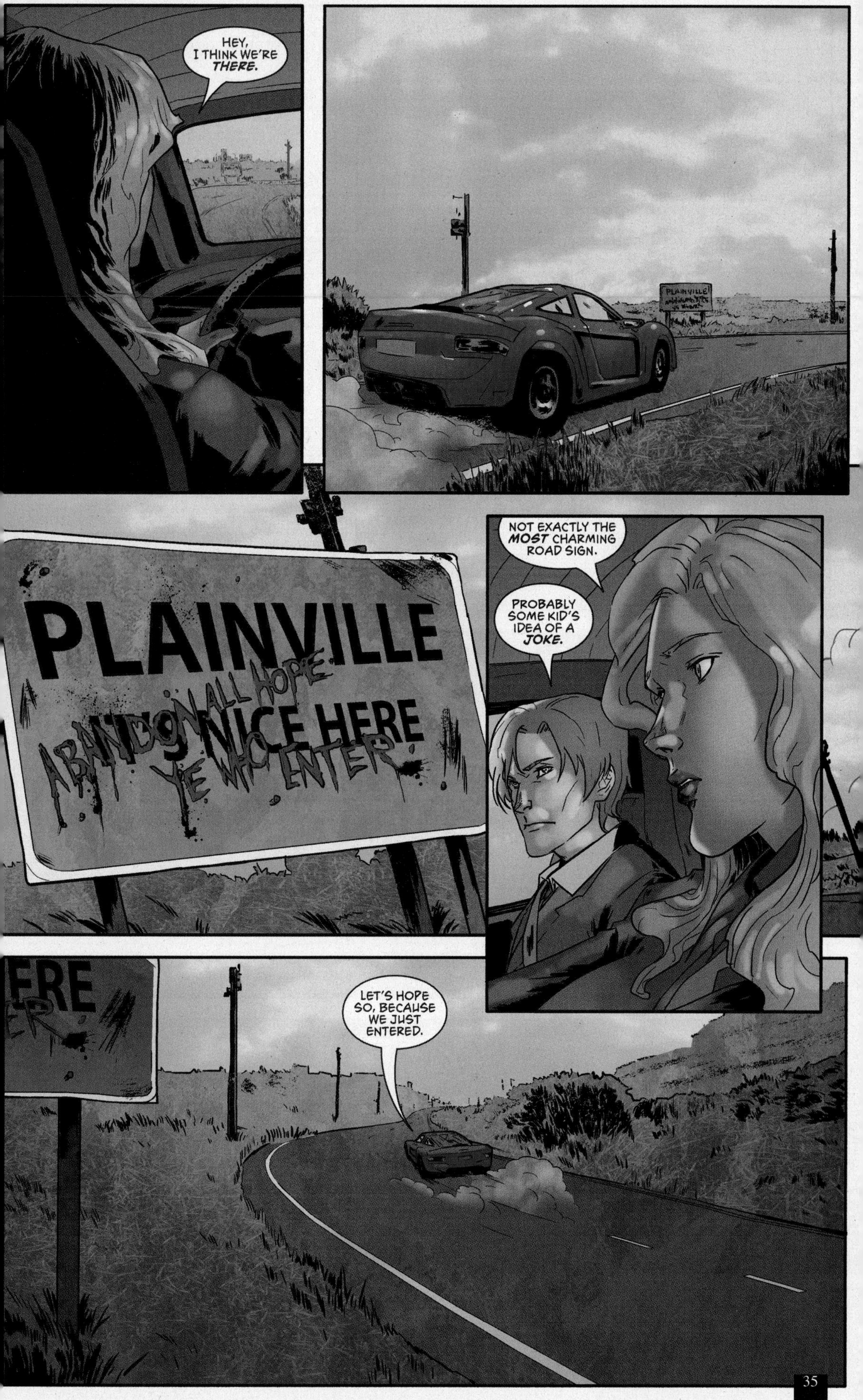
HEY, I THINK WE'RE *THERE.*
PLAINVILLE
NICE HERE
ABANDON ALL HOPE YE WHO ENTER
NOT EXACTLY THE *MOST* CHARMING ROAD SIGN.
PROBABLY SOME KID'S IDEA OF A *JOKE.*
LET'S HOPE SO, BECAUSE WE JUST ENTERED.

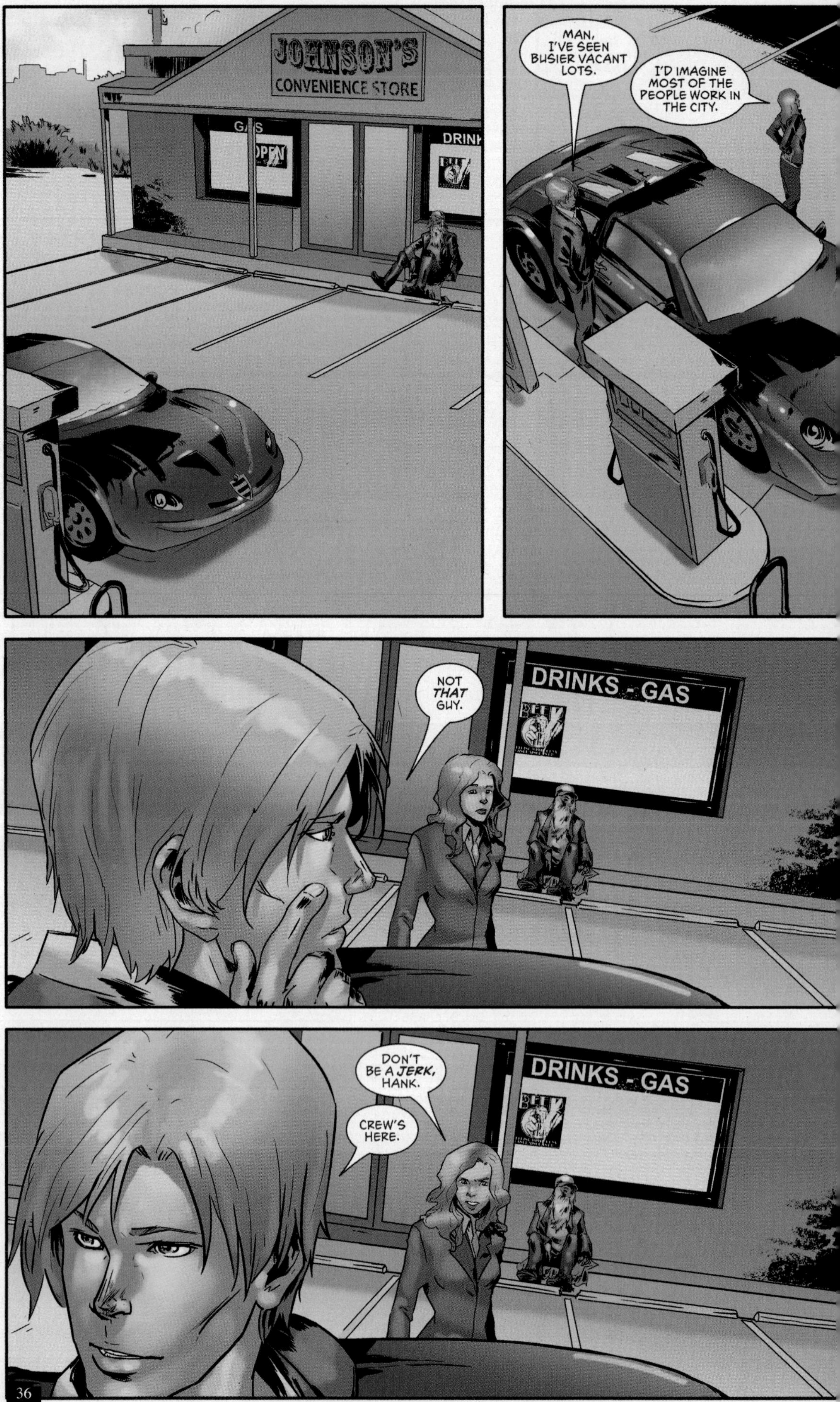
JOHNSON'S
CONVENIENCE STORE
GAS
OPEN
DRINK
MAN, I'VE SEEN BUSIER VACANT LOTS.
I'D IMAGINE MOST OF THE PEOPLE WORK IN THE CITY.
DRINKS - GAS
NOT *THAT* GUY.
DON'T BE A *JERK*, HANK.
CREW'S HERE.

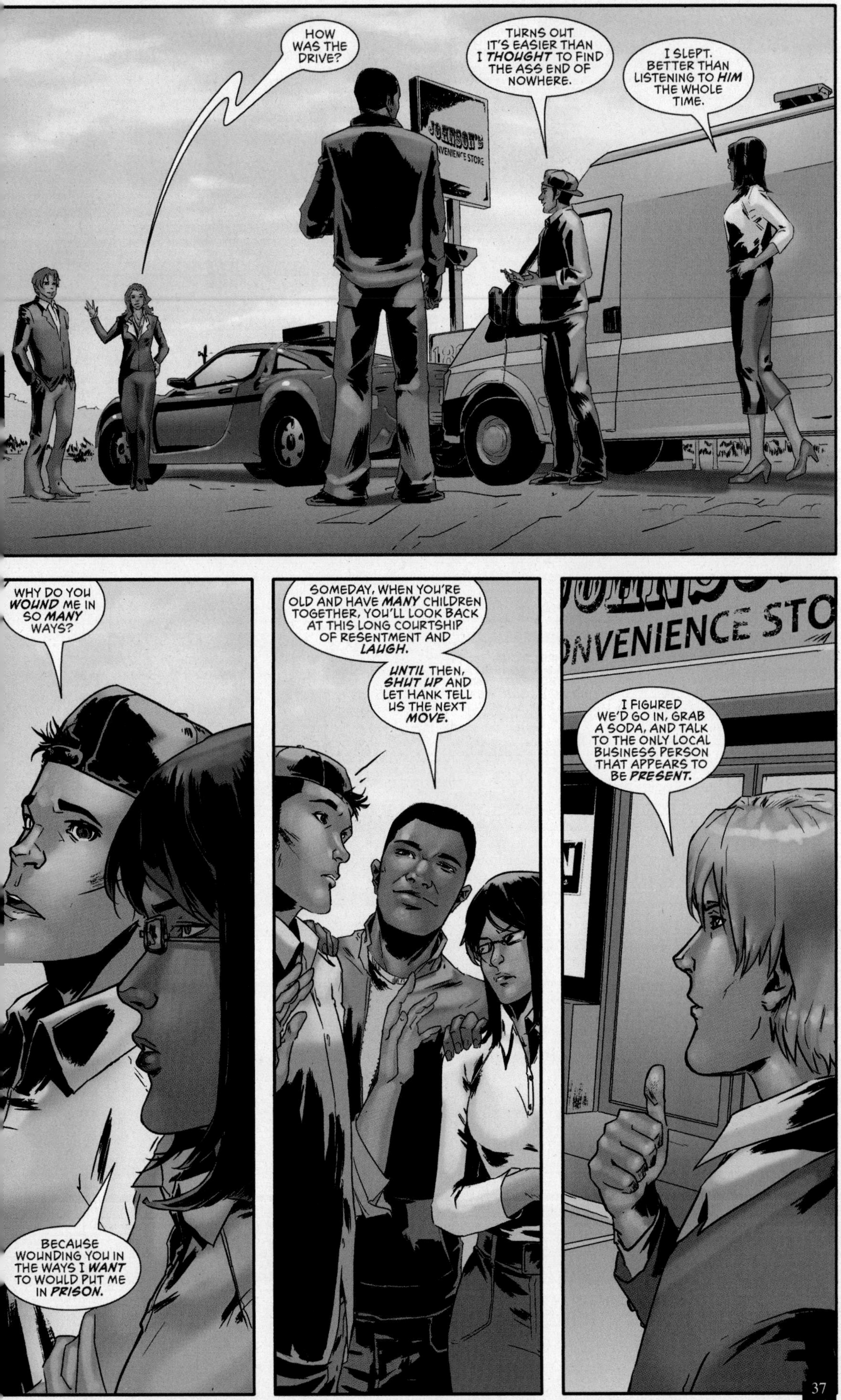
HOW WAS THE DRIVE?
TURNS OUT IT'S EASIER THAN I THOUGHT TO FIND THE ASS END OF NOWHERE.
I SLEPT. BETTER THAN LISTENING TO HIM THE WHOLE TIME.
JOHNSON'S CONVENIENCE STORE
WHY DO YOU WOUND ME IN SO MANY WAYS?
BECAUSE WOUNDING YOU IN THE WAYS I WANT TO WOULD PUT ME IN PRISON.
SOMEDAY, WHEN YOU'RE OLD AND HAVE MANY CHILDREN TOGETHER, YOU'LL LOOK BACK AT THIS LONG COURTSHIP OF RESENTMENT AND LAUGH.
UNTIL THEN, SHUT UP AND LET HANK TELL US THE NEXT MOVE.
ONVENIENCE STO
I FIGURED WE'D GO IN, GRAB A SODA, AND TALK TO THE ONLY LOCAL BUSINESS PERSON THAT APPEARS TO BE PRESENT.

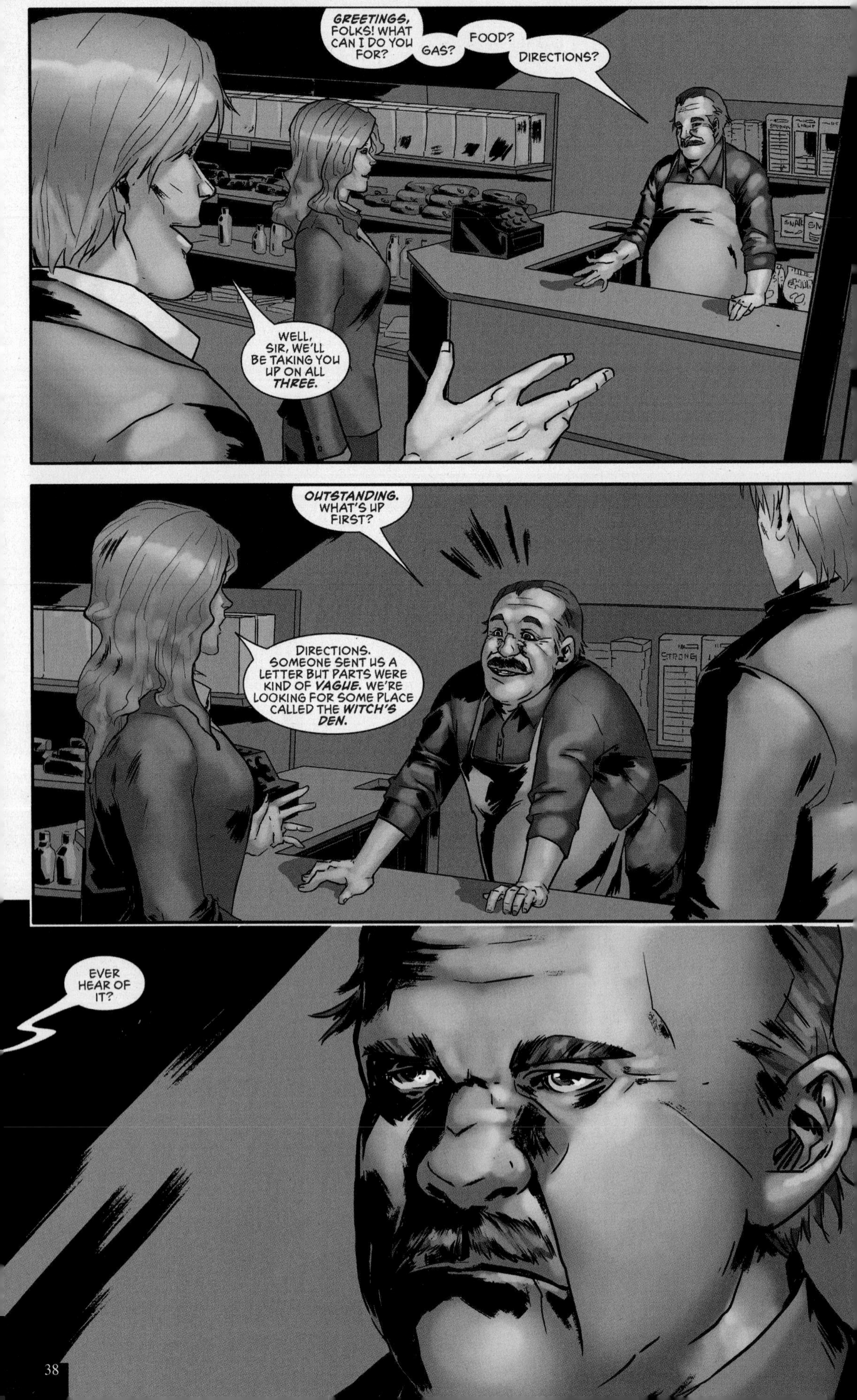
GREETINGS, FOLKS! WHAT CAN I DO YOU FOR?
GAS?
FOOD?
DIRECTIONS?
WELL, SIR, WE'LL BE TAKING YOU UP ON ALL THREE.
OUTSTANDING. WHAT'S UP FIRST?
DIRECTIONS. SOMEONE SENT US A LETTER BUT PARTS WERE KIND OF VAGUE. WE'RE LOOKING FOR SOME PLACE CALLED THE WITCH'S DEN.
EVER HEAR OF IT?

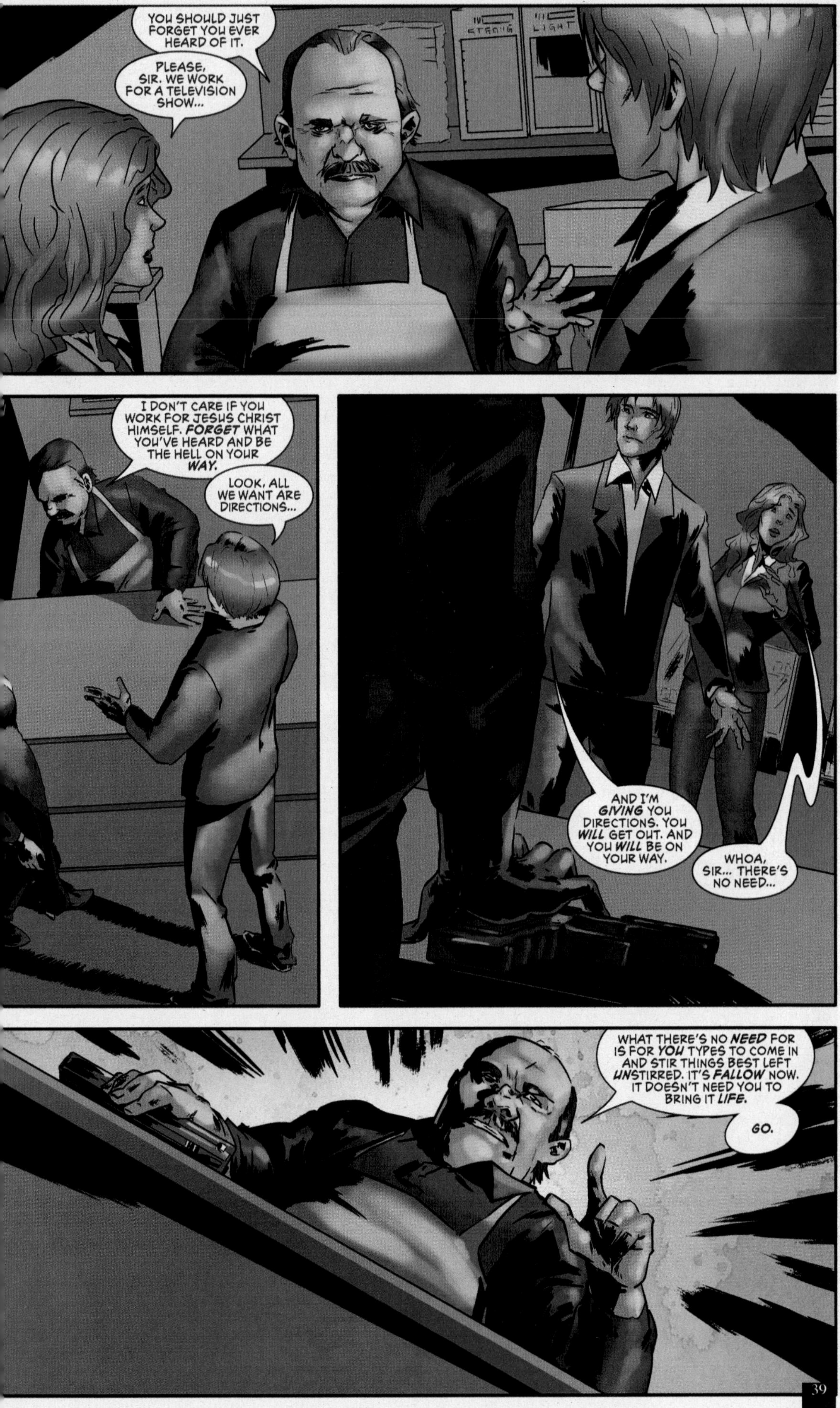

YOU SHOULD JUST FORGET YOU EVER HEARD OF IT.
PLEASE, SIR. WE WORK FOR A TELEVISION SHOW...
I DON'T CARE IF YOU WORK FOR JESUS CHRIST HIMSELF. ***FORGET*** WHAT YOU'VE HEARD AND BE THE HELL ON YOUR ***WAY.***
LOOK, ALL WE WANT ARE DIRECTIONS...
AND I'M ***GIVING*** YOU DIRECTIONS. YOU ***WILL*** GET OUT. AND YOU ***WILL*** BE ON YOUR WAY.
WHOA, SIR... THERE'S NO NEED...
WHAT THERE'S NO ***NEED*** FOR IS FOR ***YOU*** TYPES TO COME IN AND STIR THINGS BEST LEFT ***UN***STIRRED. IT'S ***FALLOW*** NOW. IT DOESN'T NEED YOU TO BRING IT ***LIFE.***
GO.

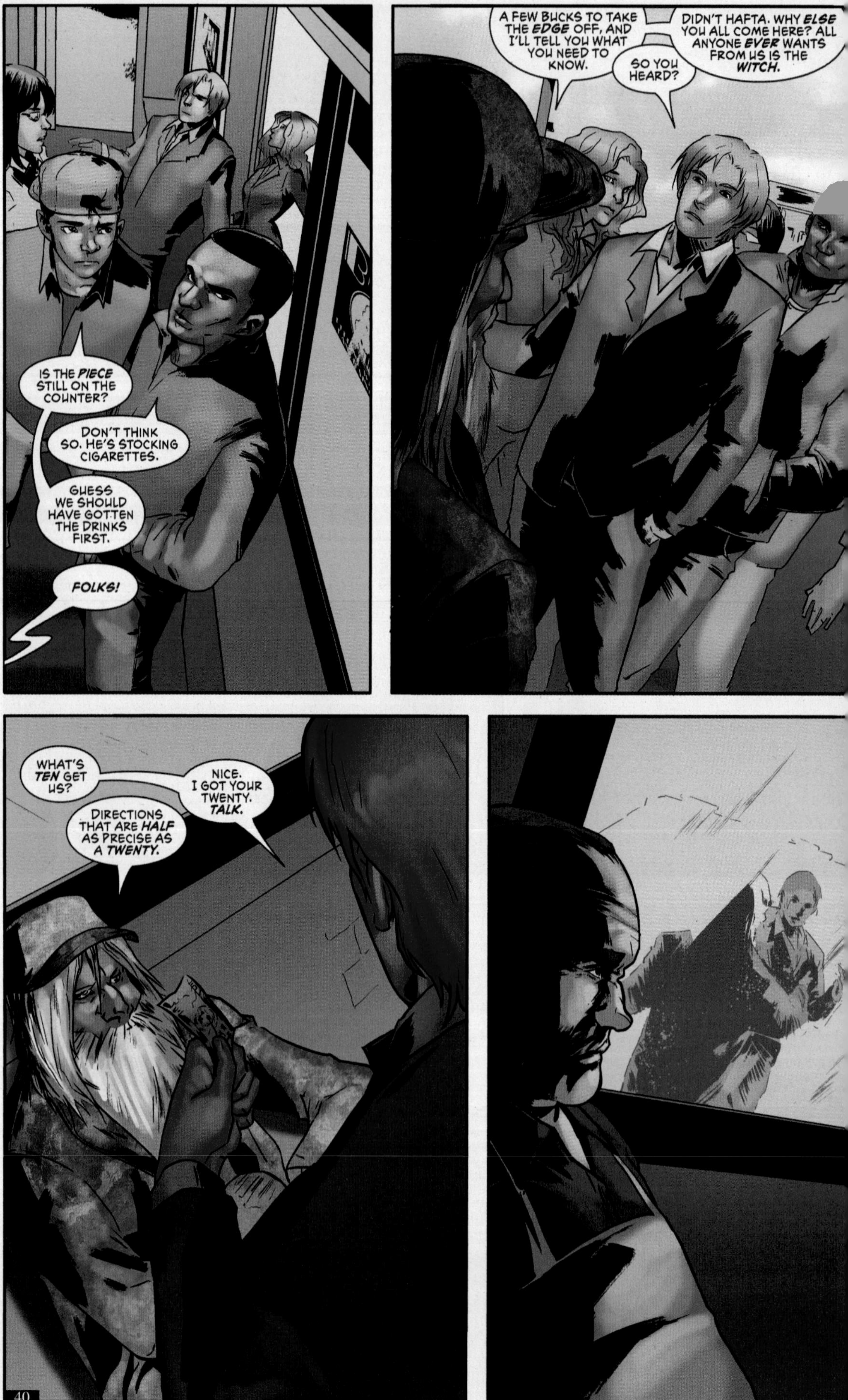
IS THE *PIECE* STILL ON THE COUNTER?
DON'T THINK SO. HE'S STOCKING CIGARETTES.
GUESS WE SHOULD HAVE GOTTEN THE DRINKS FIRST.
FOLKS!
A FEW BUCKS TO TAKE THE *EDGE* OFF, AND I'LL TELL YOU WHAT YOU NEED TO KNOW.
SO YOU HEARD?
DIDN'T HAFTA. WHY *ELSE* YOU ALL COME HERE? ALL ANYONE *EVER* WANTS FROM US IS THE *WITCH*.
WHAT'S *TEN* GET US?
DIRECTIONS THAT ARE *HALF* AS PRECISE AS A *TWENTY*.
NICE. I GOT YOUR TWENTY. *TALK*.

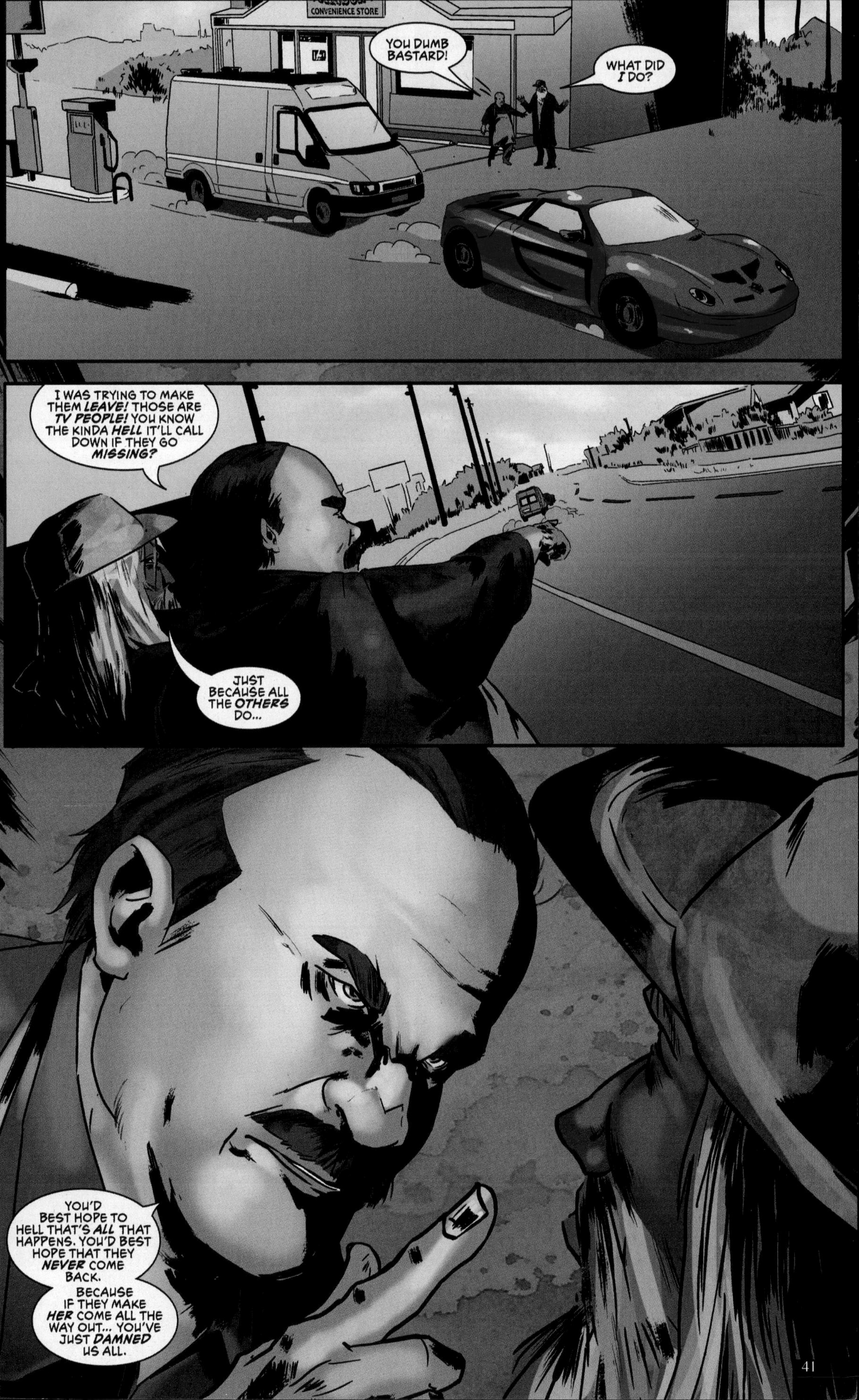
CONVENIENCE STORE
YOU DUMB BASTARD!
WHAT DID I DO?
I WAS TRYING TO MAKE THEM LEAVE! THOSE ARE TV PEOPLE! YOU KNOW THE KINDA HELL IT'LL CALL DOWN IF THEY GO MISSING?
JUST BECAUSE ALL THE OTHERS DO...
YOU'D BEST HOPE TO HELL THAT'S ALL THAT HAPPENS. YOU'D BEST HOPE THAT THEY NEVER COME BACK.
BECAUSE IF THEY MAKE HER COME ALL THE WAY OUT... YOU'VE JUST DAMNED US ALL.

THANKS FOR SIGNING THE WAIVER! ARE YOU READY TO BE ON TV?

THE WITCH'S DEN.

SURE! WHAT ARE WE TALKING ABOUT?

PLEASE COME BACK!

NO! GET AWAY FROM ME!

PLAIN HIGH S

I'VE NEVER BEEN ON TV BEFORE!

WELL, HERE'S YOUR CHANCE, MA'AM. TELL US ABOUT THE WITCH'S DEN.

OH, SONNY, YOU'D BEST BE MOVIN' ON. I'LL PRAY FOR YOU.

THAT'S NICE, MA'AM, BUT--

YOU'LL SURELY NEED IT.

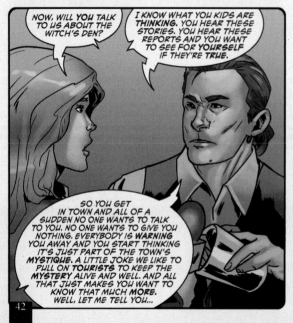

NOW, WILL YOU TALK TO US ABOUT THE WITCH'S DEN?

I KNOW WHAT YOU KIDS ARE THINKING. YOU HEAR THESE STORIES. YOU HEAR THESE REPORTS AND YOU WANT TO SEE FOR YOURSELF IF THEY'RE TRUE.

SO YOU GET IN TOWN AND ALL OF A SUDDEN NO ONE WANTS TO TALK TO YOU. NO ONE WANTS TO GIVE YOU NOTHING. EVERYBODY IS WARNING YOU AWAY AND YOU START THINKING IT'S JUST PART OF THE TOWN'S MYSTIQUE. A LITTLE JOKE WE LIKE TO PULL ON TOURISTS TO KEEP THE MYSTERY ALIVE AND WELL. AND ALL THAT JUST MAKES YOU WANT TO KNOW THAT MUCH MORE. WELL, LET ME TELL YOU...

THIS IS NO JOKE. THIS IS NOT ME TRYING TO SCARE YOU. THIS IS ME TELLING YOU I'VE LIVED IN THIS TOWN SINCE I WAS BORN AND IN ALL THOSE YEARS, EVERY YEAR WE GET PEOPLE LIKE YOU WHO COME TO TOWN FOR ONE THING AND ONE THING ONLY, AND THOSE PEOPLE, THE ONES WHO COME TO SEE THAT PLACE, THE ONES WHO DO ACTUALLY END UP FINDING IT... THEY DON'T COME BACK.

BUT WHAT--

INTERVIEW'S OVER.

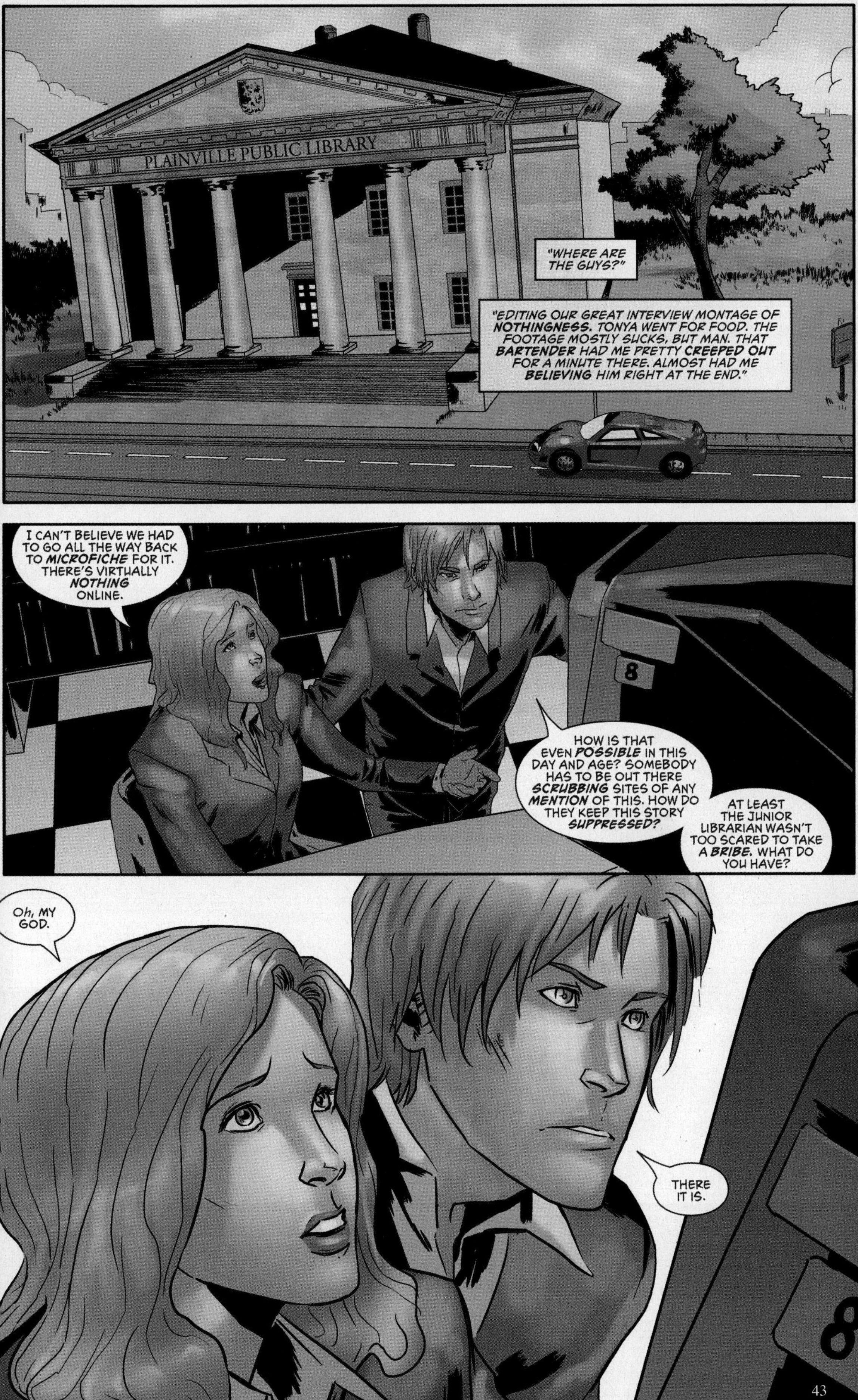
PLAINVILLE PUBLIC LIBRARY
"WHERE ARE THE GUYS?"
"EDITING OUR GREAT INTERVIEW MONTAGE OF NOTHINGNESS. TONYA WENT FOR FOOD. THE FOOTAGE MOSTLY SUCKS, BUT MAN. THAT BARTENDER HAD ME PRETTY CREEPED OUT FOR A MINUTE THERE. ALMOST HAD ME BELIEVING HIM RIGHT AT THE END."
I CAN'T BELIEVE WE HAD TO GO ALL THE WAY BACK TO MICROFICHE FOR IT. THERE'S VIRTUALLY NOTHING ONLINE.
HOW IS THAT EVEN POSSIBLE IN THIS DAY AND AGE? SOMEBODY HAS TO BE OUT THERE SCRUBBING SITES OF ANY MENTION OF THIS. HOW DO THEY KEEP THIS STORY SUPPRESSED?
AT LEAST THE JUNIOR LIBRARIAN WASN'T TOO SCARED TO TAKE A BRIBE. WHAT DO YOU HAVE?
8
Oh, MY GOD.
THERE IT IS.
8

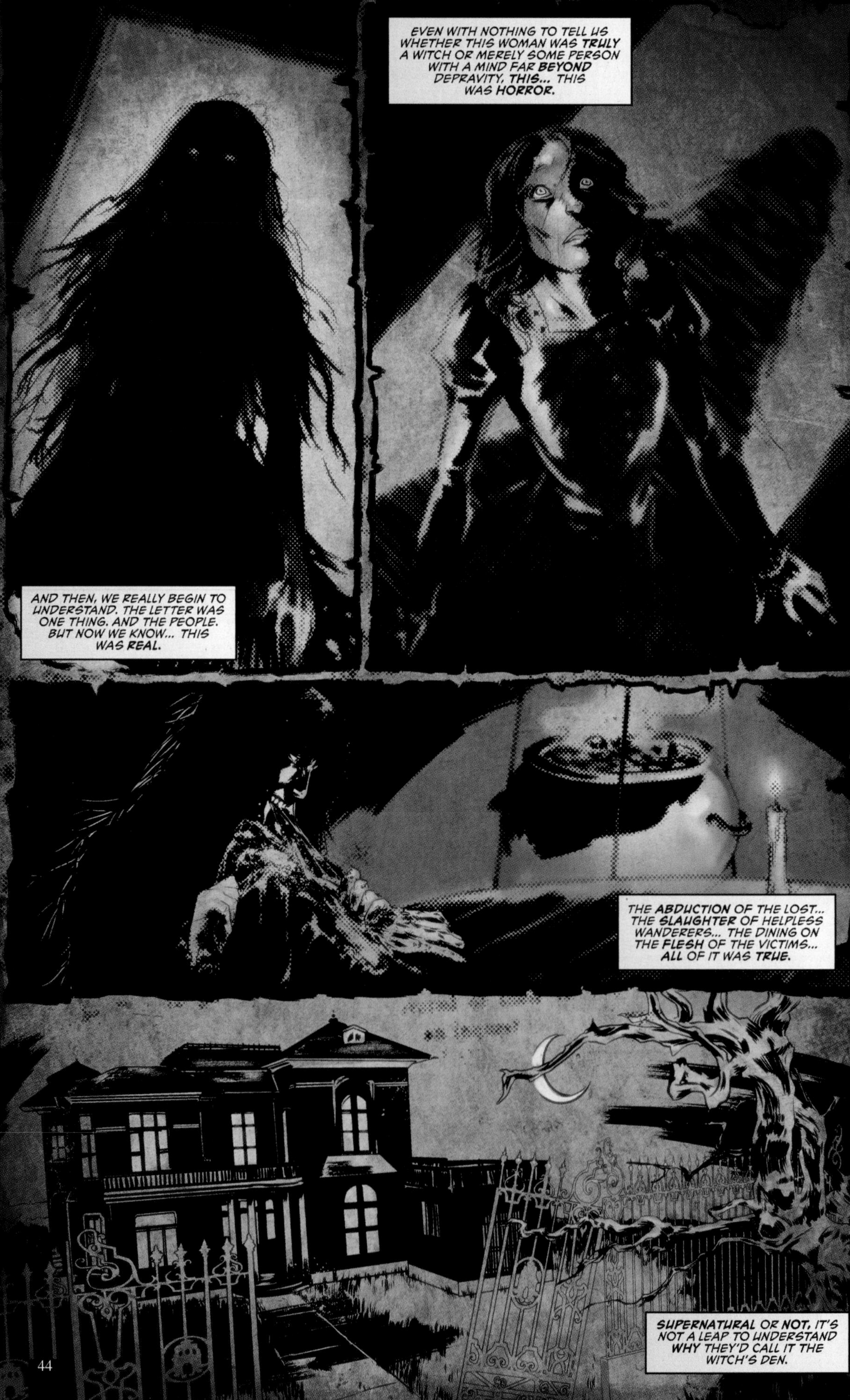
AND THEN, WE REALLY BEGIN TO UNDERSTAND. THE LETTER WAS ONE THING. AND THE PEOPLE. BUT NOW WE KNOW... THIS WAS REAL.
EVEN WITH NOTHING TO TELL US WHETHER THIS WOMAN WAS TRULY A WITCH OR MERELY SOME PERSON WITH A MIND FAR BEYOND DEPRAVITY, THIS... THIS WAS HORROR.
THE ABDUCTION OF THE LOST... THE SLAUGHTER OF HELPLESS WANDERERS... THE DINING ON THE FLESH OF THE VICTIMS... ALL OF IT WAS TRUE.
SUPERNATURAL OR NOT, IT'S NOT A LEAP TO UNDERSTAND WHY THEY'D CALL IT THE WITCH'S DEN.

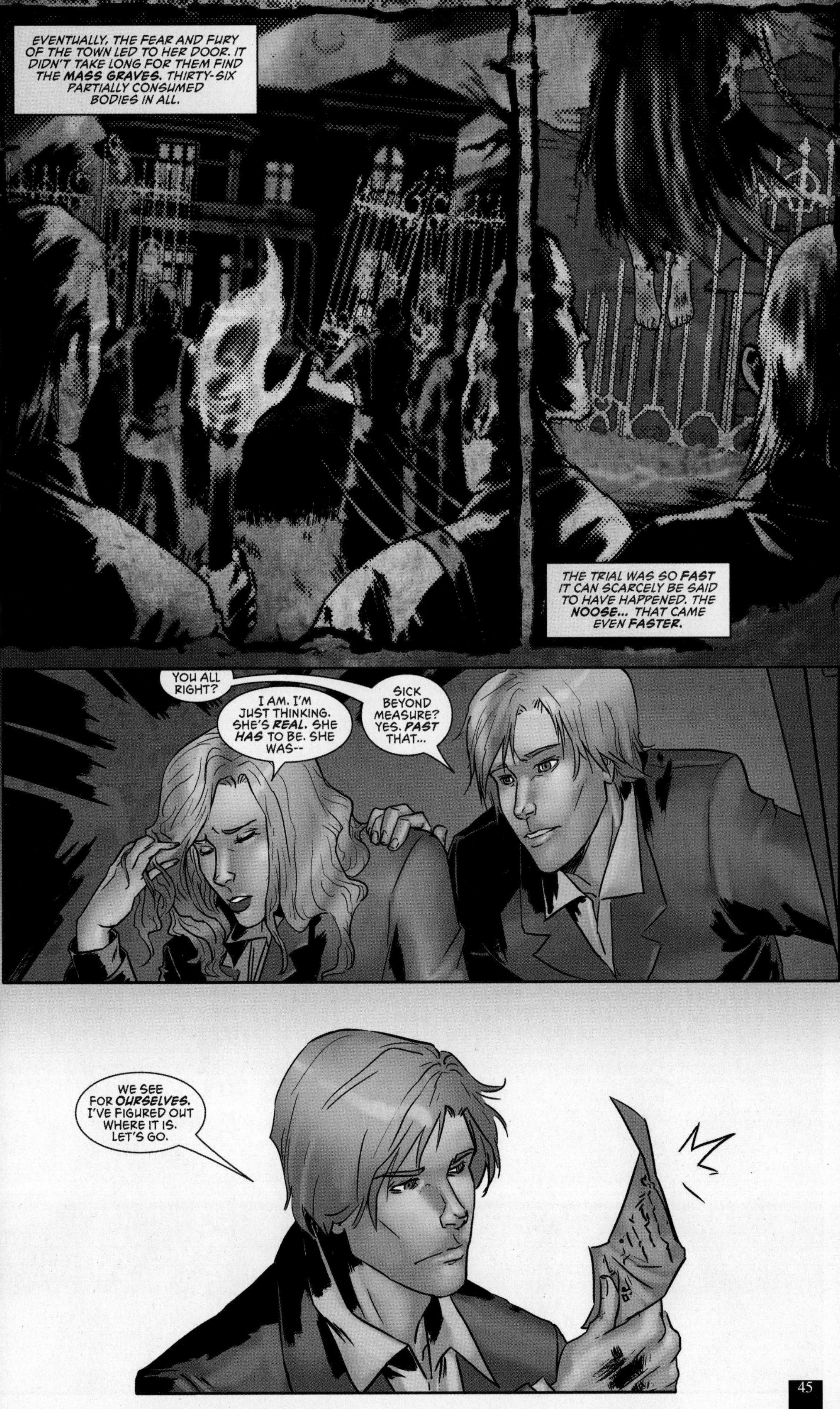

EVENTUALLY, THE FEAR AND FURY OF THE TOWN LED TO HER DOOR. IT DIDN'T TAKE LONG FOR THEM FIND THE **MASS GRAVES.** THIRTY-SIX PARTIALLY CONSUMED BODIES IN ALL.
THE TRIAL WAS SO **FAST** IT CAN SCARCELY BE SAID TO HAVE HAPPENED. THE **NOOSE...** THAT CAME EVEN **FASTER.**
YOU ALL RIGHT?
I AM. I'M JUST THINKING. SHE'S **REAL.** SHE **HAS** TO BE. SHE WAS--
SICK BEYOND MEASURE? YES. **PAST** THAT...
WE SEE FOR **OURSELVES.** I'VE FIGURED OUT WHERE IT IS. LET'S GO.

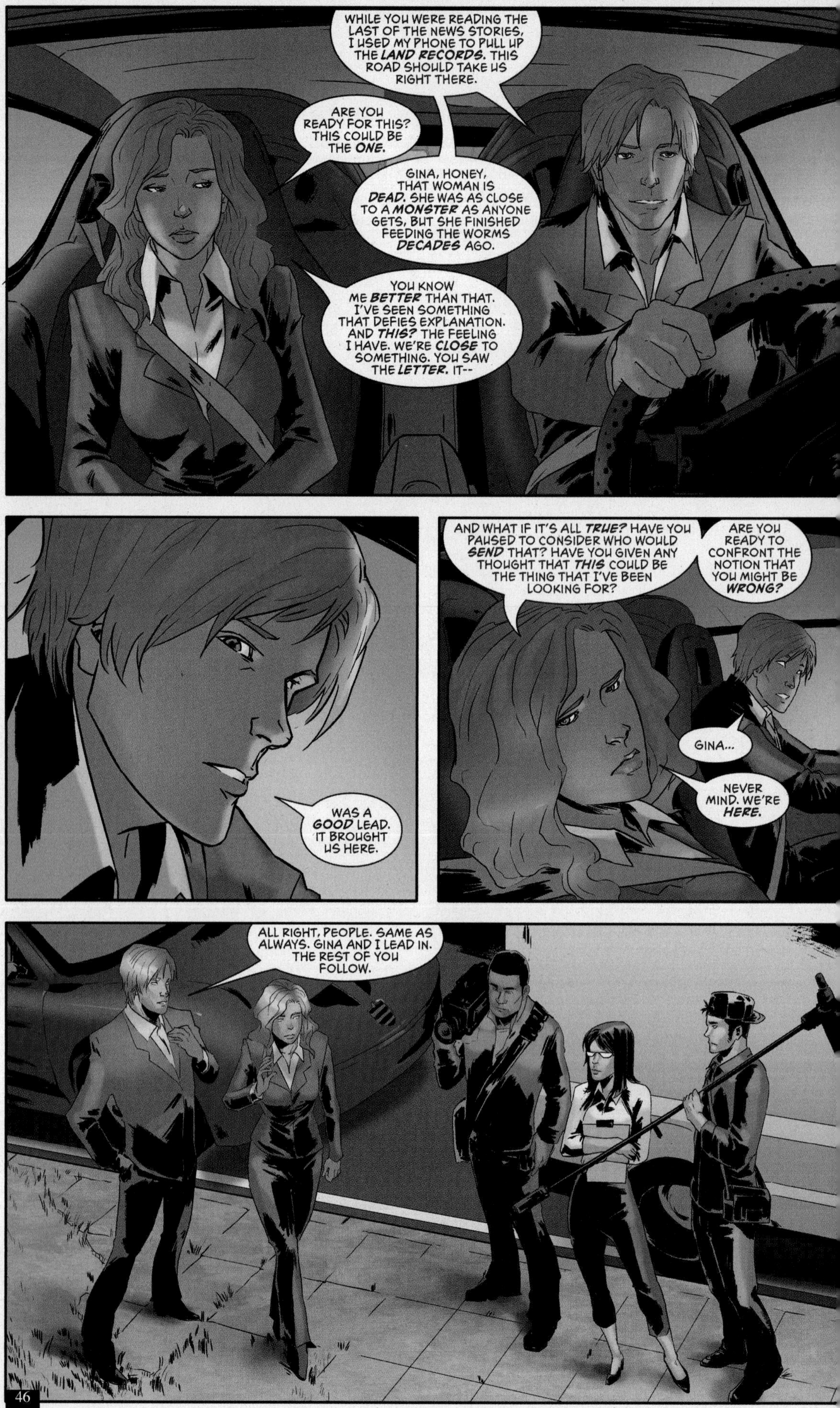

WHILE YOU WERE READING THE LAST OF THE NEWS STORIES, I USED MY PHONE TO PULL UP THE LAND RECORDS. THIS ROAD SHOULD TAKE US RIGHT THERE.
ARE YOU READY FOR THIS? THIS COULD BE THE ONE.
GINA, HONEY, THAT WOMAN IS DEAD. SHE WAS AS CLOSE TO A MONSTER AS ANYONE GETS, BUT SHE FINISHED FEEDING THE WORMS DECADES AGO.
YOU KNOW ME BETTER THAN THAT. I'VE SEEN SOMETHING THAT DEFIES EXPLANATION. AND THIS? THE FEELING I HAVE. WE'RE CLOSE TO SOMETHING. YOU SAW THE LETTER. IT--
WAS A GOOD LEAD. IT BROUGHT US HERE.
AND WHAT IF IT'S ALL TRUE? HAVE YOU PAUSED TO CONSIDER WHO WOULD SEND THAT? HAVE YOU GIVEN ANY THOUGHT THAT THIS COULD BE THE THING THAT I'VE BEEN LOOKING FOR?
ARE YOU READY TO CONFRONT THE NOTION THAT YOU MIGHT BE WRONG?
GINA...
NEVER MIND. WE'RE HERE.
ALL RIGHT, PEOPLE. SAME AS ALWAYS. GINA AND I LEAD IN. THE REST OF YOU FOLLOW.

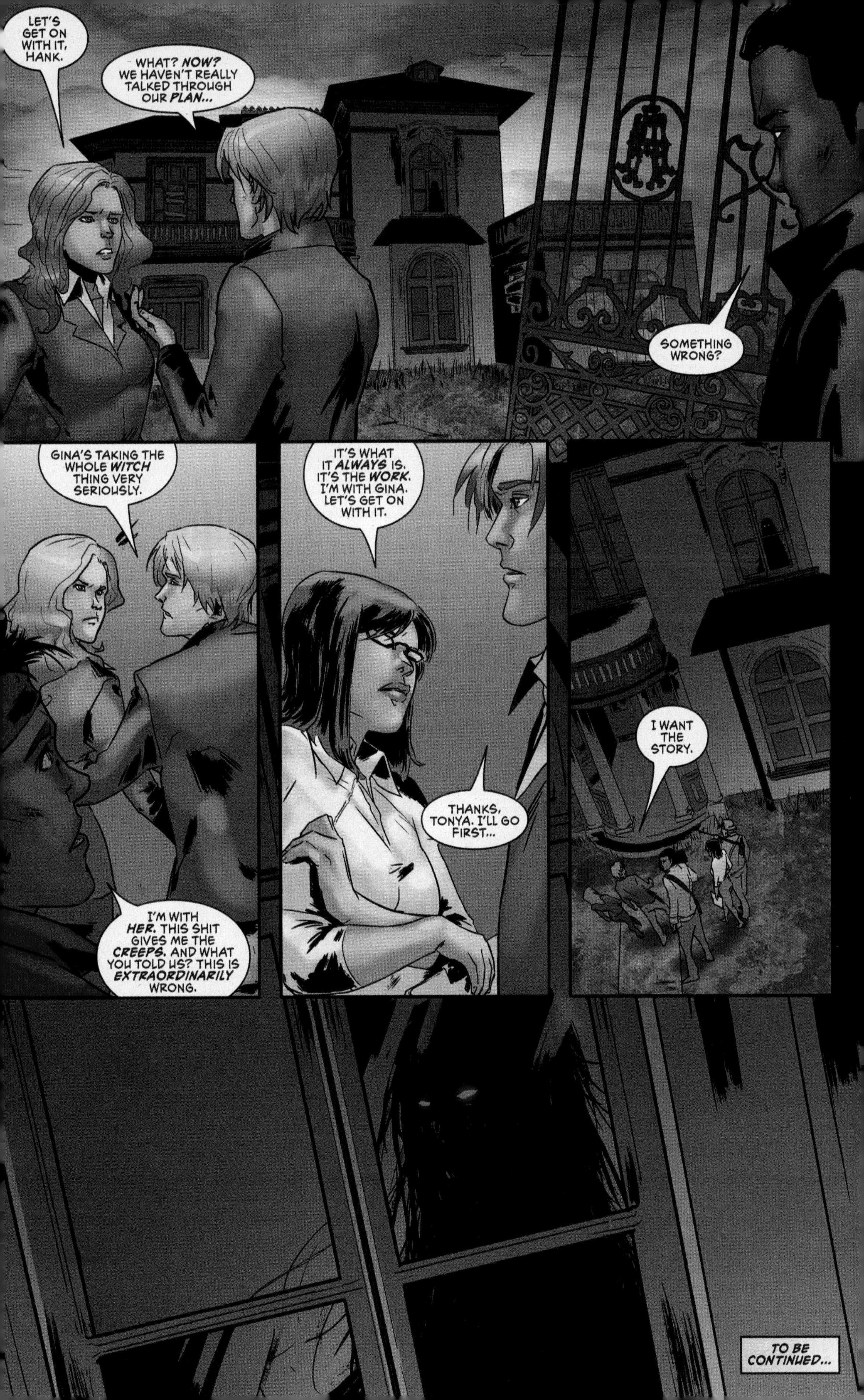

LET'S GET ON WITH IT, HANK.
WHAT? NOW? WE HAVEN'T REALLY TALKED THROUGH OUR PLAN...
SOMETHING WRONG?
GINA'S TAKING THE WHOLE WITCH THING VERY SERIOUSLY.
I'M WITH HER. THIS SHIT GIVES ME THE CREEPS. AND WHAT YOU TOLD US? THIS IS EXTRAORDINARILY WRONG.
IT'S WHAT IT ALWAYS IS. IT'S THE WORK. I'M WITH GINA. LET'S GET ON WITH IT.
THANKS, TONYA. I'LL GO FIRST...
I WANT THE STORY.
TO BE CONTINUED...

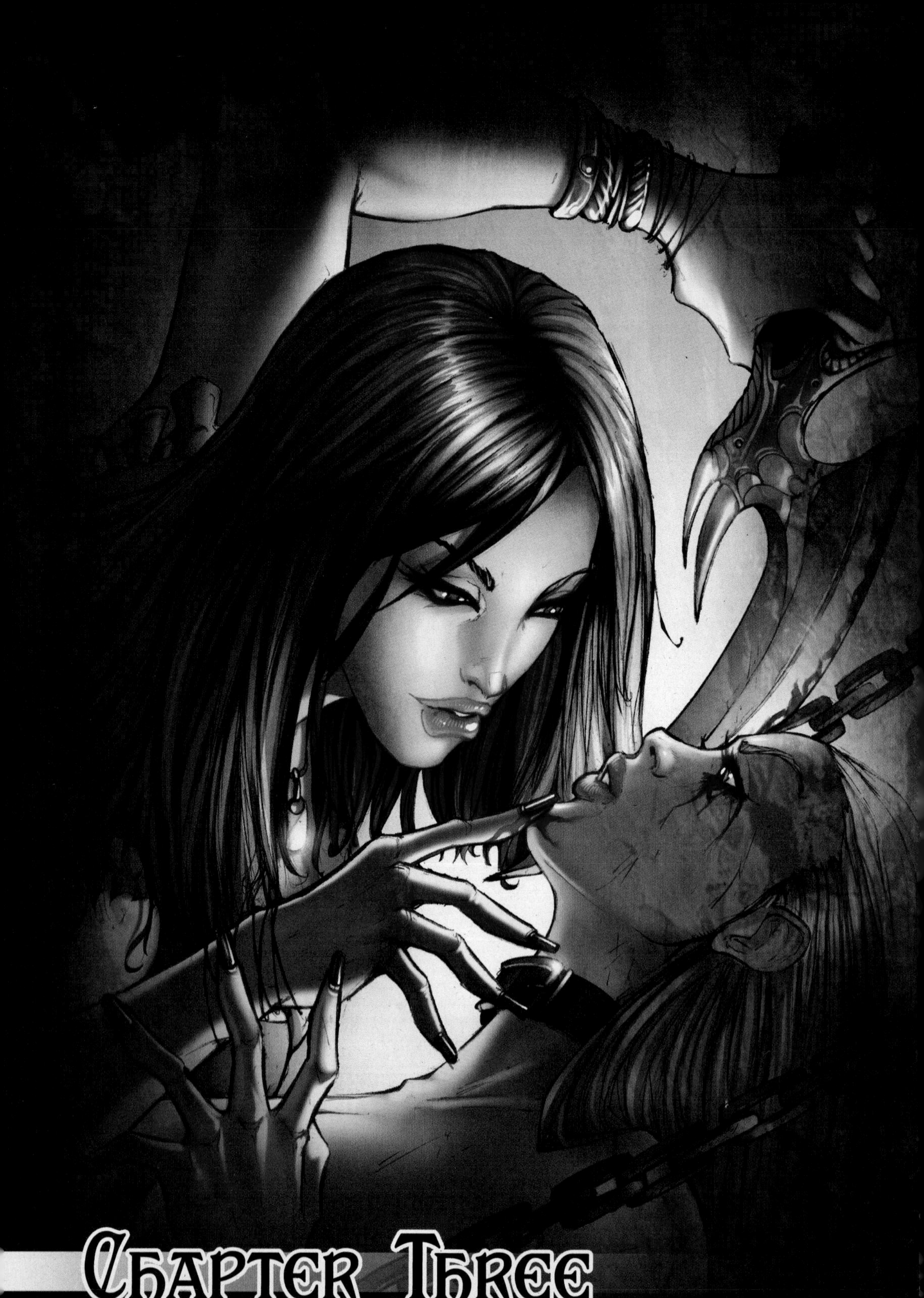

Chapter Three

Story by Raven Gregory, Joe Brusha, Ralph Tedesco and Troy Brownfield

Written by Troy Brownfield • Art by Josh Hood

Colors by Jason Embury • Letters by Jim Campbell

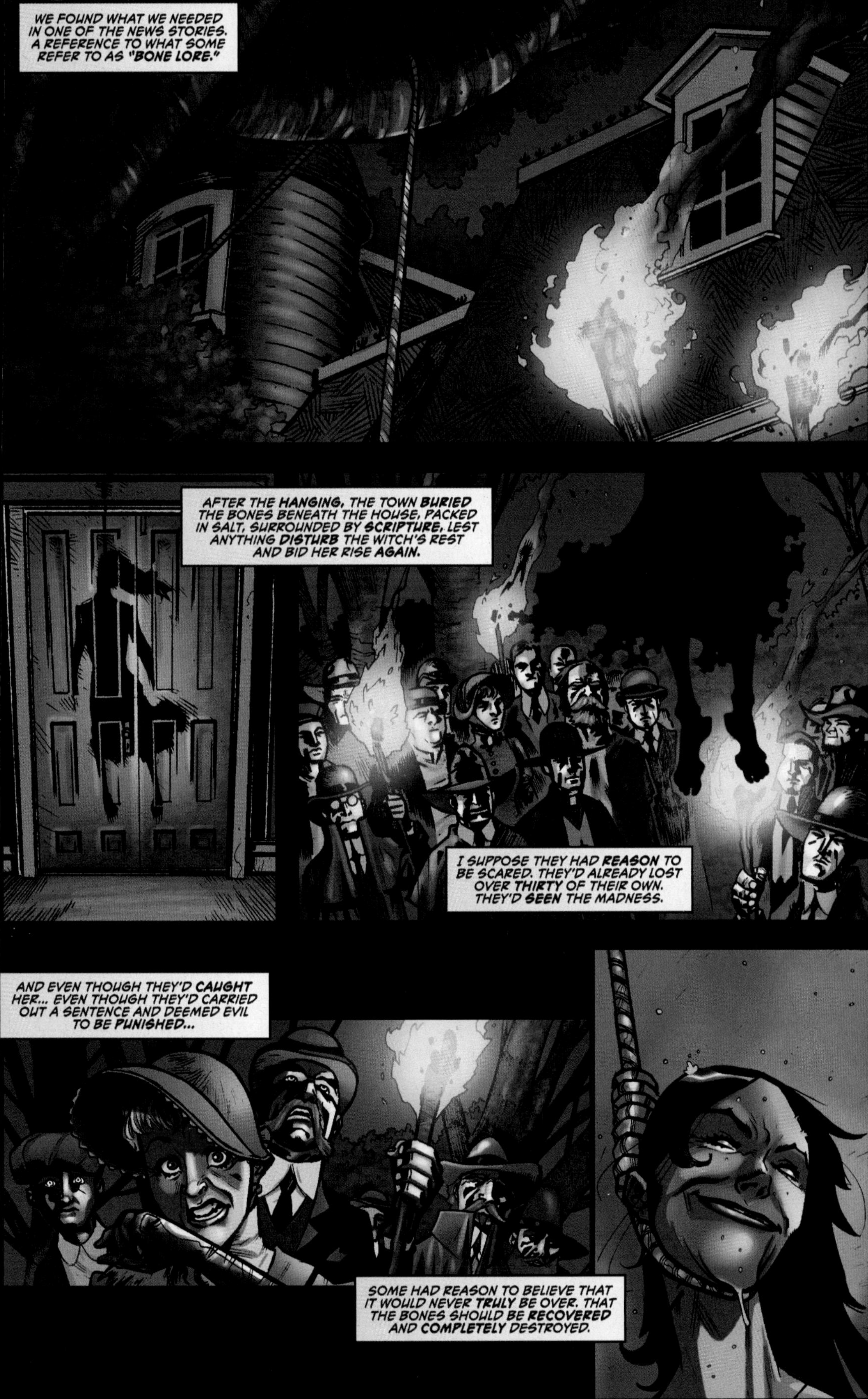
WE FOUND WHAT WE NEEDED IN ONE OF THE NEWS STORIES. A REFERENCE TO WHAT SOME REFER TO AS "BONE LORE."
AFTER THE HANGING, THE TOWN BURIED THE BONES BENEATH THE HOUSE, PACKED IN SALT, SURROUNDED BY SCRIPTURE, LEST ANYTHING DISTURB THE WITCH'S REST AND BID HER RISE AGAIN.
I SUPPOSE THEY HAD REASON TO BE SCARED. THEY'D ALREADY LOST OVER THIRTY OF THEIR OWN. THEY'D SEEN THE MADNESS.
AND EVEN THOUGH THEY'D CAUGHT HER... EVEN THOUGH THEY'D CARRIED OUT A SENTENCE AND DEEMED EVIL TO BE PUNISHED...
SOME HAD REASON TO BELIEVE THAT IT WOULD NEVER TRULY BE OVER. THAT THE BONES SHOULD BE RECOVERED AND COMPLETELY DESTROYED.

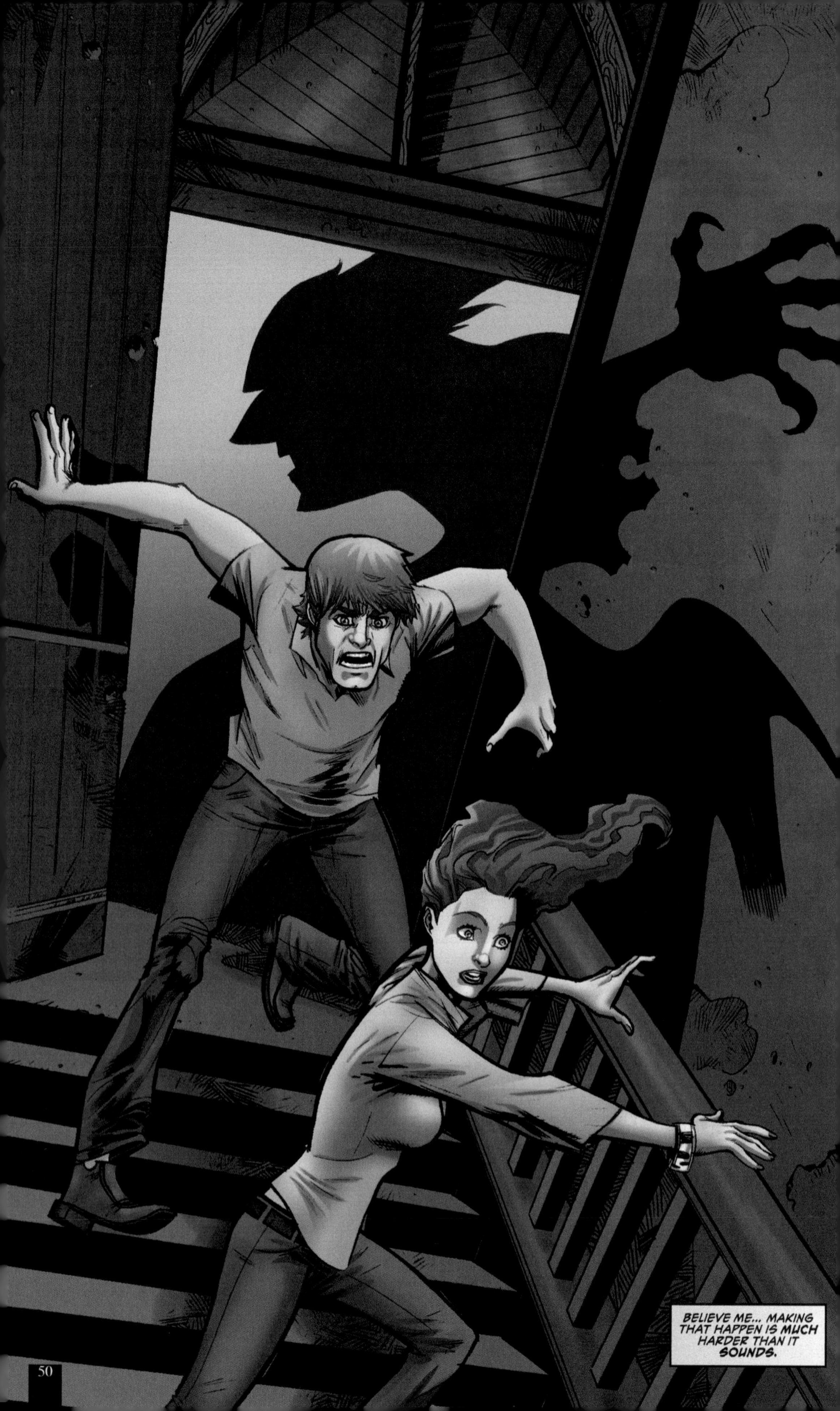
BELIEVE ME... MAKING THAT HAPPEN IS MUCH HARDER THAN IT SOUNDS.

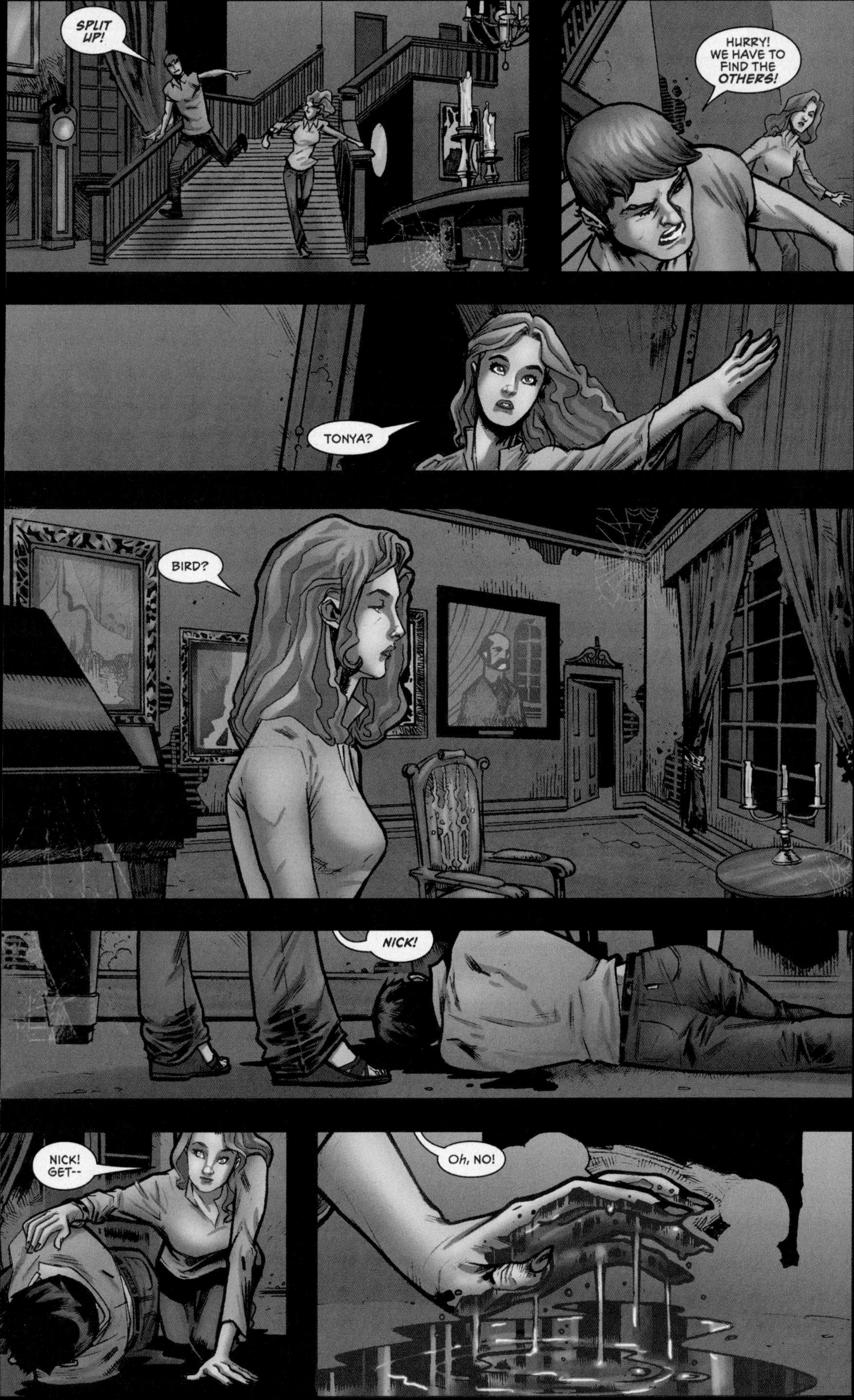
SPLIT UP!
HURRY! WE HAVE TO FIND THE OTHERS!
TONYA?
BIRD?
NICK!
NICK! GET--
Oh, NO!

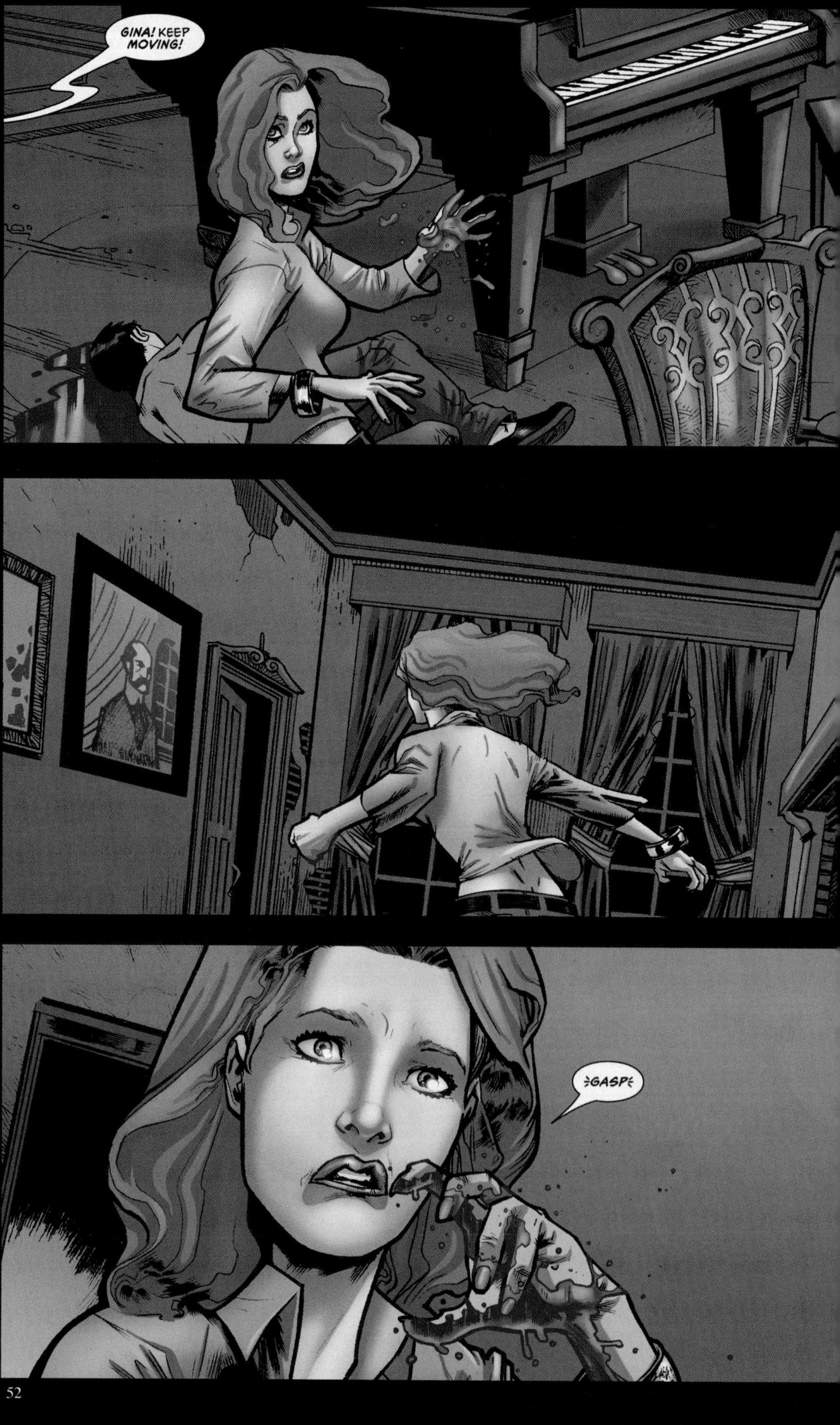
GINA! KEEP MOVING!
GASP

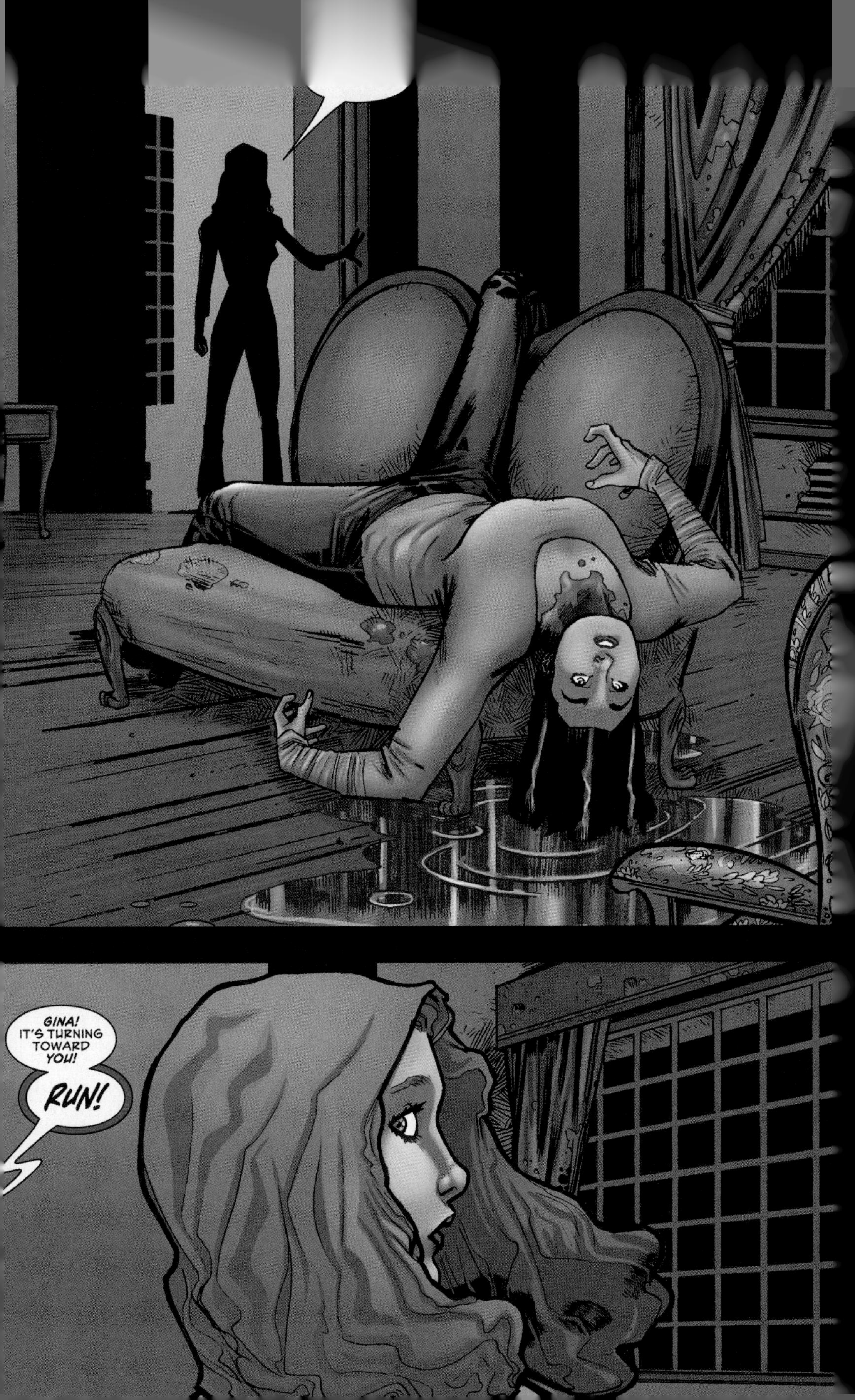
GINA! IT'S TURNING TOWARD YOU!
RUN!

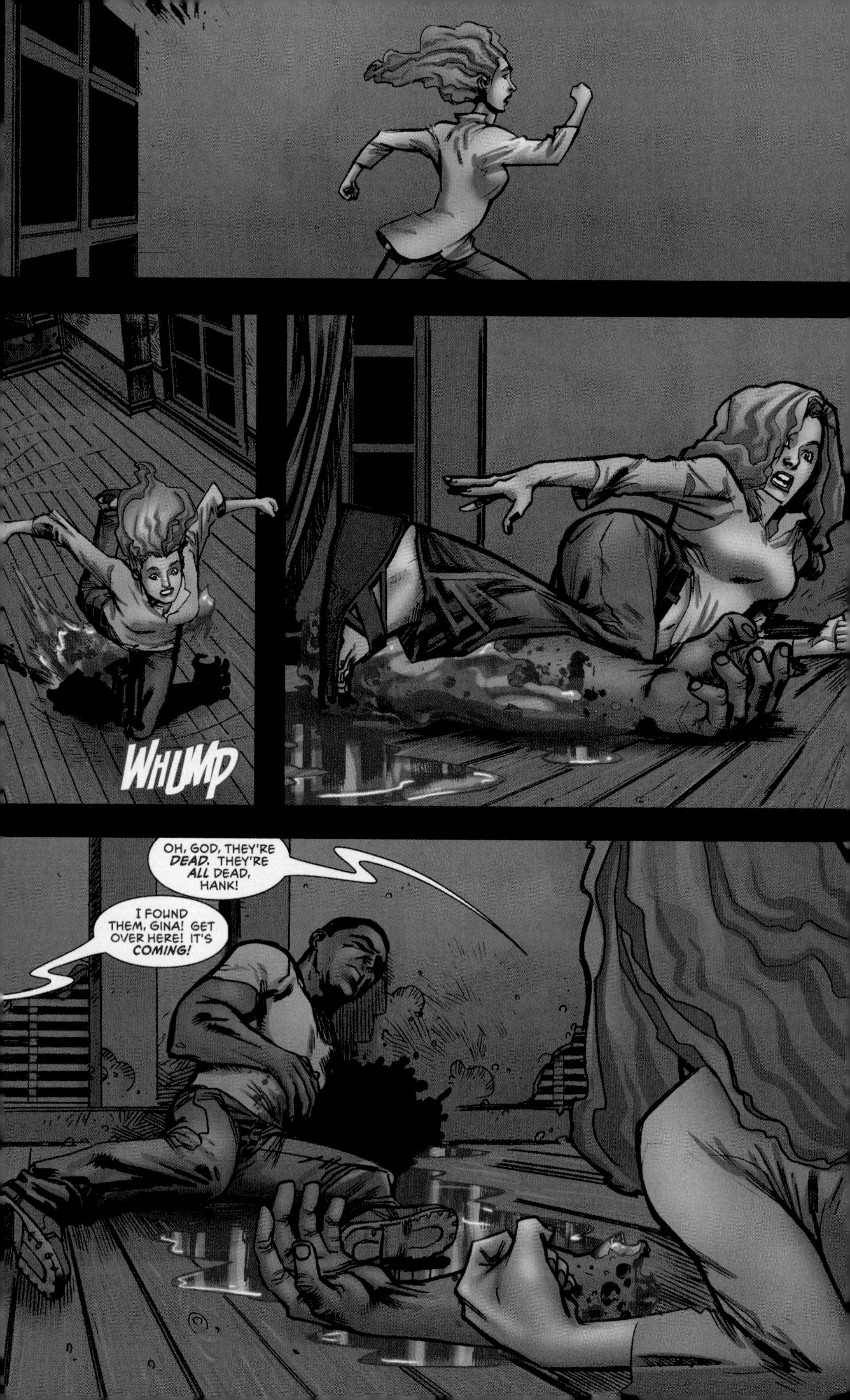
WHUMP
OH, GOD, THEY'RE DEAD. THEY'RE ALL DEAD, HANK!
I FOUND THEM, GINA! GET OVER HERE! IT'S COMING!

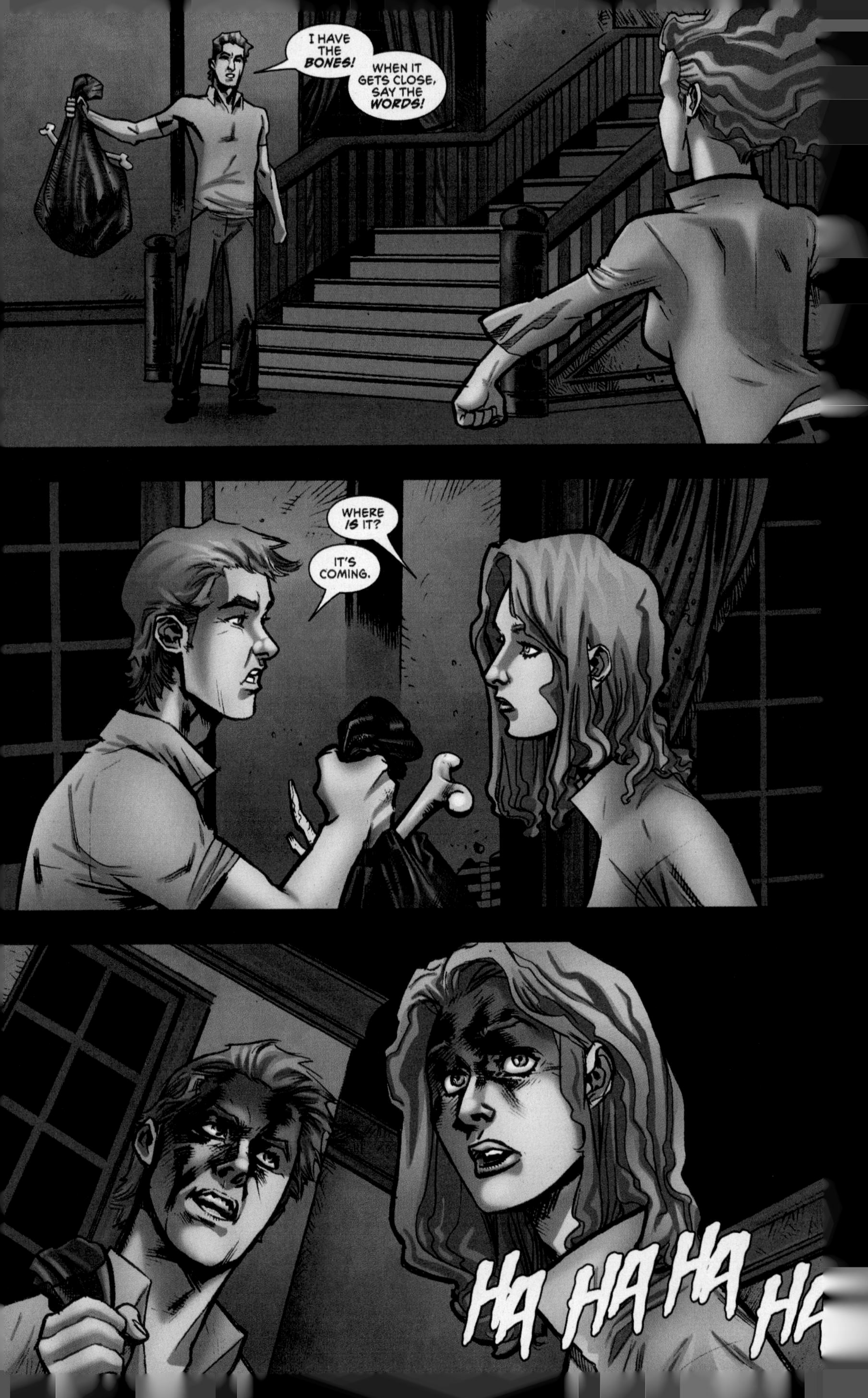
I HAVE THE BONES!
WHEN IT GETS CLOSE, SAY THE WORDS!
WHERE IS IT?
IT'S COMING.
HA HA HA HA

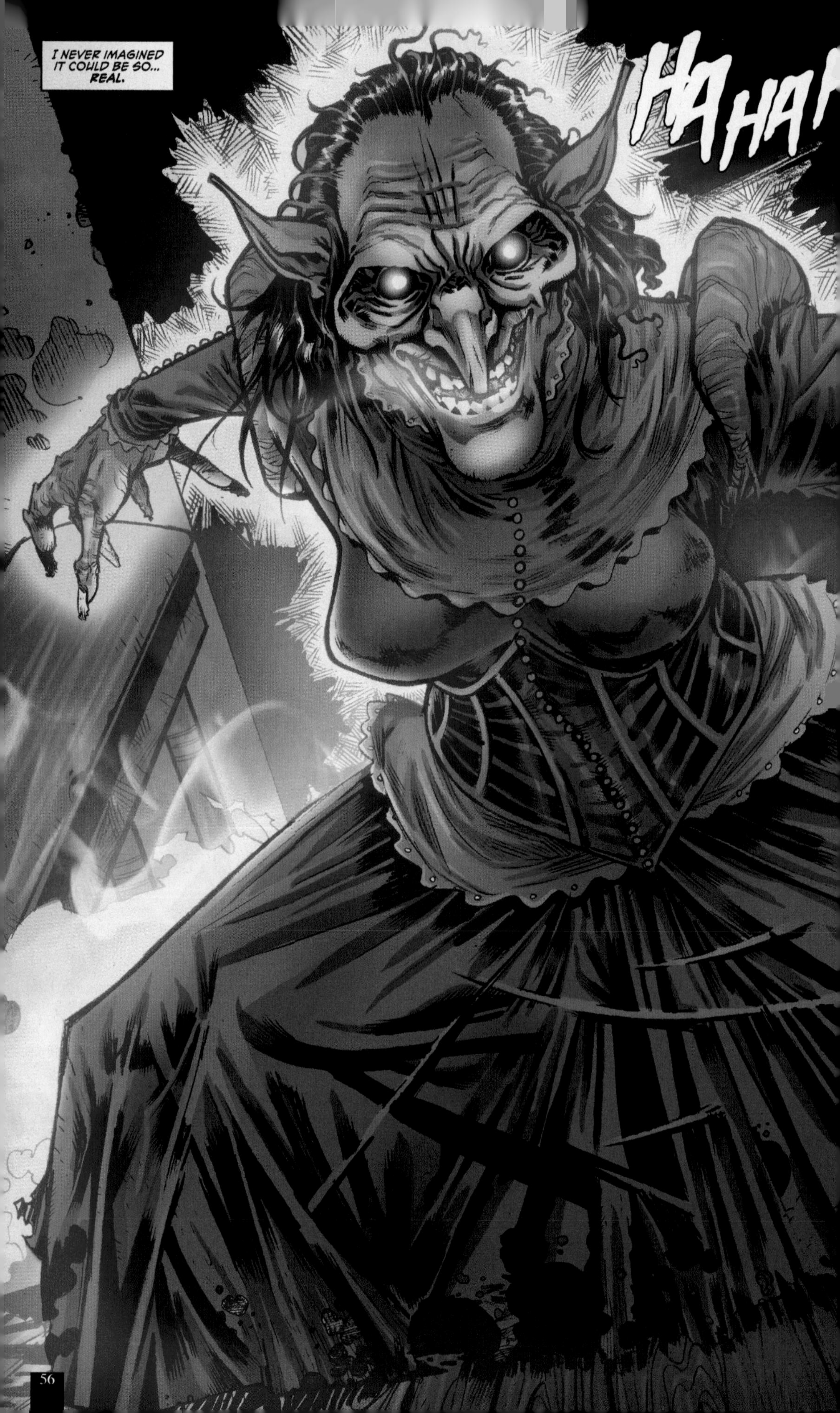
I NEVER IMAGINED IT COULD BE SO... REAL.
HAHA

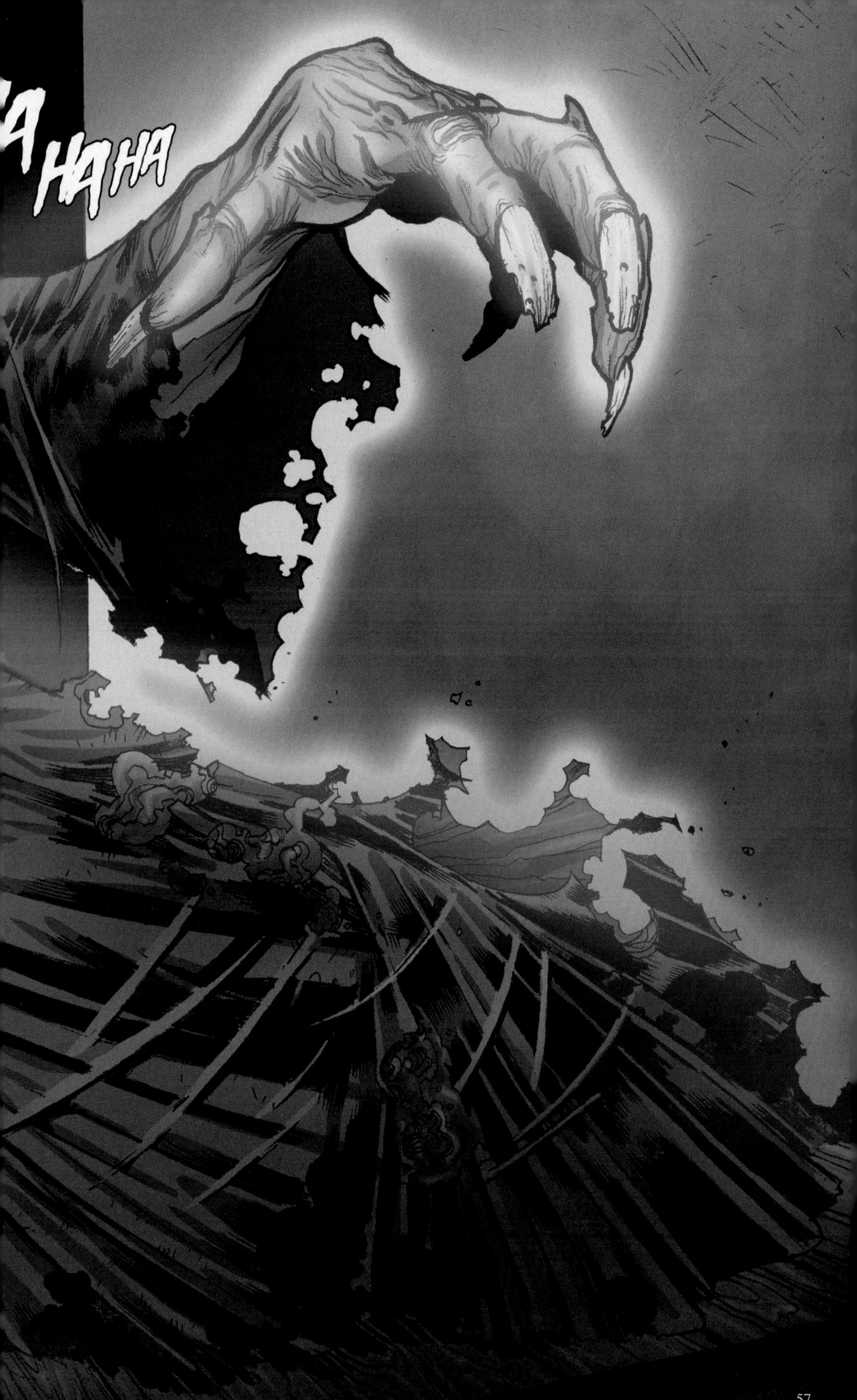
HA HA

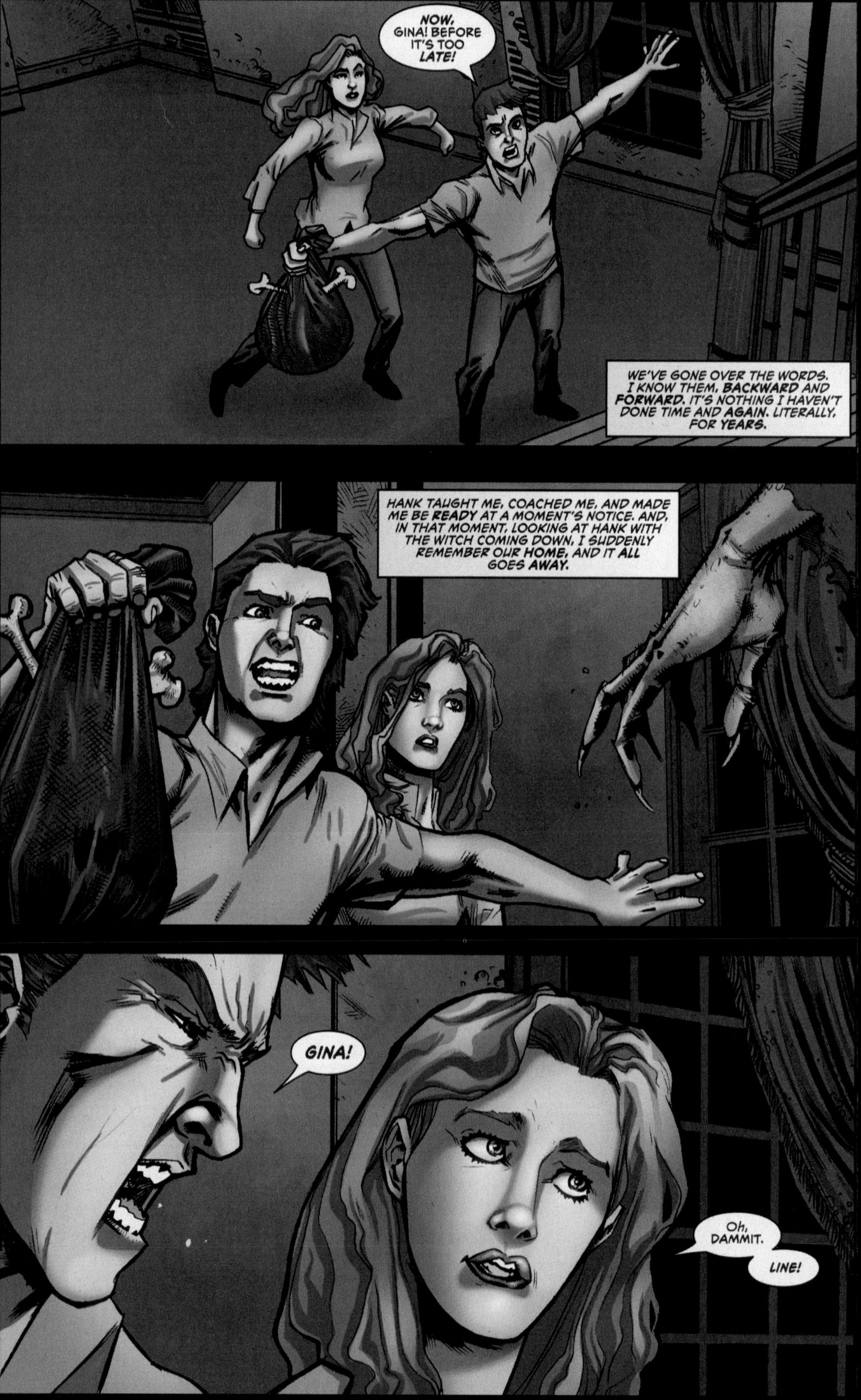
NOW, GINA! BEFORE IT'S TOO LATE!
WE'VE GONE OVER THE WORDS. I KNOW THEM. BACKWARD AND FORWARD. IT'S NOTHING I HAVEN'T DONE TIME AND AGAIN. LITERALLY. FOR YEARS.
HANK TAUGHT ME, COACHED ME, AND MADE ME BE READY AT A MOMENT'S NOTICE. AND, IN THAT MOMENT, LOOKING AT HANK WITH THE WITCH COMING DOWN, I SUDDENLY REMEMBER OUR HOME, AND IT ALL GOES AWAY.
GINA!
Oh, DAMMIT.
LINE!

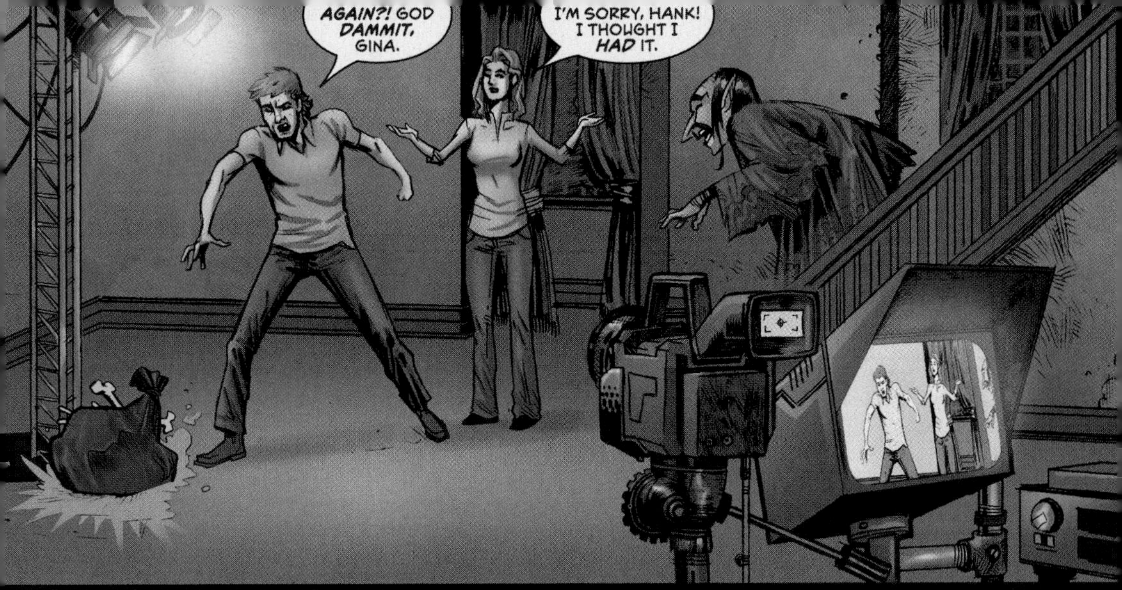
AGAIN?! GOD DAMMIT, GINA.
I'M SORRY, HANK! I THOUGHT I HAD IT.

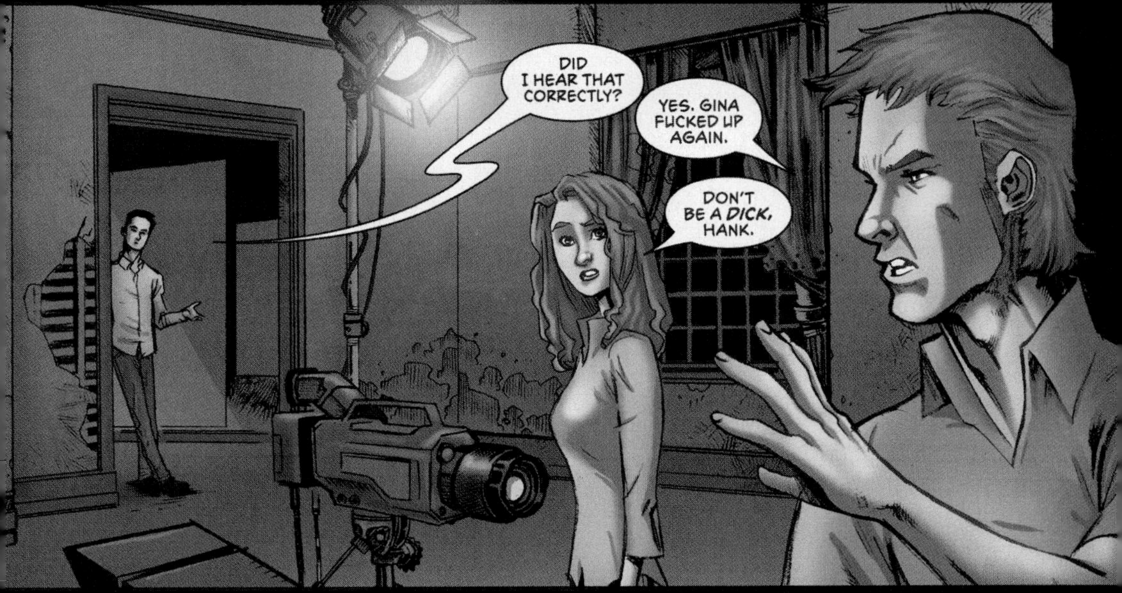
DID I HEAR THAT CORRECTLY?
YES. GINA FUCKED UP AGAIN.
DON'T BE A DICK, HANK.

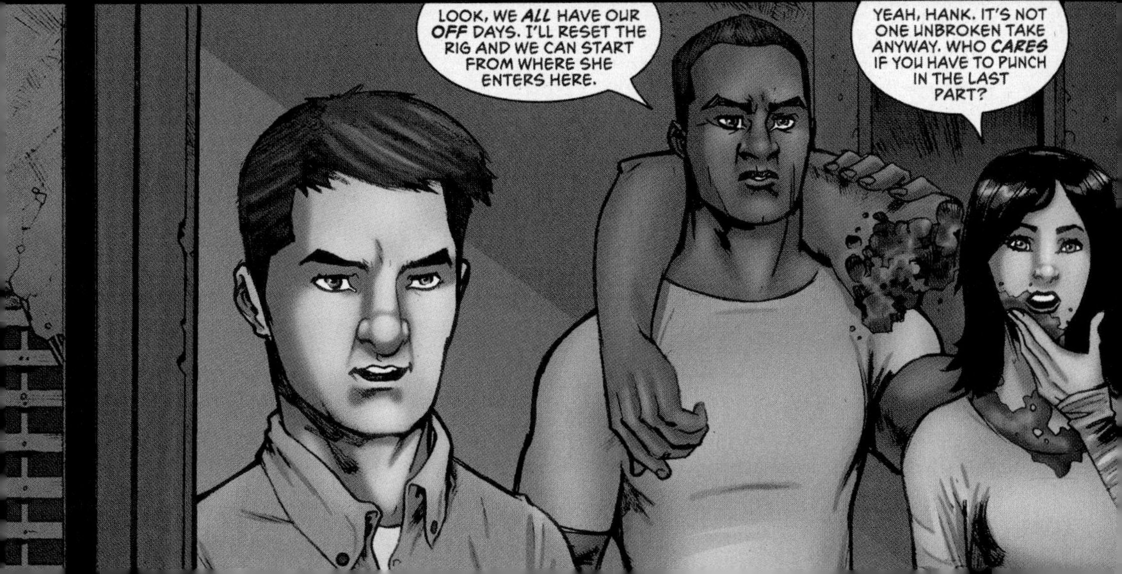
LOOK, WE ALL HAVE OUR OFF DAYS. I'LL RESET THE RIG AND WE CAN START FROM WHERE SHE ENTERS HERE.
YEAH, HANK. IT'S NOT ONE UNBROKEN TAKE ANYWAY. WHO CARES IF YOU HAVE TO PUNCH IN THE LAST PART?

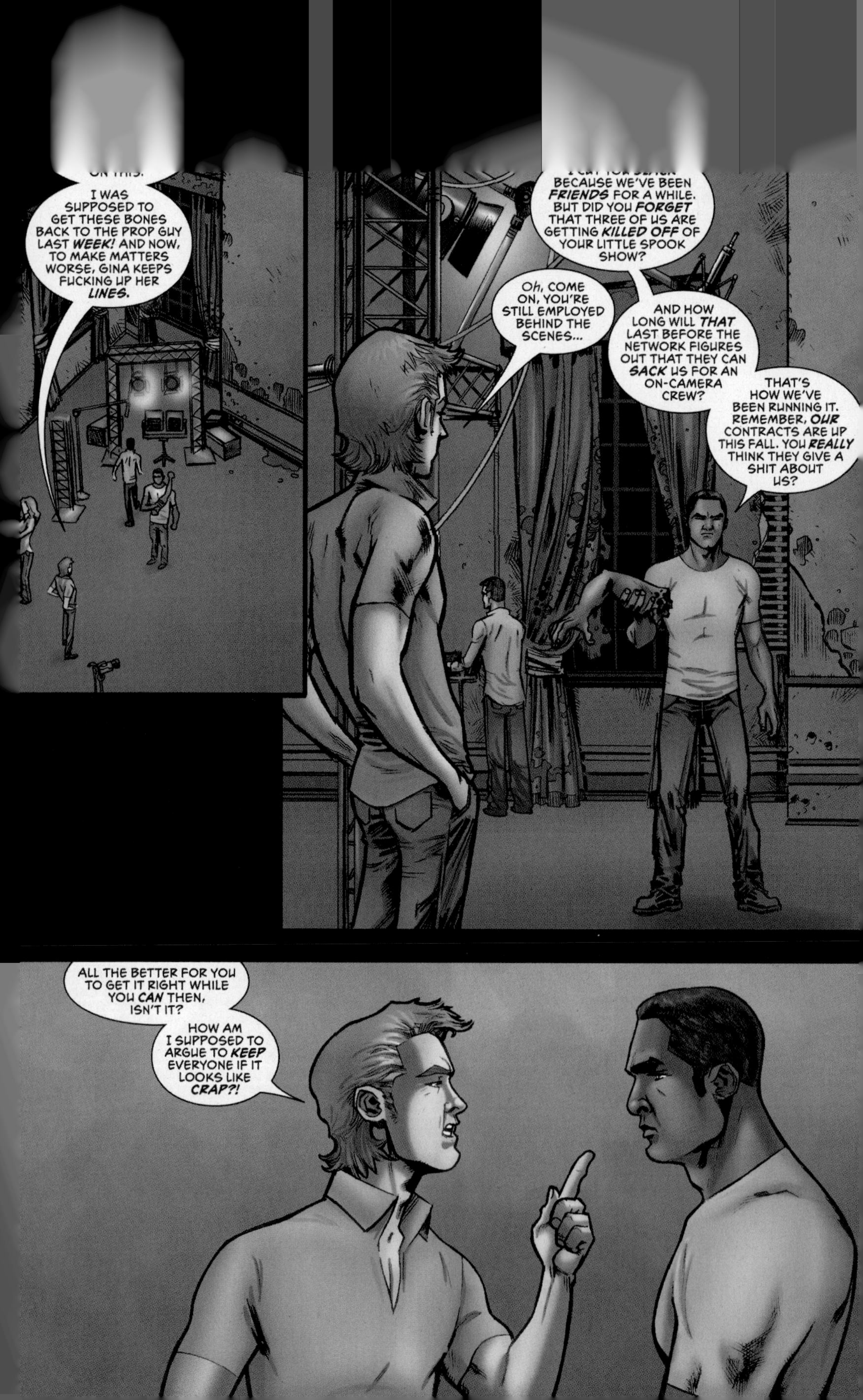

I WAS SUPPOSED TO GET THESE BONES BACK TO THE PROP GUY LAST WEEK! AND NOW, TO MAKE MATTERS WORSE, GINA KEEPS FUCKING UP HER LINES.
BECAUSE WE'VE BEEN FRIENDS FOR A WHILE. BUT DID YOU FORGET THAT THREE OF US ARE GETTING KILLED OFF OF YOUR LITTLE SPOOK SHOW?
Oh, COME ON, YOU'RE STILL EMPLOYED BEHIND THE SCENES...
AND HOW LONG WILL THAT LAST BEFORE THE NETWORK FIGURES OUT THAT THEY CAN SACK US FOR AN ON-CAMERA CREW?
THAT'S HOW WE'VE BEEN RUNNING IT. REMEMBER, OUR CONTRACTS ARE UP THIS FALL. YOU REALLY THINK THEY GIVE A SHIT ABOUT US?
ALL THE BETTER FOR YOU TO GET IT RIGHT WHILE YOU CAN THEN, ISN'T IT?
HOW AM I SUPPOSED TO ARGUE TO KEEP EVERYONE IF IT LOOKS LIKE CRAP?!

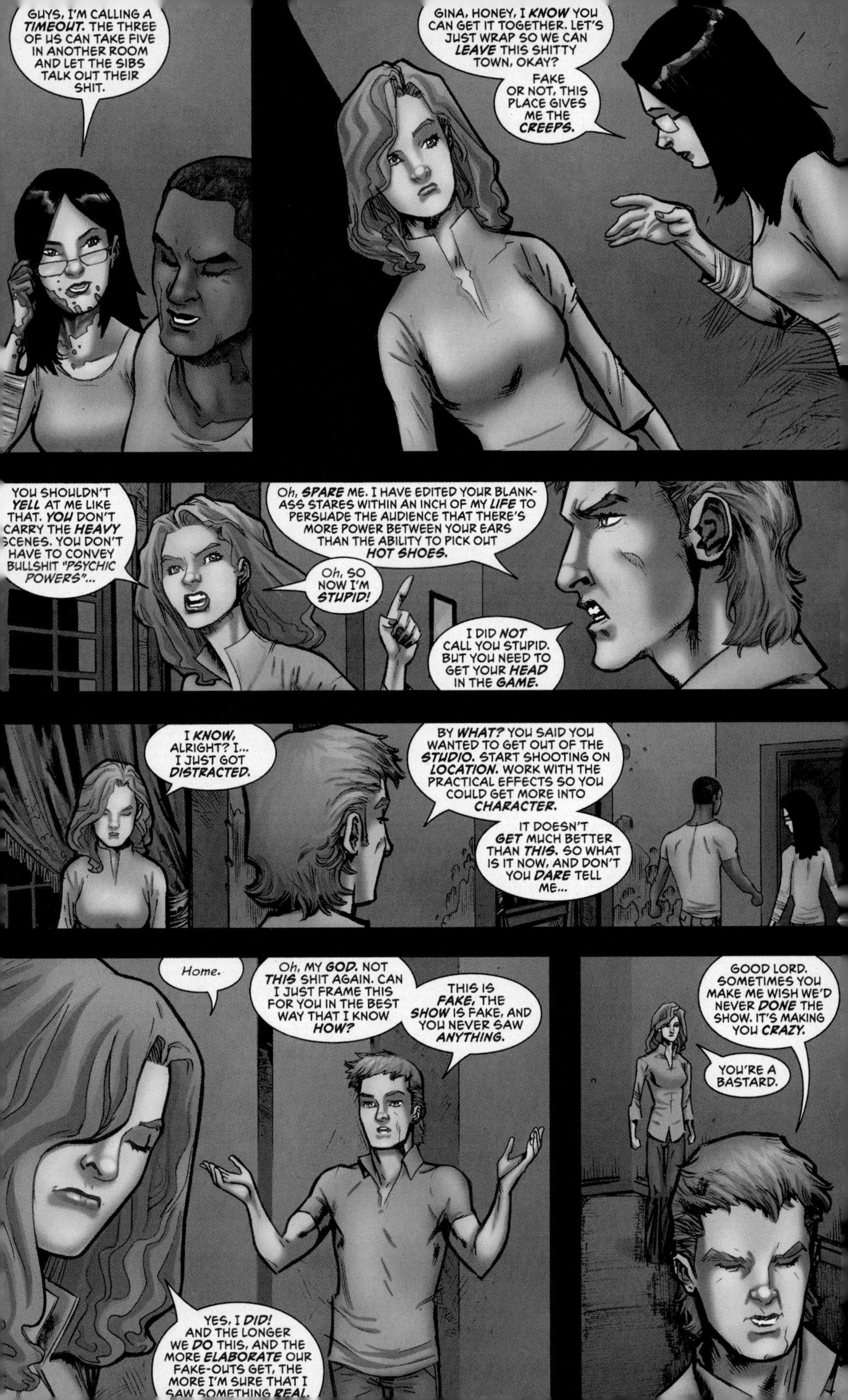
GUYS, I'M CALLING A TIMEOUT. THE THREE OF US CAN TAKE FIVE IN ANOTHER ROOM AND LET THE SIBS TALK OUT THEIR SHIT.
GINA, HONEY, I KNOW YOU CAN GET IT TOGETHER. LET'S JUST WRAP SO WE CAN LEAVE THIS SHITTY TOWN, OKAY?
FAKE OR NOT, THIS PLACE GIVES ME THE CREEPS.
YOU SHOULDN'T YELL AT ME LIKE THAT. YOU DON'T CARRY THE HEAVY SCENES. YOU DON'T HAVE TO CONVEY BULLSHIT "PSYCHIC POWERS"...
Oh, SPARE ME. I HAVE EDITED YOUR BLANK-ASS STARES WITHIN AN INCH OF MY LIFE TO PERSUADE THE AUDIENCE THAT THERE'S MORE POWER BETWEEN YOUR EARS THAN THE ABILITY TO PICK OUT HOT SHOES.
Oh, SO NOW I'M STUPID!
I DID NOT CALL YOU STUPID. BUT YOU NEED TO GET YOUR HEAD IN THE GAME.
I KNOW, ALRIGHT? I... I JUST GOT DISTRACTED.
BY WHAT? YOU SAID YOU WANTED TO GET OUT OF THE STUDIO. START SHOOTING ON LOCATION. WORK WITH THE PRACTICAL EFFECTS SO YOU COULD GET MORE INTO CHARACTER.
IT DOESN'T GET MUCH BETTER THAN THIS. SO WHAT IS IT NOW, AND DON'T YOU DARE TELL ME...
Home.
Oh, MY GOD. NOT THIS SHIT AGAIN. CAN I JUST FRAME THIS FOR YOU IN THE BEST WAY THAT I KNOW HOW?
THIS IS FAKE, THE SHOW IS FAKE, AND YOU NEVER SAW ANYTHING.
YES, I DID! AND THE LONGER WE DO THIS, AND THE MORE ELABORATE OUR FAKE-OUTS GET, THE MORE I'M SURE THAT I SAW SOMETHING REAL.
GOOD LORD. SOMETIMES YOU MAKE ME WISH WE'D NEVER DONE THE SHOW. IT'S MAKING YOU CRAZY.
YOU'RE A BASTARD.

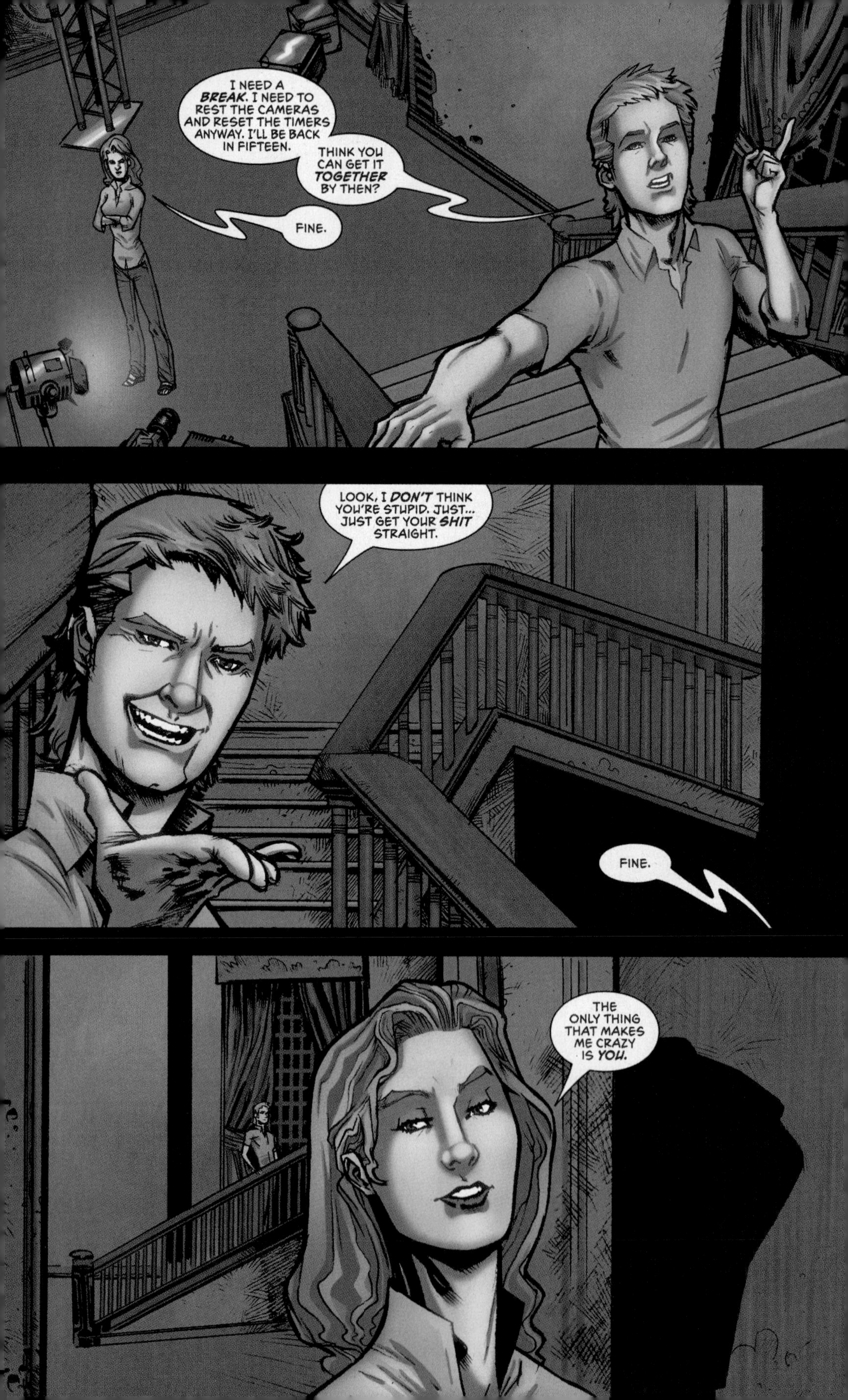
I NEED A BREAK. I NEED TO REST THE CAMERAS AND RESET THE TIMERS ANYWAY. I'LL BE BACK IN FIFTEEN.
THINK YOU CAN GET IT TOGETHER BY THEN?
FINE.
LOOK, I DON'T THINK YOU'RE STUPID. JUST... JUST GET YOUR SHIT STRAIGHT.
FINE.
THE ONLY THING THAT MAKES ME CRAZY IS YOU.

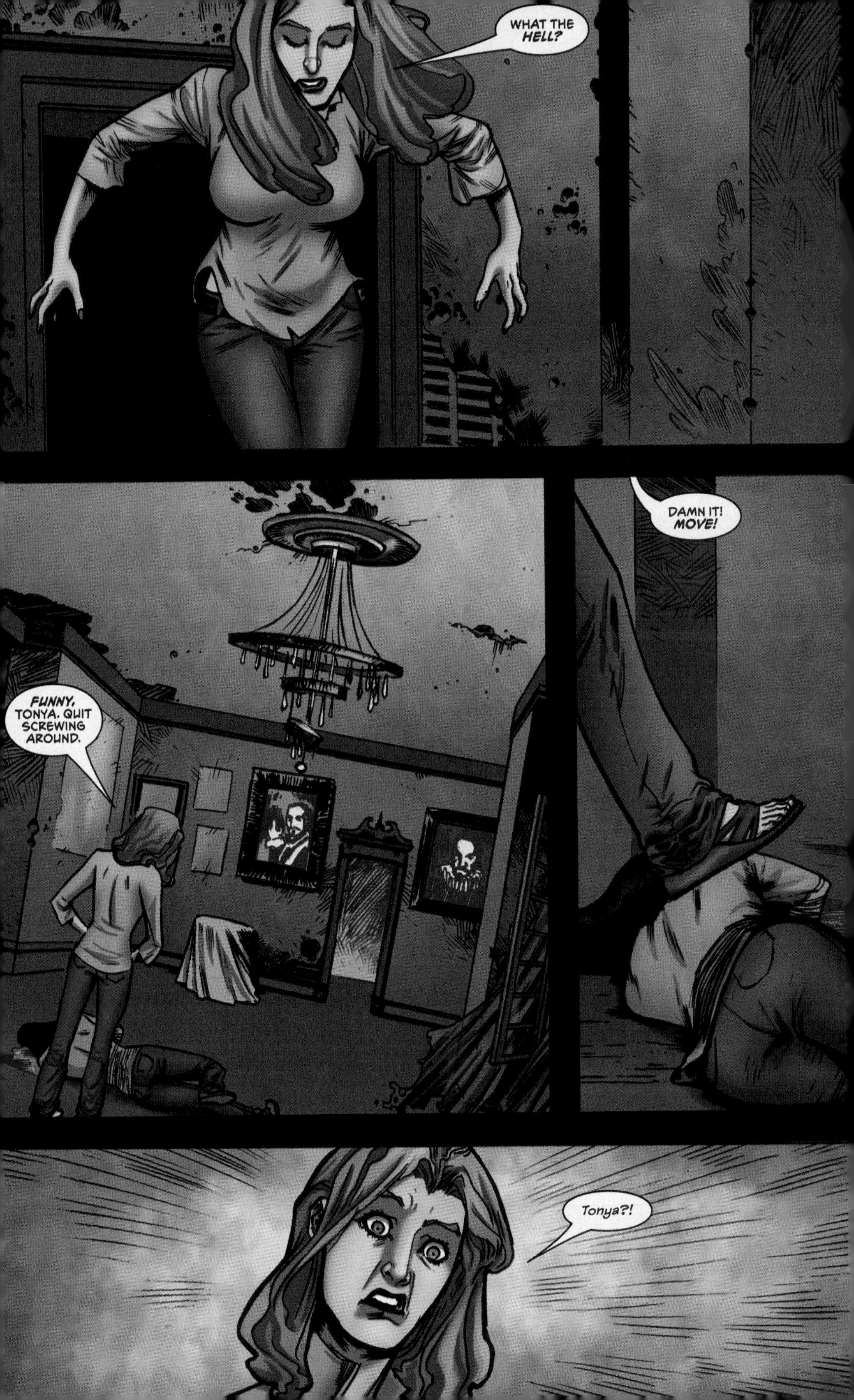
WHAT THE HELL?
FUNNY, TONYA. QUIT SCREWING AROUND.
DAMN IT! MOVE!
Tonya?!

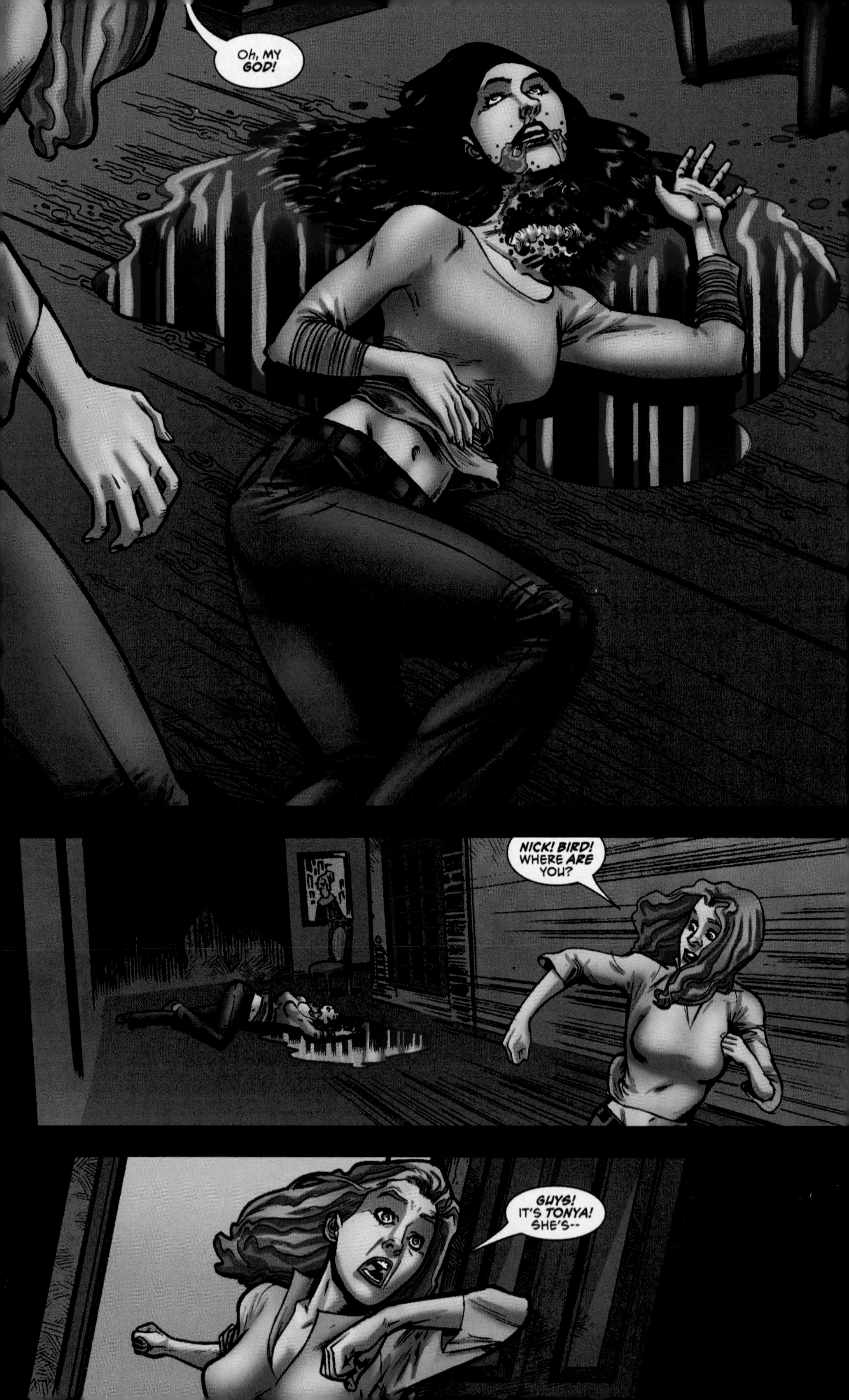
Oh, MY GOD!
NICK! BIRD! WHERE ARE YOU?
GUYS! IT'S TONYA! SHE'S--

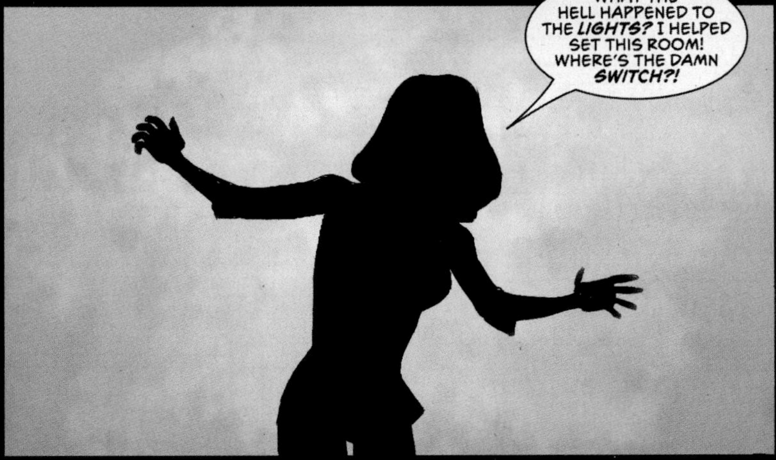
WHAT THE HELL HAPPENED TO THE LIGHTS? I HELPED SET THIS ROOM! WHERE'S THE DAMN SWITCH?!

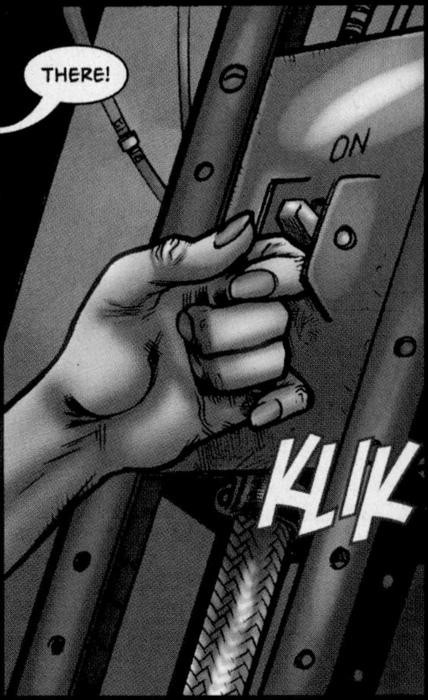
THERE!
ON
KLIK

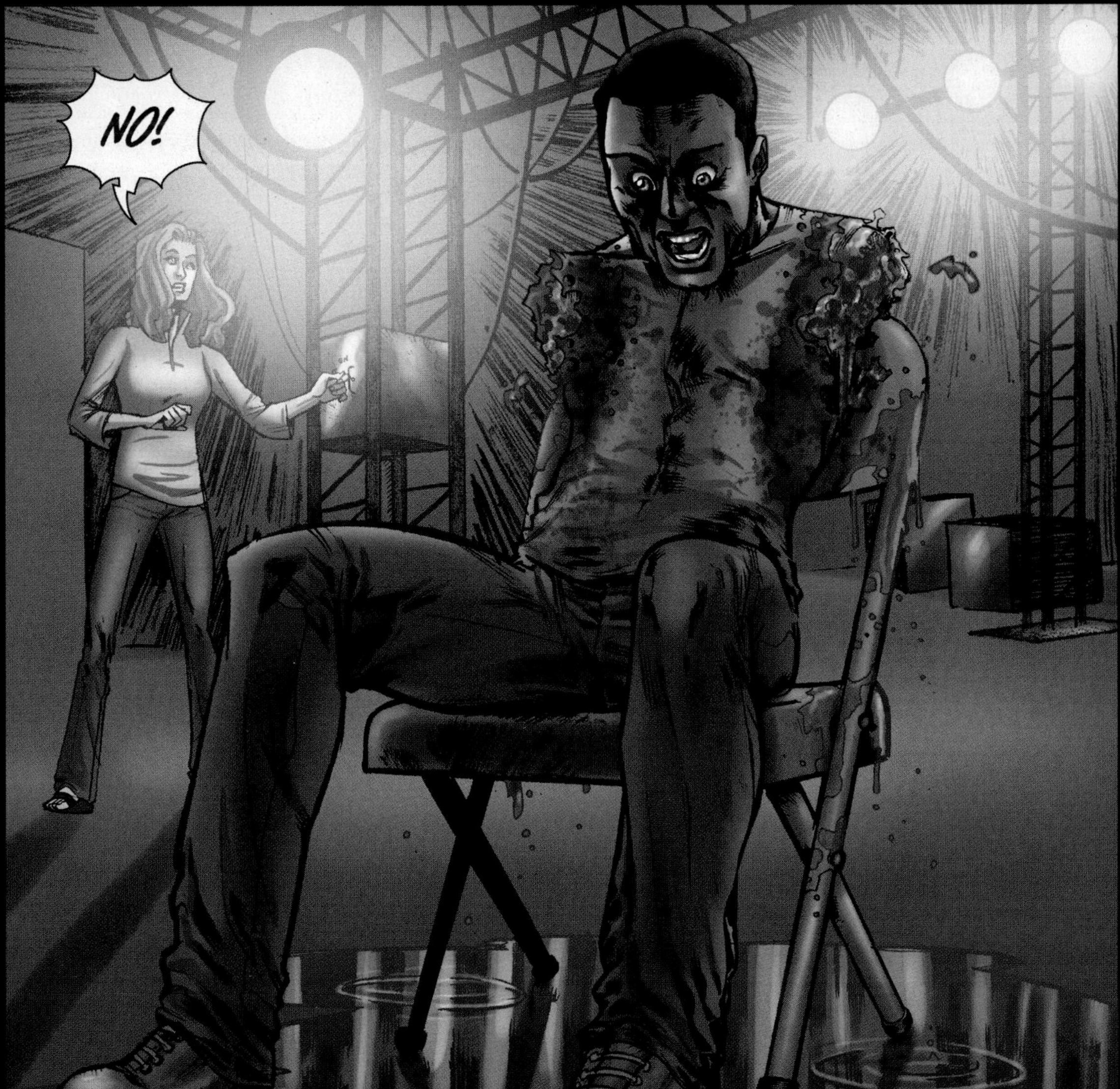
NO!

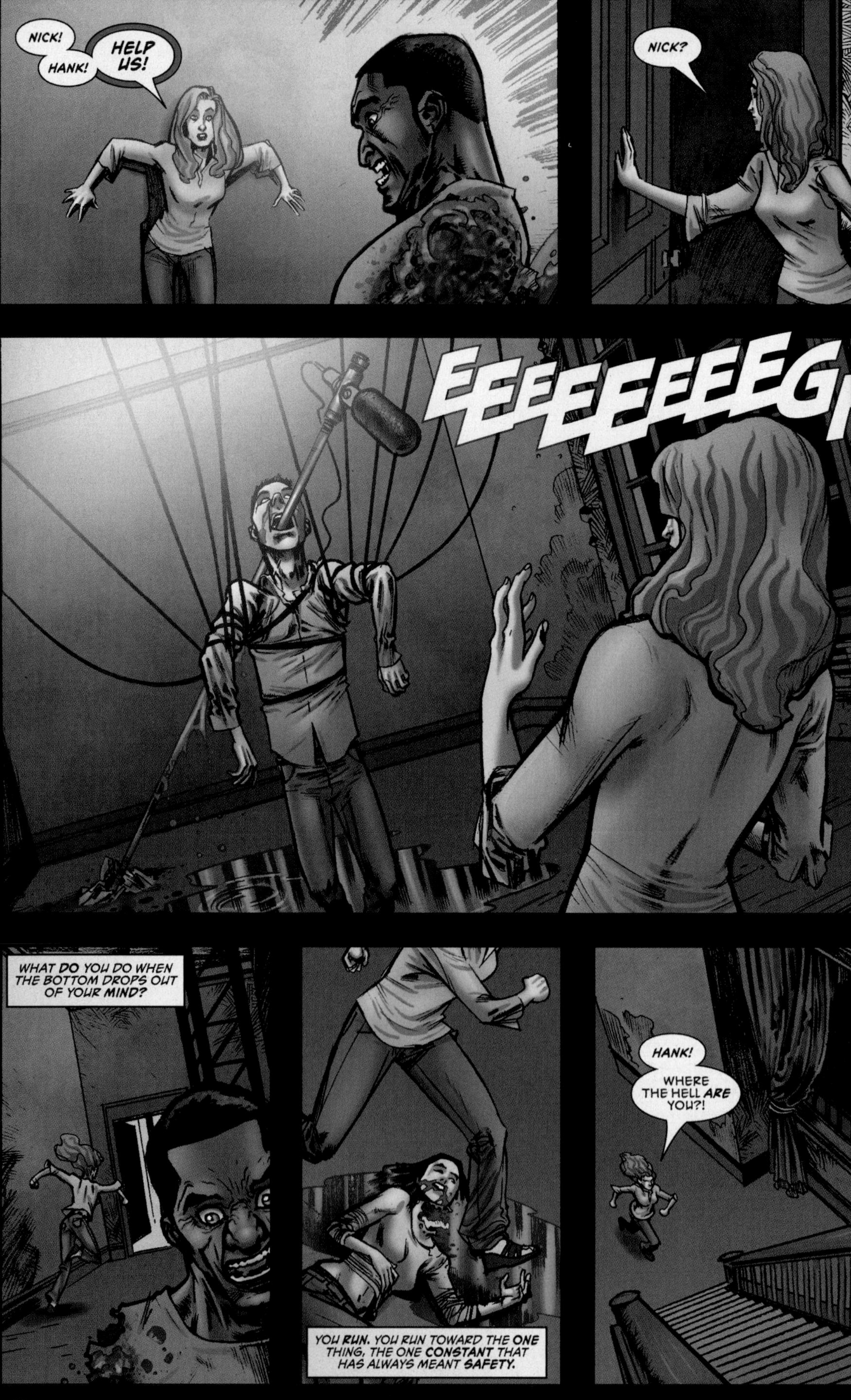
NICK!
HANK!
HELP US!
NICK?
EEEEEEEEEG
WHAT DO YOU DO WHEN THE BOTTOM DROPS OUT OF YOUR MIND?
YOU RUN. YOU RUN TOWARD THE ONE THING, THE ONE CONSTANT THAT HAS ALWAYS MEANT SAFETY.
HANK!
WHERE THE HELL ARE YOU?!

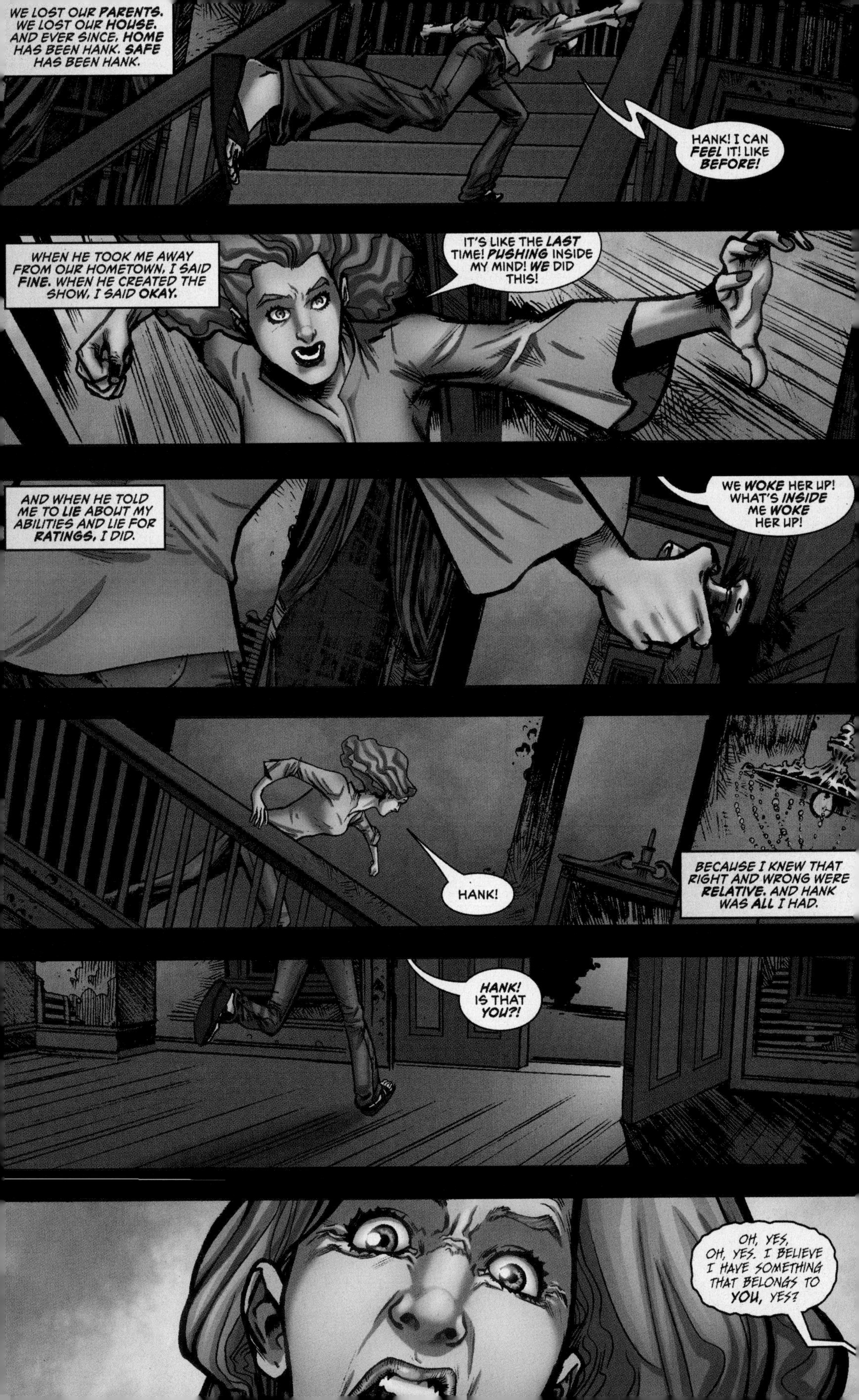

WE LOST OUR PARENTS. WE LOST OUR HOUSE. AND EVER SINCE, HOME HAS BEEN HANK. SAFE HAS BEEN HANK.
HANK! I CAN FEEL IT! LIKE BEFORE!
WHEN HE TOOK ME AWAY FROM OUR HOMETOWN, I SAID FINE. WHEN HE CREATED THE SHOW, I SAID OKAY.
IT'S LIKE THE LAST TIME! PUSHING INSIDE MY MIND! WE DID THIS!
AND WHEN HE TOLD ME TO LIE ABOUT MY ABILITIES AND LIE FOR RATINGS, I DID.
WE WOKE HER UP! WHAT'S INSIDE ME WOKE HER UP!
HANK!
BECAUSE I KNEW THAT RIGHT AND WRONG WERE RELATIVE. AND HANK WAS ALL I HAD.
HANK! IS THAT YOU?!
OH, YES, OH, YES. I BELIEVE I HAVE SOMETHING THAT BELONGS TO YOU, YES?

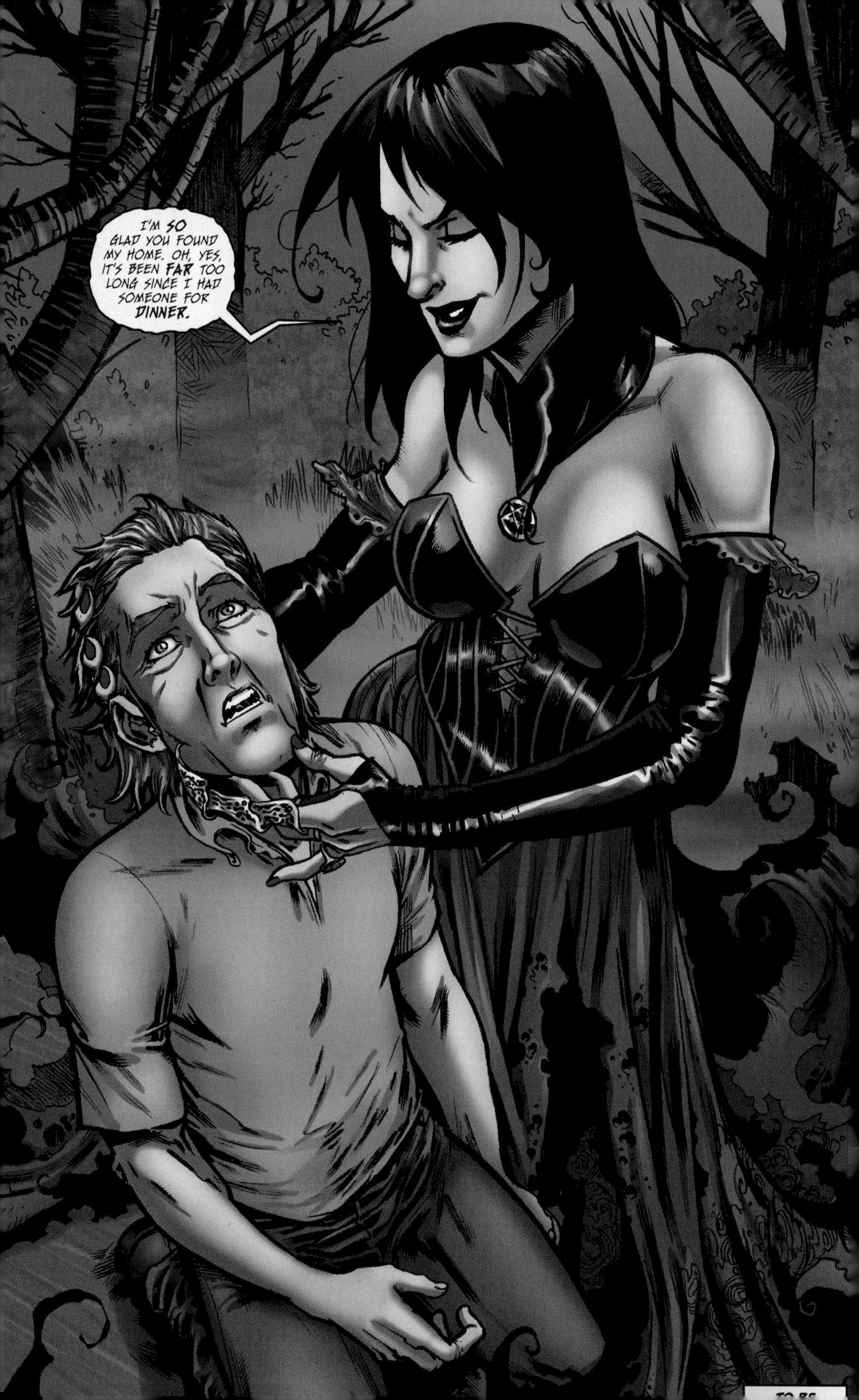
I'M SO GLAD YOU FOUND MY HOME. OH, YES, IT'S BEEN FAR TOO LONG SINCE I HAD SOMEONE FOR DINNER.

Grimm Fairy Tales
Myths & Legends

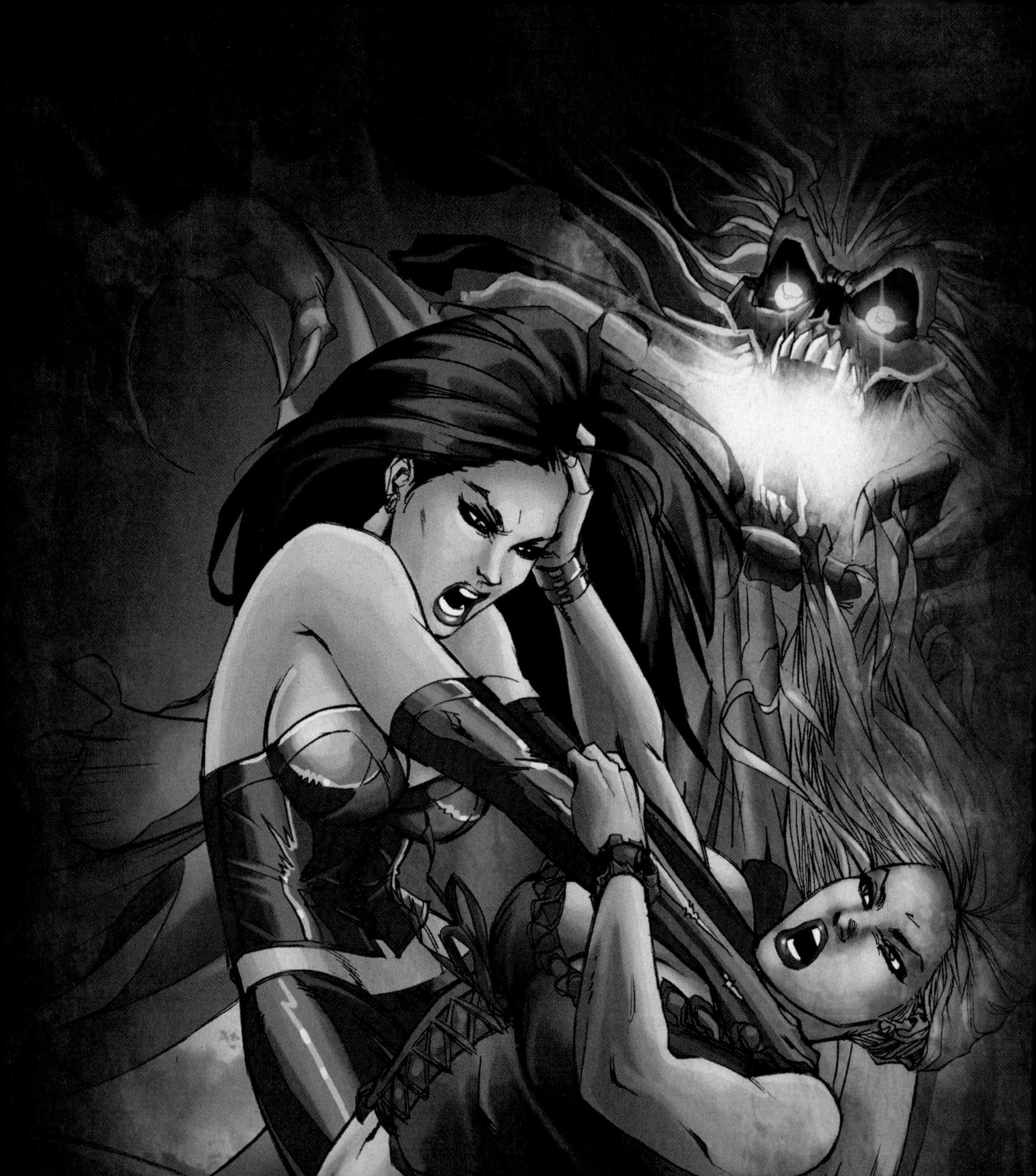

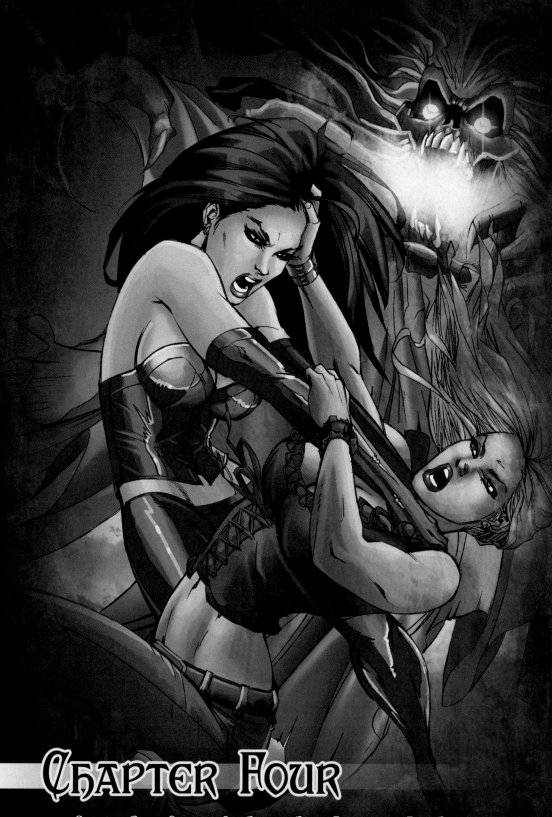

CHAPTER FOUR

Story by Raven Gregory, Joe Brusha, Ralph Tedesco and Troy Brownfield

Written by Troy Brownfield • Art by Amancay Nahuelpan and Ayhan Hayrula

Colors by Marc Lewis • Letters by Jim Campbell

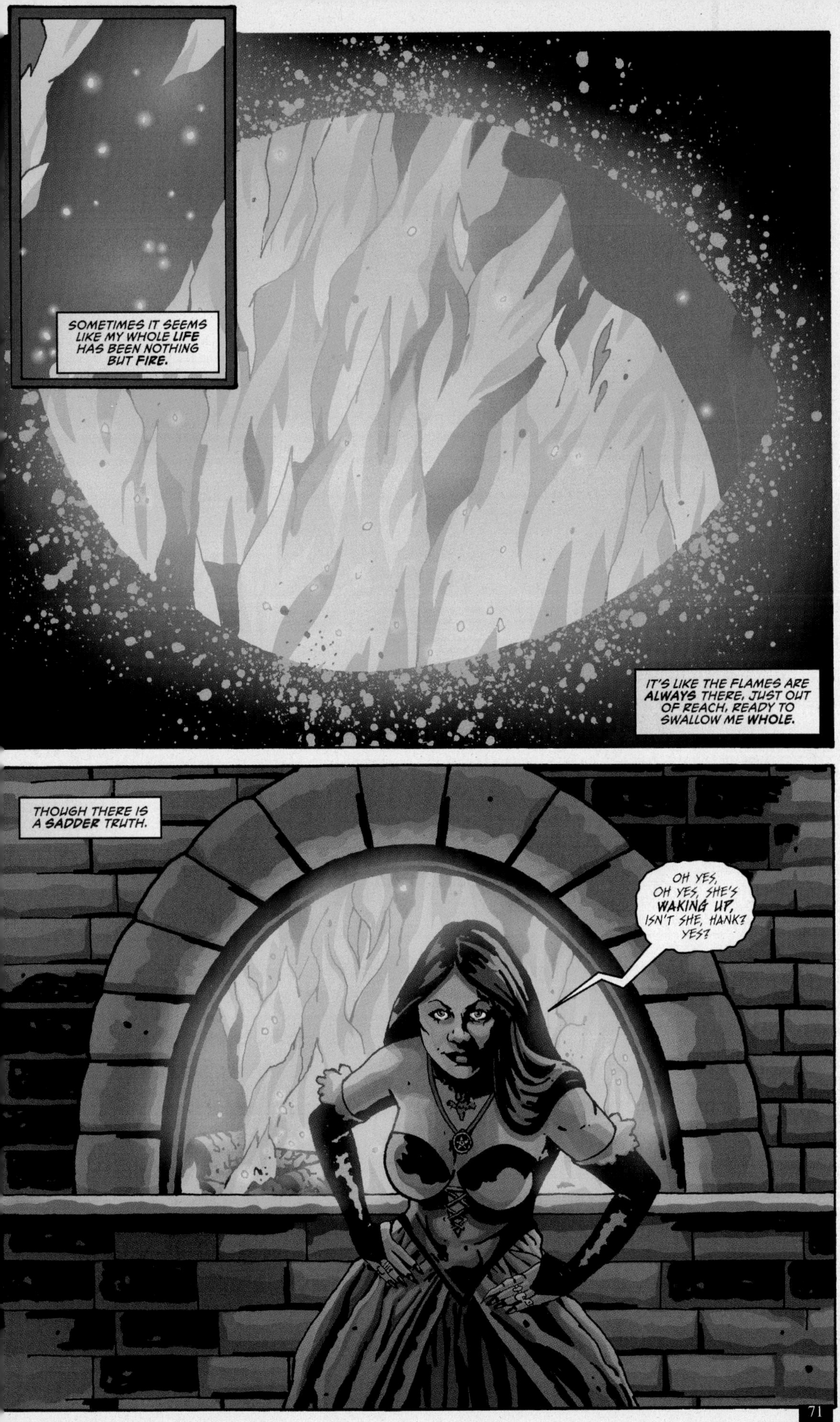
SOMETIMES IT SEEMS LIKE MY WHOLE LIFE HAS BEEN NOTHING BUT FIRE.
IT'S LIKE THE FLAMES ARE ALWAYS THERE, JUST OUT OF REACH, READY TO SWALLOW ME WHOLE.
THOUGH THERE IS A SADDER TRUTH.
OH YES, OH YES, SHE'S WAKING UP, ISN'T SHE, HANK? YES?

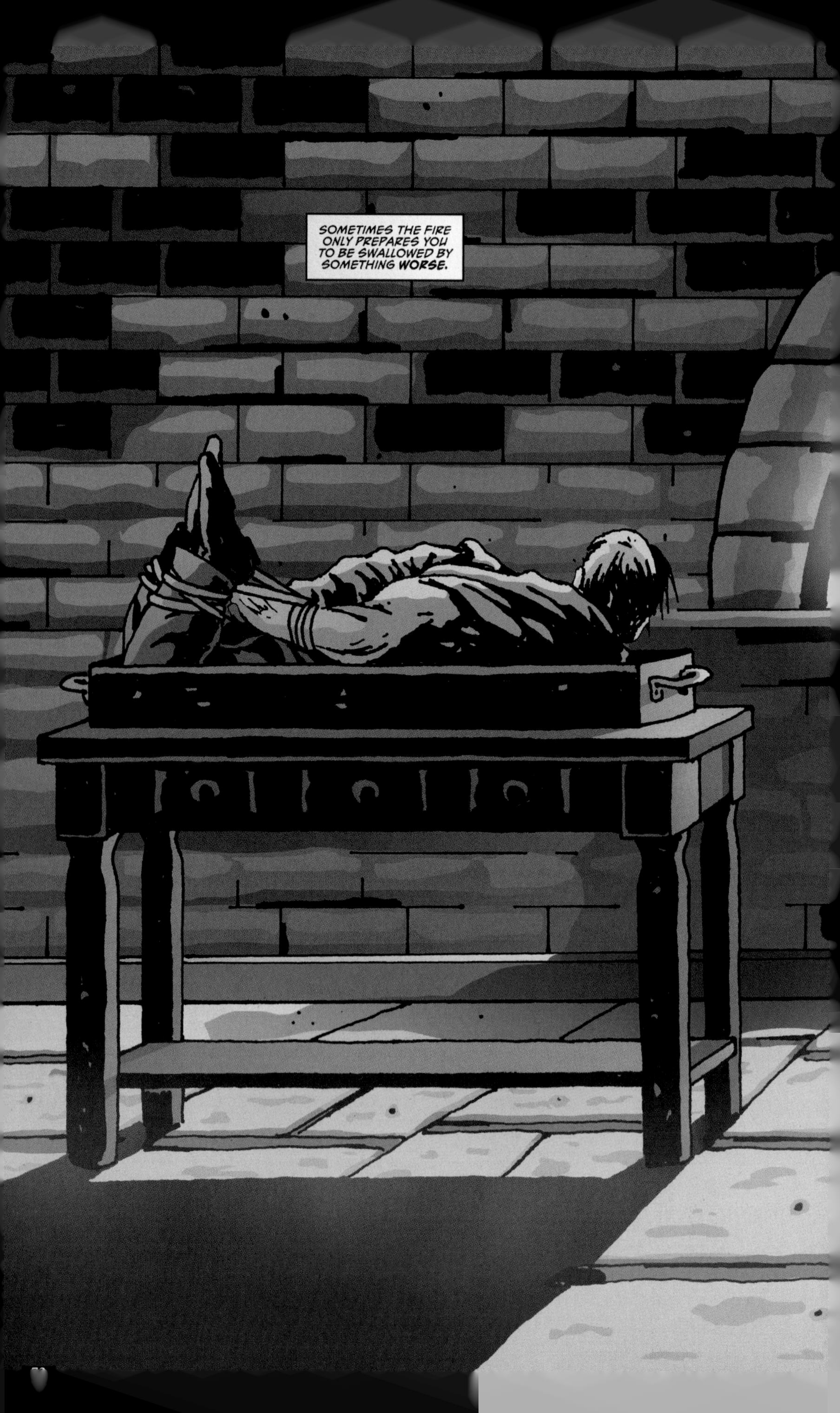
SOMETIMES THE FIRE ONLY PREPARES YOU TO BE SWALLOWED BY SOMETHING WORSE.

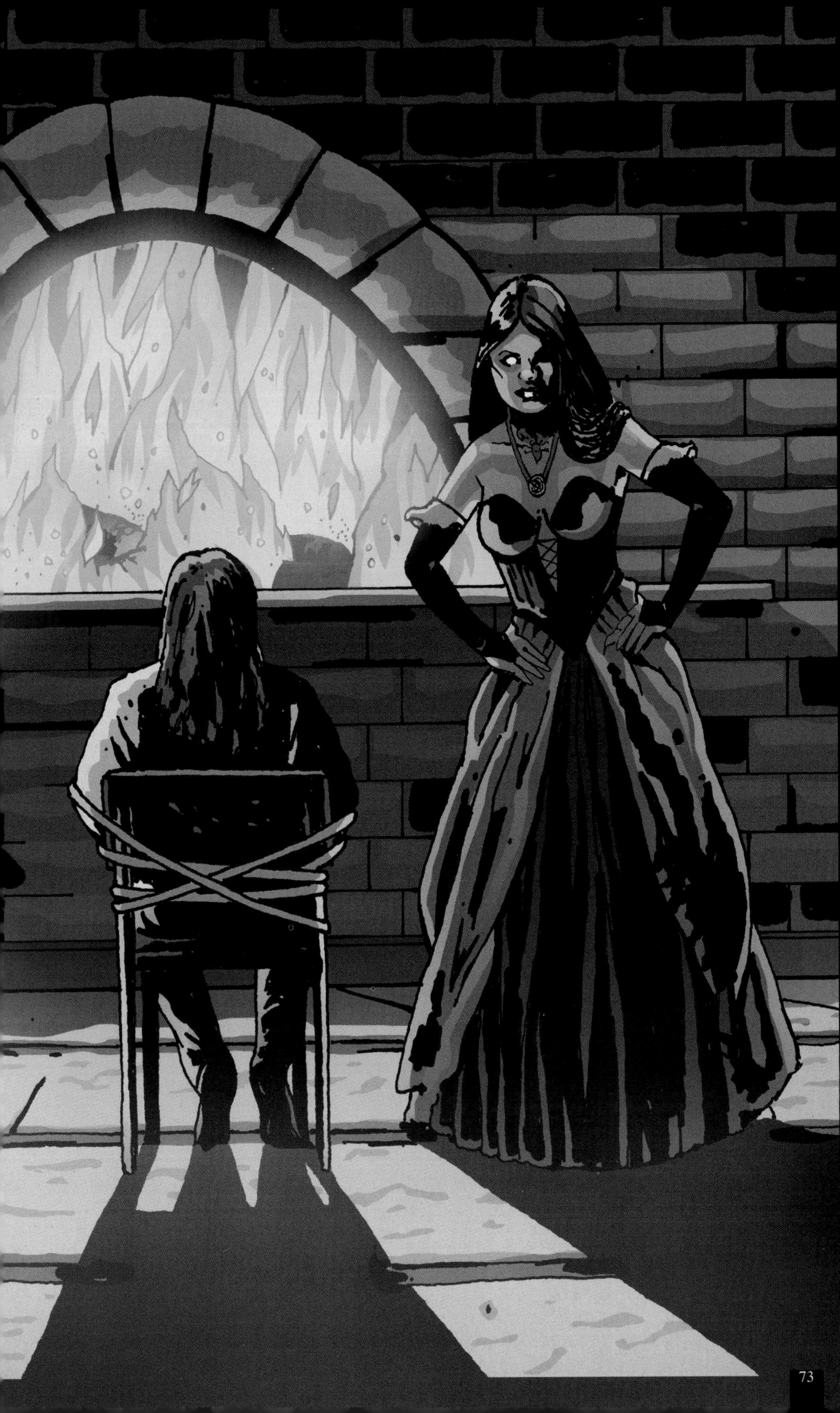

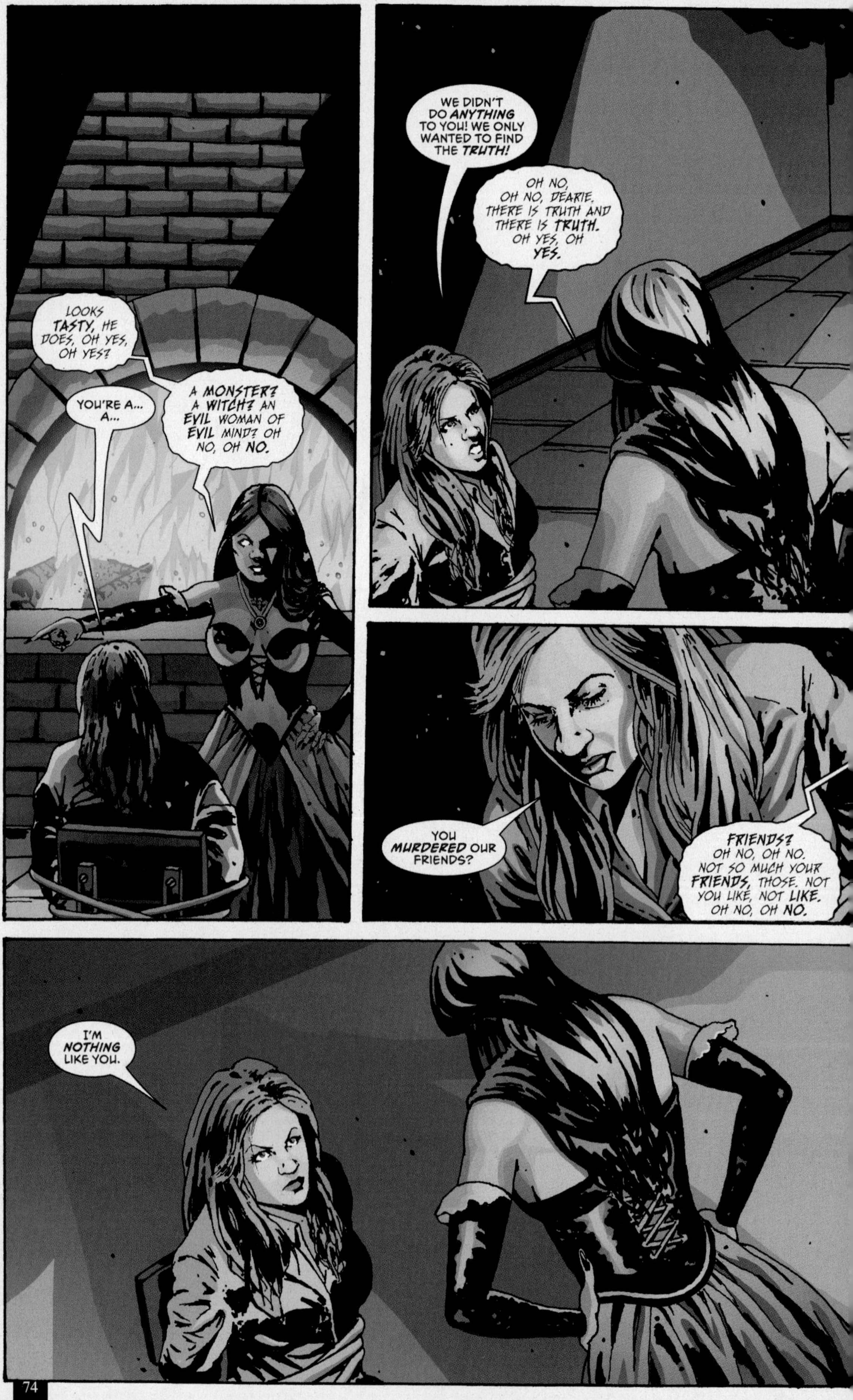
LOOKS TASTY, HE DOES, OH YES, OH YES?
YOU'RE A... A...
A MONSTER? A WITCH? AN EVIL WOMAN OF EVIL MIND? OH NO, OH NO.
WE DIDN'T DO ANYTHING TO YOU! WE ONLY WANTED TO FIND THE TRUTH!
OH NO, OH NO, DEARIE. THERE IS TRUTH AND THERE IS TRUTH. OH YES, OH YES.
YOU MURDERED OUR FRIENDS?
FRIENDS? OH NO, OH NO. NOT SO MUCH YOUR FRIENDS, THOSE. NOT YOU LIKE, NOT LIKE. OH NO, OH NO.
I'M NOTHING LIKE YOU.

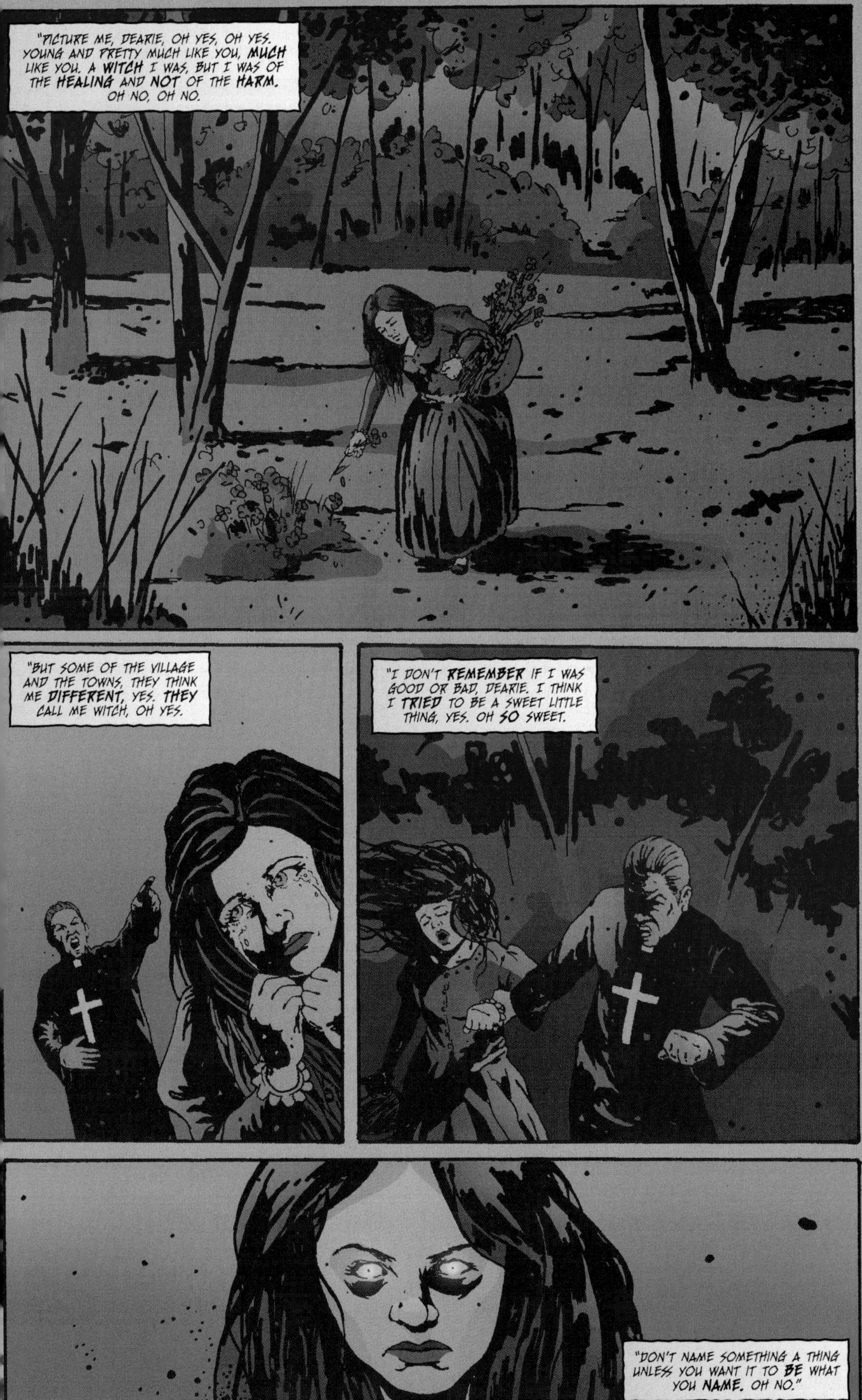
"PICTURE ME, DEARIE, OH YES, OH YES. YOUNG AND PRETTY MUCH LIKE YOU, MUCH LIKE YOU. A WITCH I WAS, BUT I WAS OF THE HEALING AND NOT OF THE HARM. OH NO, OH NO.
"BUT SOME OF THE VILLAGE AND THE TOWNS, THEY THINK ME DIFFERENT, YES. THEY CALL ME WITCH, OH YES.
"I DON'T REMEMBER IF I WAS GOOD OR BAD, DEARIE. I THINK I TRIED TO BE A SWEET LITTLE THING, YES. OH SO SWEET.
"DON'T NAME SOMETHING A THING UNLESS YOU WANT IT TO BE WHAT YOU NAME. OH NO."

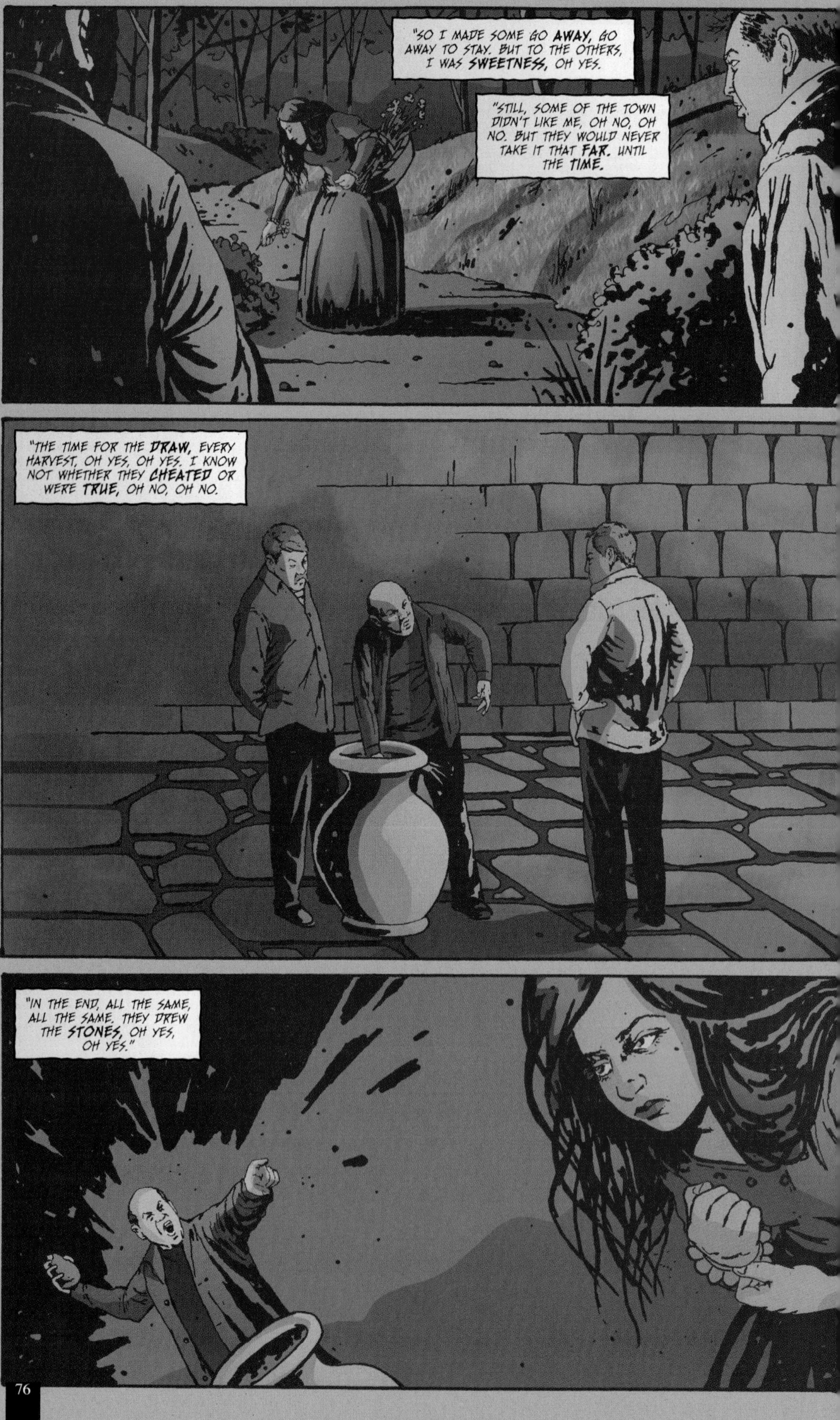
"SO I MADE SOME GO AWAY, GO AWAY TO STAY. BUT TO THE OTHERS, I WAS SWEETNESS, OH YES.
"STILL, SOME OF THE TOWN DIDN'T LIKE ME, OH NO, OH NO. BUT THEY WOULD NEVER TAKE IT THAT FAR. UNTIL THE TIME.
"THE TIME FOR THE DRAW, EVERY HARVEST, OH YES, OH YES. I KNOW NOT WHETHER THEY CHEATED OR WERE TRUE, OH NO, OH NO.
"IN THE END, ALL THE SAME, ALL THE SAME. THEY DREW THE STONES, OH YES, OH YES."

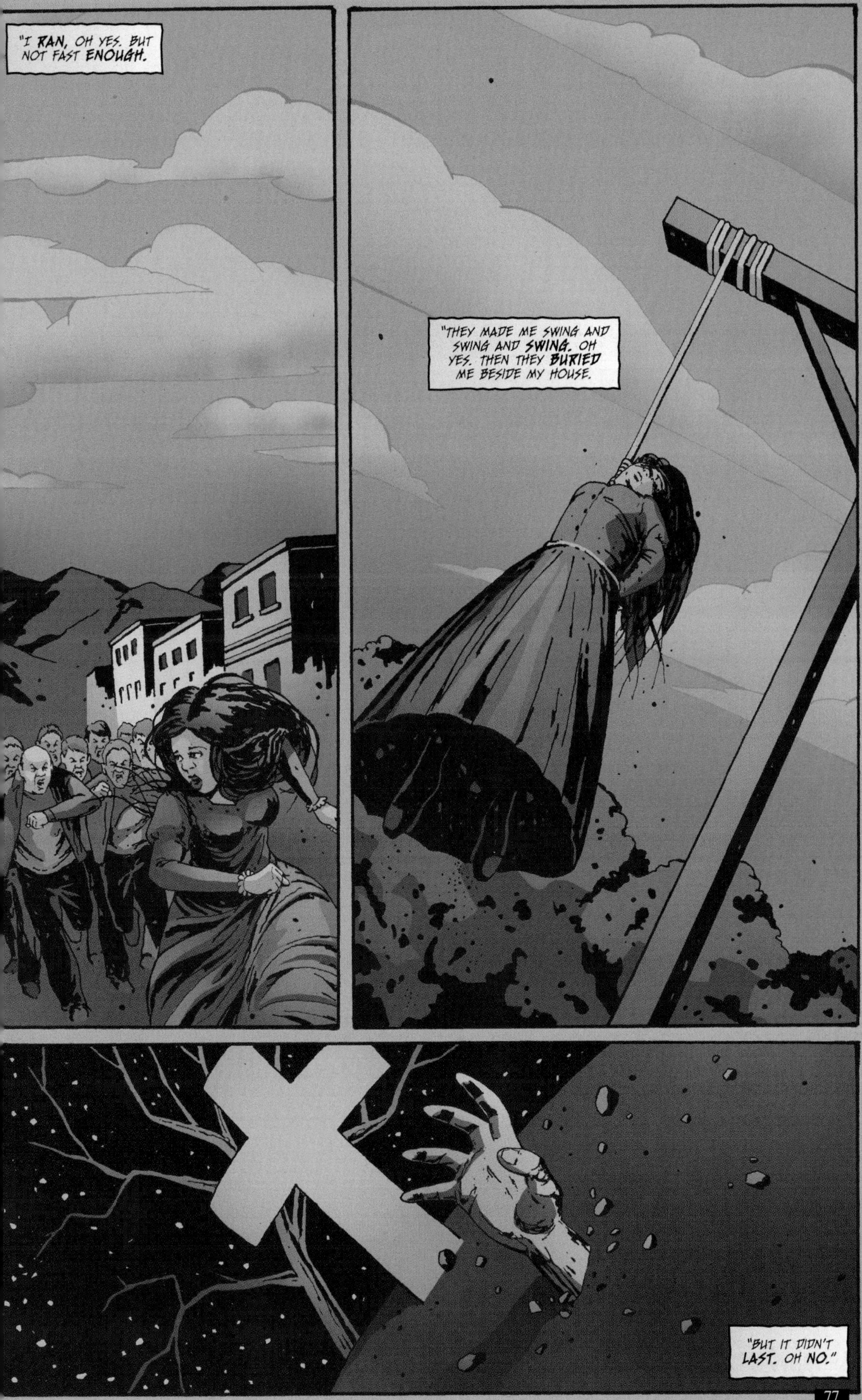
"I RAN, OH YES. BUT NOT FAST ENOUGH.
"THEY MADE ME SWING AND SWING AND SWING. OH YES. THEN THEY BURIED ME BESIDE MY HOUSE.
"BUT IT DIDN'T LAST. OH NO."

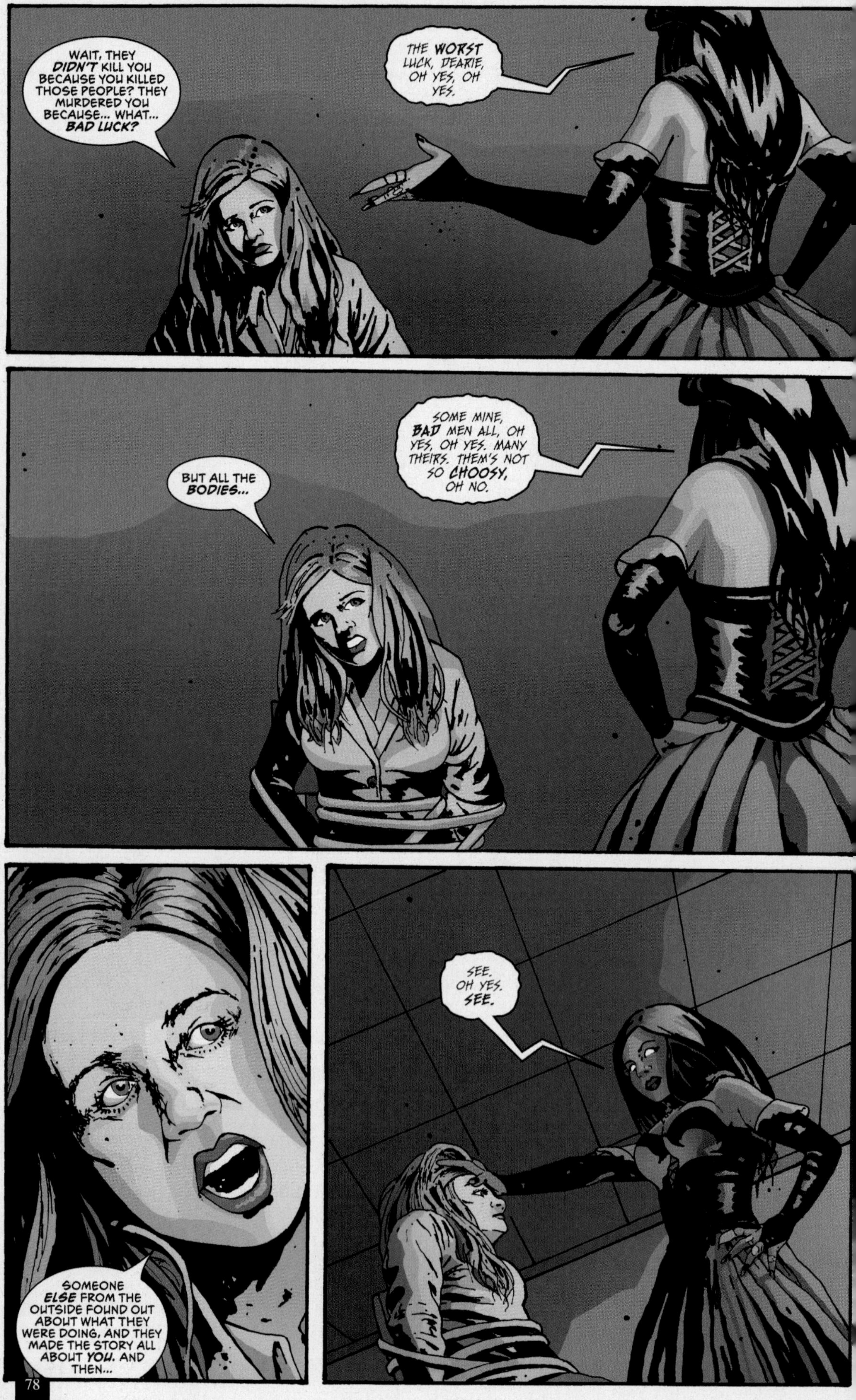

WAIT, THEY DIDN'T KILL YOU BECAUSE YOU KILLED THOSE PEOPLE? THEY MURDERED YOU BECAUSE... WHAT... BAD LUCK?
THE WORST LUCK, DEARIE, OH YES, OH YES.
BUT ALL THE BODIES...
SOME MINE, BAD MEN ALL, OH YES, OH YES. MANY THEIRS. THEM'S NOT SO CHOOSY, OH NO.
SOMEONE ELSE FROM THE OUTSIDE FOUND OUT ABOUT WHAT THEY WERE DOING, AND THEY MADE THE STORY ALL ABOUT YOU. AND THEN...
SEE. OH YES. SEE.

"CAN YOU FEEL IT? OH YES, OH YES. THE STICKS... THEY POUND, THEY CUT.

"BONES BREAK, OH YES. MY JAW, MY RIBS. I OPEN MY MOUTH TO CRY, AND A MIDWIFE'S THROW TAKES MOST OF MY TEETH. OH YES.

"AND THEN THE GRABBING AND THE DRAGGING, OH YES, OH YES.

"AND THE HANGING. DEED DONE, CROPS COME. WHAT'S A MURDERESS, IF THE CROPS THEY GROW? OH YES, OH YES."

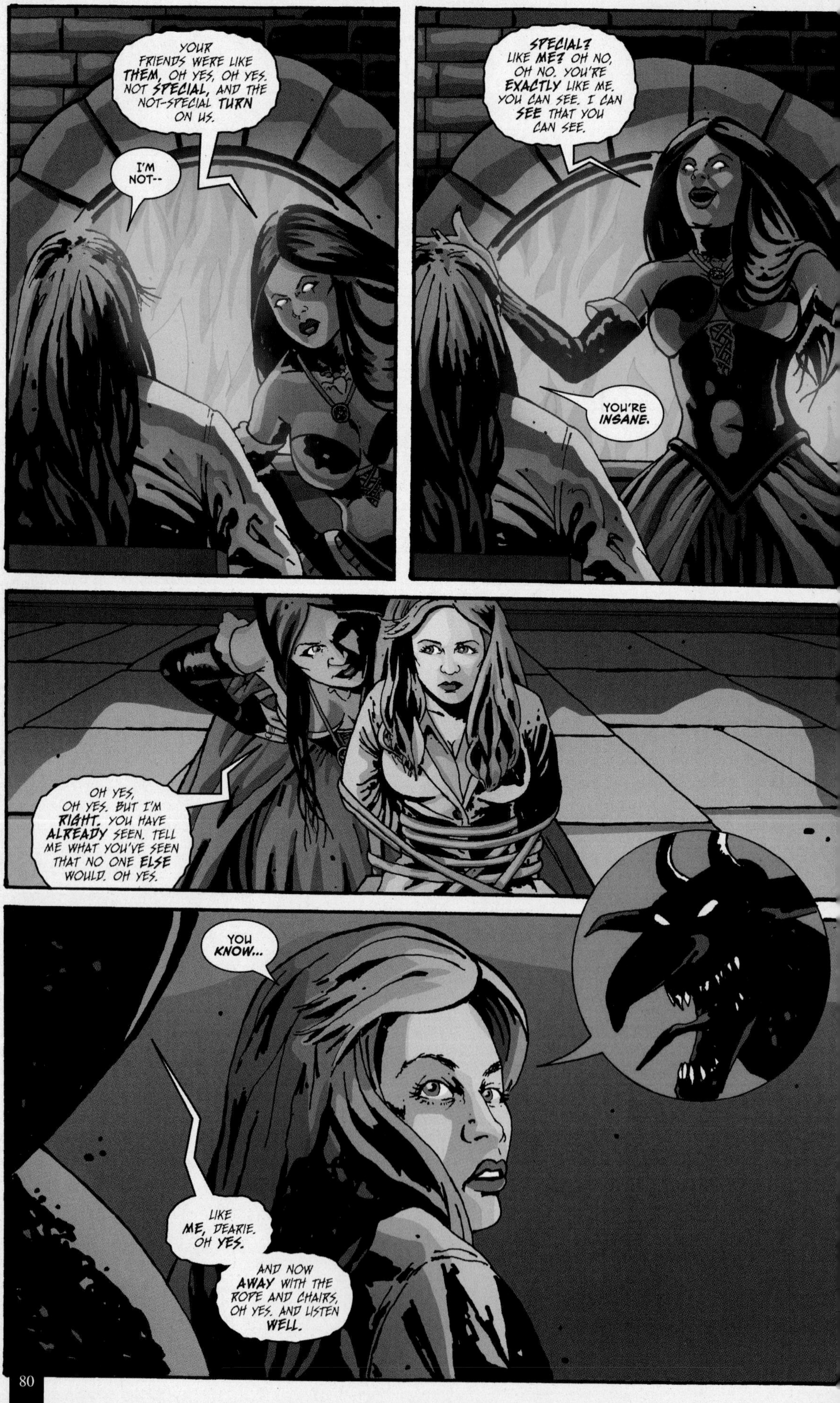
YOUR FRIENDS WERE LIKE THEM, OH YES, OH YES. NOT SPECIAL, AND THE NOT-SPECIAL TURN ON US.
I'M NOT--
SPECIAL? LIKE ME? OH NO, OH NO. YOU'RE EXACTLY LIKE ME. YOU CAN SEE. I CAN SEE THAT YOU CAN SEE.
YOU'RE INSANE.
OH YES, OH YES. BUT I'M RIGHT. YOU HAVE ALREADY SEEN. TELL ME WHAT YOU'VE SEEN THAT NO ONE ELSE WOULD. OH YES.
YOU KNOW...
LIKE ME, DEARIE. OH YES.
AND NOW AWAY WITH THE ROPE AND CHAIRS, OH YES. AND LISTEN WELL.

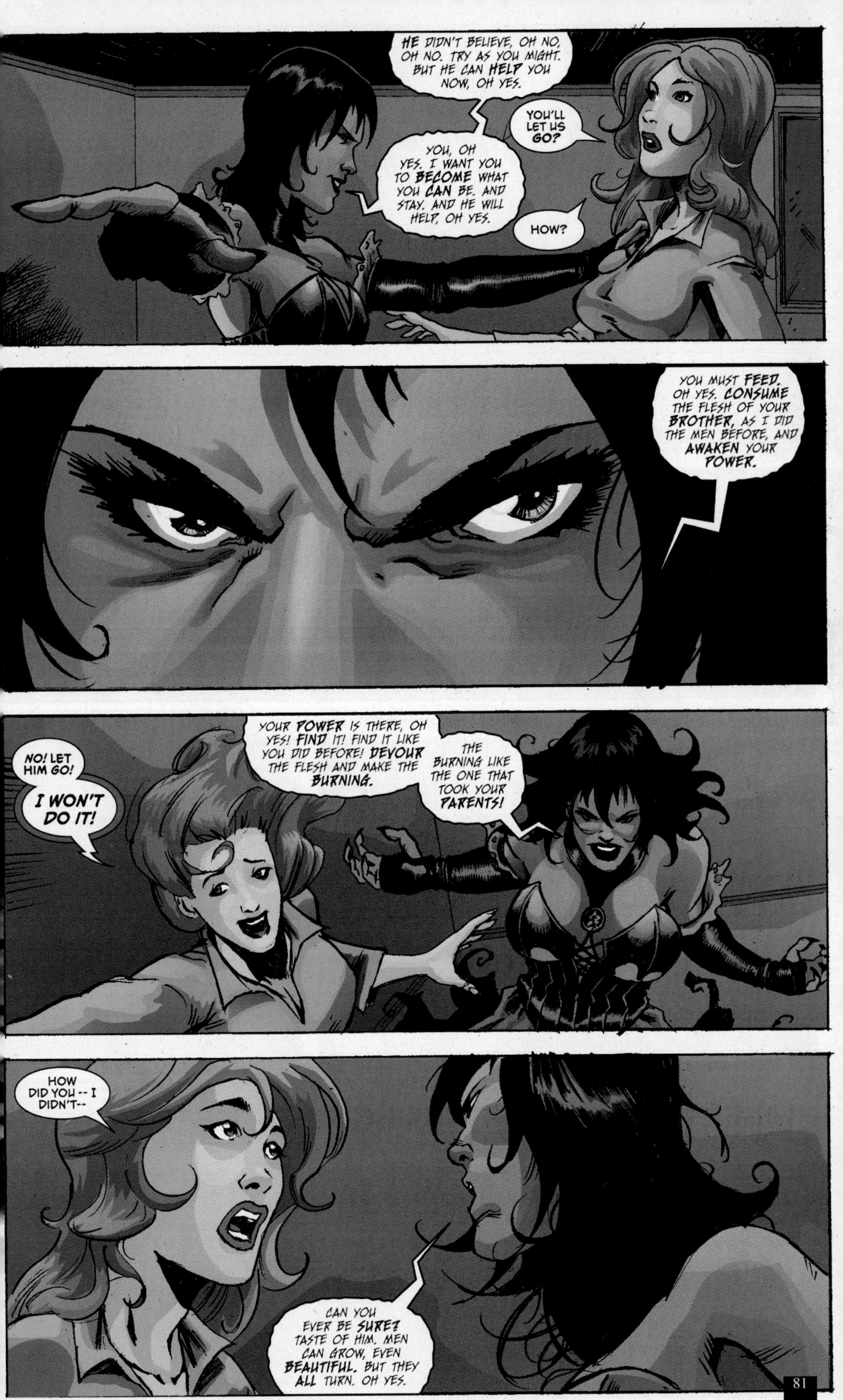
HE DIDN'T BELIEVE, OH NO, OH NO. TRY AS YOU MIGHT. BUT HE CAN HELP YOU NOW, OH YES.
YOU'LL LET US GO?
YOU, OH YES. I WANT YOU TO BECOME WHAT YOU CAN BE. AND STAY. AND HE WILL HELP, OH YES.
HOW?
YOU MUST FEED. OH YES. CONSUME THE FLESH OF YOUR BROTHER, AS I DID THE MEN BEFORE, AND AWAKEN YOUR POWER.
NO! LET HIM GO!
I WON'T DO IT!
YOUR POWER IS THERE, OH YES! FIND IT! FIND IT LIKE YOU DID BEFORE! DEVOUR THE FLESH AND MAKE THE BURNING.
THE BURNING LIKE THE ONE THAT TOOK YOUR PARENTS!
HOW DID YOU -- I DIDN'T--
CAN YOU EVER BE SURE? TASTE OF HIM. MEN CAN GROW, EVEN BEAUTIFUL. BUT THEY ALL TURN. OH YES.

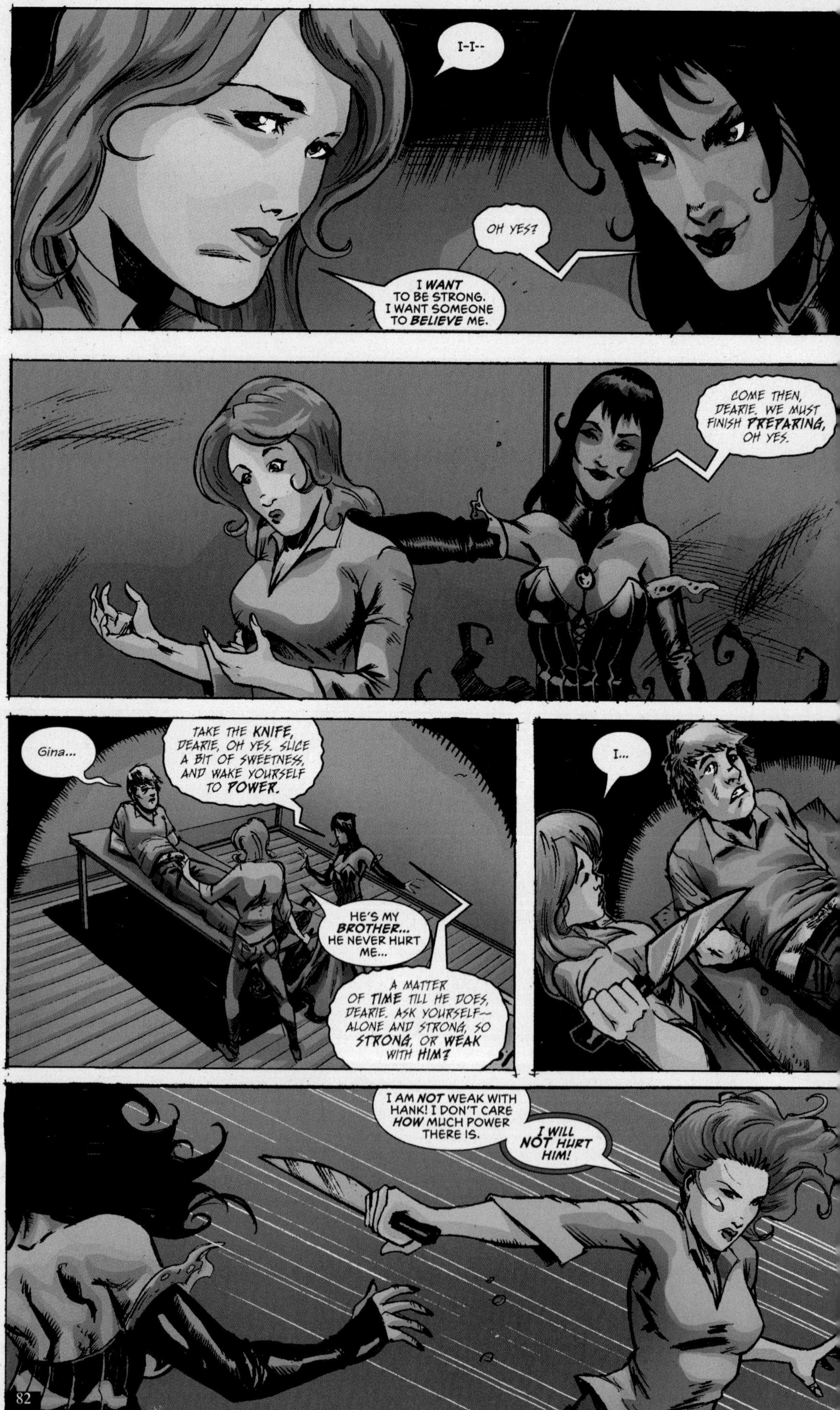
I-I--
I WANT TO BE STRONG. I WANT SOMEONE TO BELIEVE ME.
OH YES?
COME THEN, DEARIE. WE MUST FINISH PREPARING, OH YES.
Gina...
TAKE THE KNIFE, DEARIE, OH YES. SLICE A BIT OF SWEETNESS, AND WAKE YOURSELF TO POWER.
HE'S MY BROTHER... HE NEVER HURT ME...
A MATTER OF TIME TILL HE DOES, DEARIE. ASK YOURSELF-- ALONE AND STRONG, SO STRONG, OR WEAK WITH HIM?
I...
I AM NOT WEAK WITH HANK! I DON'T CARE HOW MUCH POWER THERE IS.
I WILL NOT HURT HIM!

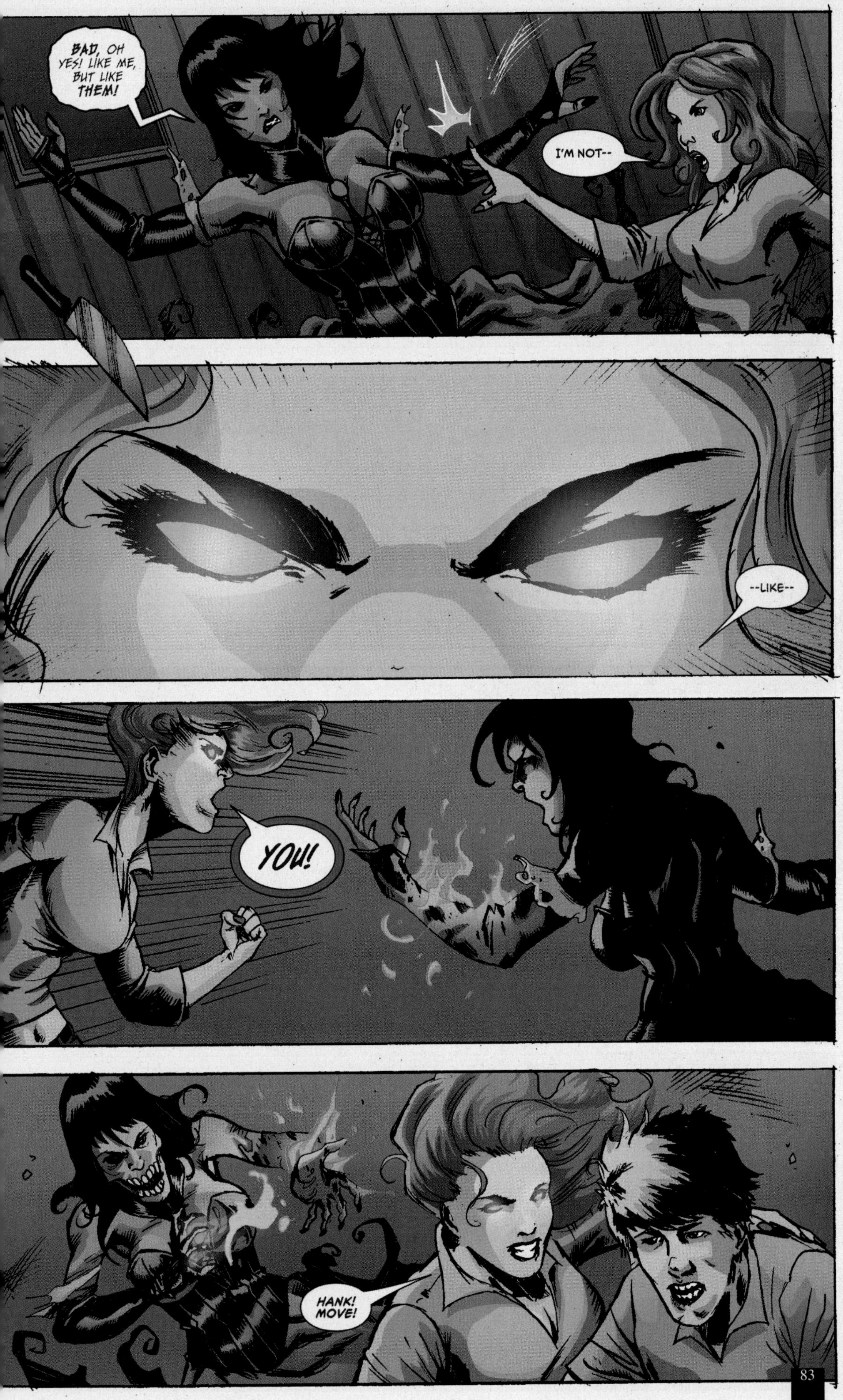
BAD, OH YES! LIKE ME, BUT LIKE THEM!
I'M NOT--
--LIKE--
YOU!
HANK! MOVE!

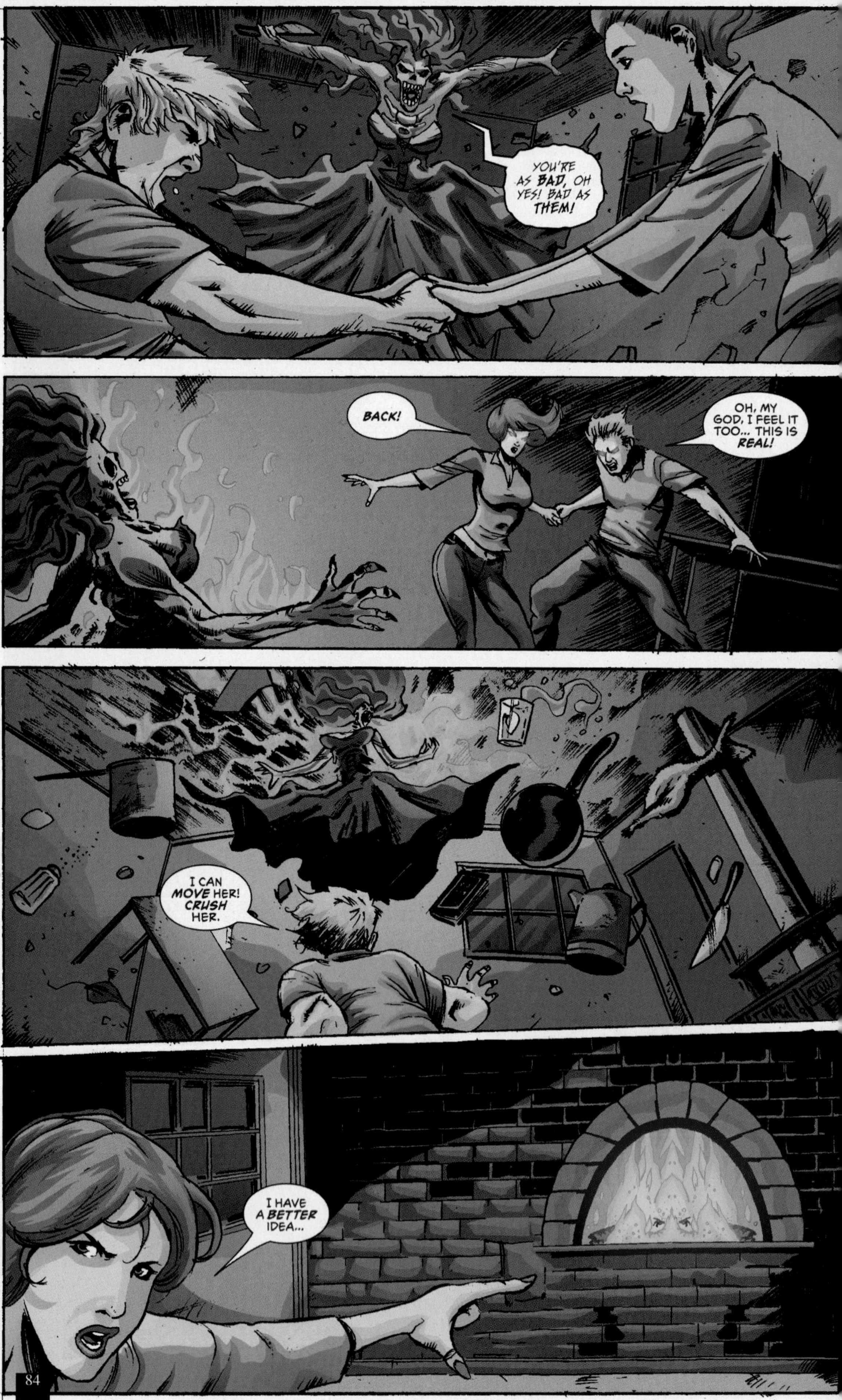
YOU'RE AS BAD, OH YES! BAD AS THEM!
BACK!
OH, MY GOD, I FEEL IT TOO... THIS IS REAL!
I CAN MOVE HER! CRUSH HER.
I HAVE A BETTER IDEA...

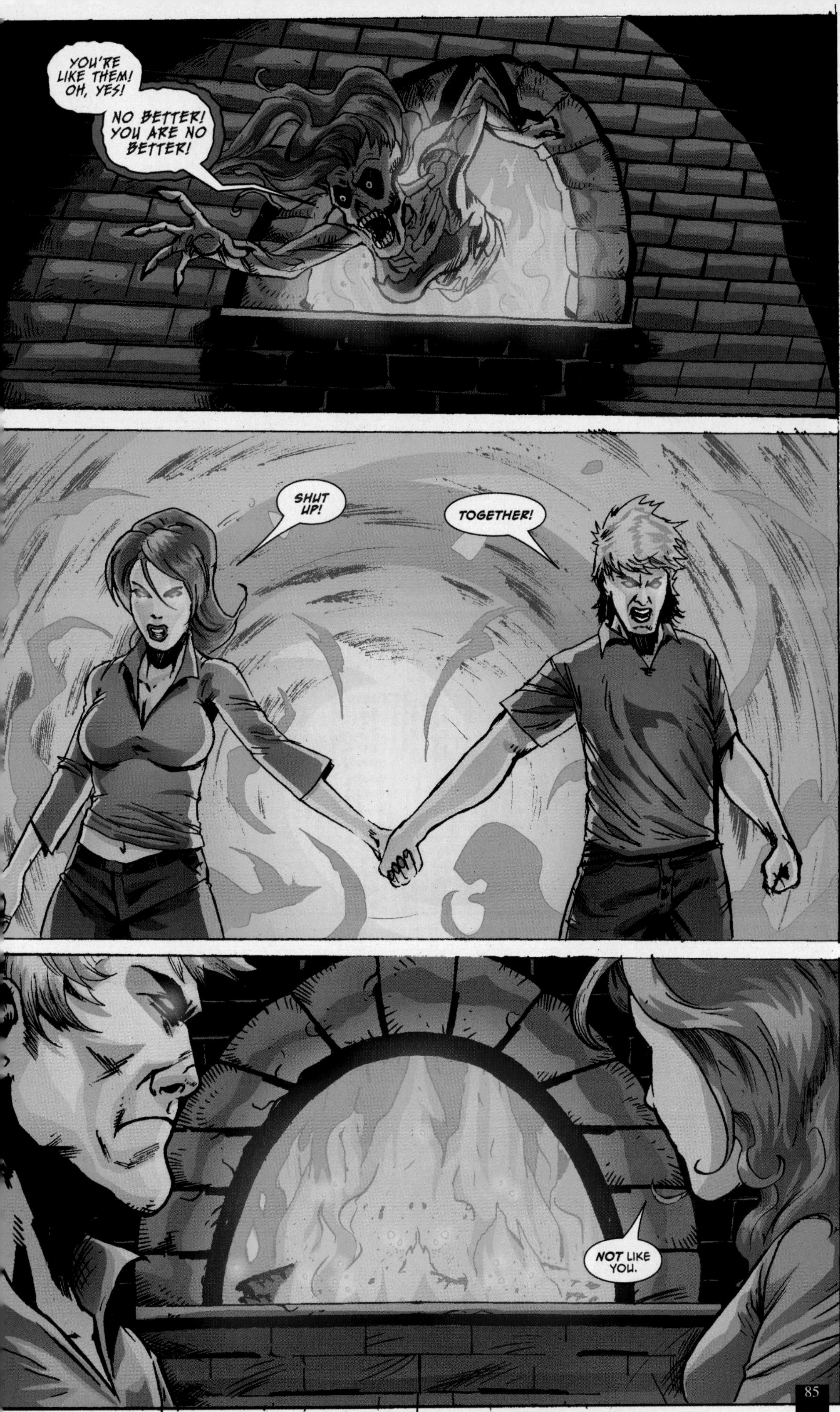
YOU'RE LIKE THEM! OH, YES!
NO BETTER! YOU ARE NO BETTER!
SHUT UP!
TOGETHER!
NOT LIKE YOU.

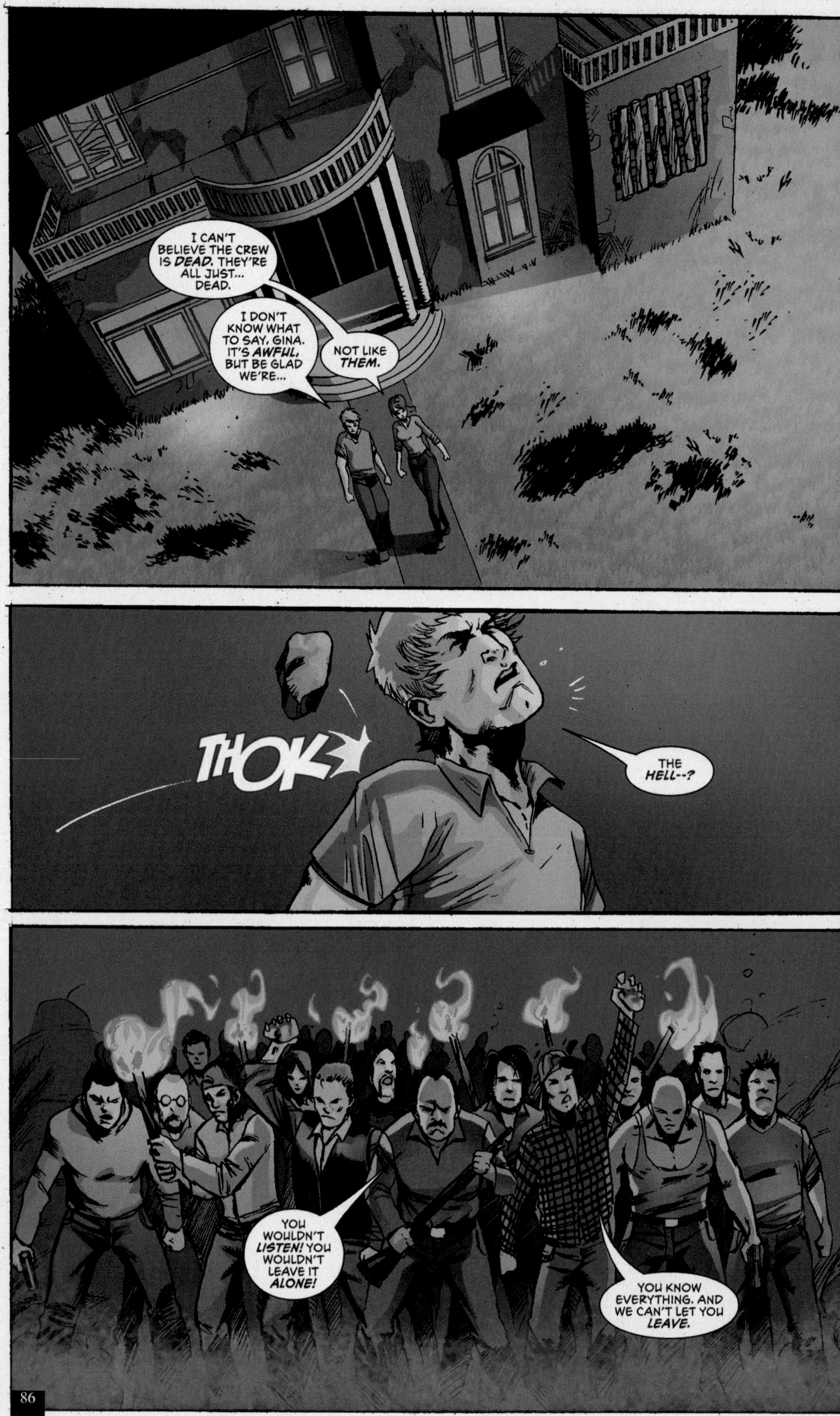
I CAN'T BELIEVE THE CREW IS *DEAD*. THEY'RE ALL JUST... DEAD.
I DON'T KNOW WHAT TO SAY, GINA. IT'S *AWFUL*, BUT BE GLAD WE'RE...
NOT LIKE *THEM*.
THOK
THE *HELL*--?
YOU WOULDN'T *LISTEN!* YOU WOULDN'T LEAVE IT *ALONE!*
YOU KNOW EVERYTHING. AND WE CAN'T LET YOU *LEAVE*.

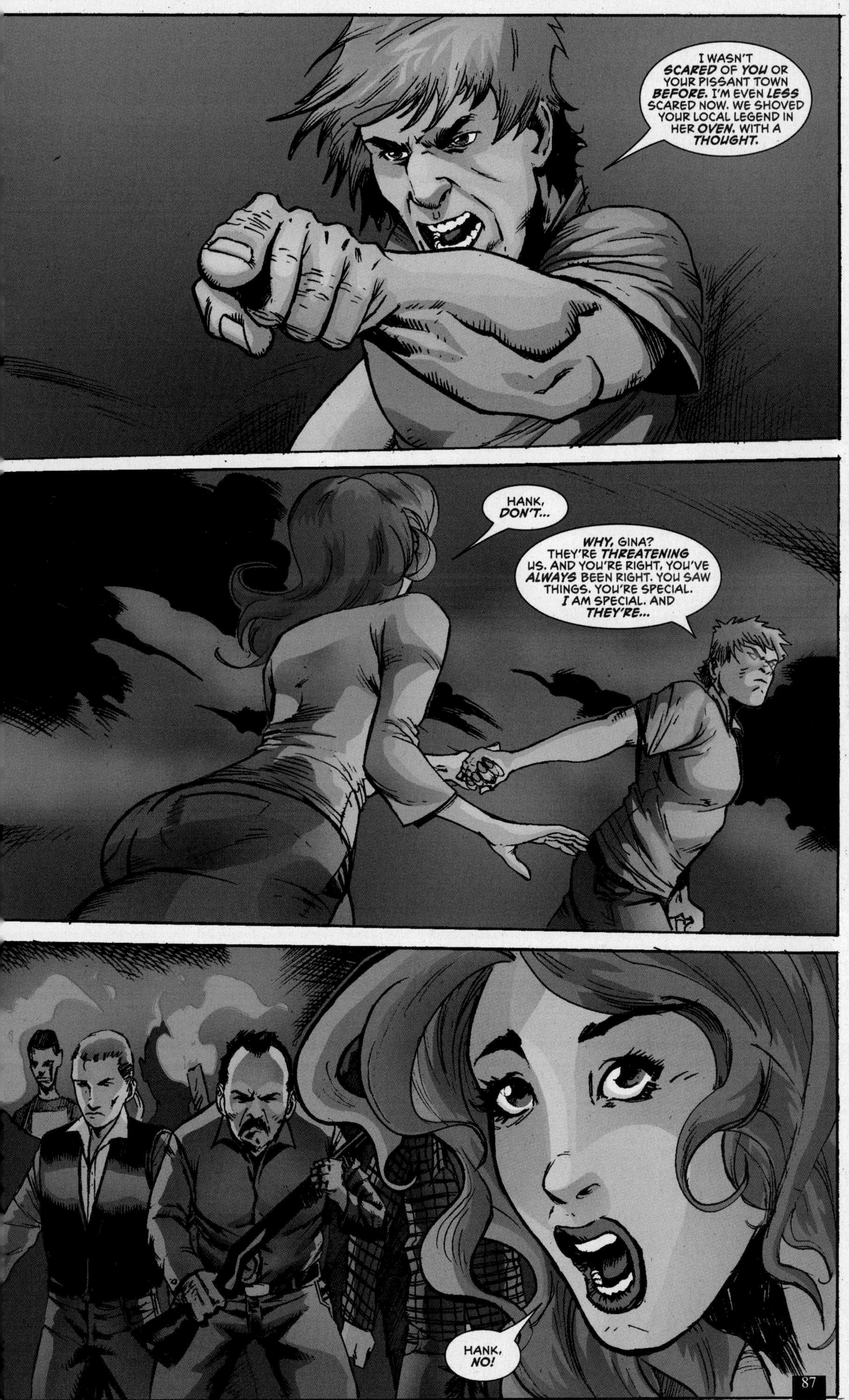
I WASN'T SCARED OF YOU OR YOUR PISSANT TOWN BEFORE. I'M EVEN LESS SCARED NOW. WE SHOVED YOUR LOCAL LEGEND IN HER OVEN. WITH A THOUGHT.
HANK, DON'T...
WHY, GINA? THEY'RE THREATENING US. AND YOU'RE RIGHT, YOU'VE ALWAYS BEEN RIGHT. YOU SAW THINGS. YOU'RE SPECIAL. I AM SPECIAL. AND THEY'RE...
HANK, NO!

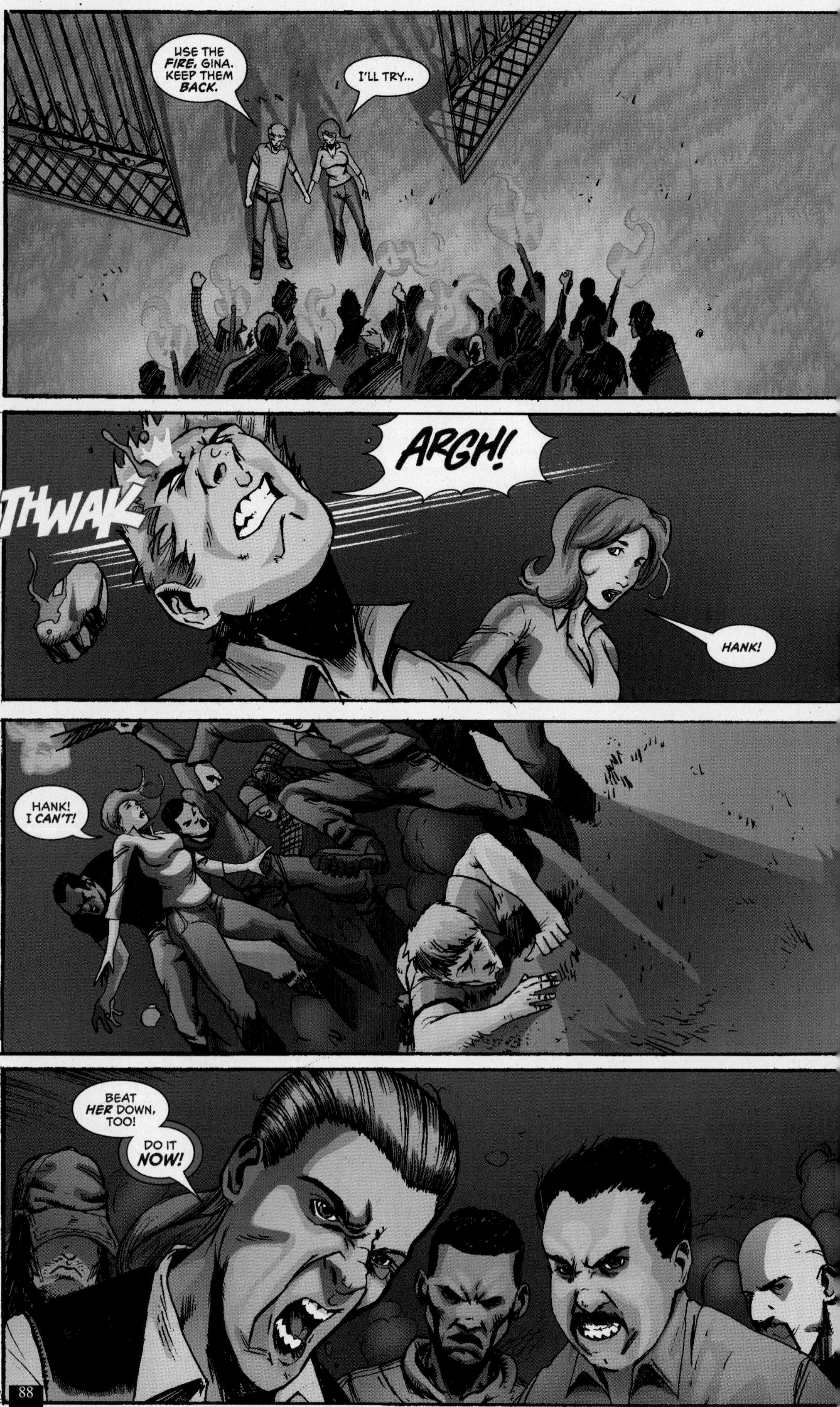
USE THE FIRE, GINA. KEEP THEM BACK.
I'LL TRY...
THWAK
ARGH!
HANK!
HANK! I CAN'T!
BEAT HER DOWN, TOO!
DO IT NOW!

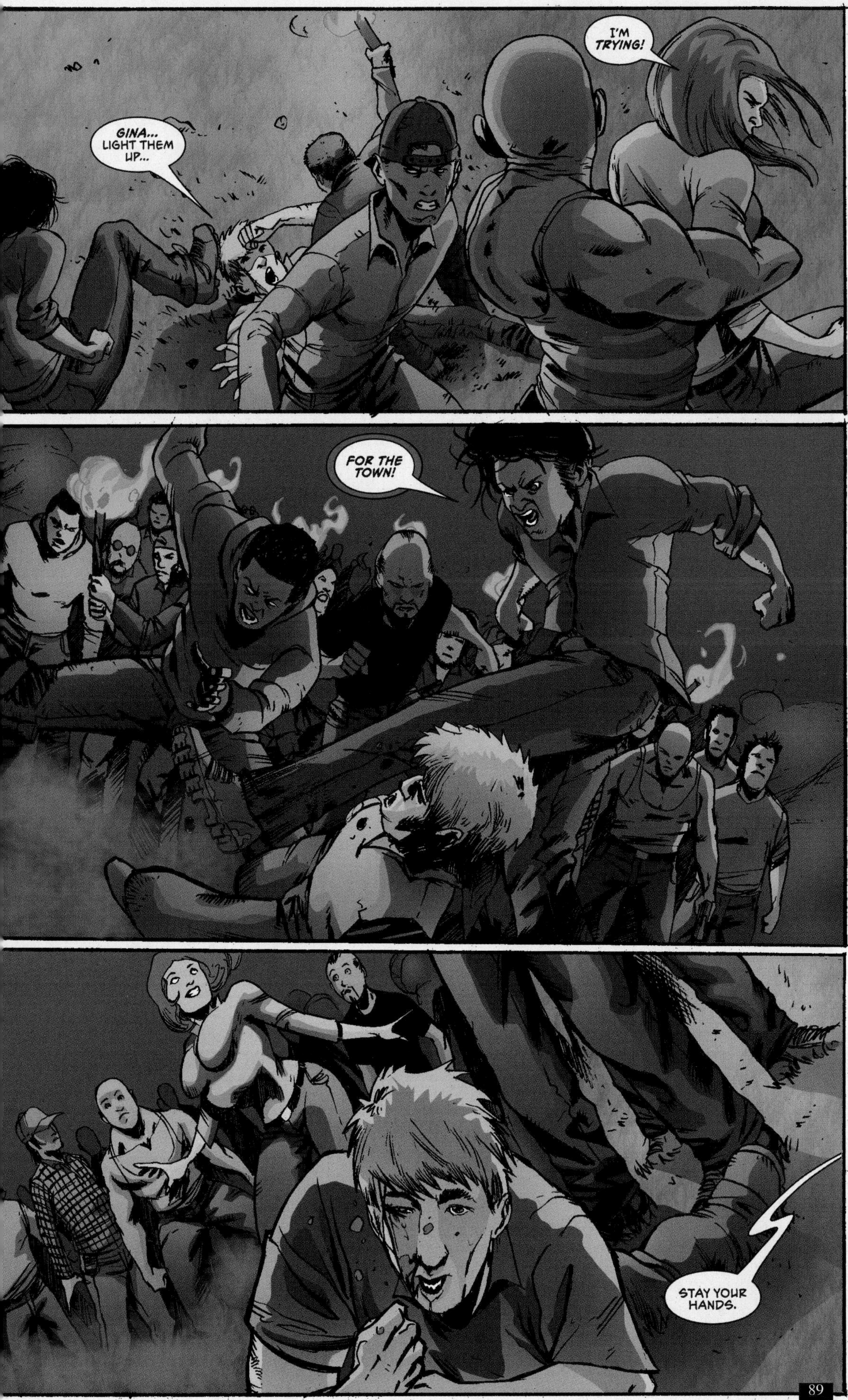
GINA... LIGHT THEM UP...
I'M TRYING!
FOR THE TOWN!
STAY YOUR HANDS.

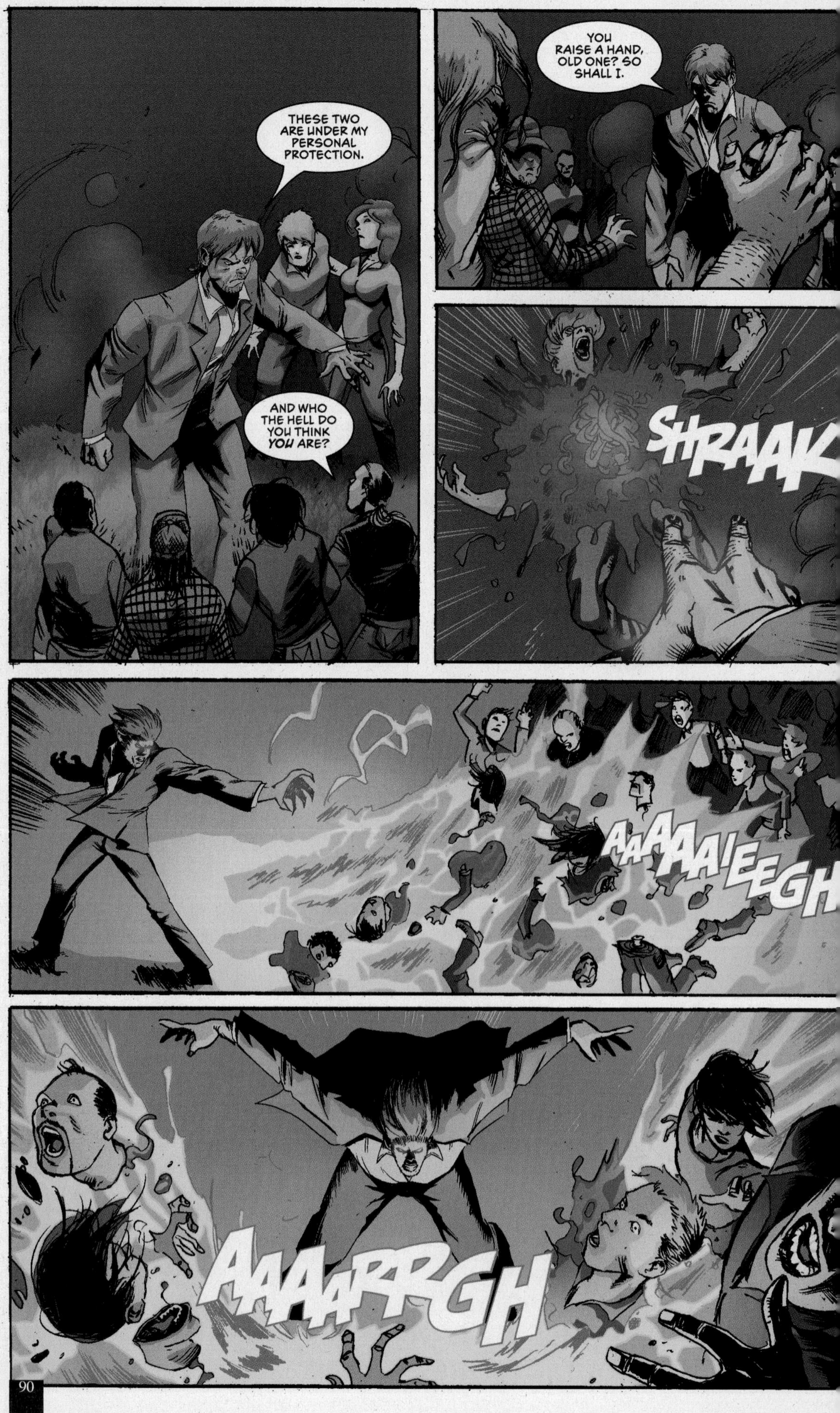
THESE TWO ARE UNDER MY PERSONAL PROTECTION.
AND WHO THE HELL DO YOU THINK YOU ARE?
YOU RAISE A HAND, OLD ONE? SO SHALL I.
SHRAAK
AAAAAAIEEGH
AAAARRGH

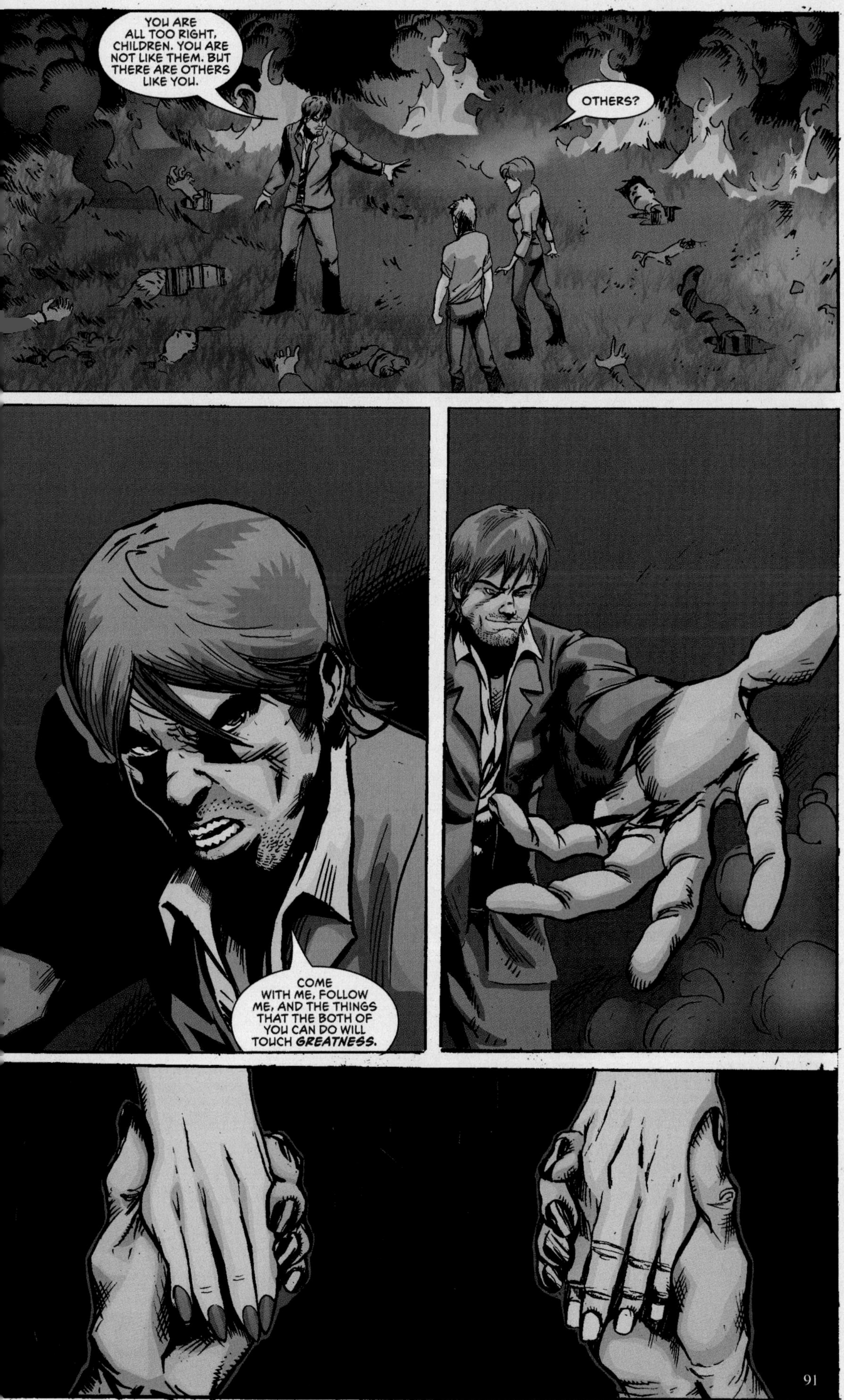
YOU ARE ALL TOO RIGHT, CHILDREN. YOU ARE NOT LIKE THEM. BUT THERE ARE OTHERS LIKE YOU.
OTHERS?
COME WITH ME, FOLLOW ME, AND THE THINGS THAT THE BOTH OF YOU CAN DO WILL TOUCH *GREATNESS*.

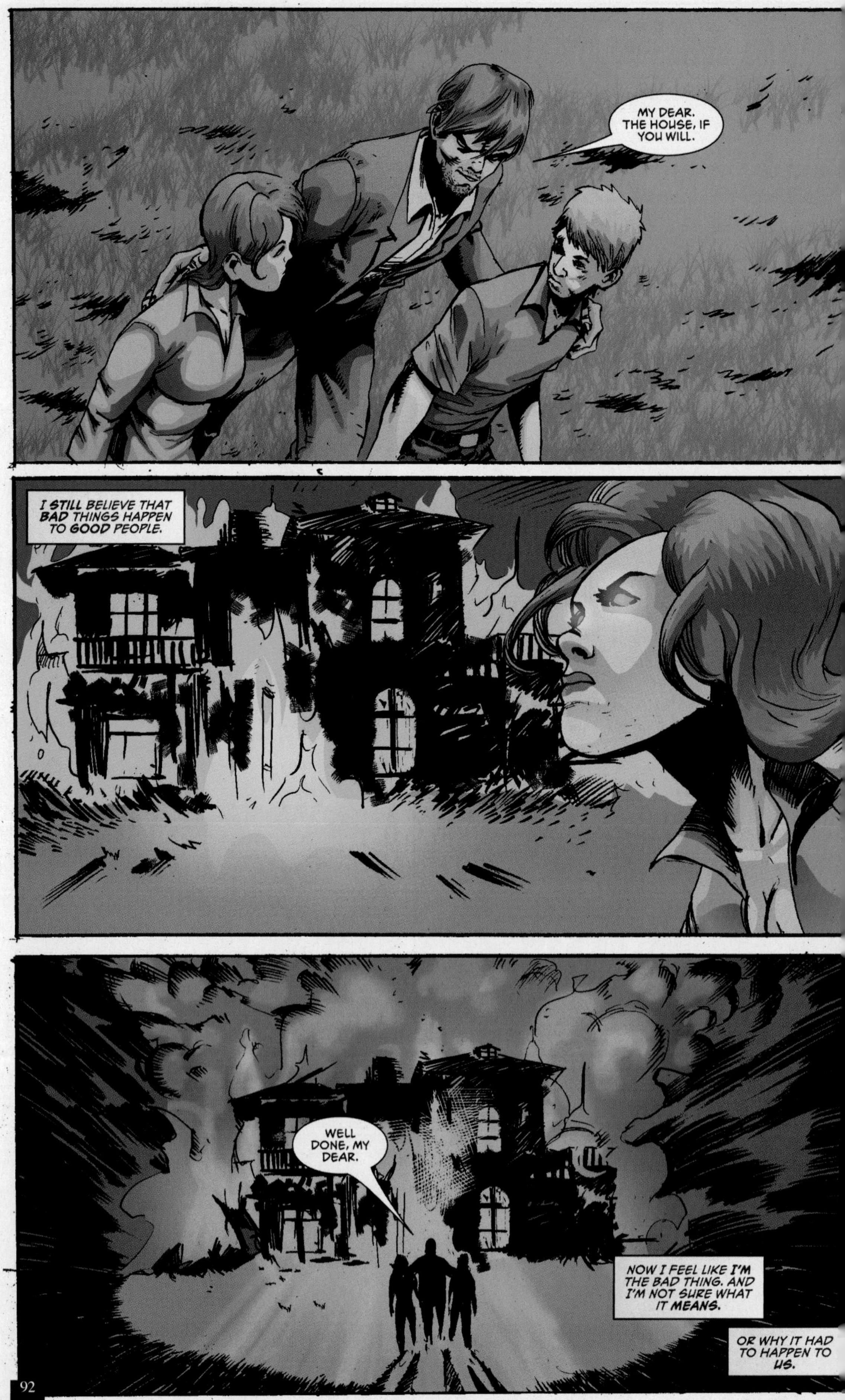
MY DEAR. THE HOUSE, IF YOU WILL.
I STILL BELIEVE THAT BAD THINGS HAPPEN TO GOOD PEOPLE.
WELL DONE, MY DEAR.
NOW I FEEL LIKE I'M THE BAD THING. AND I'M NOT SURE WHAT IT MEANS.
OR WHY IT HAD TO HAPPEN TO US.

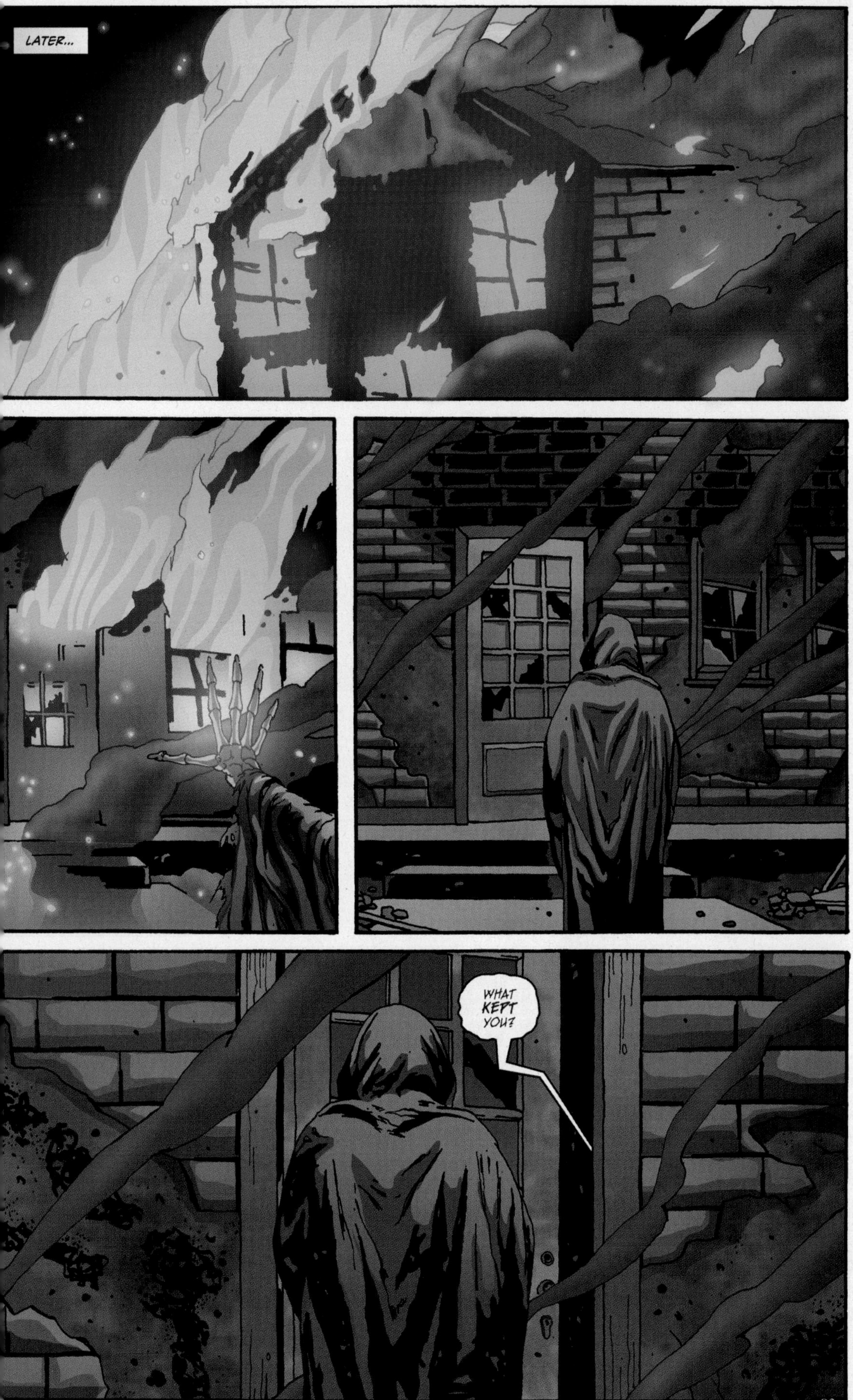

LATER...
WHAT KEPT YOU?

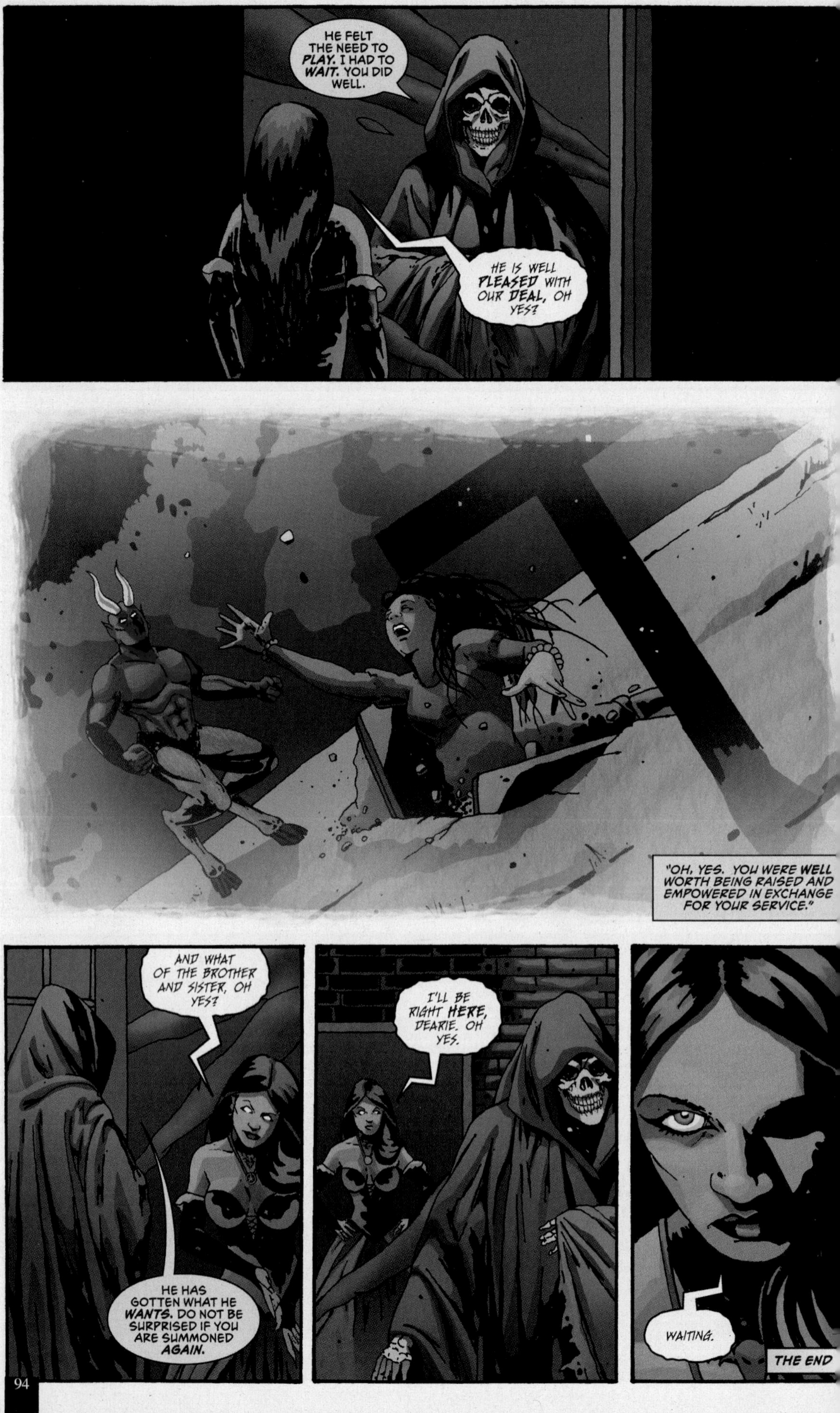

HE FELT THE NEED TO PLAY. I HAD TO WAIT. YOU DID WELL.
HE IS WELL PLEASED WITH OUR DEAL, OH YES?
"OH, YES. YOU WERE WELL WORTH BEING RAISED AND EMPOWERED IN EXCHANGE FOR YOUR SERVICE."
AND WHAT OF THE BROTHER AND SISTER, OH YES?
HE HAS GOTTEN WHAT HE WANTS. DO NOT BE SURPRISED IF YOU ARE SUMMONED AGAIN.
I'LL BE RIGHT HERE, DEARIE. OH YES.
WAITING.
THE END

Grimm Fairy Tales
MYTHS & LEGENDS

A SPECIAL REPRINTING OF

GRIMM FAIRY TALES #3

HANSEL & GRETEL

Written and Story by Joe Tyler and Ralph Tedesco
Art by Alexander Benhossi • Colors by Eric Rodriguez
Letters by Artmonkeys

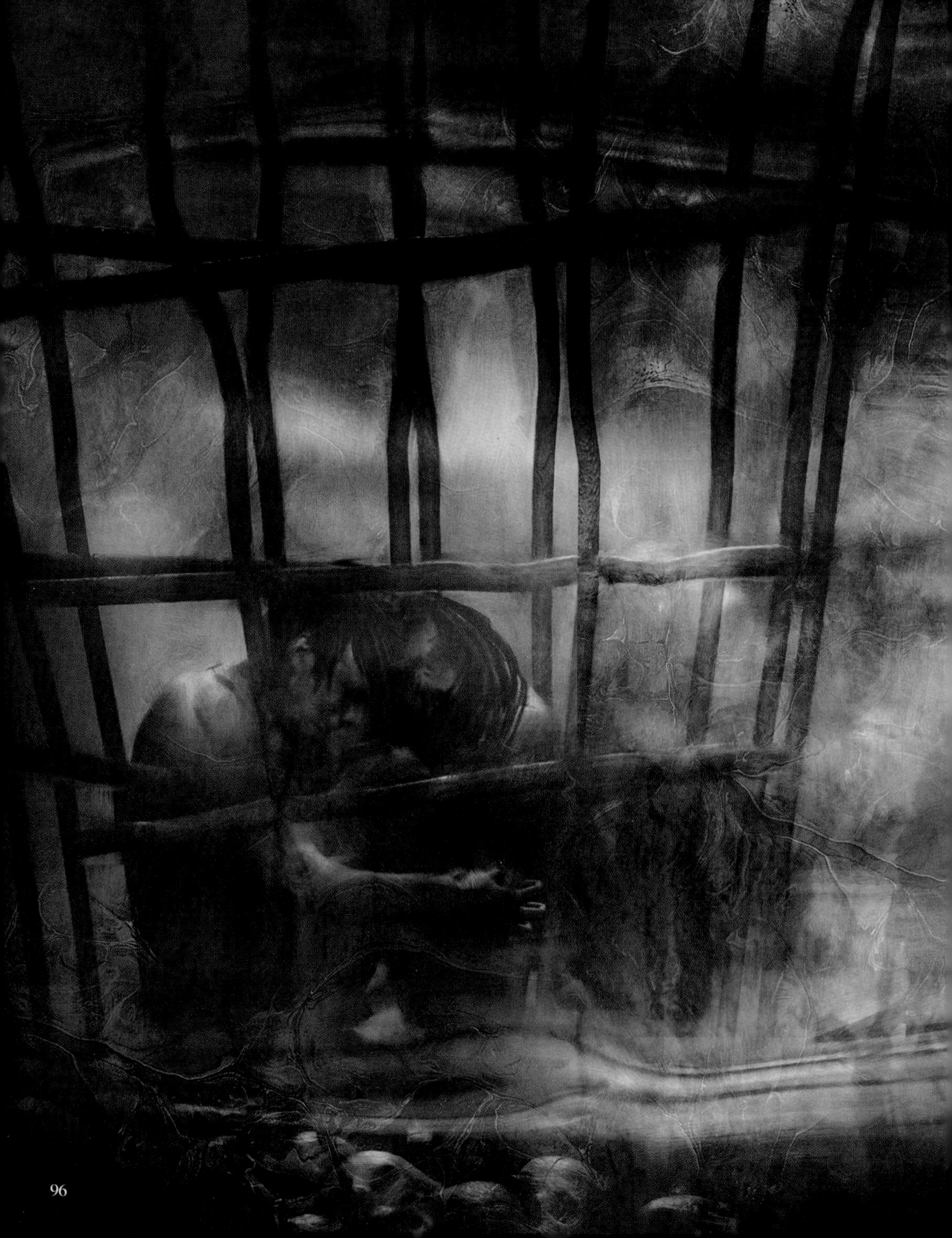

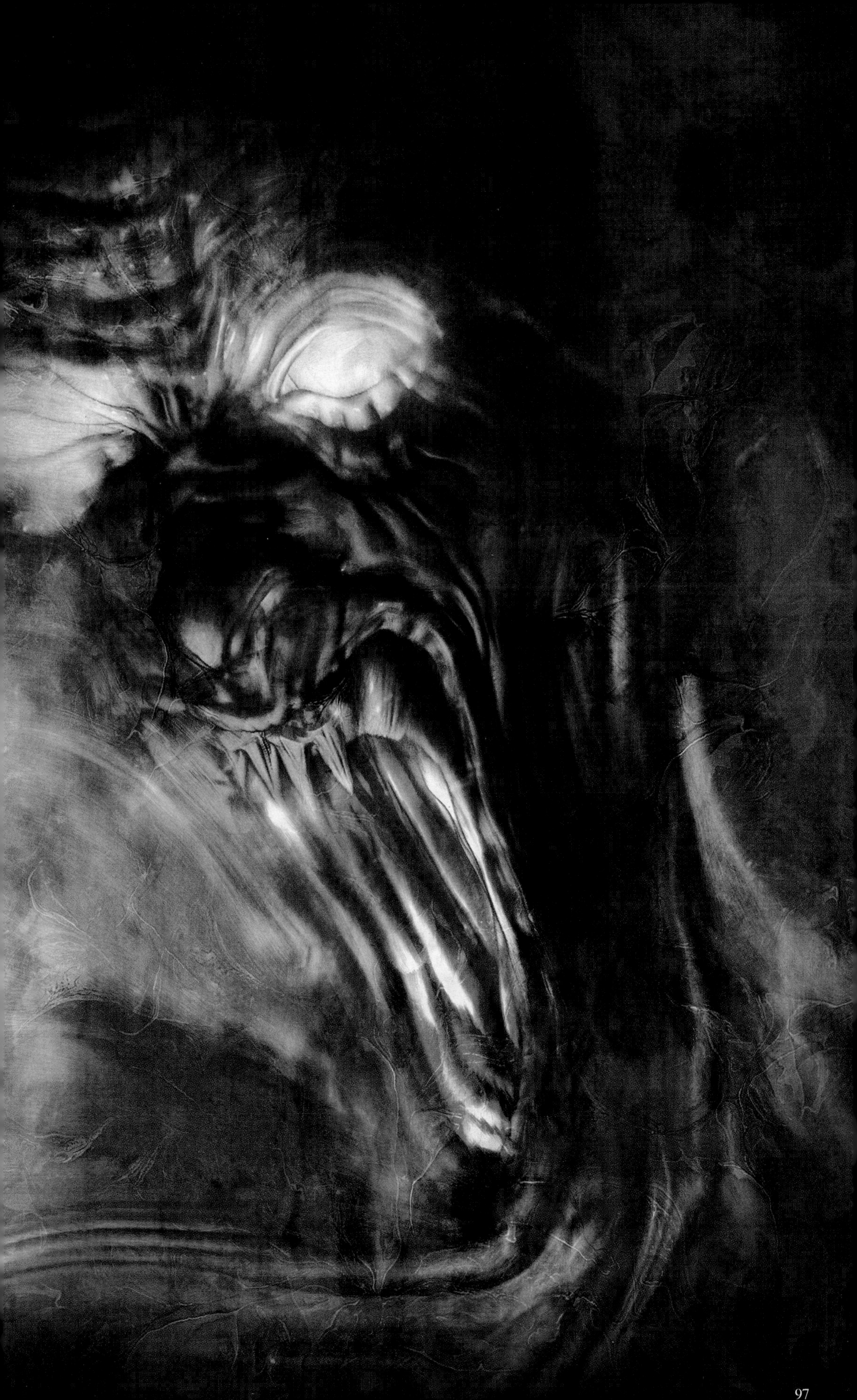

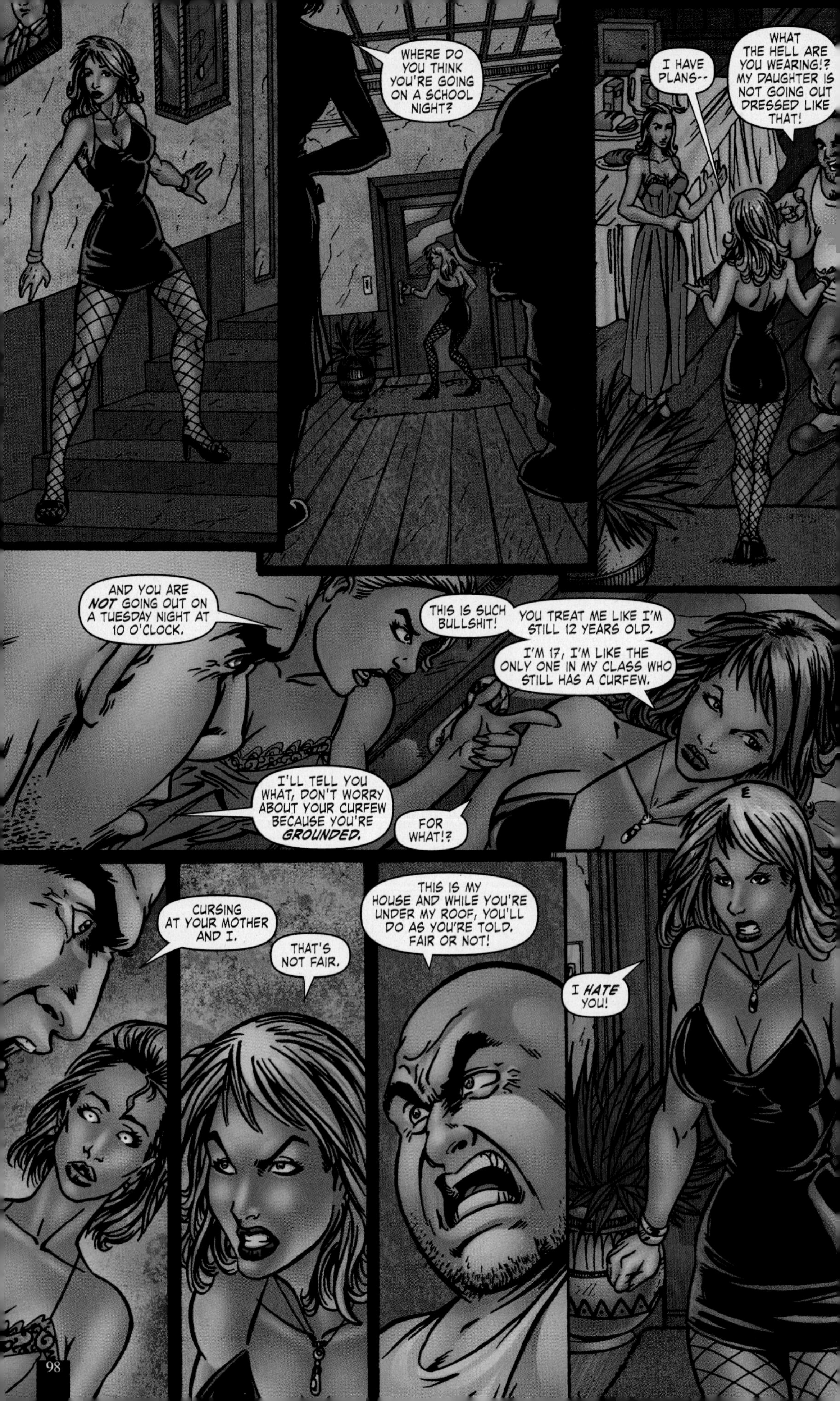
WHERE DO YOU THINK YOU'RE GOING ON A SCHOOL NIGHT?
I HAVE PLANS--
WHAT THE HELL ARE YOU WEARING!? MY DAUGHTER IS NOT GOING OUT DRESSED LIKE THAT!
AND YOU ARE NOT GOING OUT ON A TUESDAY NIGHT AT 10 O'CLOCK.
THIS IS SUCH BULLSHIT!
YOU TREAT ME LIKE I'M STILL 12 YEARS OLD.
I'M 17, I'M LIKE THE ONLY ONE IN MY CLASS WHO STILL HAS A CURFEW.
I'LL TELL YOU WHAT, DON'T WORRY ABOUT YOUR CURFEW BECAUSE YOU'RE GROUNDED.
FOR WHAT!?
CURSING AT YOUR MOTHER AND I.
THAT'S NOT FAIR.
THIS IS MY HOUSE AND WHILE YOU'RE UNDER MY ROOF, YOU'LL DO AS YOU'RE TOLD. FAIR OR NOT!
I HATE YOU!

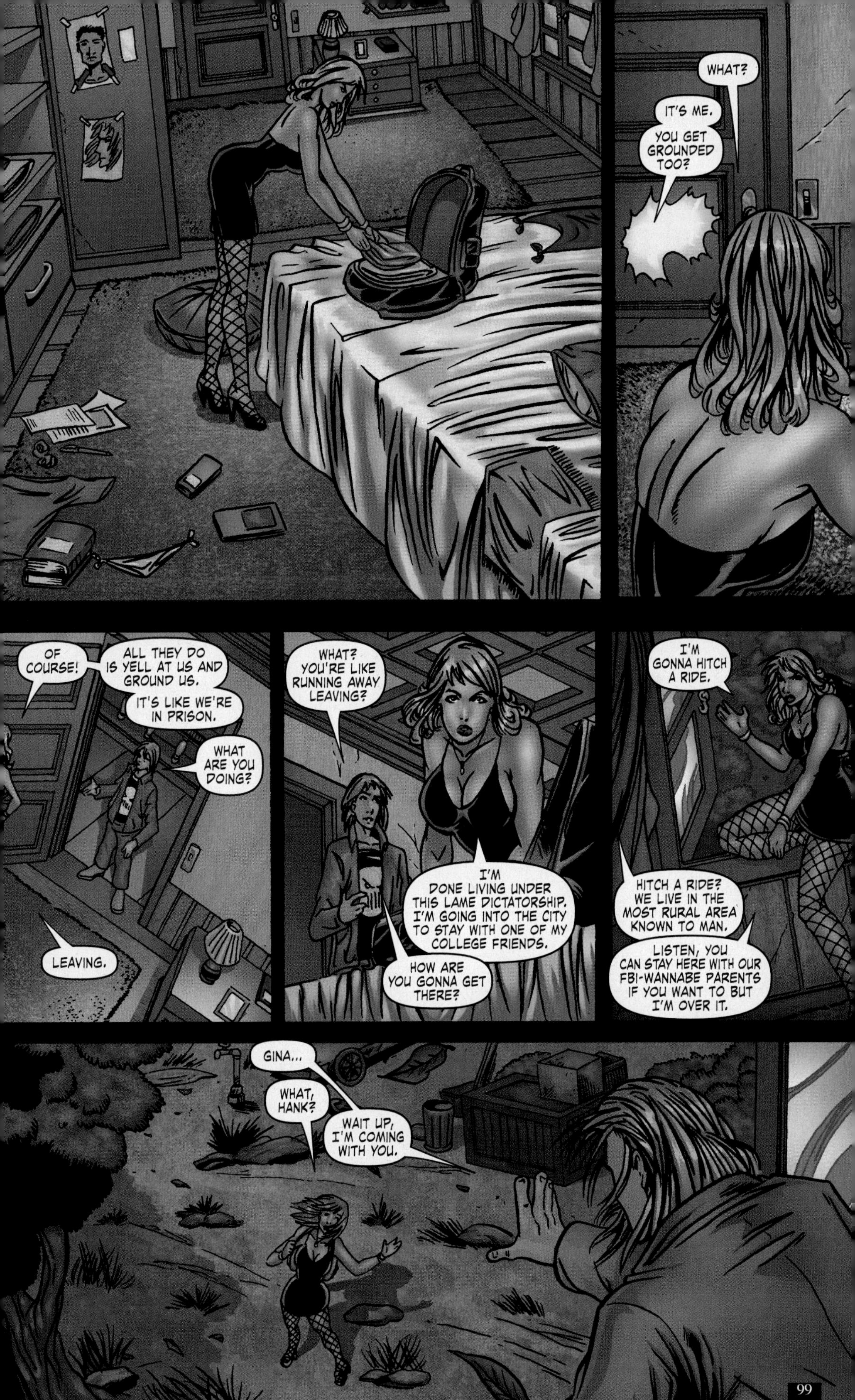
WHAT?
IT'S ME.
YOU GET GROUNDED TOO?
OF COURSE!
ALL THEY DO IS YELL AT US AND GROUND US.
IT'S LIKE WE'RE IN PRISON.
WHAT ARE YOU DOING?
LEAVING.
WHAT? YOU'RE LIKE RUNNING AWAY LEAVING?
I'M DONE LIVING UNDER THIS LAME DICTATORSHIP. I'M GOING INTO THE CITY TO STAY WITH ONE OF MY COLLEGE FRIENDS.
HOW ARE YOU GONNA GET THERE?
I'M GONNA HITCH A RIDE.
HITCH A RIDE? WE LIVE IN THE MOST RURAL AREA KNOWN TO MAN.
LISTEN, YOU CAN STAY HERE WITH OUR FBI-WANNABE PARENTS IF YOU WANT TO BUT I'M OVER IT.
GINA...
WHAT, HANK?
WAIT UP, I'M COMING WITH YOU.

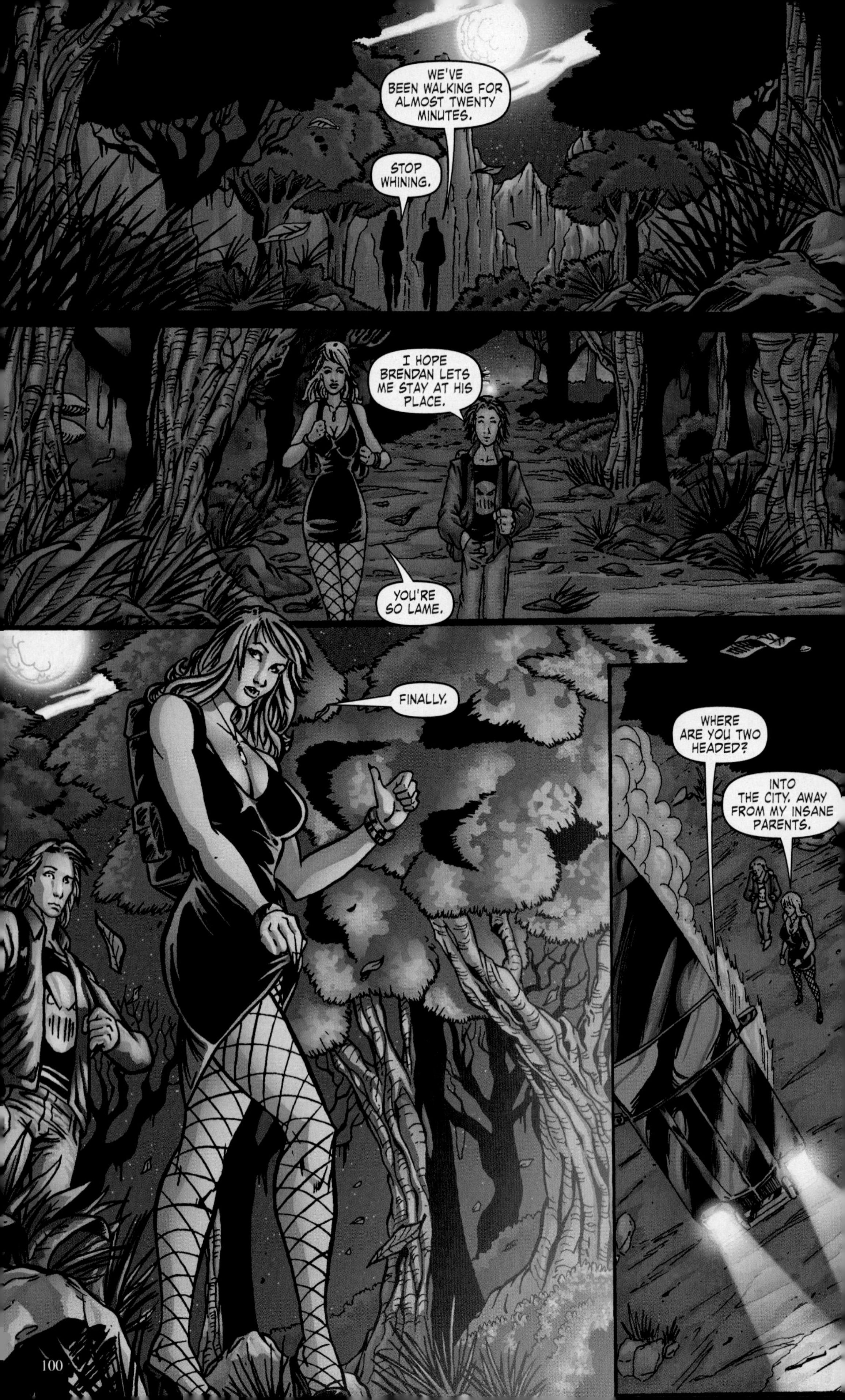
WE'VE BEEN WALKING FOR ALMOST TWENTY MINUTES.
STOP WHINING.
I HOPE BRENDAN LETS ME STAY AT HIS PLACE.
YOU'RE SO LAME.
FINALLY.
WHERE ARE YOU TWO HEADED?
INTO THE CITY. AWAY FROM MY INSANE PARENTS.

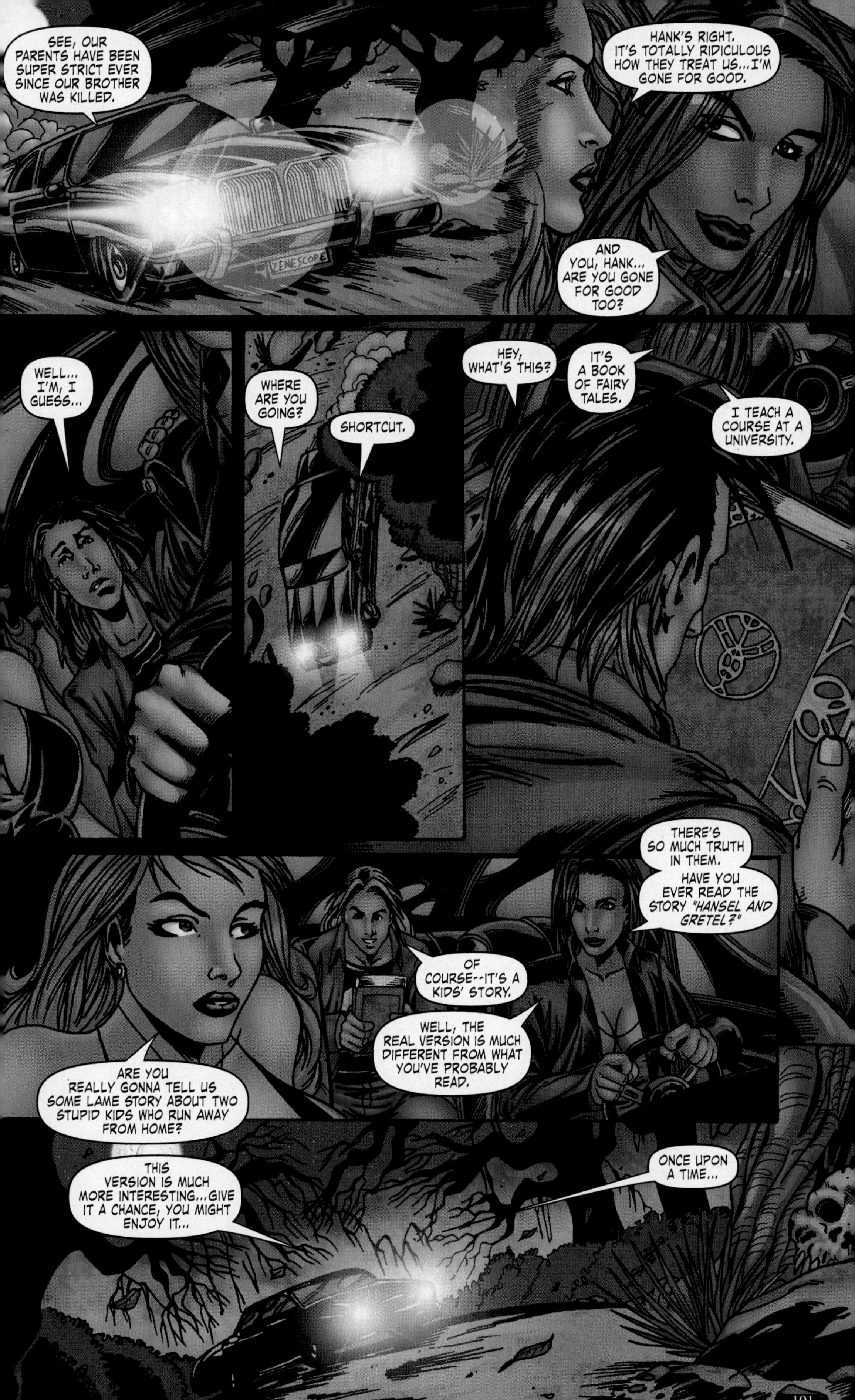
SEE, OUR PARENTS HAVE BEEN SUPER STRICT EVER SINCE OUR BROTHER WAS KILLED.
ZENESCOPE
HANK'S RIGHT. IT'S TOTALLY RIDICULOUS HOW THEY TREAT US...I'M GONE FOR GOOD.
AND YOU, HANK... ARE YOU GONE FOR GOOD TOO?
WELL... I'M, I GUESS...
WHERE ARE YOU GOING?
SHORTCUT.
HEY, WHAT'S THIS?
IT'S A BOOK OF FAIRY TALES.
I TEACH A COURSE AT A UNIVERSITY.
THERE'S SO MUCH TRUTH IN THEM.
HAVE YOU EVER READ THE STORY "HANSEL AND GRETEL?"
OF COURSE--IT'S A KIDS' STORY.
WELL, THE REAL VERSION IS MUCH DIFFERENT FROM WHAT YOU'VE PROBABLY READ.
ARE YOU REALLY GONNA TELL US SOME LAME STORY ABOUT TWO STUPID KIDS WHO RUN AWAY FROM HOME?
THIS VERSION IS MUCH MORE INTERESTING...GIVE IT A CHANCE, YOU MIGHT ENJOY IT...
ONCE UPON A TIME...

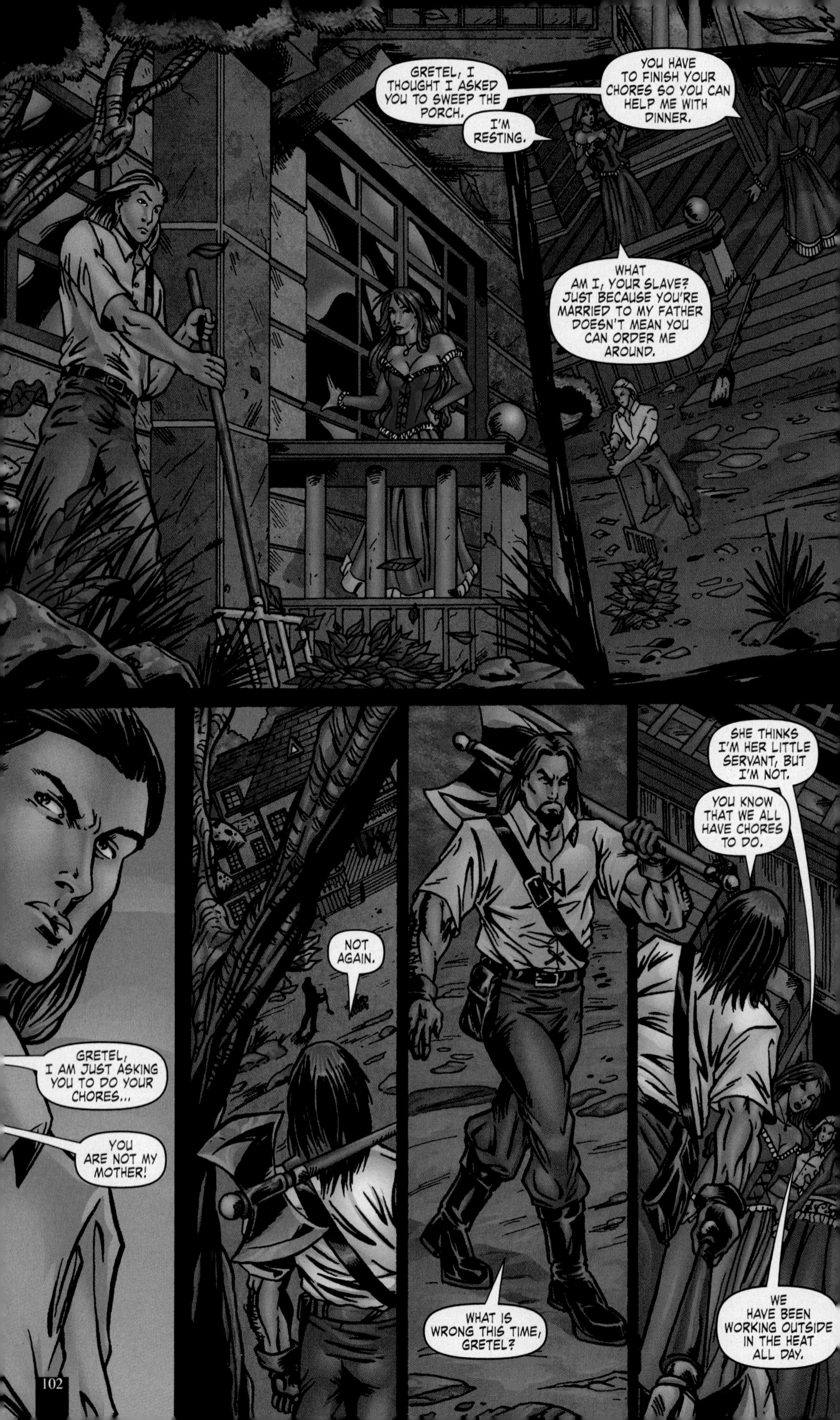
GRETEL, I THOUGHT I ASKED YOU TO SWEEP THE PORCH.
YOU HAVE TO FINISH YOUR CHORES SO YOU CAN HELP ME WITH DINNER.
I'M RESTING.
WHAT AM I, YOUR SLAVE? JUST BECAUSE YOU'RE MARRIED TO MY FATHER DOESN'T MEAN YOU CAN ORDER ME AROUND.
GRETEL, I AM JUST ASKING YOU TO DO YOUR CHORES...
YOU ARE NOT MY MOTHER!
NOT AGAIN.
WHAT IS WRONG THIS TIME, GRETEL?
SHE THINKS I'M HER LITTLE SERVANT, BUT I'M NOT.
YOU KNOW THAT WE ALL HAVE CHORES TO DO.
WE HAVE BEEN WORKING OUTSIDE IN THE HEAT ALL DAY.

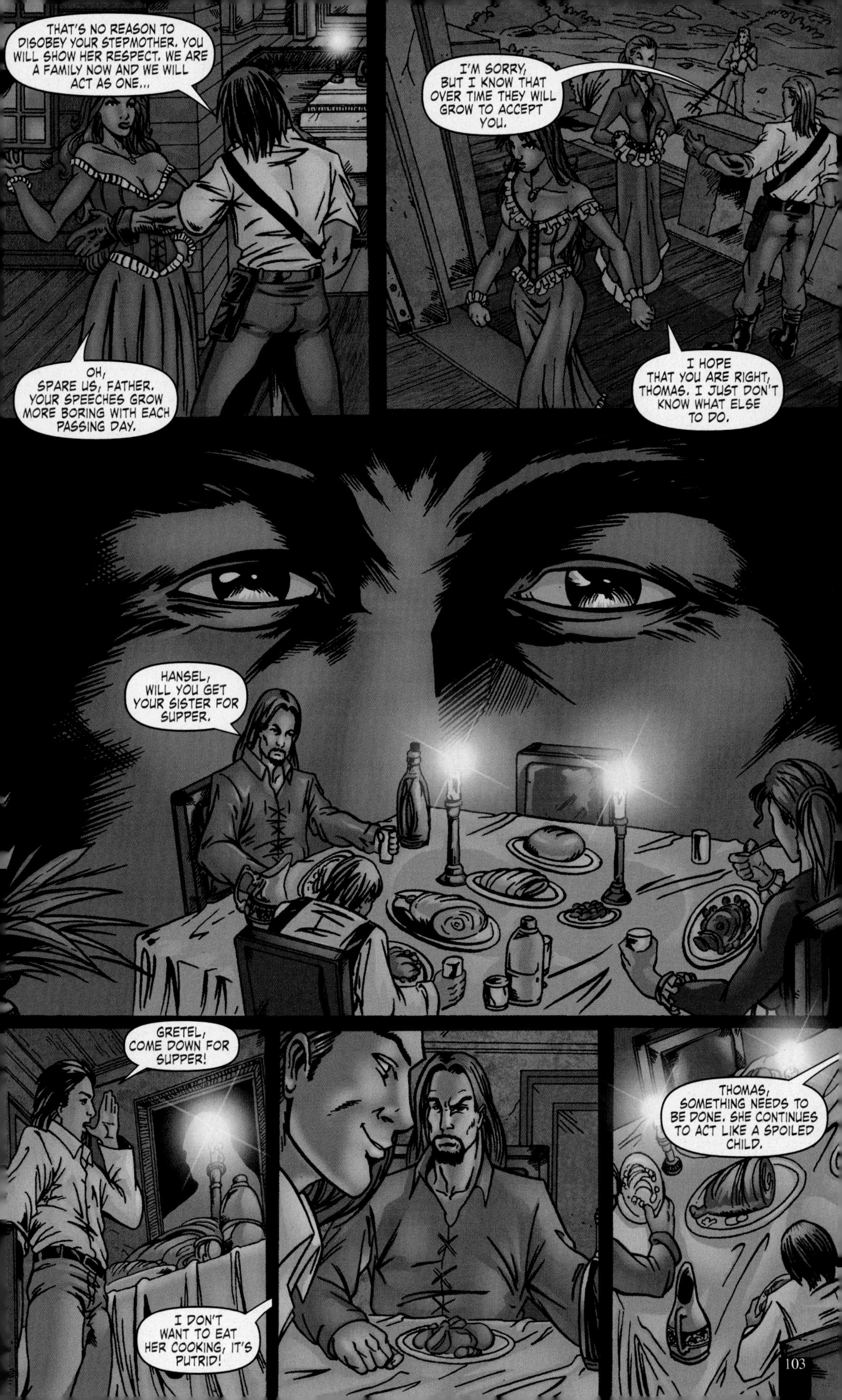

THAT'S NO REASON TO DISOBEY YOUR STEPMOTHER. YOU WILL SHOW HER RESPECT. WE ARE A FAMILY NOW AND WE WILL ACT AS ONE...
OH, SPARE US, FATHER. YOUR SPEECHES GROW MORE BORING WITH EACH PASSING DAY.
I'M SORRY, BUT I KNOW THAT OVER TIME THEY WILL GROW TO ACCEPT YOU.
I HOPE THAT YOU ARE RIGHT, THOMAS. I JUST DON'T KNOW WHAT ELSE TO DO.
HANSEL, WILL YOU GET YOUR SISTER FOR SUPPER.
GRETEL, COME DOWN FOR SUPPER!
I DON'T WANT TO EAT HER COOKING, IT'S PUTRID!
THOMAS, SOMETHING NEEDS TO BE DONE. SHE CONTINUES TO ACT LIKE A SPOILED CHILD.

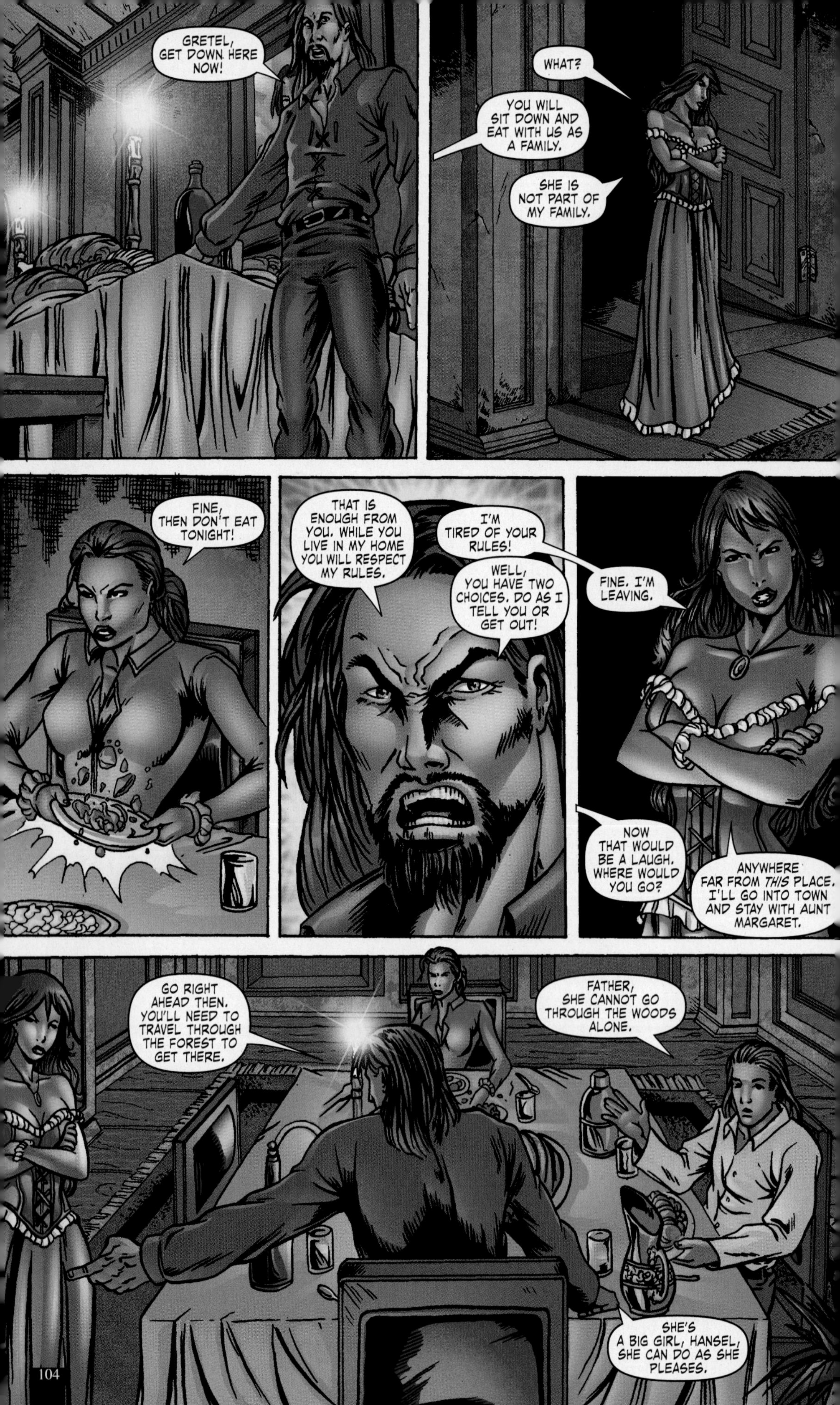
GRETEL, GET DOWN HERE NOW!
WHAT?
YOU WILL SIT DOWN AND EAT WITH US AS A FAMILY.
SHE IS NOT PART OF MY FAMILY.
FINE, THEN DON'T EAT TONIGHT!
THAT IS ENOUGH FROM YOU. WHILE YOU LIVE IN MY HOME YOU WILL RESPECT MY RULES.
I'M TIRED OF YOUR RULES!
WELL, YOU HAVE TWO CHOICES. DO AS I TELL YOU OR GET OUT!
FINE. I'M LEAVING.
NOW THAT WOULD BE A LAUGH. WHERE WOULD YOU GO?
ANYWHERE FAR FROM *THIS* PLACE. I'LL GO INTO TOWN AND STAY WITH AUNT MARGARET.
GO RIGHT AHEAD THEN. YOU'LL NEED TO TRAVEL THROUGH THE FOREST TO GET THERE.
FATHER, SHE CANNOT GO THROUGH THE WOODS ALONE.
SHE'S A BIG GIRL, HANSEL, SHE CAN DO AS SHE PLEASES.

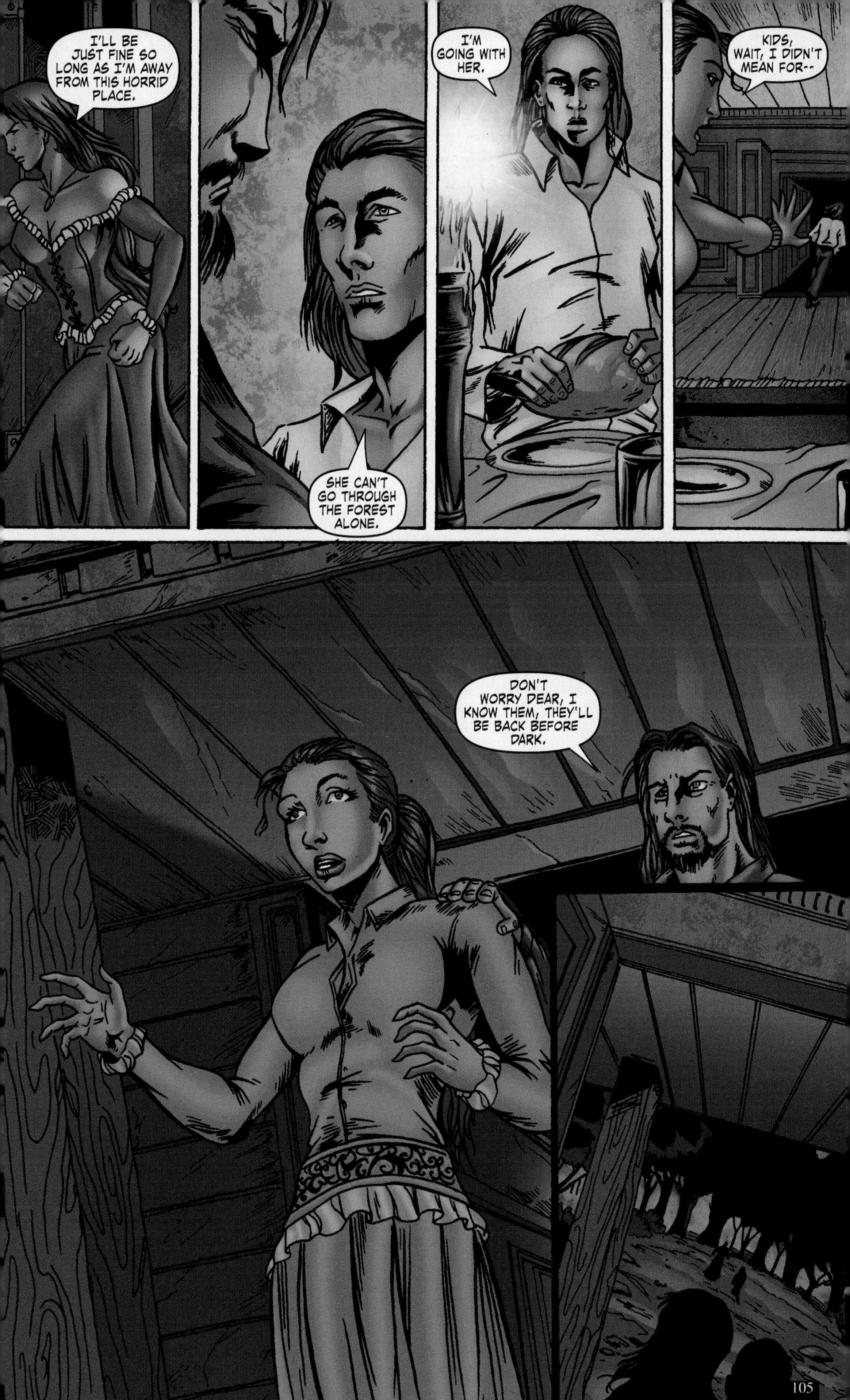
I'LL BE JUST FINE SO LONG AS I'M AWAY FROM THIS HORRID PLACE.
SHE CAN'T GO THROUGH THE FOREST ALONE.
I'M GOING WITH HER.
KIDS, WAIT, I DIDN'T MEAN FOR--
DON'T WORRY DEAR, I KNOW THEM, THEY'LL BE BACK BEFORE DARK.

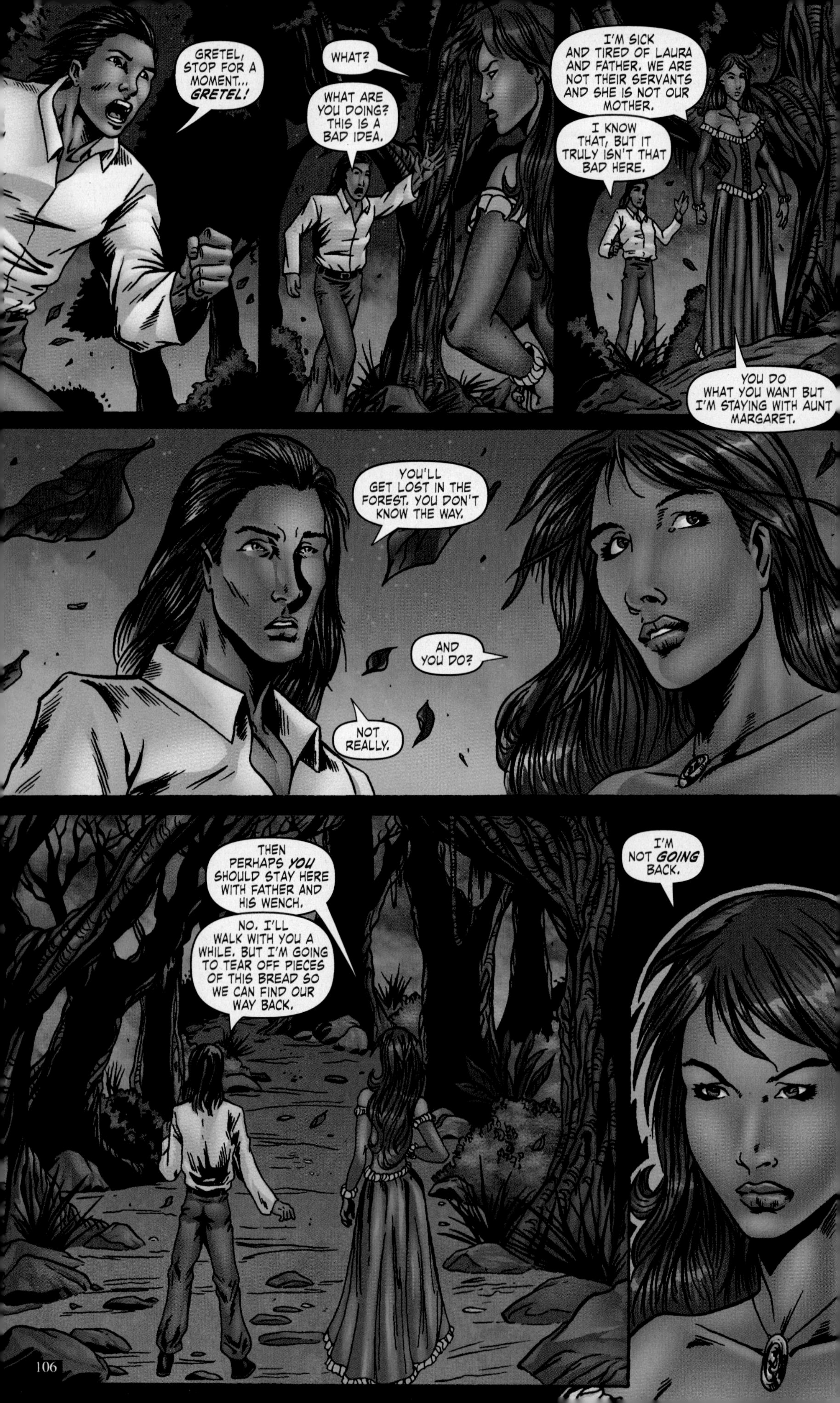
GRETEL, STOP FOR A MOMENT... GRETEL!
WHAT?
WHAT ARE YOU DOING? THIS IS A BAD IDEA.
I'M SICK AND TIRED OF LAURA AND FATHER. WE ARE NOT THEIR SERVANTS AND SHE IS NOT OUR MOTHER.
I KNOW THAT, BUT IT TRULY ISN'T THAT BAD HERE.
YOU DO WHAT YOU WANT BUT I'M STAYING WITH AUNT MARGARET.
YOU'LL GET LOST IN THE FOREST. YOU DON'T KNOW THE WAY.
AND YOU DO?
NOT REALLY.
THEN PERHAPS YOU SHOULD STAY HERE WITH FATHER AND HIS WENCH.
NO. I'LL WALK WITH YOU A WHILE. BUT I'M GOING TO TEAR OFF PIECES OF THIS BREAD SO WE CAN FIND OUR WAY BACK.
I'M NOT GOING BACK.

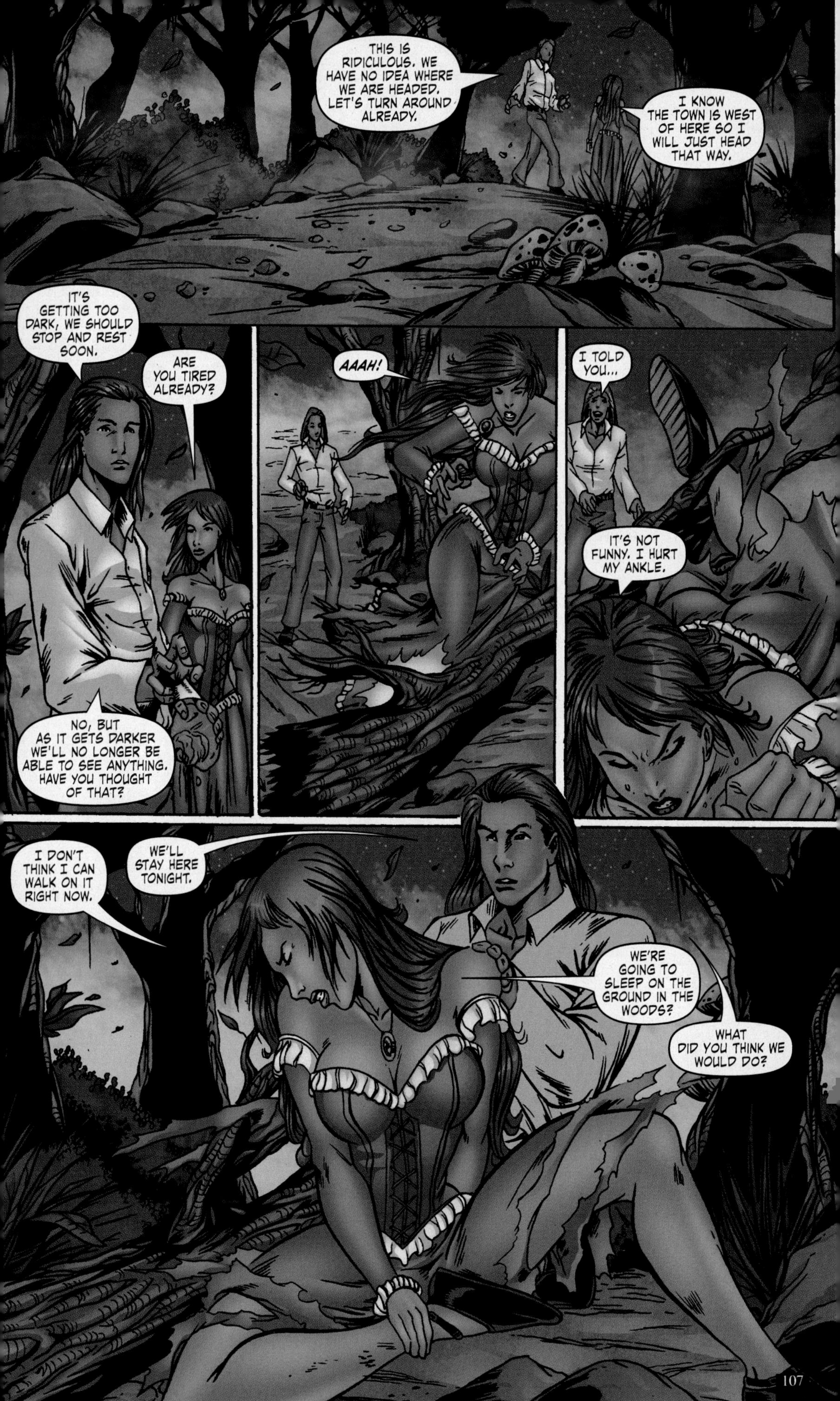
THIS IS RIDICULOUS. WE HAVE NO IDEA WHERE WE ARE HEADED. LET'S TURN AROUND ALREADY.
I KNOW THE TOWN IS WEST OF HERE SO I WILL JUST HEAD THAT WAY.
IT'S GETTING TOO DARK, WE SHOULD STOP AND REST SOON.
ARE YOU TIRED ALREADY?
NO, BUT AS IT GETS DARKER WE'LL NO LONGER BE ABLE TO SEE ANYTHING. HAVE YOU THOUGHT OF THAT?
AAAH!
I TOLD YOU...
IT'S NOT FUNNY. I HURT MY ANKLE.
I DON'T THINK I CAN WALK ON IT RIGHT NOW.
WE'LL STAY HERE TONIGHT.
WE'RE GOING TO SLEEP ON THE GROUND IN THE WOODS?
WHAT DID YOU THINK WE WOULD DO?

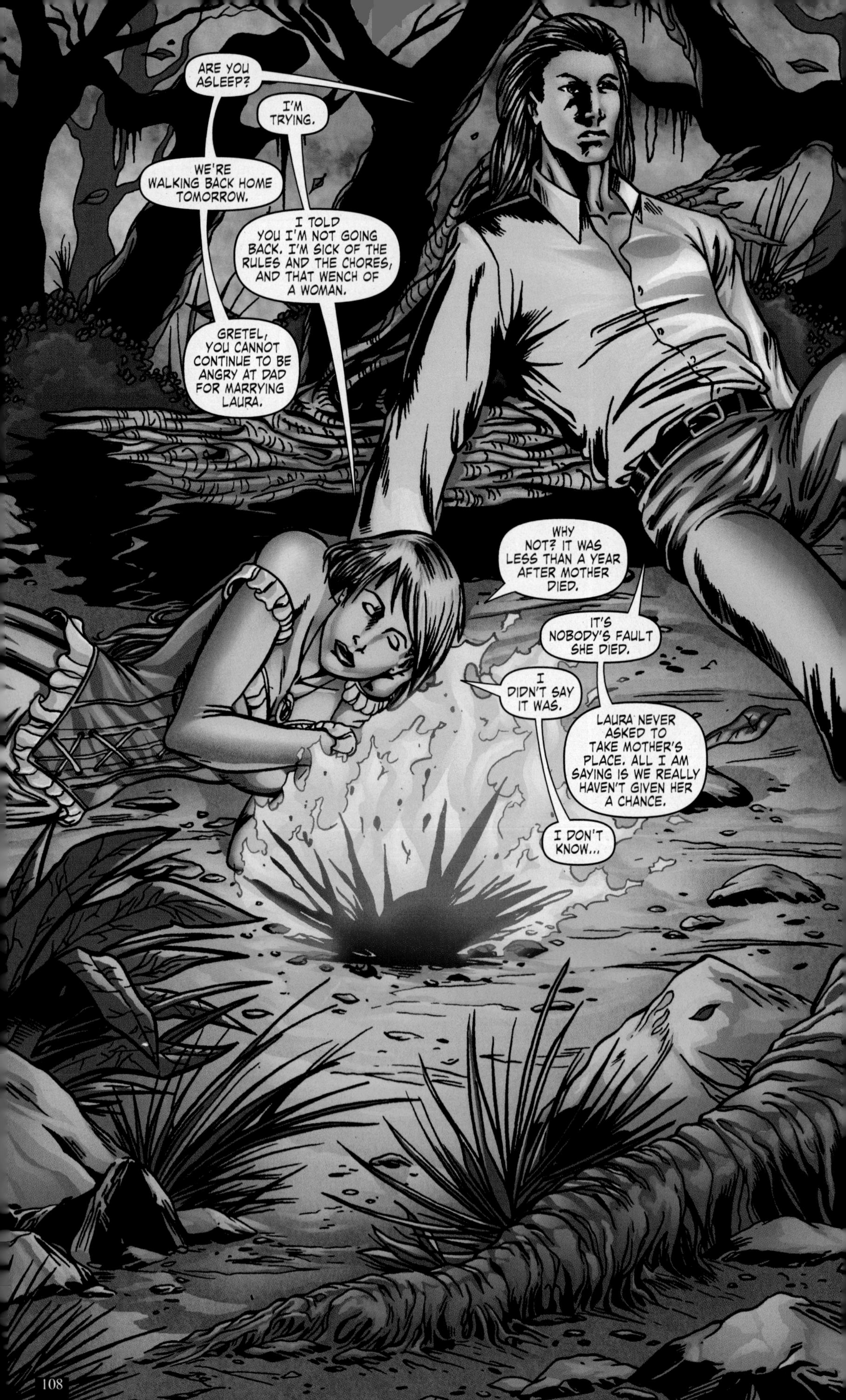
ARE YOU ASLEEP?
I'M TRYING.
WE'RE WALKING BACK HOME TOMORROW.
I TOLD YOU I'M NOT GOING BACK. I'M SICK OF THE RULES AND THE CHORES, AND THAT WENCH OF A WOMAN.
GRETEL, YOU CANNOT CONTINUE TO BE ANGRY AT DAD FOR MARRYING LAURA.
WHY NOT? IT WAS LESS THAN A YEAR AFTER MOTHER DIED.
IT'S NOBODY'S FAULT SHE DIED.
I DIDN'T SAY IT WAS.
LAURA NEVER ASKED TO TAKE MOTHER'S PLACE. ALL I AM SAYING IS WE REALLY HAVEN'T GIVEN HER A CHANCE.
I DON'T KNOW...

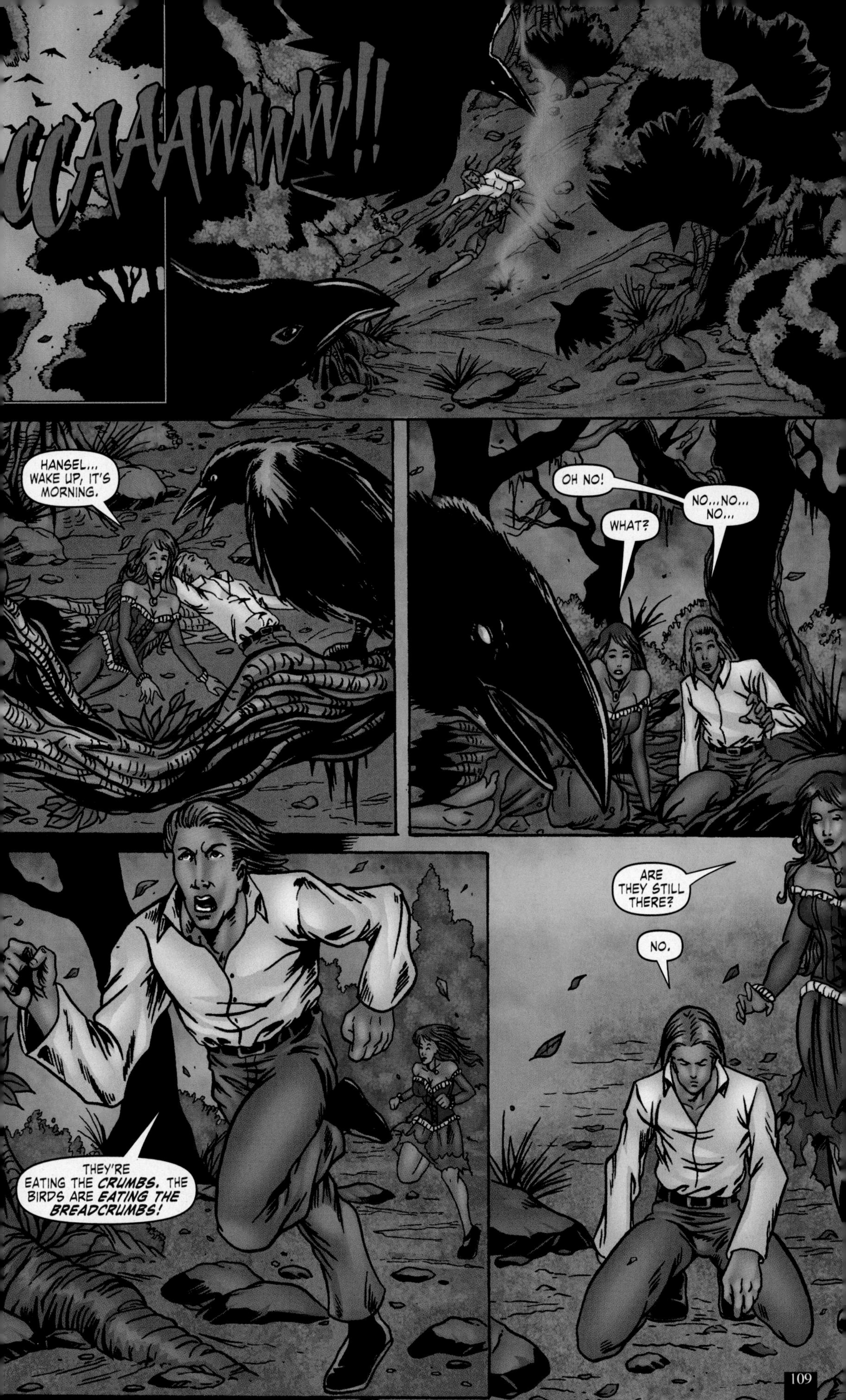
CCAAAWWW!!
HANSEL... WAKE UP, IT'S MORNING.
OH NO!
WHAT?
NO...NO... NO...
THEY'RE EATING THE CRUMBS. THE BIRDS ARE EATING THE BREADCRUMBS!
ARE THEY STILL THERE?
NO.

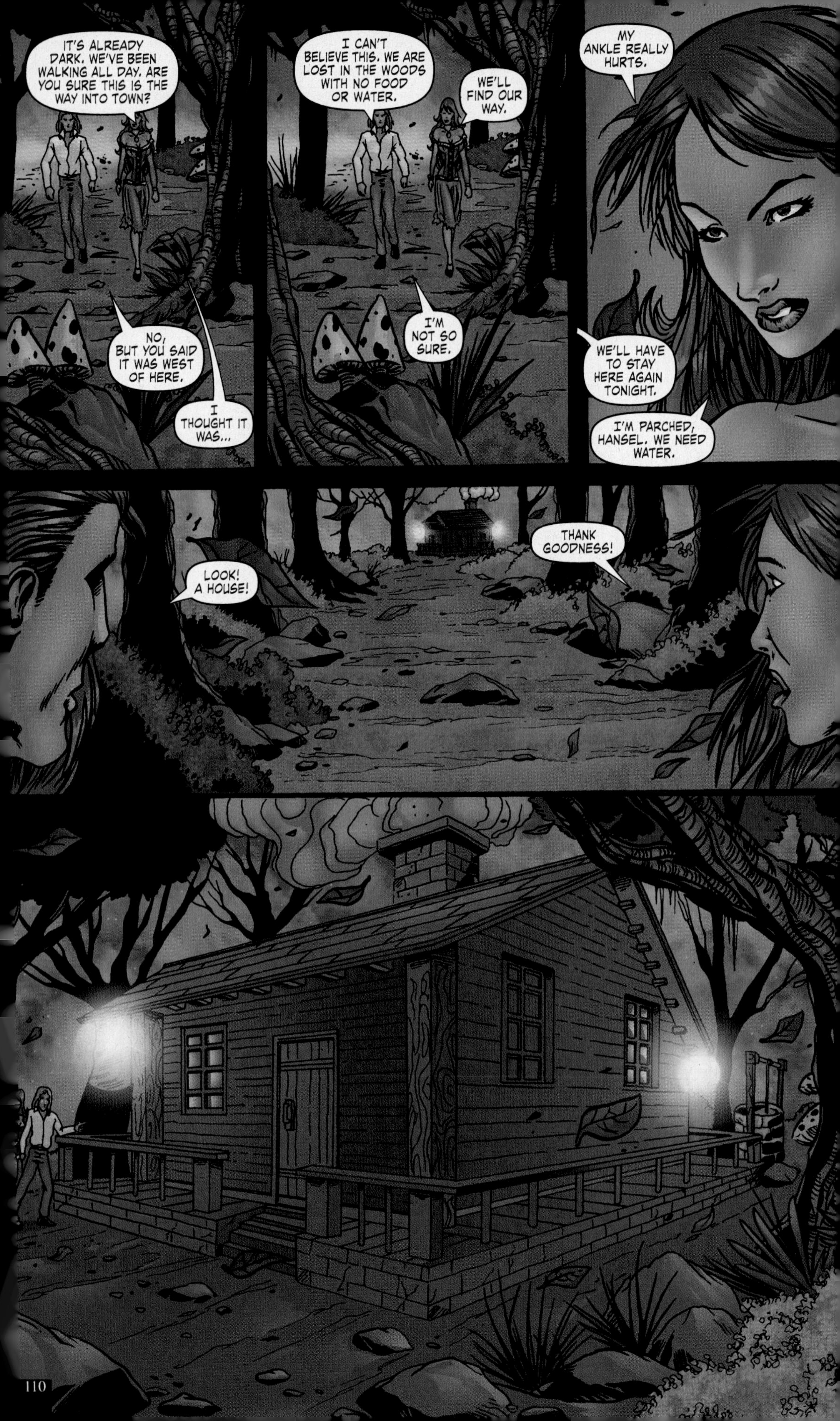
IT'S ALREADY DARK. WE'VE BEEN WALKING ALL DAY. ARE YOU SURE THIS IS THE WAY INTO TOWN?
NO, BUT YOU SAID IT WAS WEST OF HERE.
I THOUGHT IT WAS...
I CAN'T BELIEVE THIS. WE ARE LOST IN THE WOODS WITH NO FOOD OR WATER.
WE'LL FIND OUR WAY.
I'M NOT SO SURE.
MY ANKLE REALLY HURTS.
WE'LL HAVE TO STAY HERE AGAIN TONIGHT.
I'M PARCHED, HANSEL. WE NEED WATER.
LOOK! A HOUSE!
THANK GOODNESS!

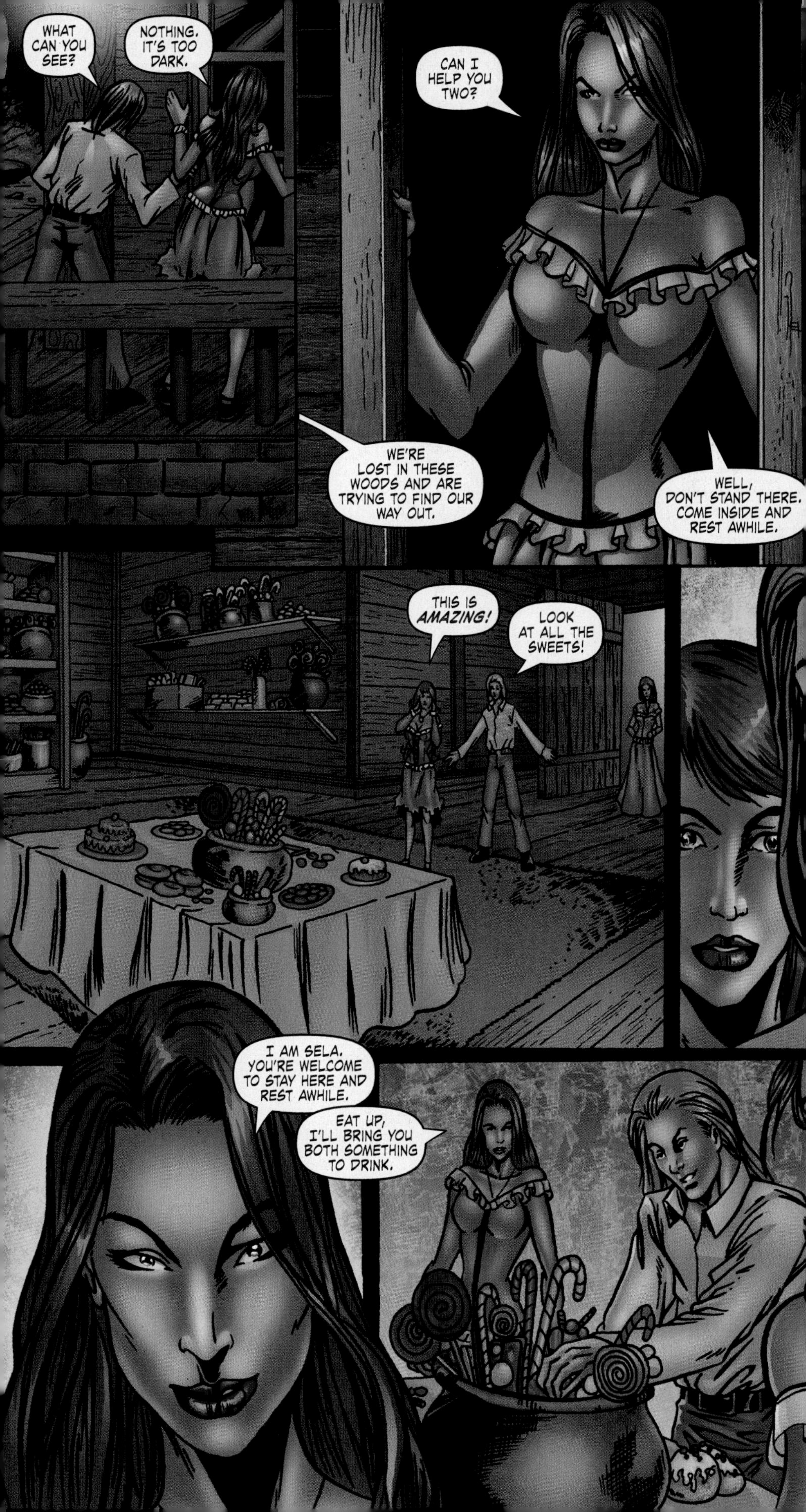

WHAT CAN YOU SEE?
NOTHING. IT'S TOO DARK.
CAN I HELP YOU TWO?
WE'RE LOST IN THESE WOODS AND ARE TRYING TO FIND OUR WAY OUT.
WELL, DON'T STAND THERE. COME INSIDE AND REST AWHILE.
THIS IS *AMAZING!*
LOOK AT ALL THE SWEETS!
I AM SELA. YOU'RE WELCOME TO STAY HERE AND REST AWHILE.
EAT UP, I'LL BRING YOU BOTH SOMETHING TO DRINK.

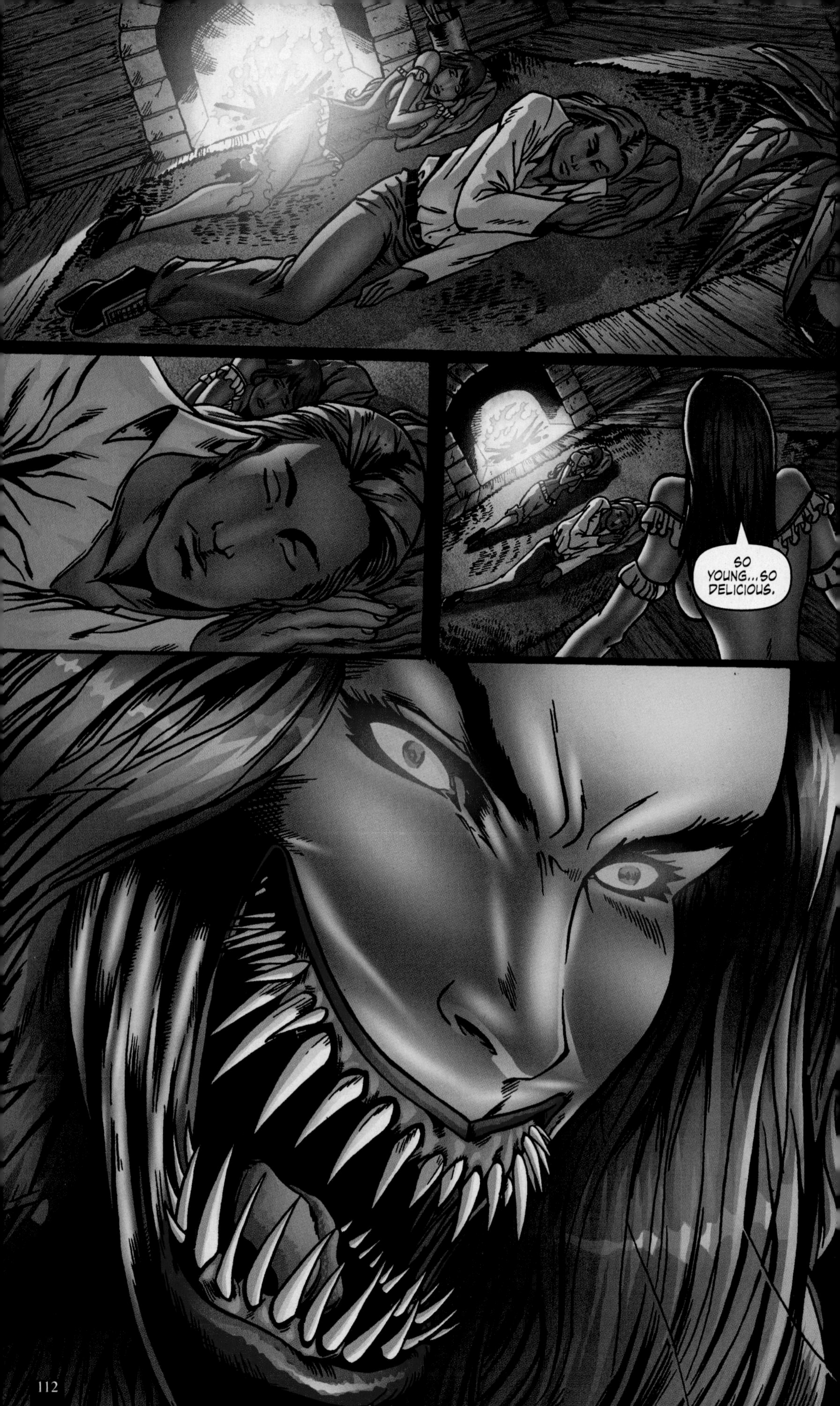
SO YOUNG...SO DELICIOUS.

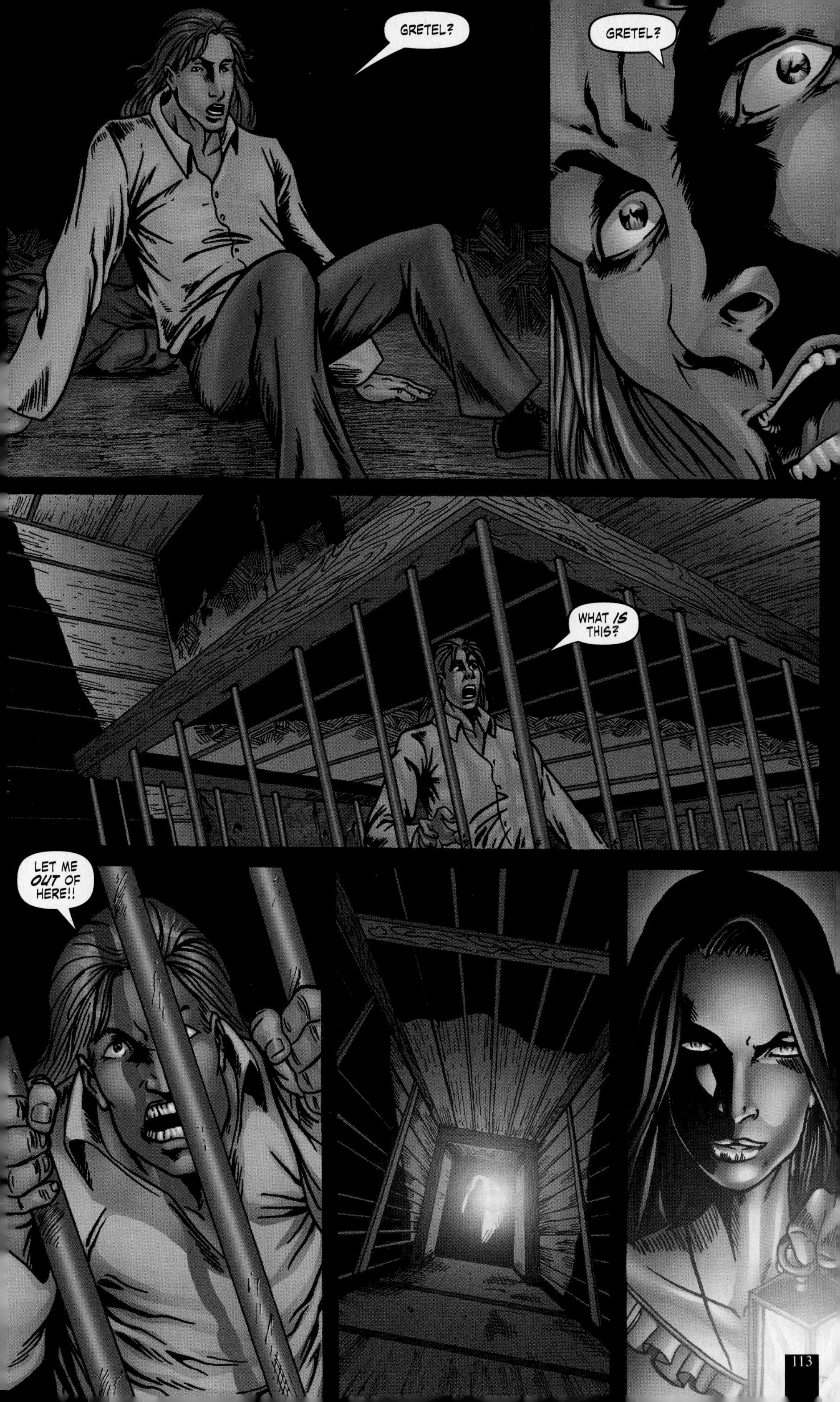
GRETEL?
GRETEL?
WHAT IS THIS?
LET ME OUT OF HERE!!

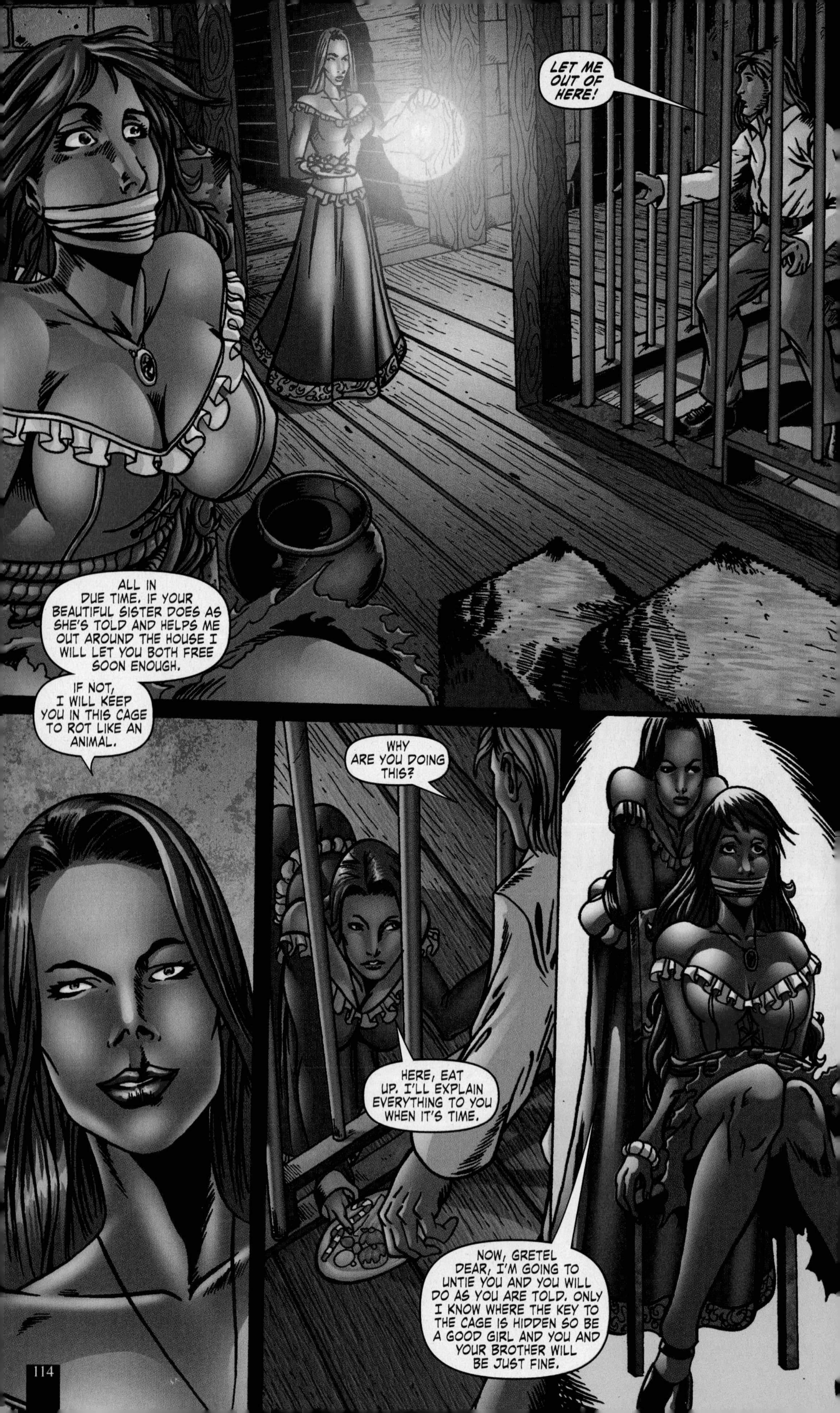
LET ME OUT OF HERE!
ALL IN DUE TIME. IF YOUR BEAUTIFUL SISTER DOES AS SHE'S TOLD AND HELPS ME OUT AROUND THE HOUSE I WILL LET YOU BOTH FREE SOON ENOUGH.
IF NOT, I WILL KEEP YOU IN THIS CAGE TO ROT LIKE AN ANIMAL.
WHY ARE YOU DOING THIS?
HERE, EAT UP. I'LL EXPLAIN EVERYTHING TO YOU WHEN IT'S TIME.
NOW, GRETEL DEAR, I'M GOING TO UNTIE YOU AND YOU WILL DO AS YOU ARE TOLD. ONLY I KNOW WHERE THE KEY TO THE CAGE IS HIDDEN SO BE A GOOD GIRL AND YOU AND YOUR BROTHER WILL BE JUST FINE.

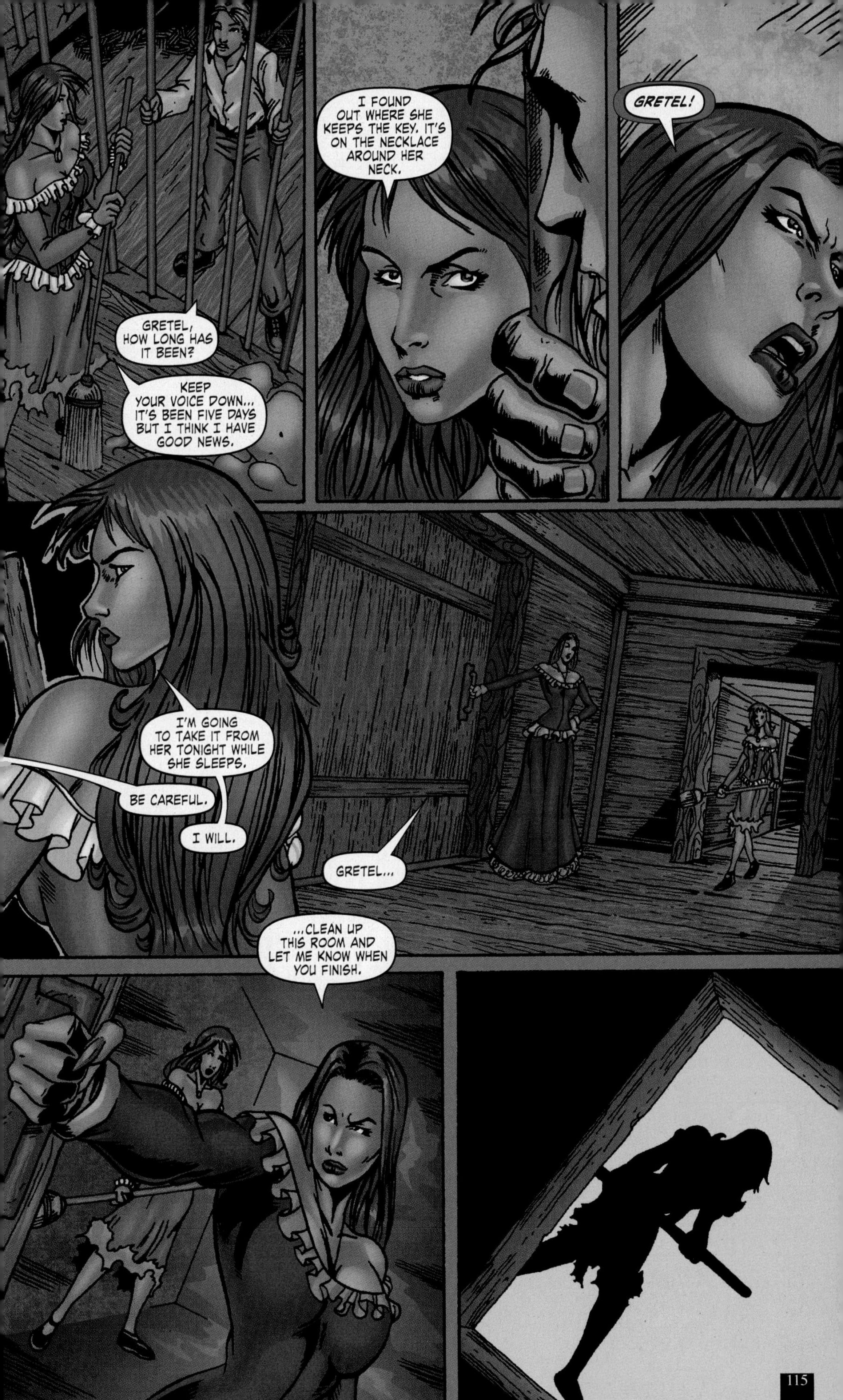
GRETEL, HOW LONG HAS IT BEEN?
KEEP YOUR VOICE DOWN... IT'S BEEN FIVE DAYS BUT I THINK I HAVE GOOD NEWS.
I FOUND OUT WHERE SHE KEEPS THE KEY. IT'S ON THE NECKLACE AROUND HER NECK.
GRETEL!
I'M GOING TO TAKE IT FROM HER TONIGHT WHILE SHE SLEEPS.
BE CAREFUL.
I WILL.
GRETEL...
...CLEAN UP THIS ROOM AND LET ME KNOW WHEN YOU FINISH.

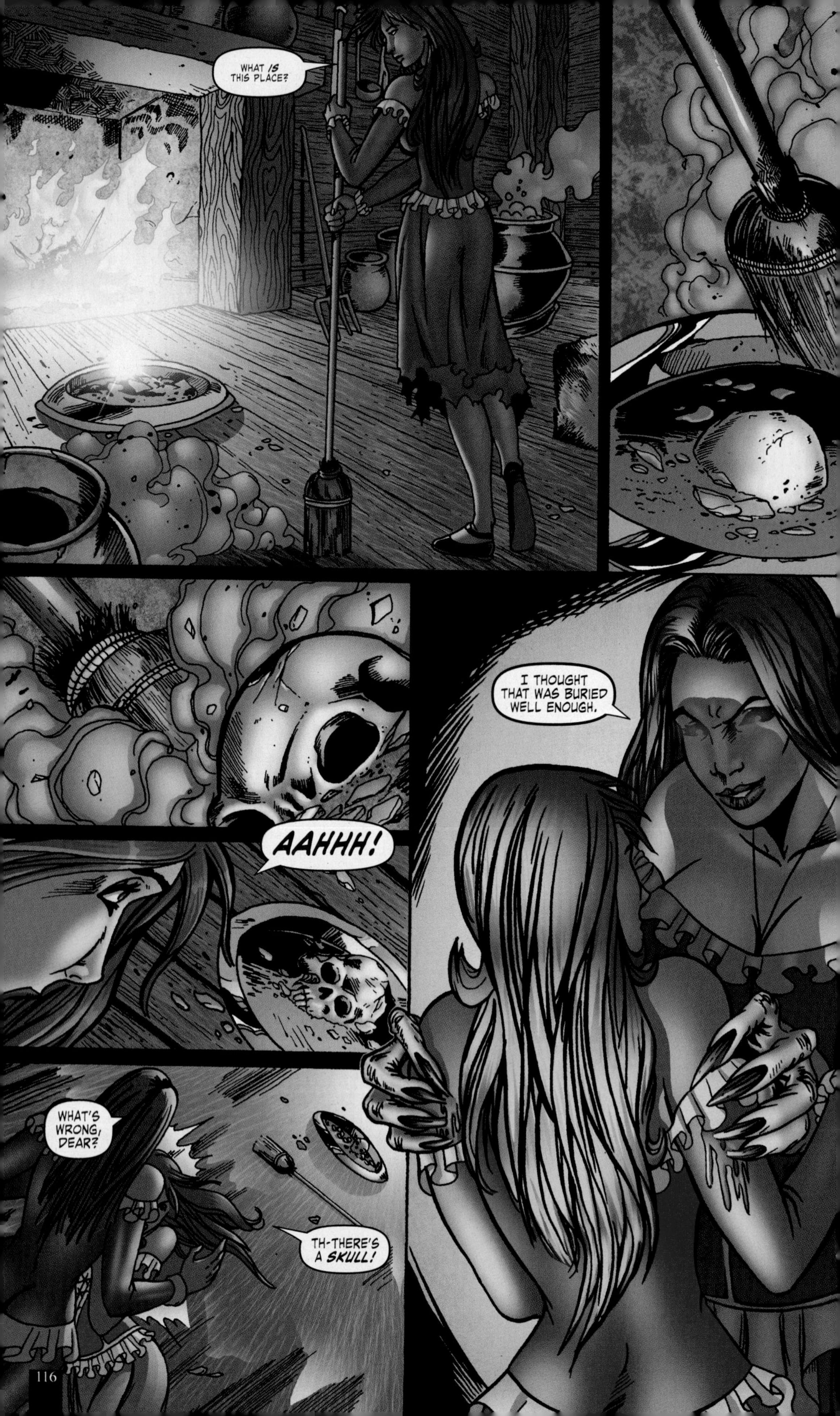
WHAT IS THIS PLACE?
AAHHH!
I THOUGHT THAT WAS BURIED WELL ENOUGH.
WHAT'S WRONG, DEAR?
TH-THERE'S A SKULL!

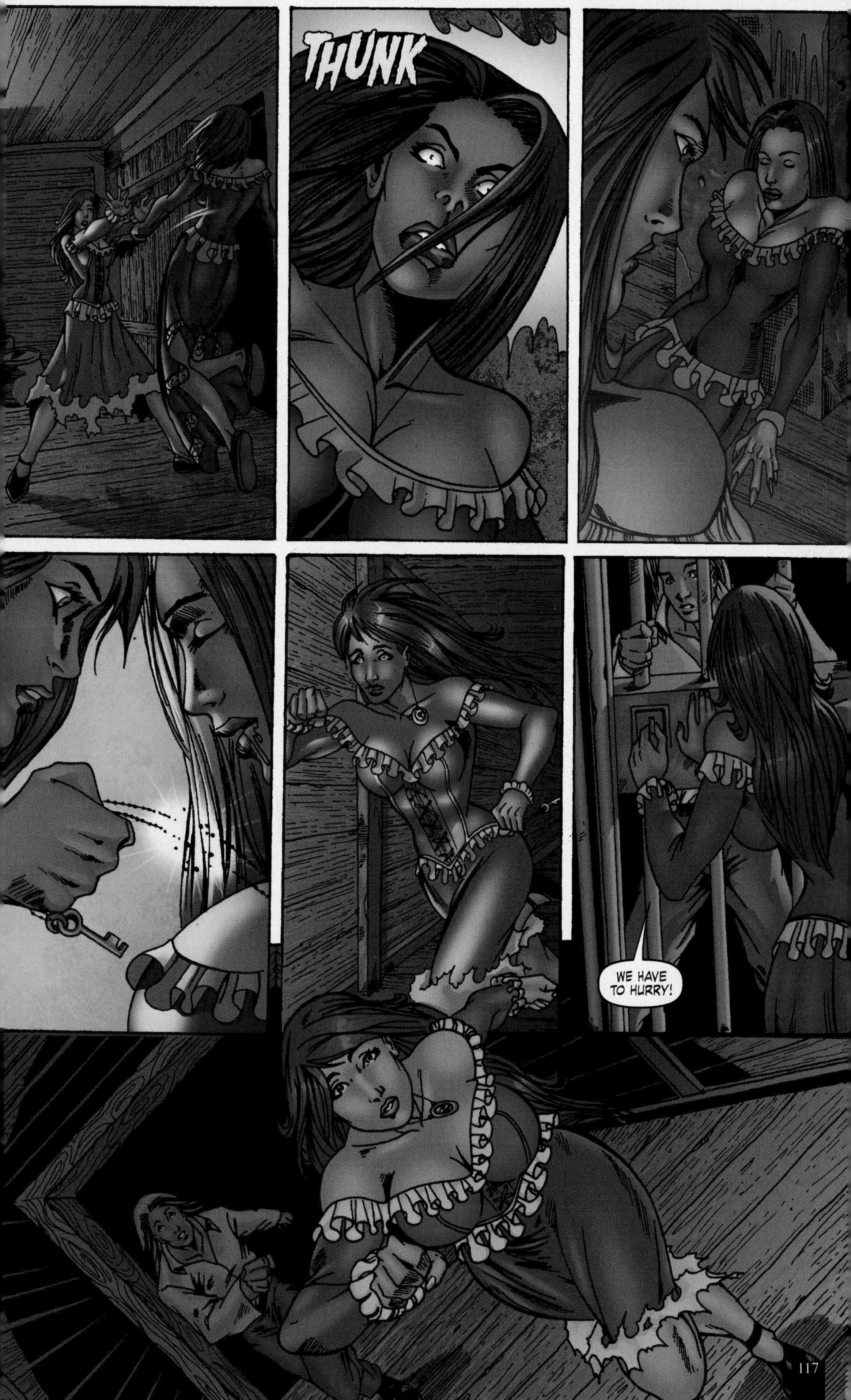
THUNK
WE HAVE TO HURRY!

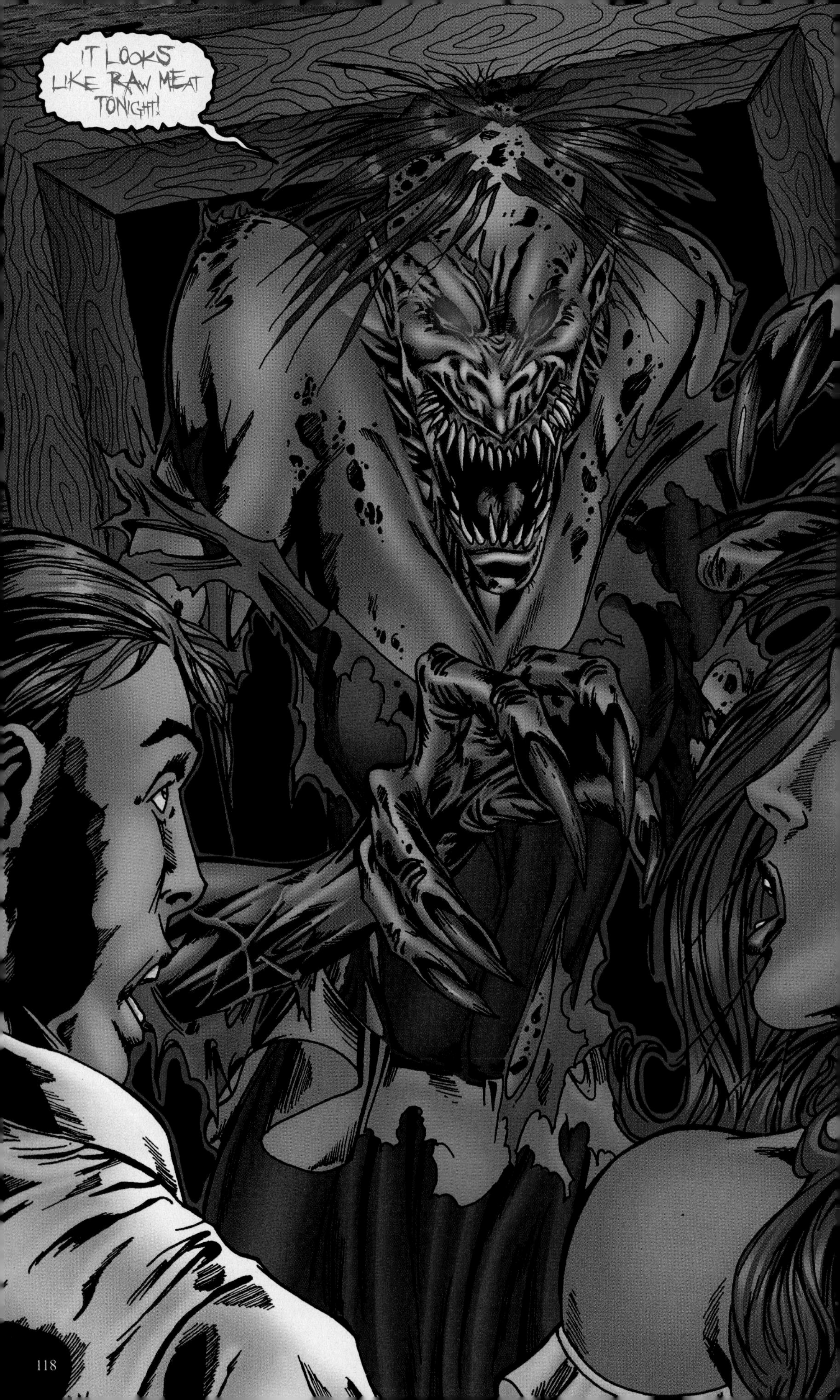
IT LOOKS LIKE RAW MEAT TONIGHT!

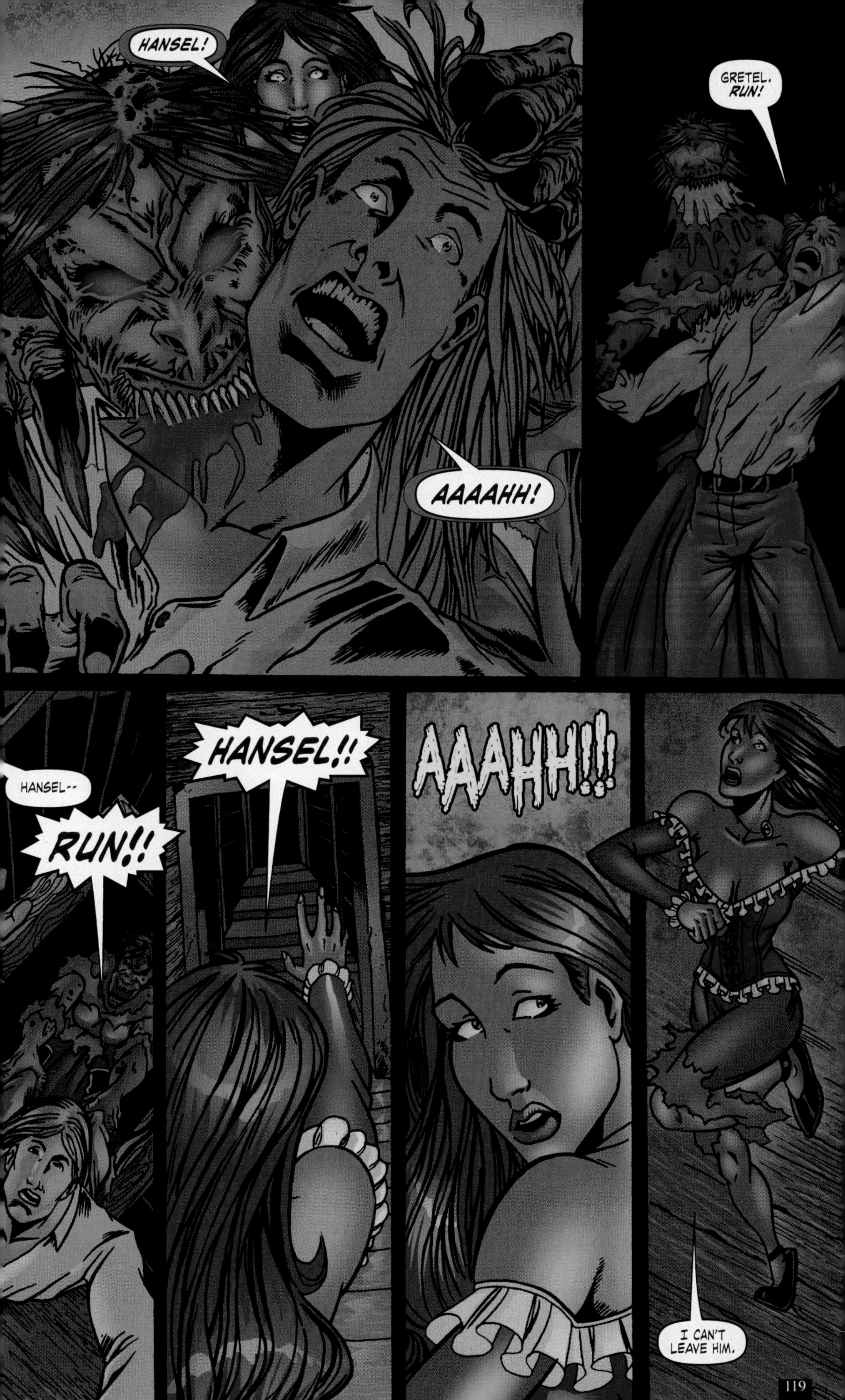
HANSEL!
AAAAHH!
GRETEL. RUN!
HANSEL--
RUN!!
HANSEL!!
AAAHH!!!
I CAN'T LEAVE HIM.

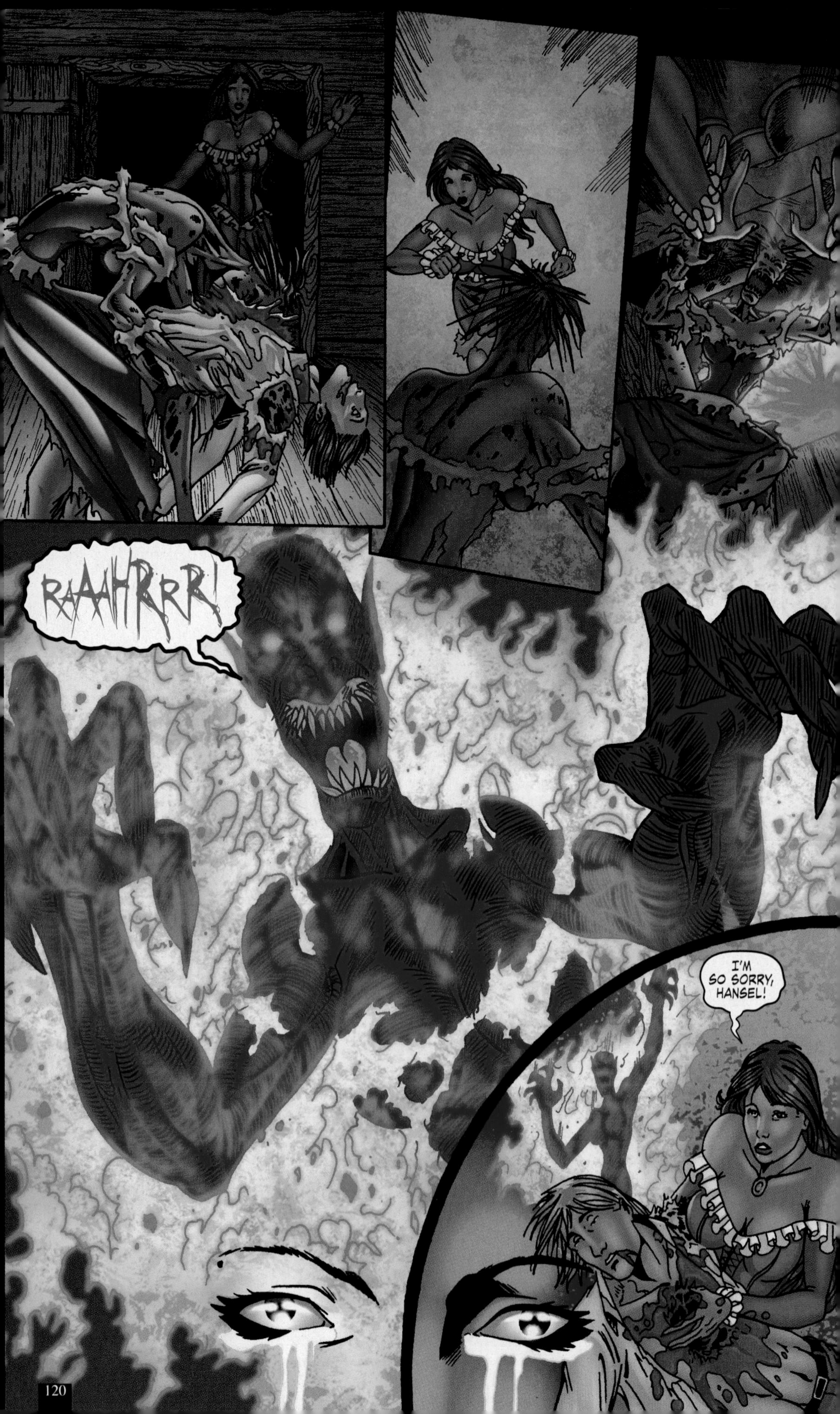
RAAAHRRRR!
I'M SO SORRY, HANSEL!

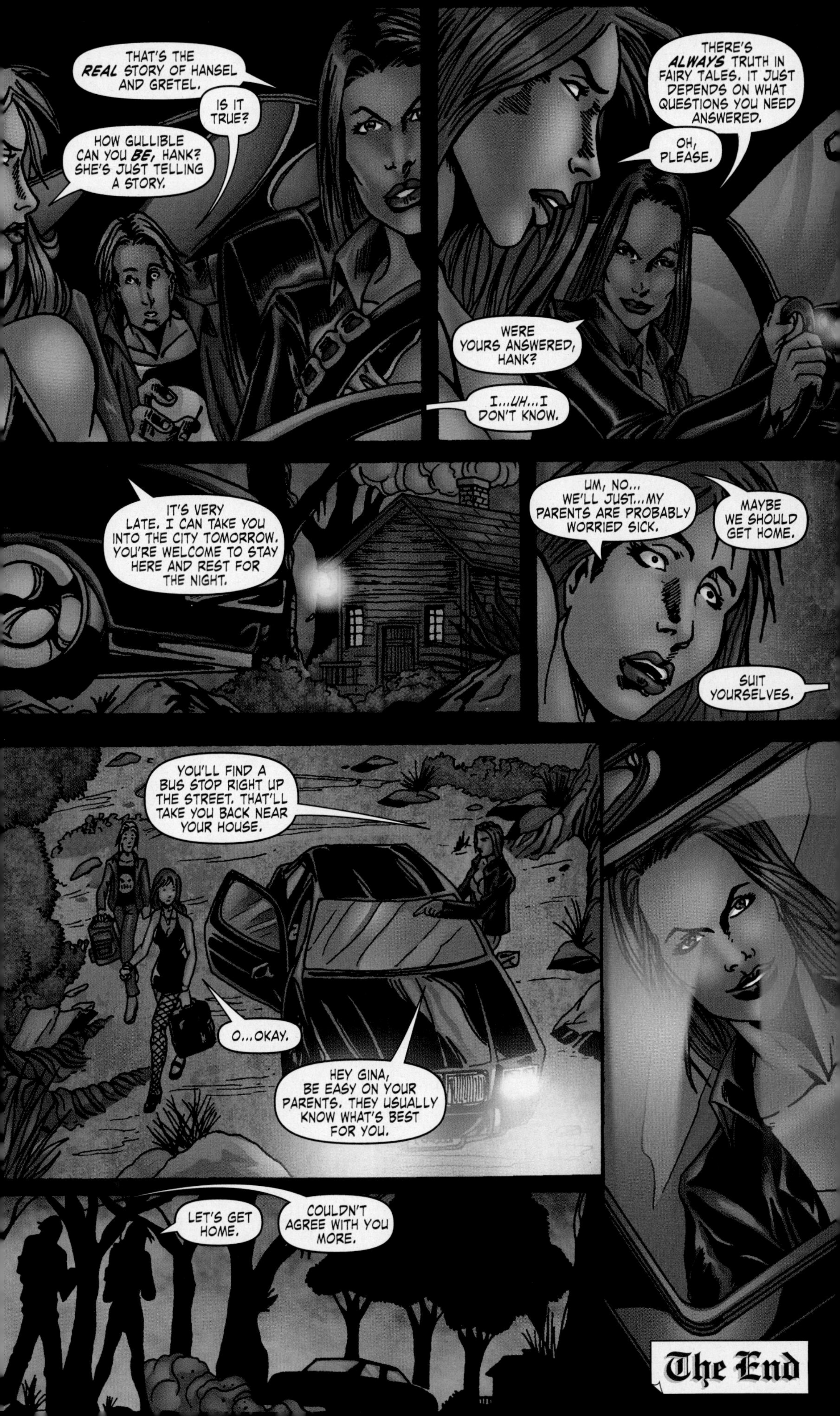
THAT'S THE *REAL* STORY OF HANSEL AND GRETEL.
IS IT TRUE?
HOW GULLIBLE CAN YOU *BE,* HANK? SHE'S JUST TELLING A STORY.
THERE'S *ALWAYS* TRUTH IN FAIRY TALES. IT JUST DEPENDS ON WHAT QUESTIONS YOU NEED ANSWERED.
OH, PLEASE.
WERE YOURS ANSWERED, HANK?
I...*UH*...I DON'T KNOW.
IT'S VERY LATE. I CAN TAKE YOU INTO THE CITY TOMORROW. YOU'RE WELCOME TO STAY HERE AND REST FOR THE NIGHT.
UM, NO... WE'LL JUST...MY PARENTS ARE PROBABLY WORRIED SICK.
MAYBE WE SHOULD GET HOME.
SUIT YOURSELVES.
YOU'LL FIND A BUS STOP RIGHT UP THE STREET. THAT'LL TAKE YOU BACK NEAR YOUR HOUSE.
O...OKAY.
HEY GINA, BE EASY ON YOUR PARENTS. THEY USUALLY KNOW WHAT'S BEST FOR YOU.
LET'S GET HOME.
COULDN'T AGREE WITH YOU MORE.
The End

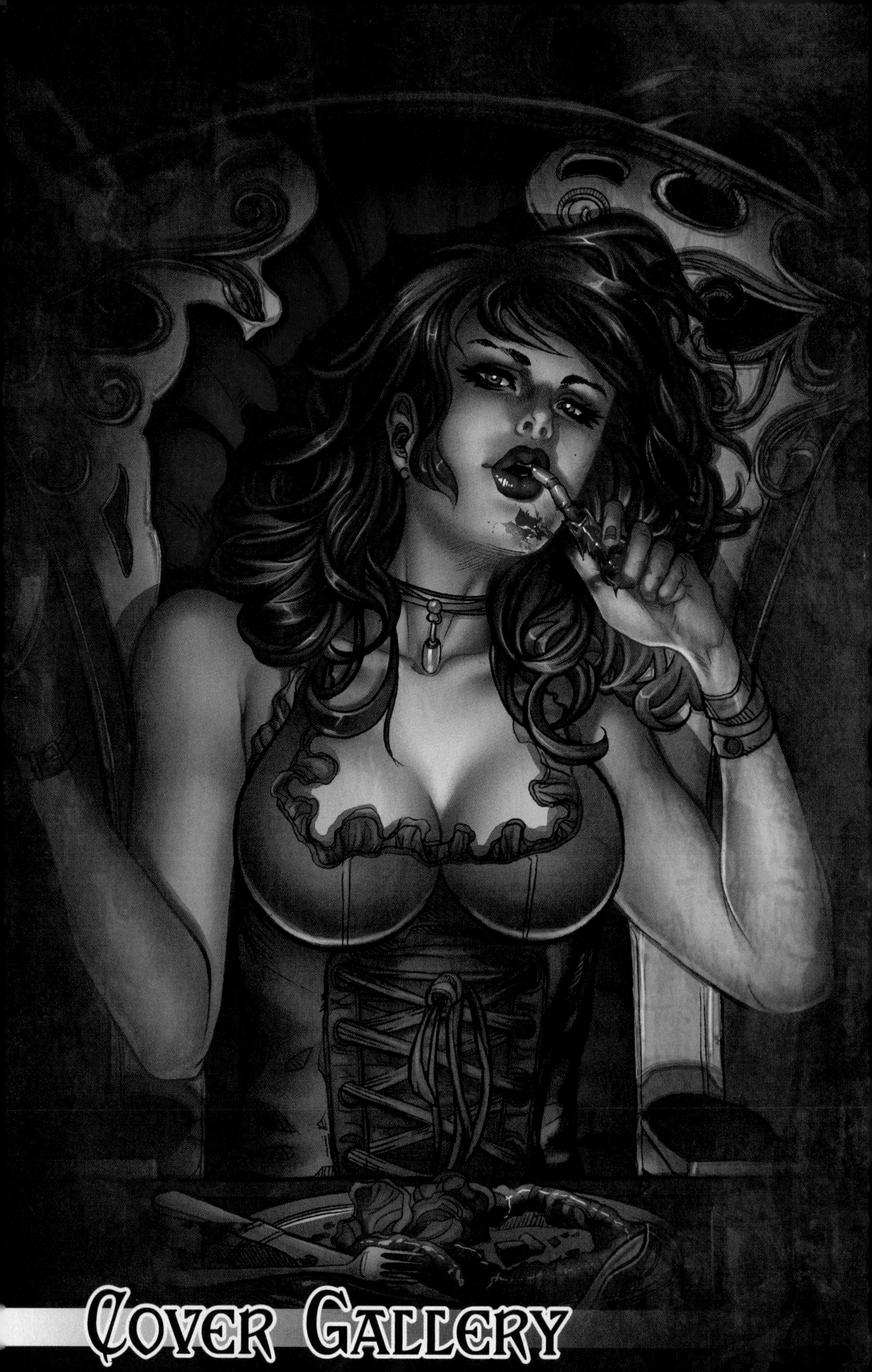

Cover Gallery

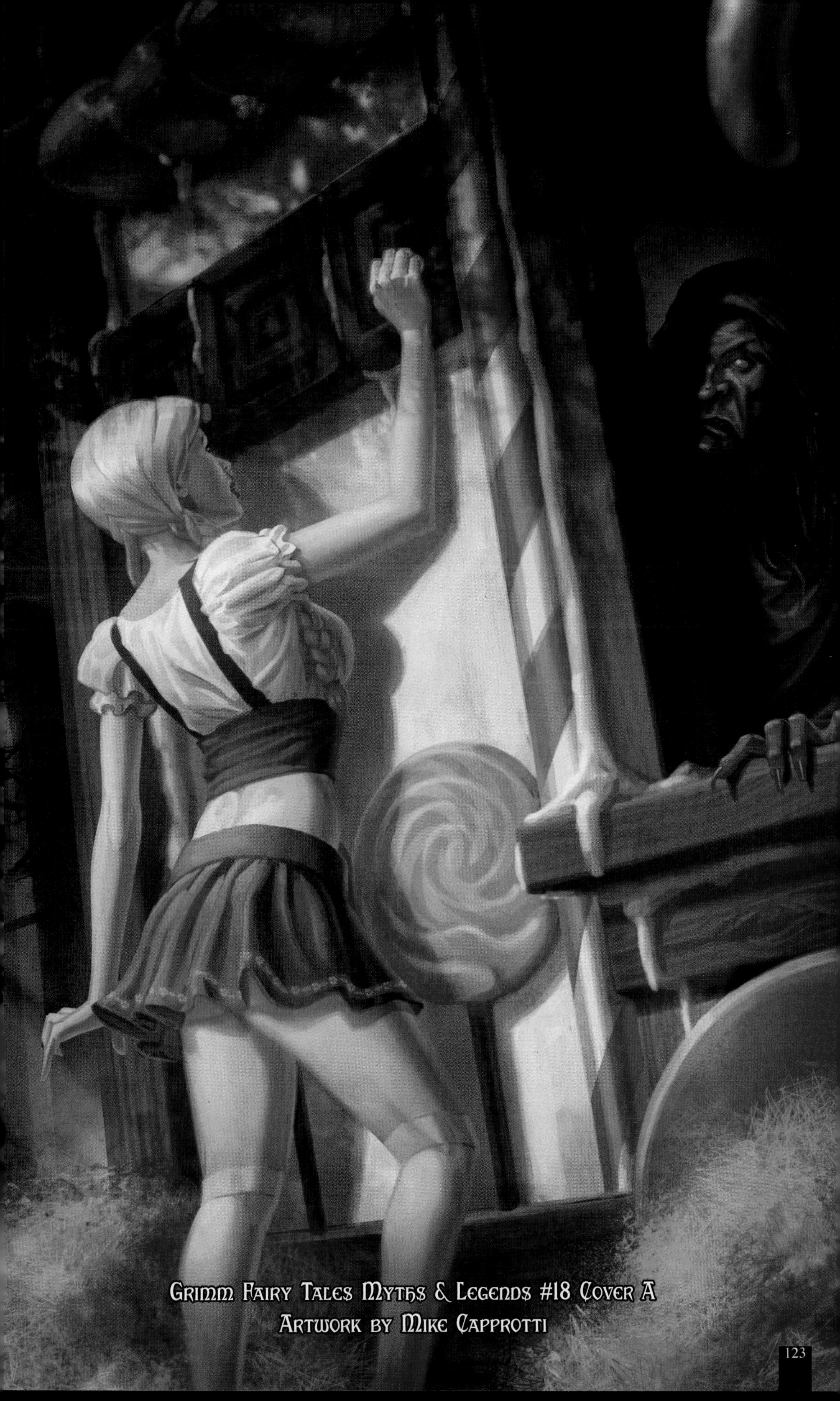

Grimm Fairy Tales Myths & Legends #18 Cover A
Artwork by Mike Capprotti

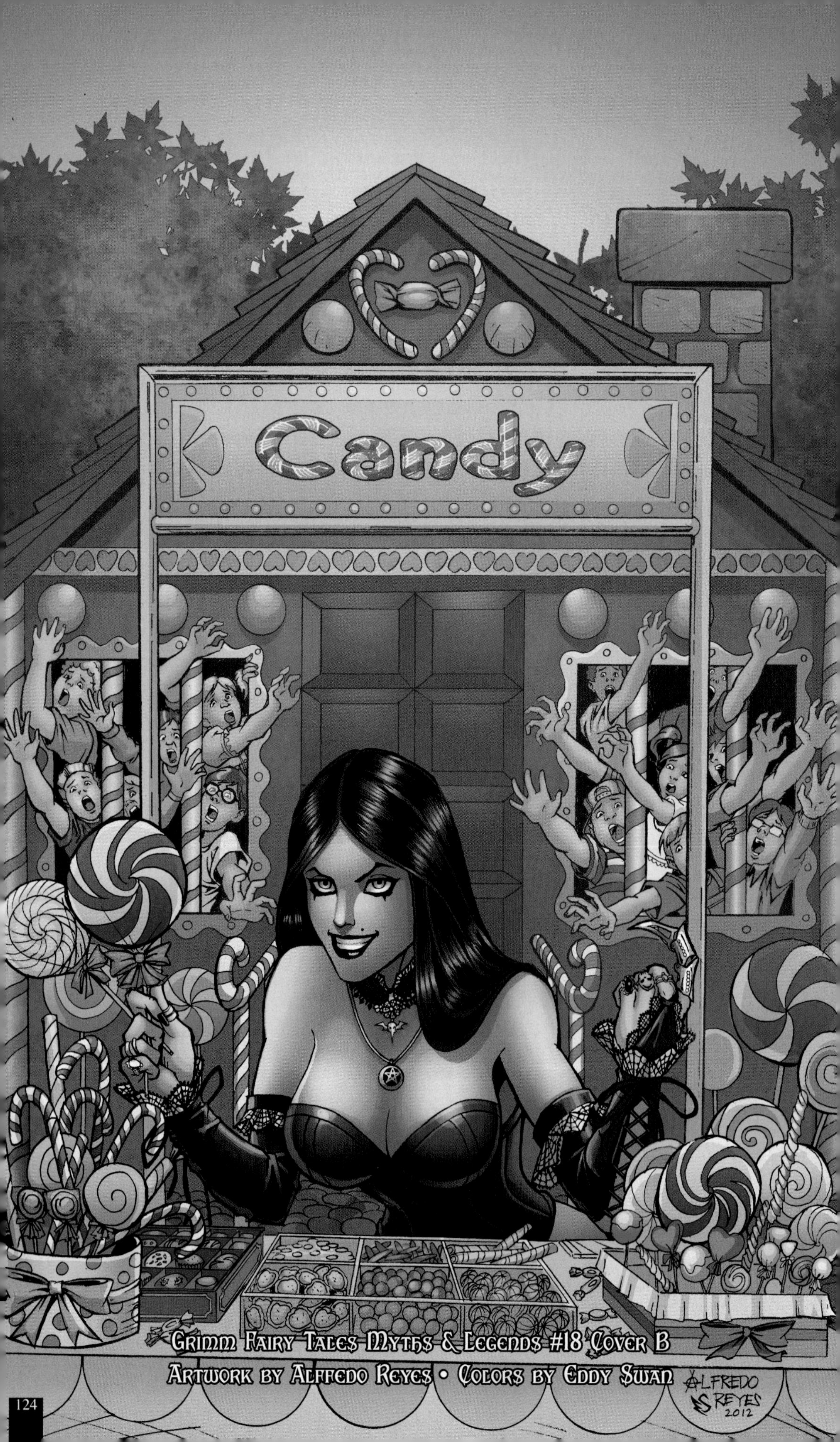
Candy
ALFREDO REYES 2012

Grimm Fairy Tales Myths & Legends #18 Cover B
Artwork by Alfredo Reyes • Colors by Eddy Swan

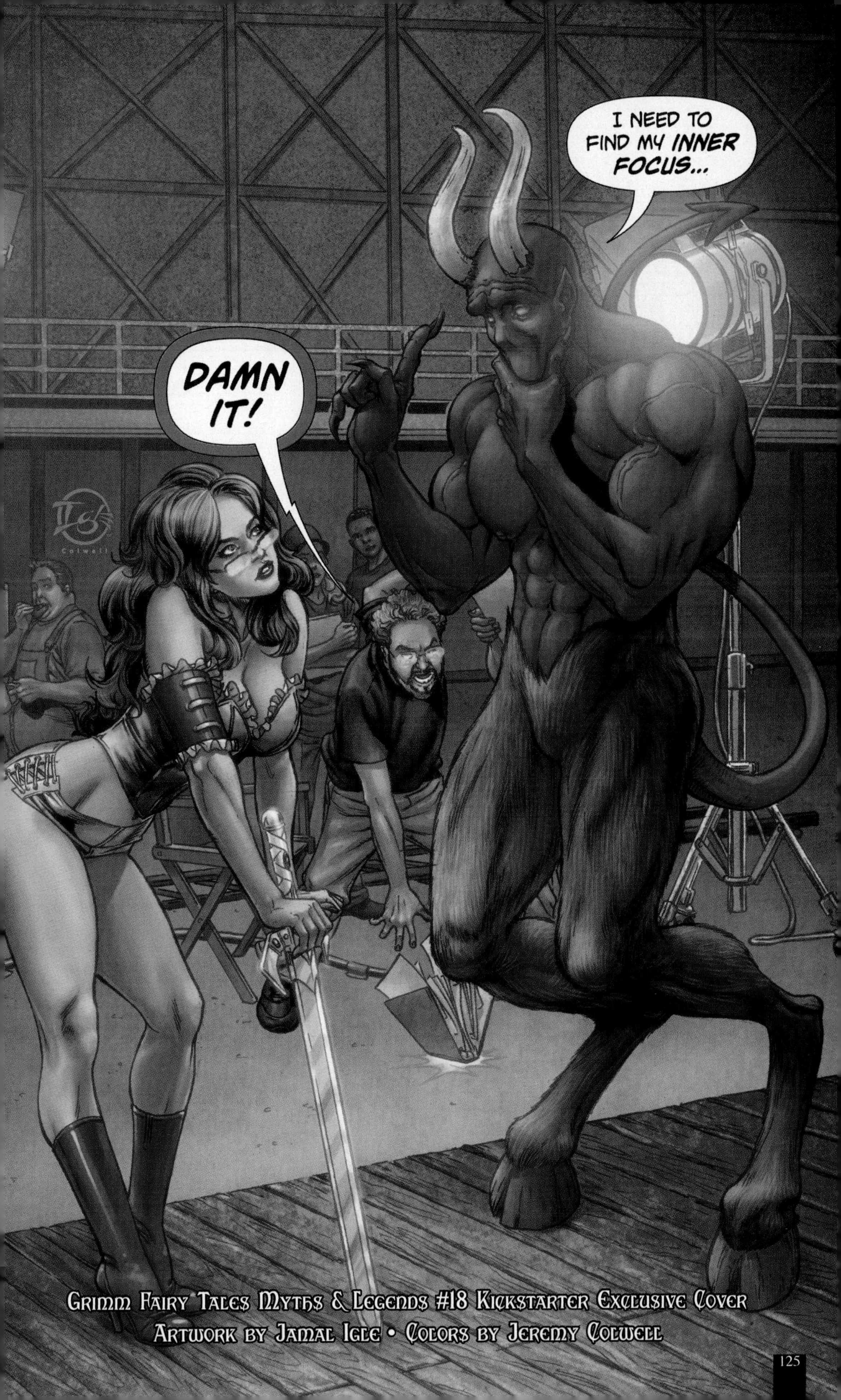
DAMN IT!
I NEED TO FIND MY INNER FOCUS...
Colwell

Grimm Fairy Tales Myths & Legends #18 Kickstarter Exclusive Cover
Artwork by Jamal Igle • Colors by Jeremy Colwell

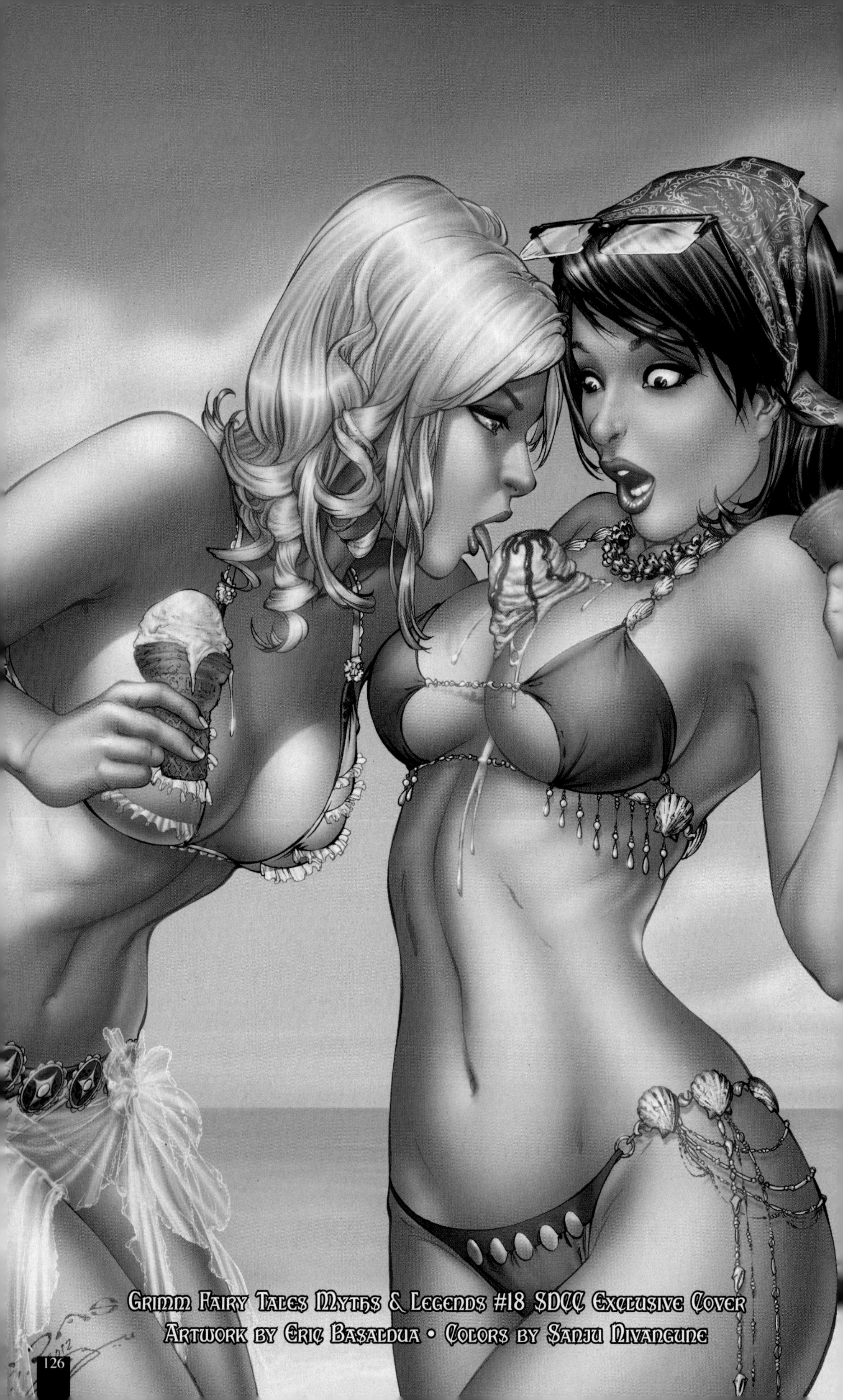

Grimm Fairy Tales Myths & Legends #18 SDCC Exclusive Cover
Artwork by Eric Basaldua • Colors by Sanju Nivangune

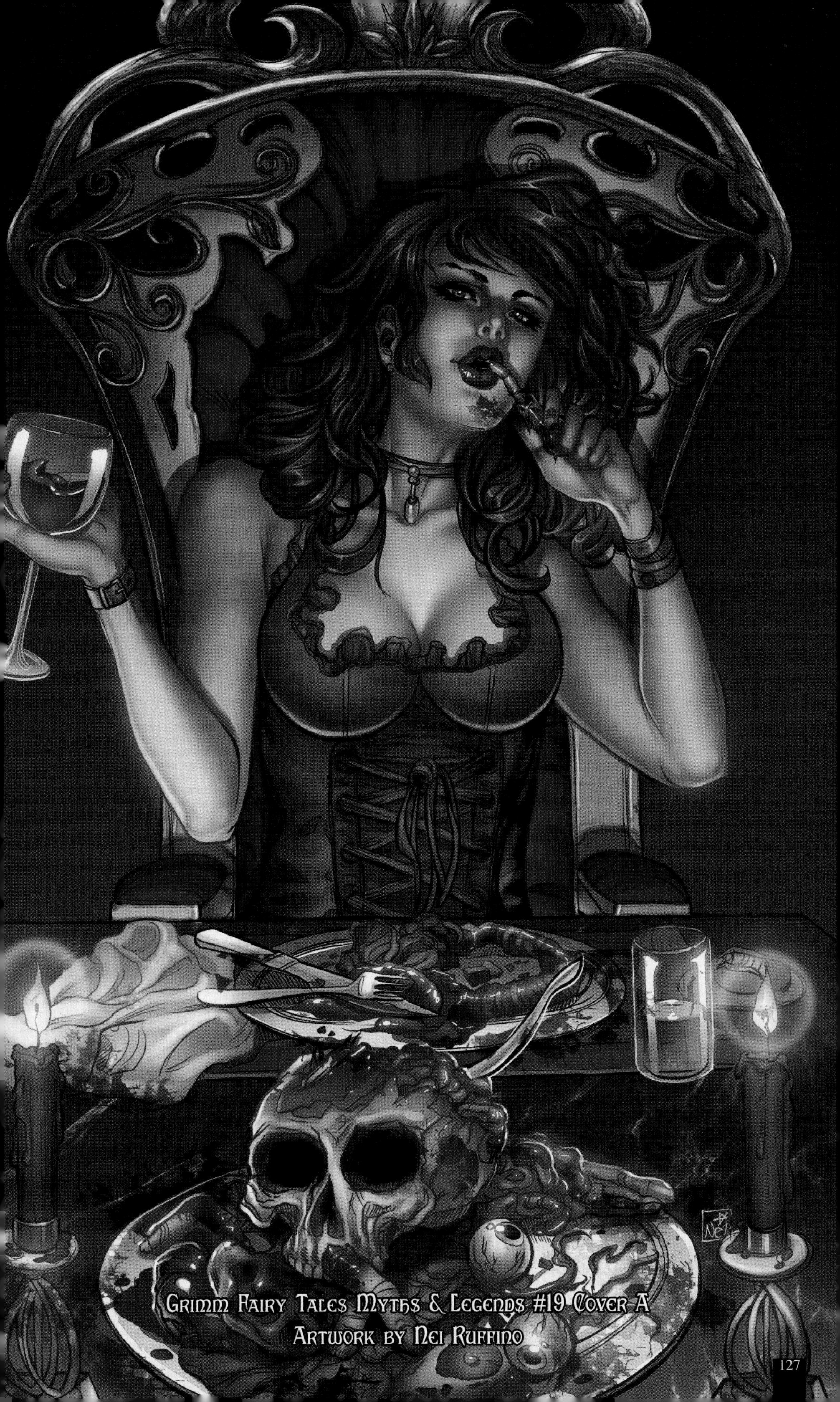

Grimm Fairy Tales Myths & Legends #19 Cover A
Artwork by Nei Ruffino

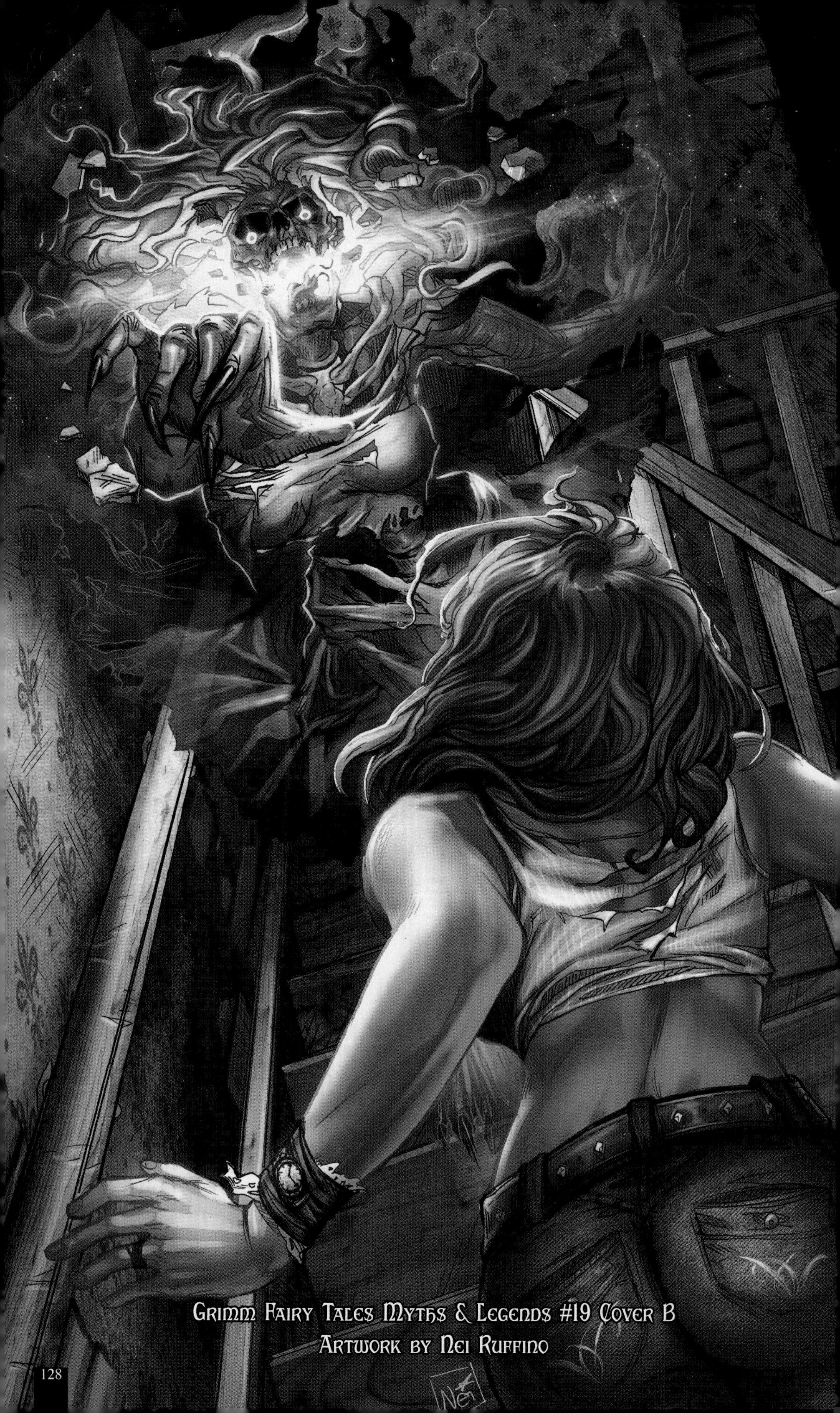

Grimm Fairy Tales Myths & Legends #19 Cover B
Artwork by Nei Ruffino

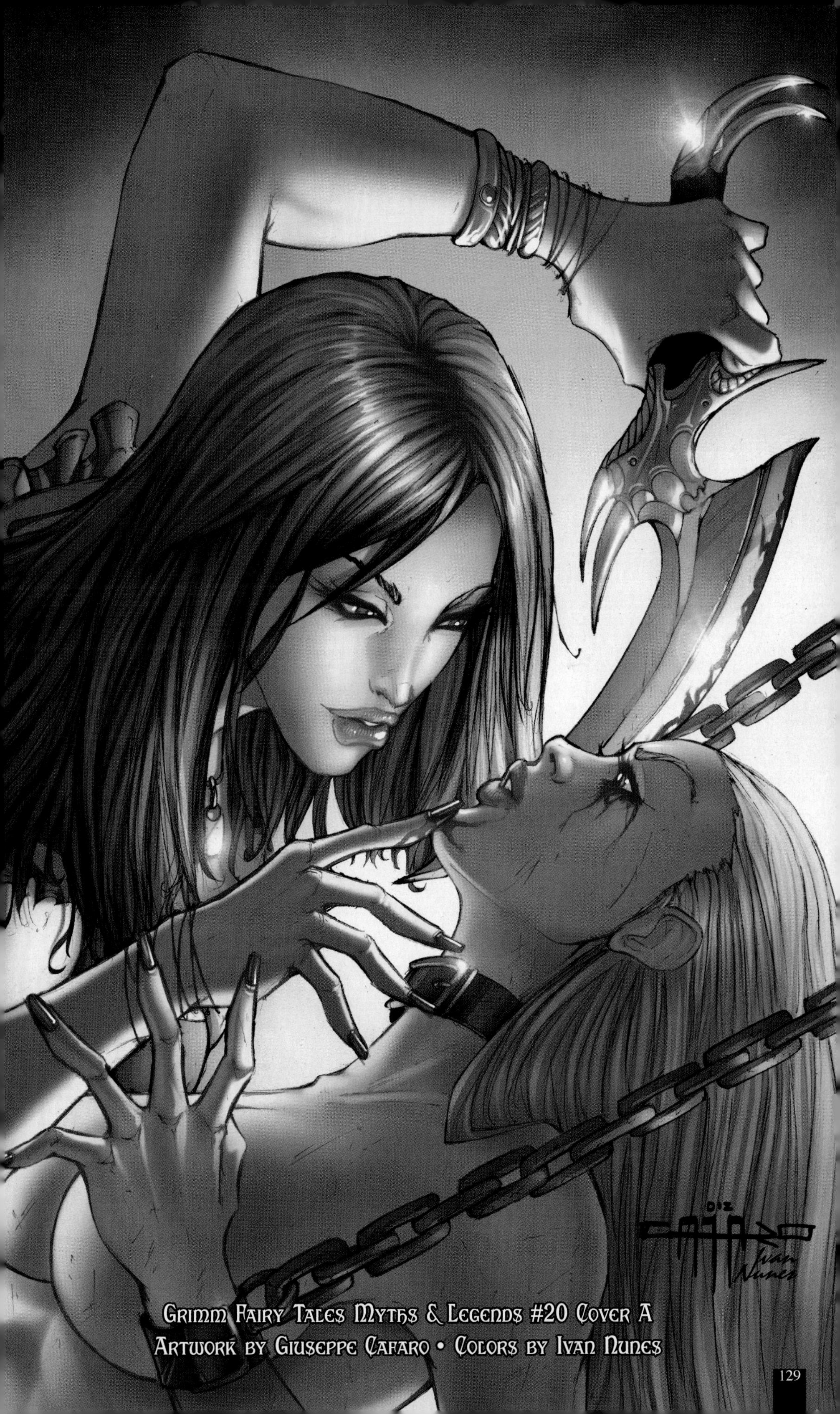

Grimm Fairy Tales Myths & Legends #20 Cover A
Artwork by Giuseppe Cafaro • Colors by Ivan Nunes

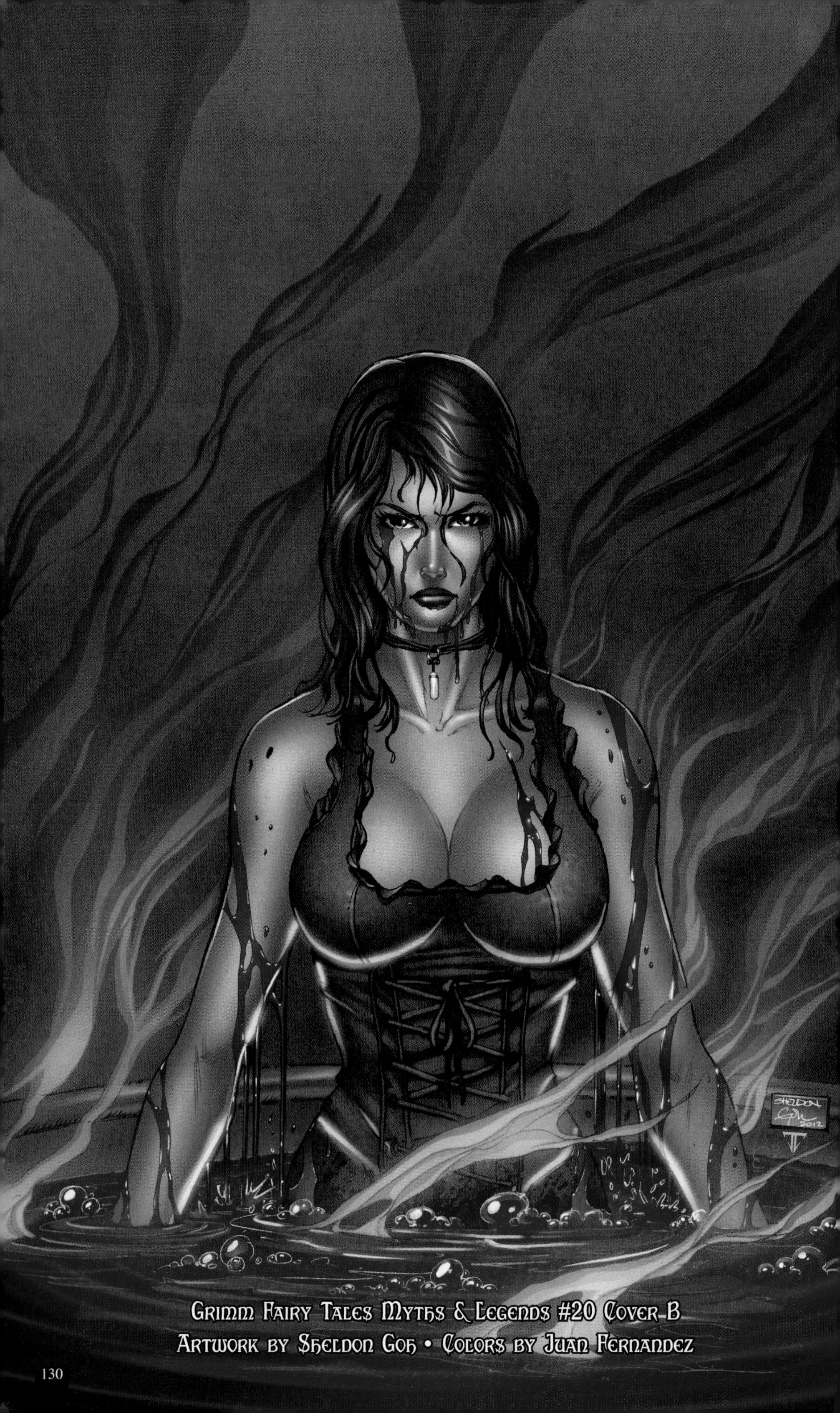

Grimm Fairy Tales Myths & Legends #20 Cover B
Artwork by Sheldon Goh • Colors by Juan Fernandez

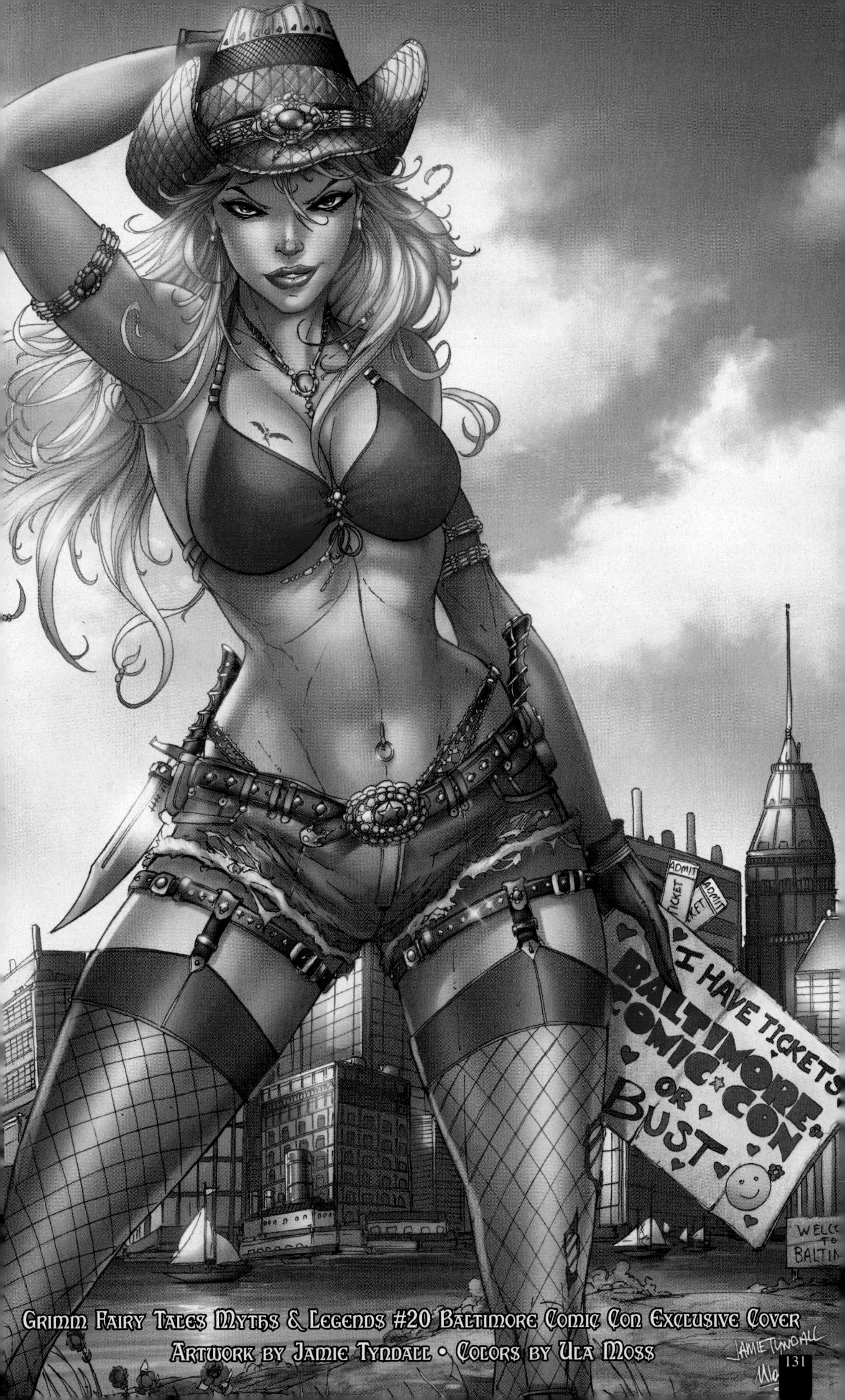
ADMIT
TICKET
ADMIT
TICKET
I HAVE TICKETS
BALTIMORE COMIC CON OR BUST
WELCO TO BALTIM
JAMIE TYNDALL

Grimm Fairy Tales Myths & Legends #20 Baltimore Comic Con Exclusive Cover
Artwork by Jamie Tyndall • Colors by Ula Moss

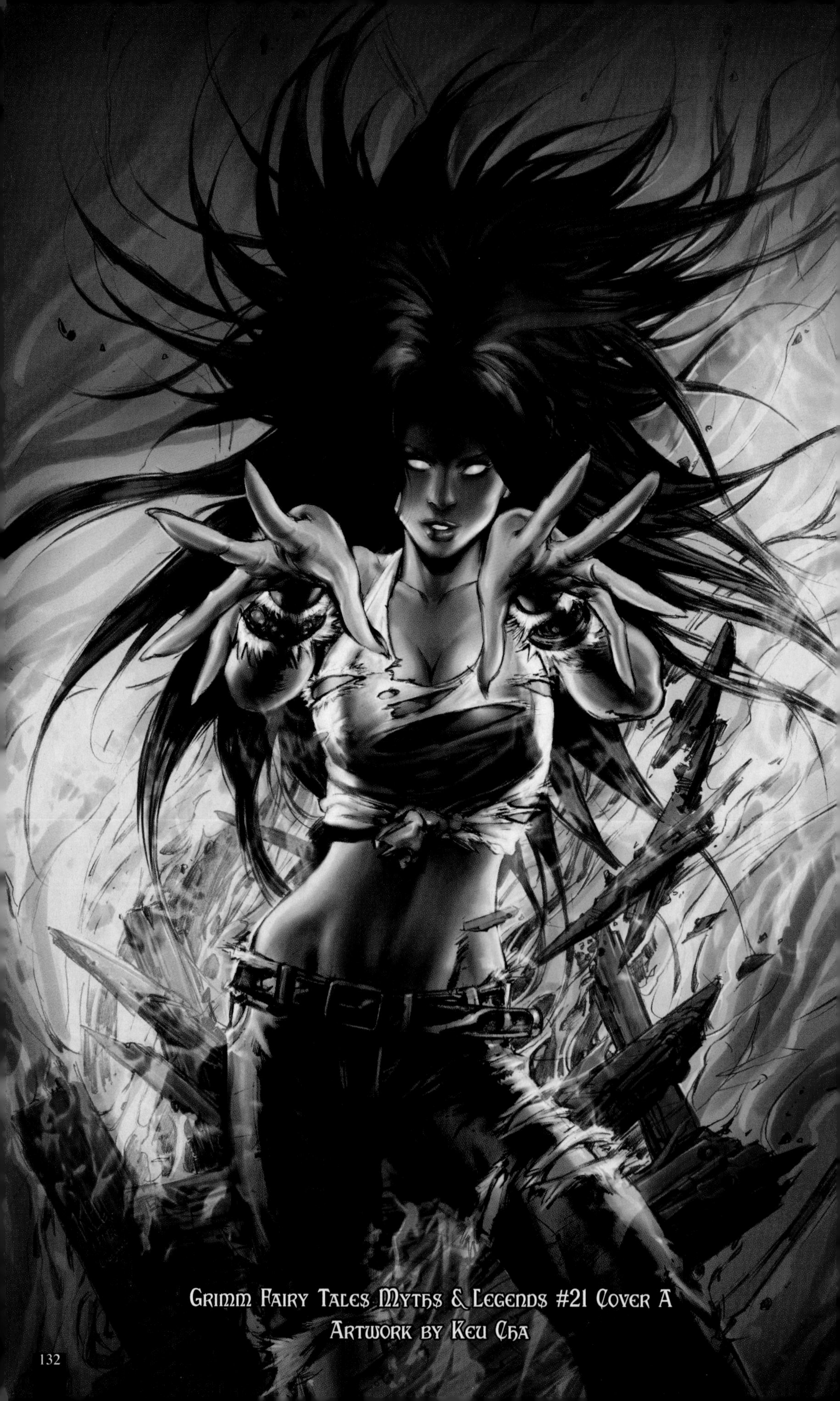

Grimm Fairy Tales Myths & Legends #21 Cover A
Artwork by Keu Cha

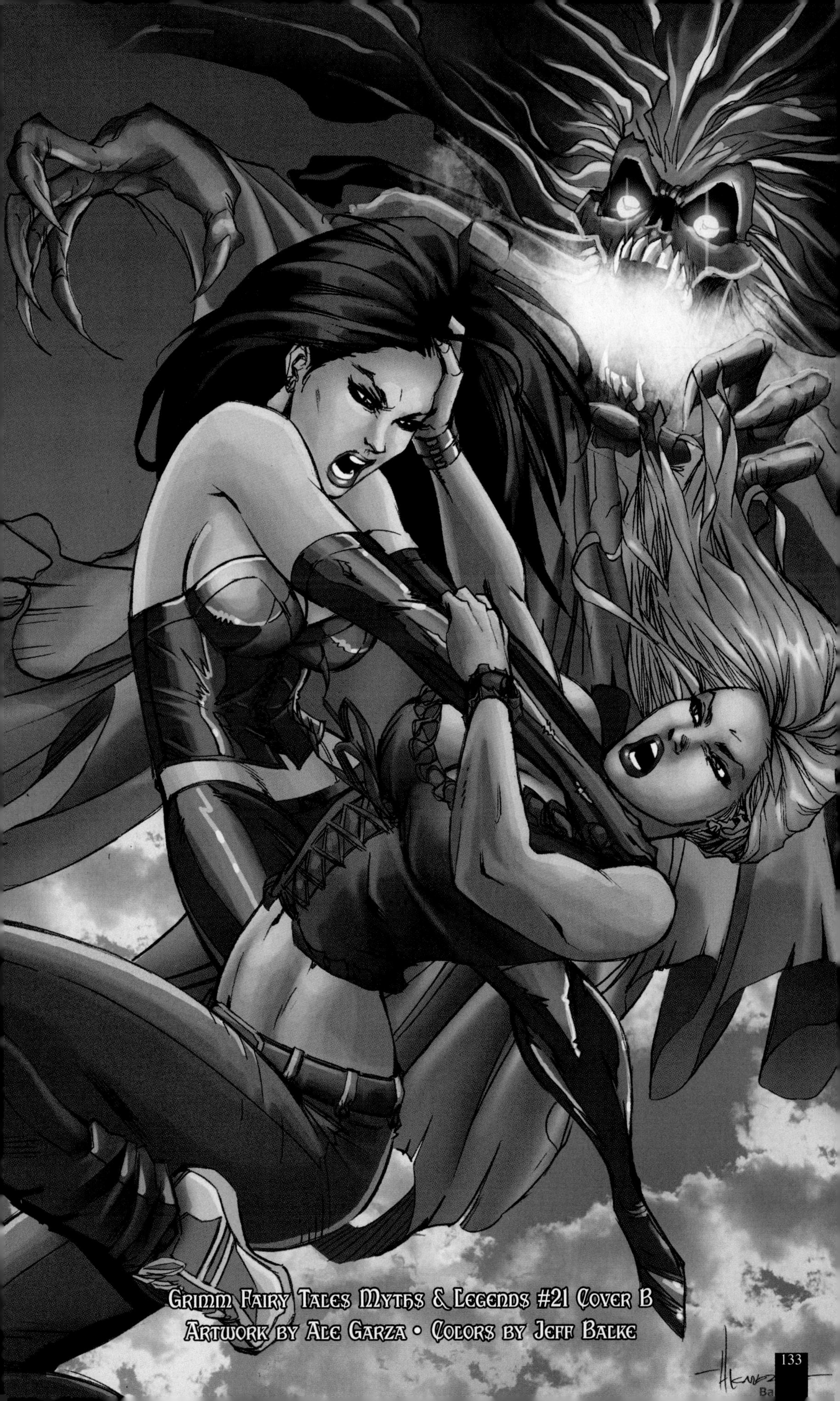

Grimm Fairy Tales Myths & Legends #21 Cover B
Artwork by Ale Garza • Colors by Jeff Balke

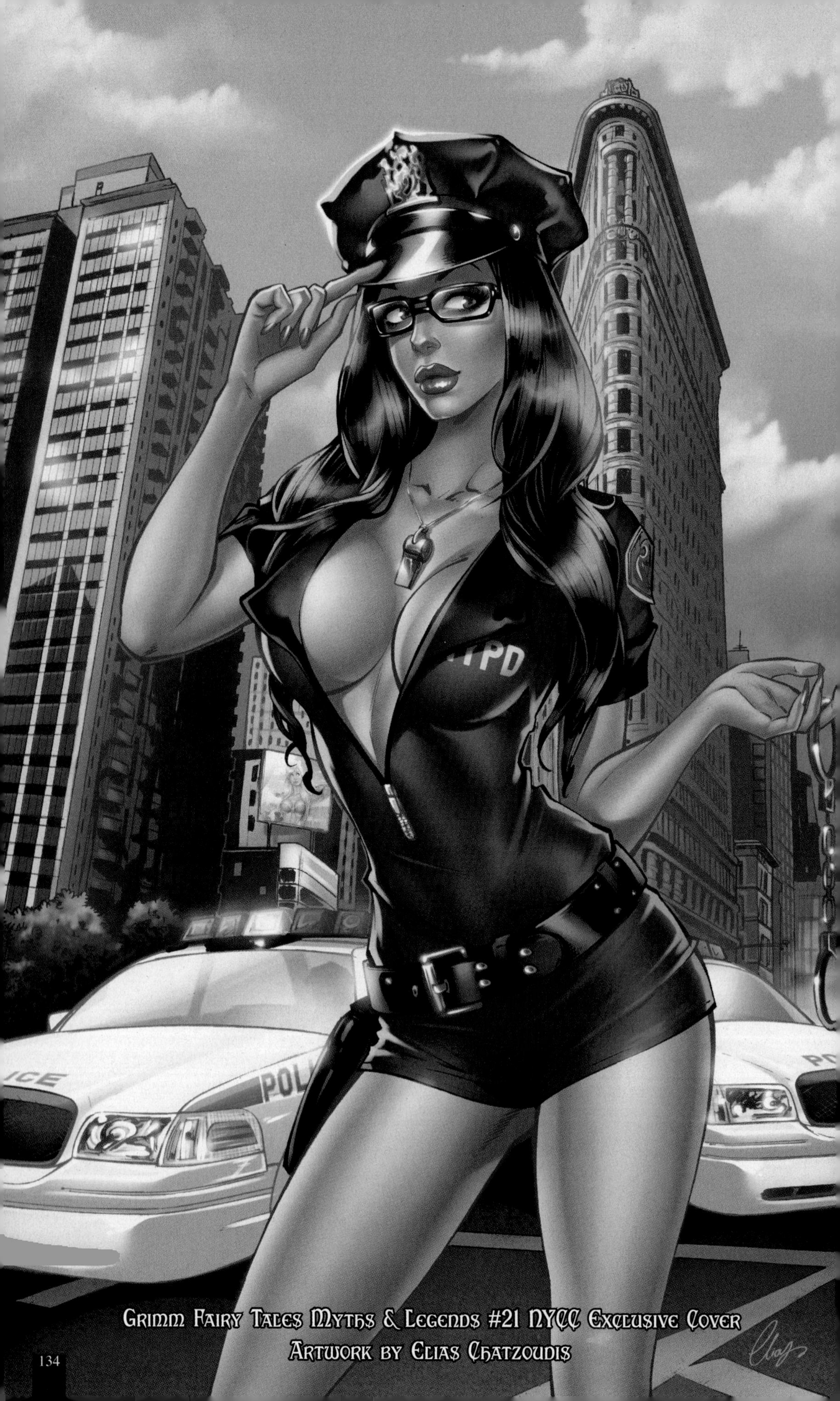

Grimm Fairy Tales Myths & Legends #21 NYCC Exclusive Cover
Artwork by Elias Chatzoudis

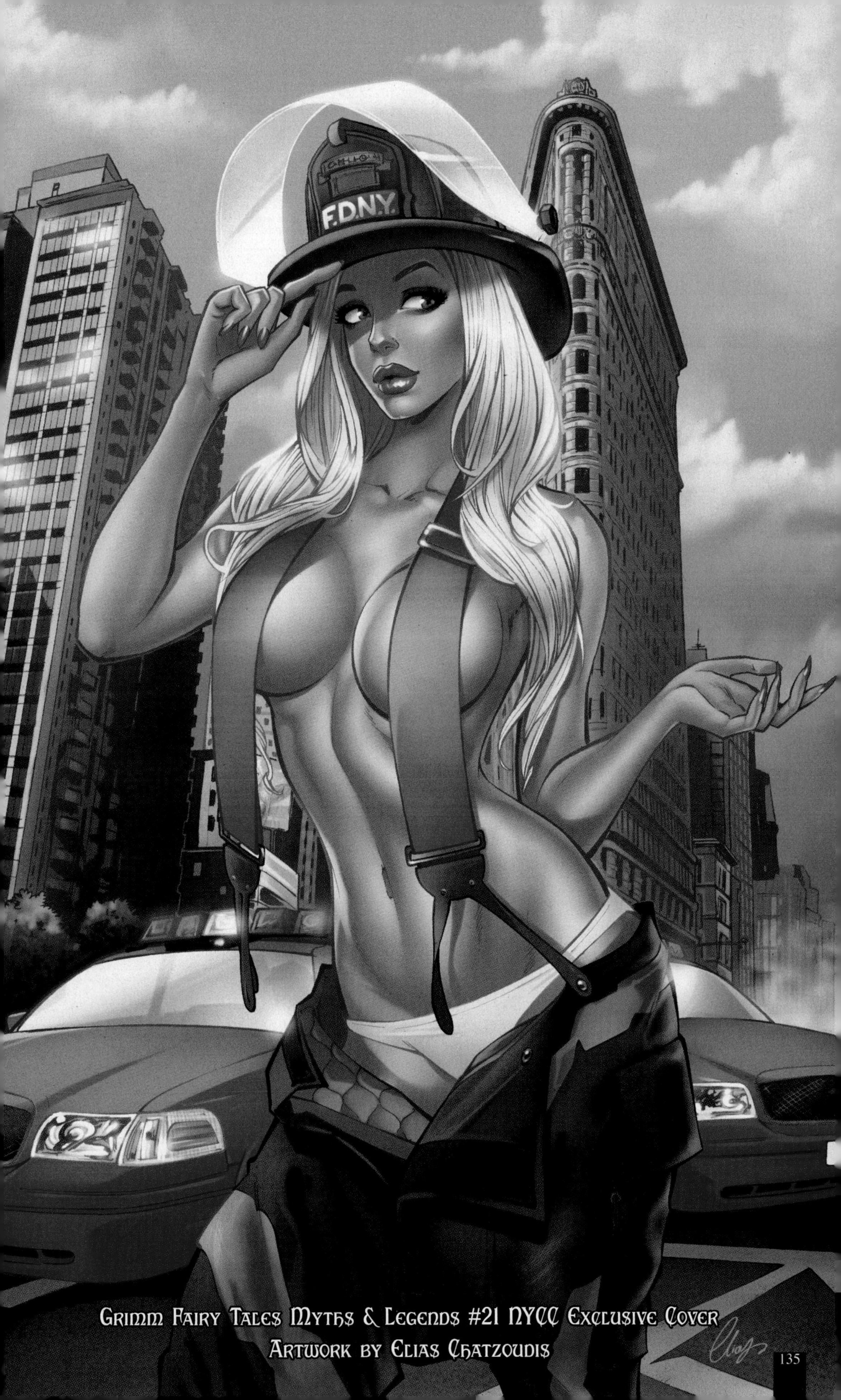
F.D.N.Y.

Grimm Fairy Tales Myths & Legends #21 NYCC Exclusive Cover
Artwork by Elias Chatzoudis

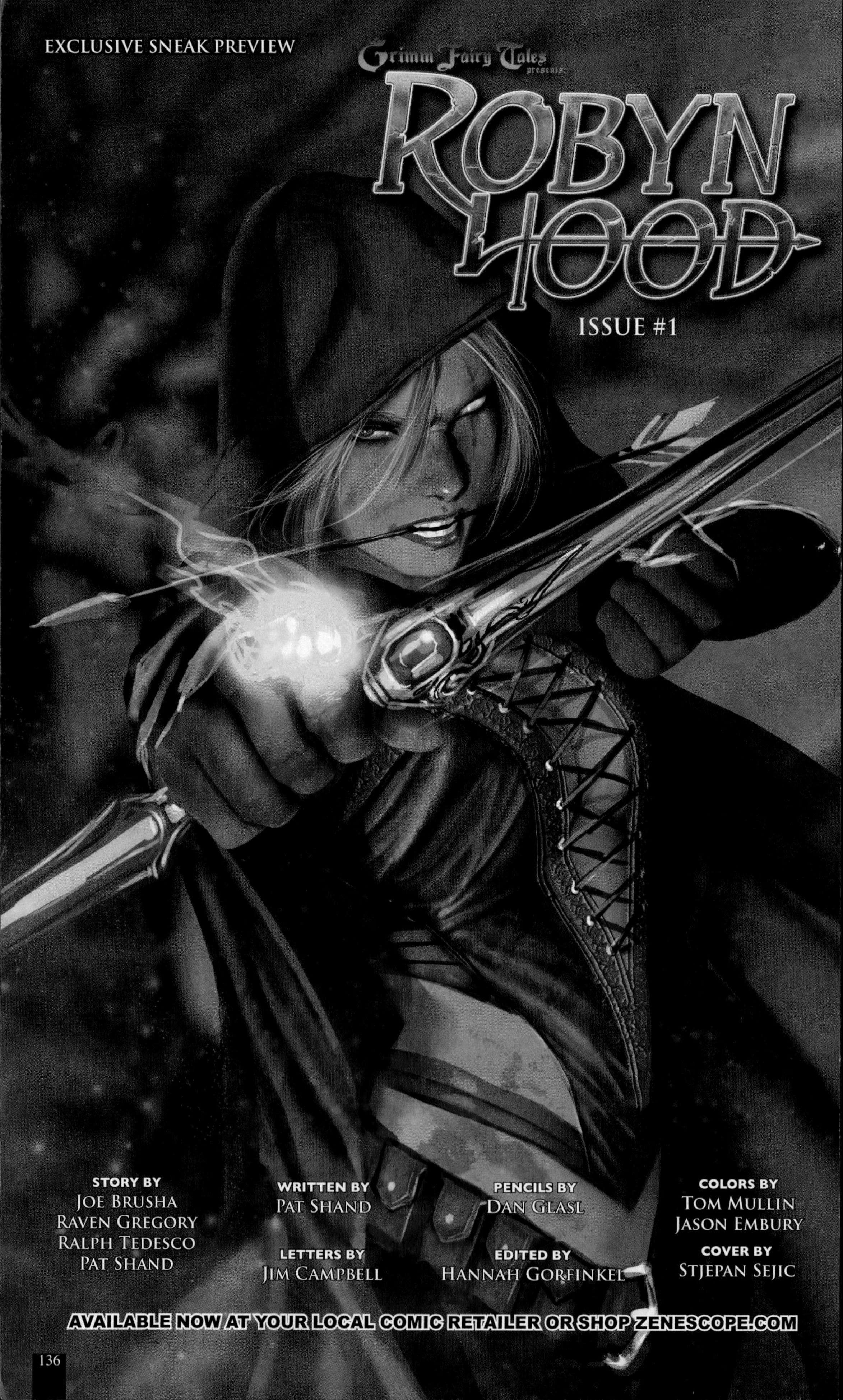
EXCLUSIVE SNEAK PREVIEW
Grimm Fairy Tales presents:
ROBYN HOOD
ISSUE #1
STORY BY
JOE BRUSHA
RAVEN GREGORY
RALPH TEDESCO
PAT SHAND
WRITTEN BY
PAT SHAND
PENCILS BY
DAN GLASL
COLORS BY
TOM MULLIN
JASON EMBURY
LETTERS BY
JIM CAMPBELL
EDITED BY
HANNAH GORFINKEL
COVER BY
STJEPAN SEJIC
AVAILABLE NOW AT YOUR LOCAL COMIC RETAILER OR SHOP ZENESCOPE.COM

Story So Far…

For centuries, it was assumed that fairy tales and fables were fictional stories passed down from generation to generation. However, that is not entirely true. Beings from four different realms linked to Earth do in fact exist. These realms are known as Myst, Neverland, Wonderland and Oz.

The ones born of these powerful realms are known as "Highborns" and those with both human and highborn blood are known as "Falsebloods." Each of these beings has some form of supernatural ability that sets them far apart from mortal men. And while many of these beings are good, there are many others who carry evil inside of them. Not all falsebloods have yet realized their destinies and as they discover their abilities, all will eventually need to choose a side in the war between good and evil that is on the horizon…

This is the story of Robyn Hood.

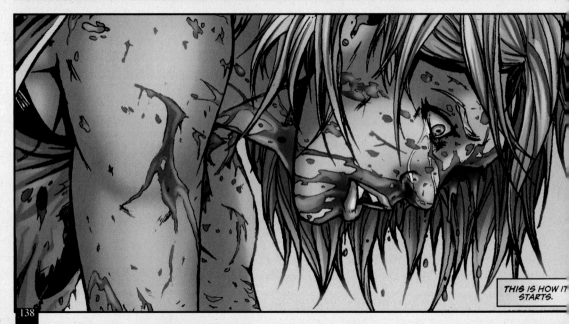

THIS IS HOW IT STARTS.

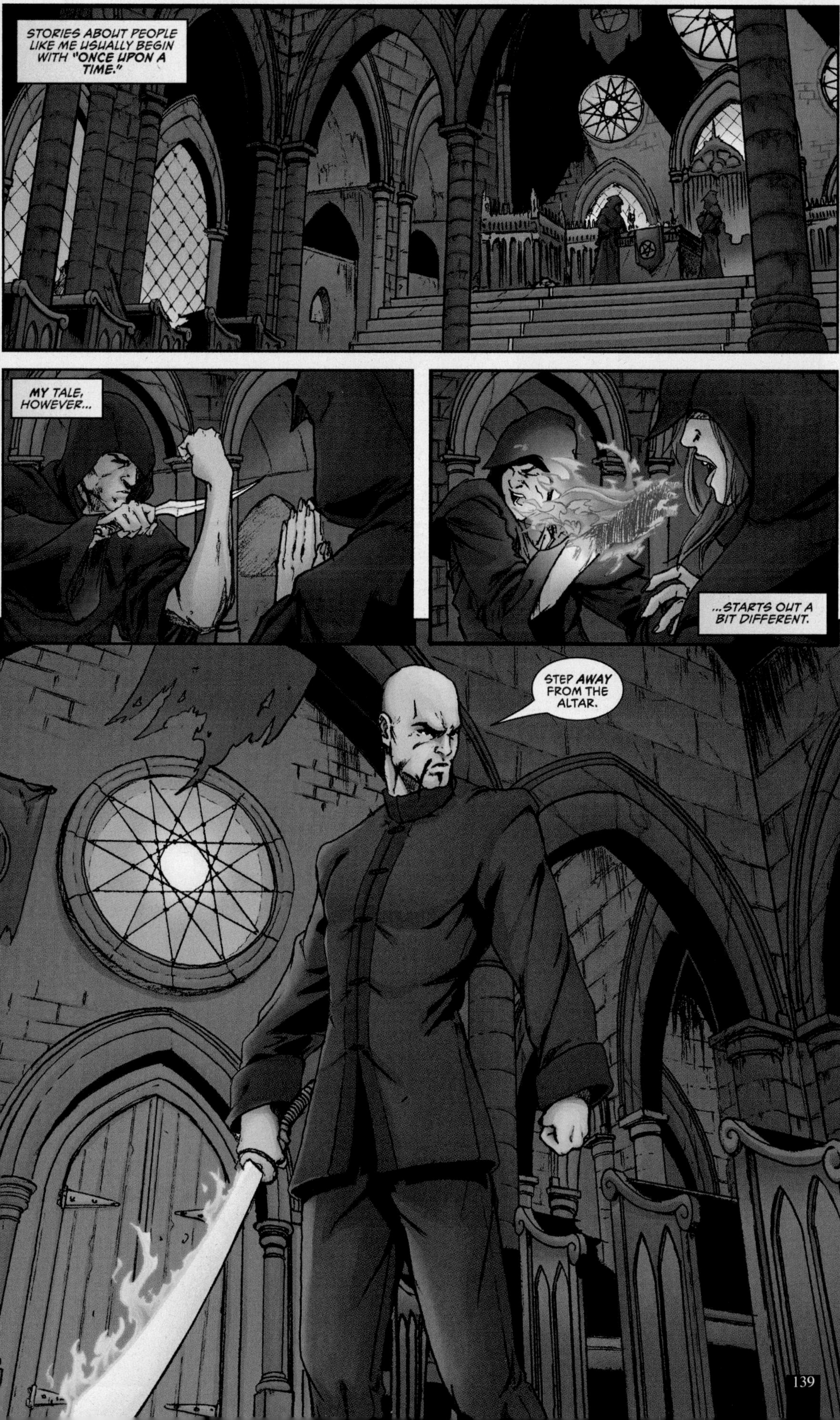
STORIES ABOUT PEOPLE LIKE ME USUALLY BEGIN WITH "ONCE UPON A TIME."
MY TALE, HOWEVER...
...STARTS OUT A BIT DIFFERENT.
STEP AWAY FROM THE ALTAR.

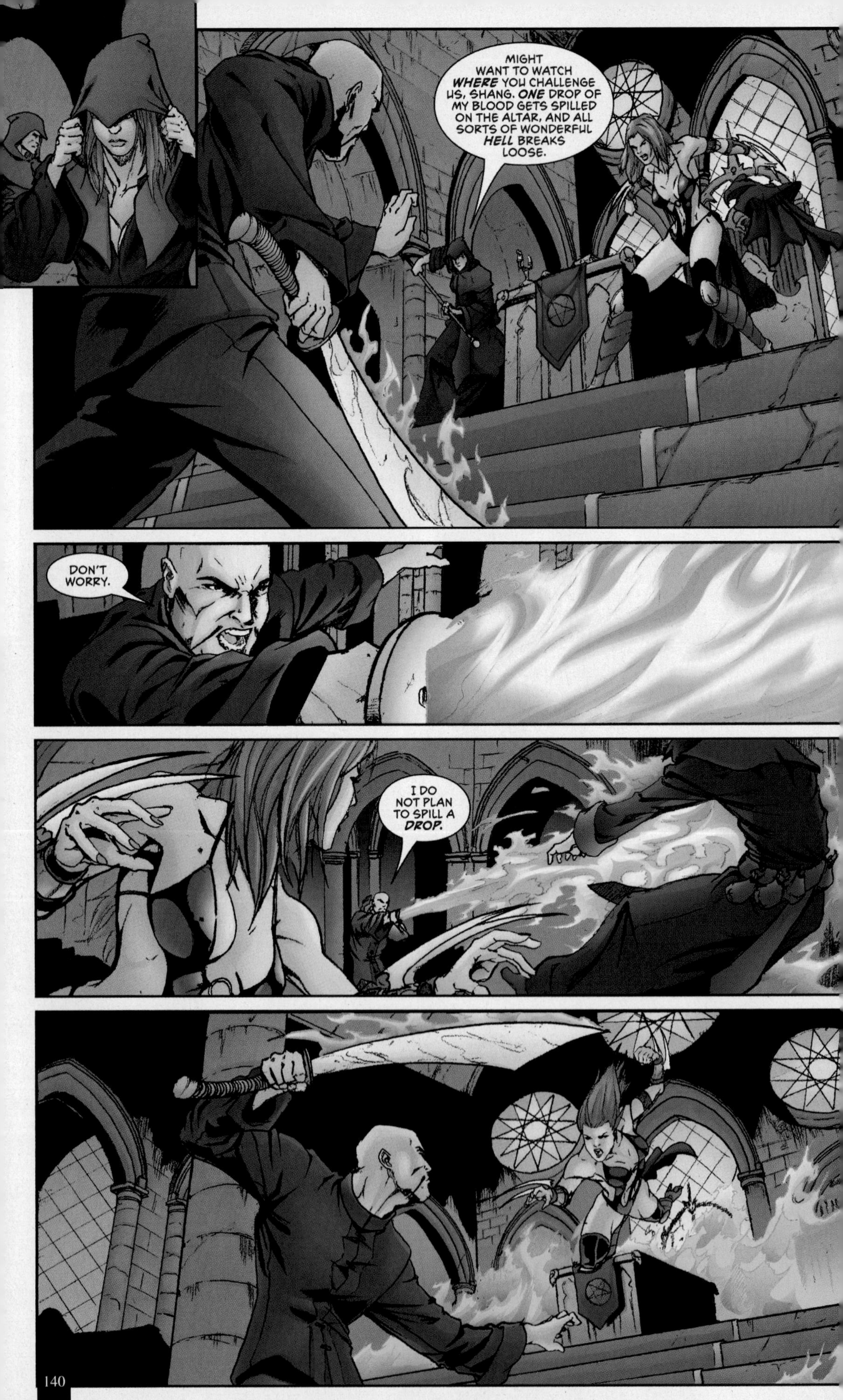
MIGHT WANT TO WATCH WHERE YOU CHALLENGE US, SHANG. ONE DROP OF MY BLOOD GETS SPILLED ON THE ALTAR, AND ALL SORTS OF WONDERFUL HELL BREAKS LOOSE.
DON'T WORRY.
I DO NOT PLAN TO SPILL A DROP.

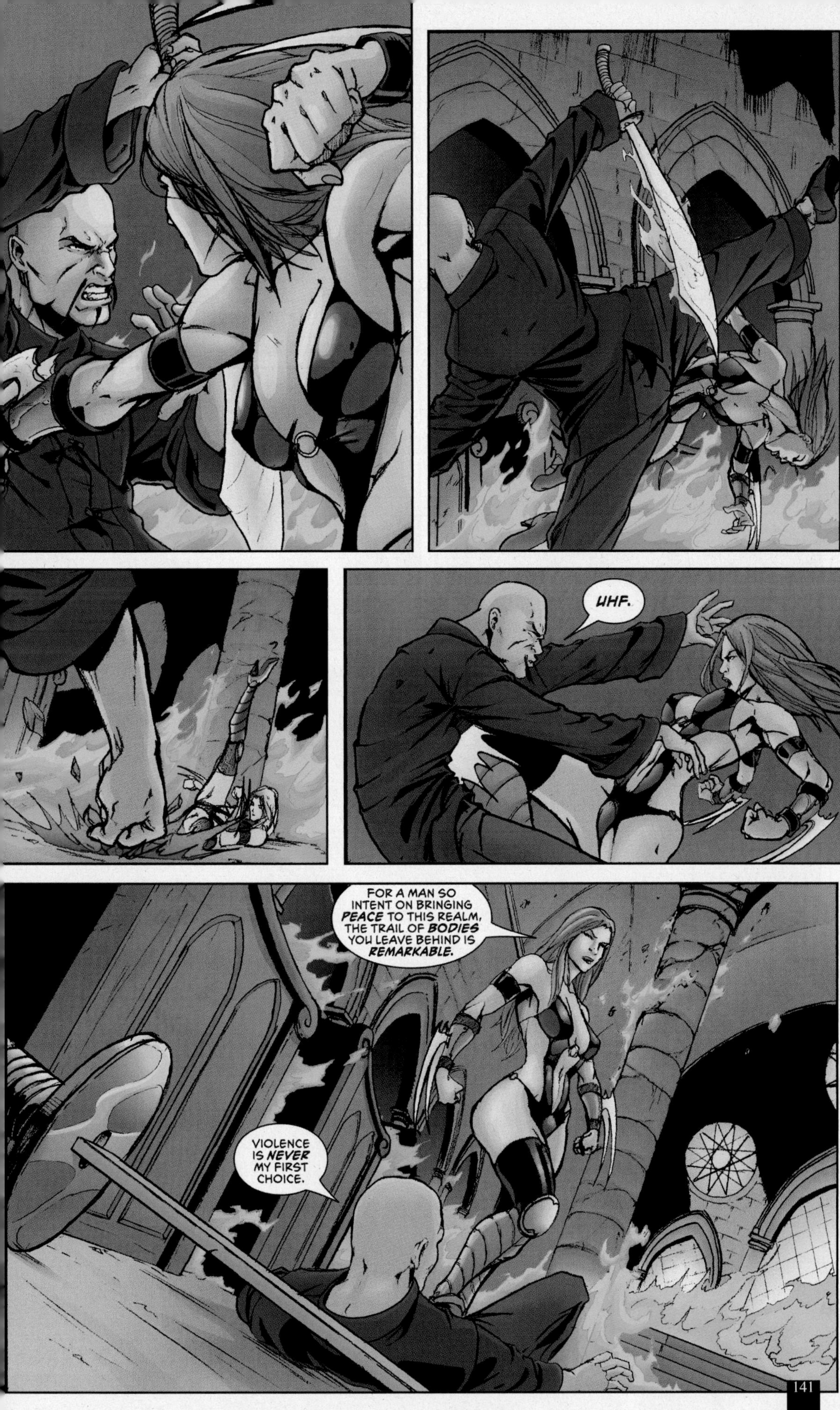
UHF.
FOR A MAN SO INTENT ON BRINGING PEACE TO THIS REALM, THE TRAIL OF BODIES YOU LEAVE BEHIND IS REMARKABLE.
VIOLENCE IS NEVER MY FIRST CHOICE.

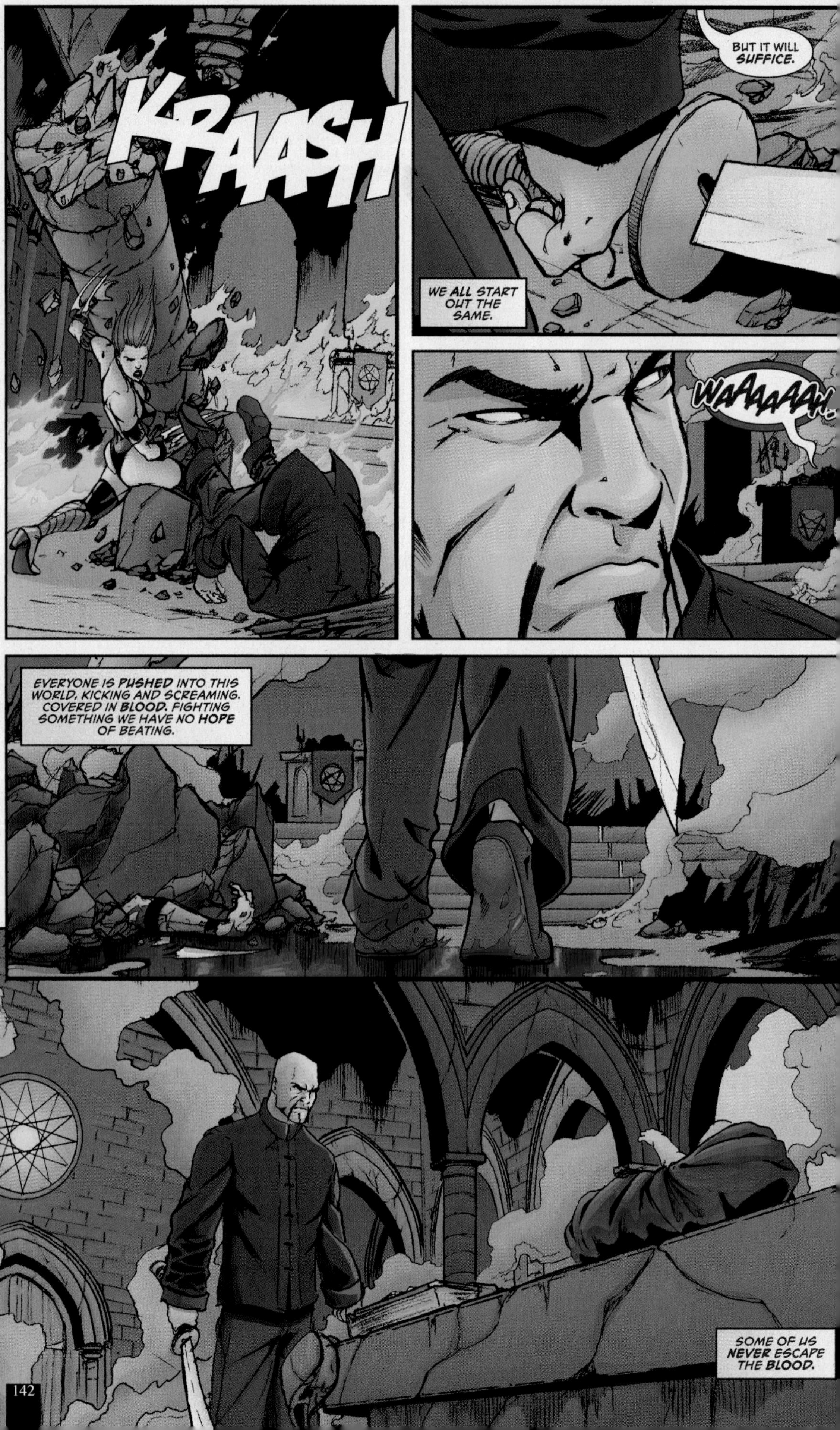

KRAASH
BUT IT WILL SUFFICE.
WE ALL START OUT THE SAME.
WAAAAAAH.
EVERYONE IS PUSHED INTO THIS WORLD, KICKING AND SCREAMING. COVERED IN BLOOD. FIGHTING SOMETHING WE HAVE NO HOPE OF BEATING.
SOME OF US NEVER ESCAPE THE BLOOD.

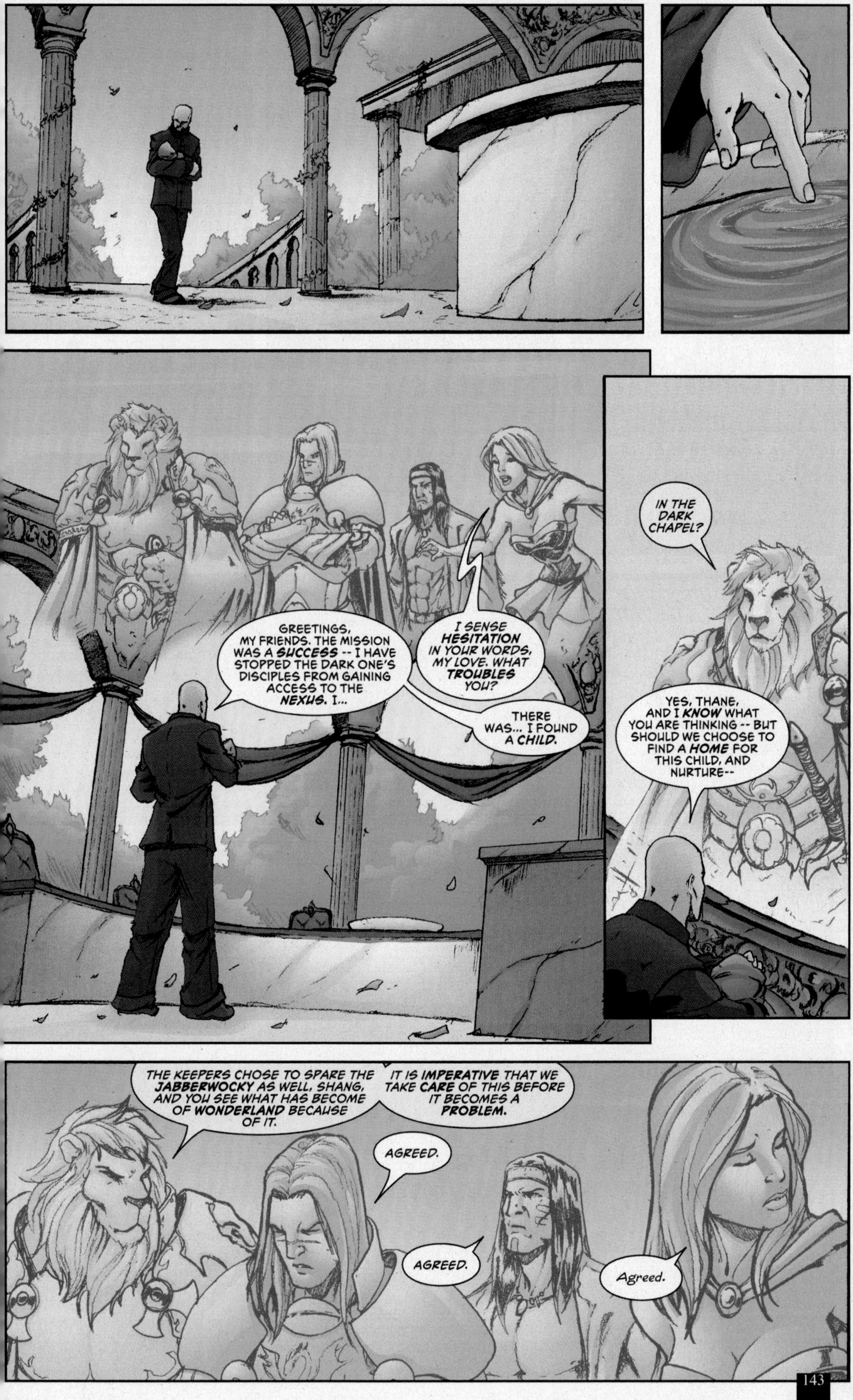

IN THE DARK CHAPEL?
GREETINGS, MY FRIENDS. THE MISSION WAS A SUCCESS -- I HAVE STOPPED THE DARK ONE'S DISCIPLES FROM GAINING ACCESS TO THE NEXUS. I...
I SENSE HESITATION IN YOUR WORDS, MY LOVE. WHAT TROUBLES YOU?
THERE WAS... I FOUND A CHILD.
YES, THANE, AND I KNOW WHAT YOU ARE THINKING -- BUT SHOULD WE CHOOSE TO FIND A HOME FOR THIS CHILD, AND NURTURE--
THE KEEPERS CHOSE TO SPARE THE JABBERWOCKY AS WELL, SHANG, AND YOU SEE WHAT HAS BECOME OF WONDERLAND BECAUSE OF IT.
IT IS IMPERATIVE THAT WE TAKE CARE OF THIS BEFORE IT BECOMES A PROBLEM.
AGREED.
AGREED.
Agreed.

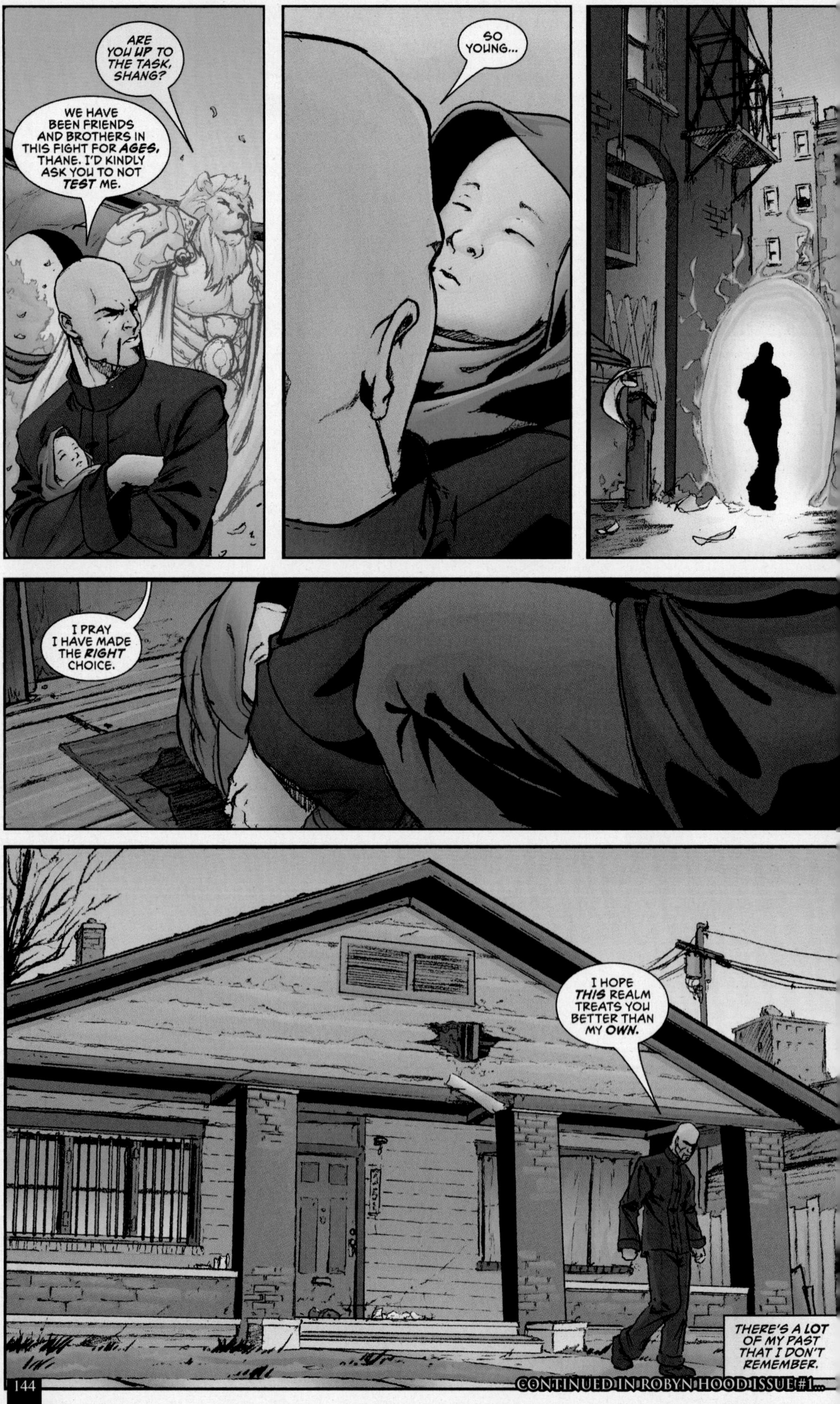
ARE YOU UP TO THE TASK, SHANG?
WE HAVE BEEN FRIENDS AND BROTHERS IN THIS FIGHT FOR AGES, THANE. I'D KINDLY ASK YOU TO NOT TEST ME.
SO YOUNG...
I PRAY I HAVE MADE THE RIGHT CHOICE.
I HOPE THIS REALM TREATS YOU BETTER THAN MY OWN.
THERE'S A LOT OF MY PAST THAT I DON'T REMEMBER.

CONTINUED IN ROBYN HOOD ISSUE #1...

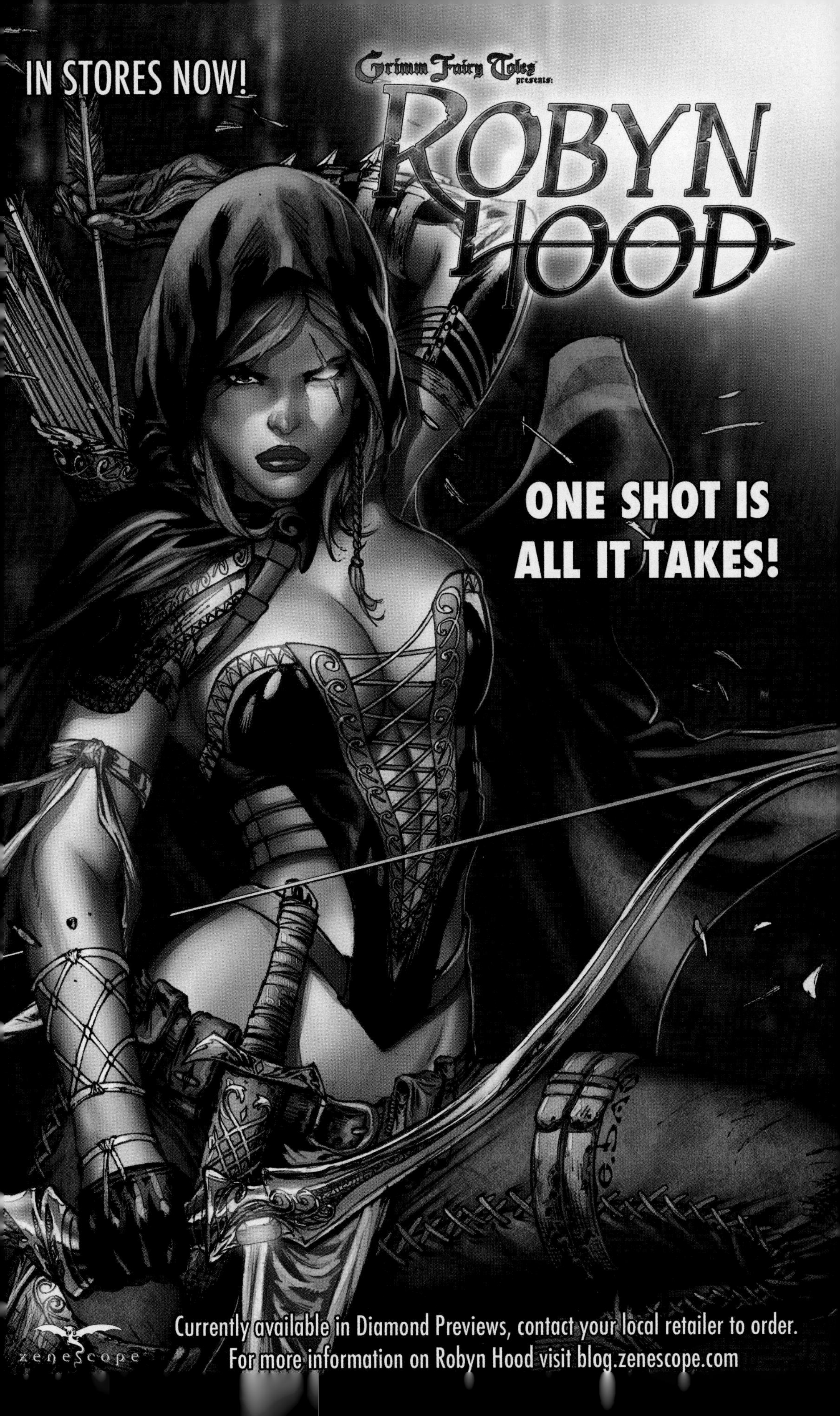
IN STORES NOW!
Grimm Fairy Tales presents:
ROBYN HOOD
ONE SHOT IS ALL IT TAKES!
Currently available in Diamond Previews, contact your local retailer to order.
For more information on Robyn Hood visit blog.zenescope.com
zenescope

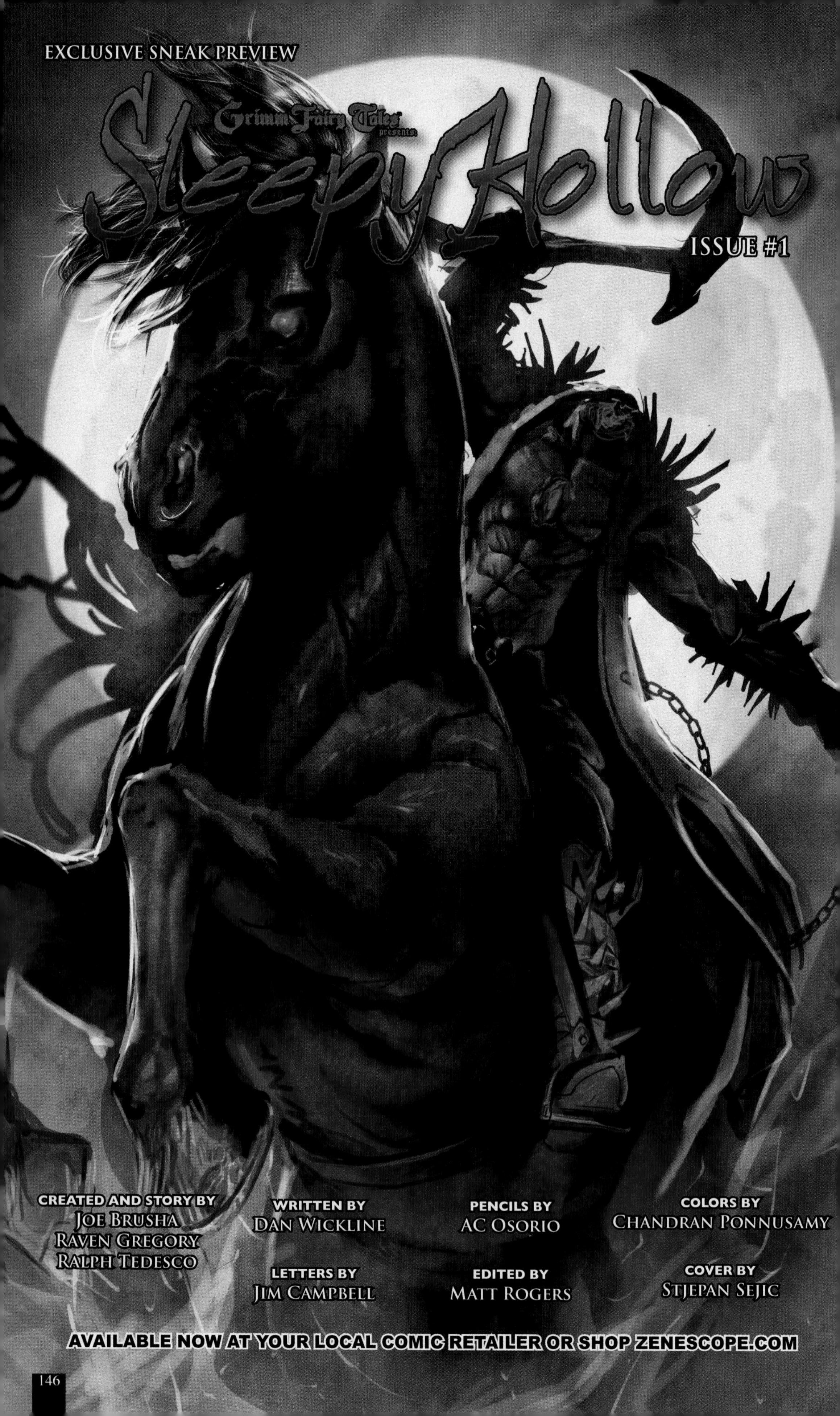
EXCLUSIVE SNEAK PREVIEW
Grimm Fairy Tales presents:
Sleepy Hollow
ISSUE #1
CREATED AND STORY BY
JOE BRUSHA
RAVEN GREGORY
RALPH TEDESCO
WRITTEN BY
DAN WICKLINE
PENCILS BY
AC OSORIO
COLORS BY
CHANDRAN PONNUSAMY
LETTERS BY
JIM CAMPBELL
EDITED BY
MATT ROGERS
COVER BY
STJEPAN SEJIC
AVAILABLE NOW AT YOUR LOCAL COMIC RETAILER OR SHOP ZENESCOPE.COM

STORY SO FAR...

IN THE SMALL TOWN OF TARRYTOWN, NEW YORK, THE STORY OF THE HEADLESS HORSEMAN OF SLEEPY HOLLOW HAS BECOME SOMETHING OF MYTH AND LEGEND. AND THIS LEGEND IS ABOUT TO BECOME ALL TOO REAL.

TEACHER'S AIDE CRAIG MARSTERS SEEMS TO HAVE THE WORLD AT HIS FINGERTIPS. HE HAS A GREAT HEAD ON HIS SHOULDERS, A BEAUTIFUL GIRLFRIEND AND AN ALL-TOO BRIGHT FUTURE. BUT THERE ARE THOSE IN THIS WORLD WHO CHOOSE TO TAKE FROM OTHERS RATHER THAN EARN THEIR OWN WAY IN LIFE, AND CRAIG FINDS HE'S IN THE CROSSHAIRS OF THOSE VERY PEOPLE.

ENTER A WORLD WHERE MORALITY IS CONSTANTLY TESTED AND THE SHOCKING REPERCUSSIONS OF ONE'S CHOICES MUST ALWAYS BE FACED... ENTER THE WORLD OF GRIMM FAIRY TALES.

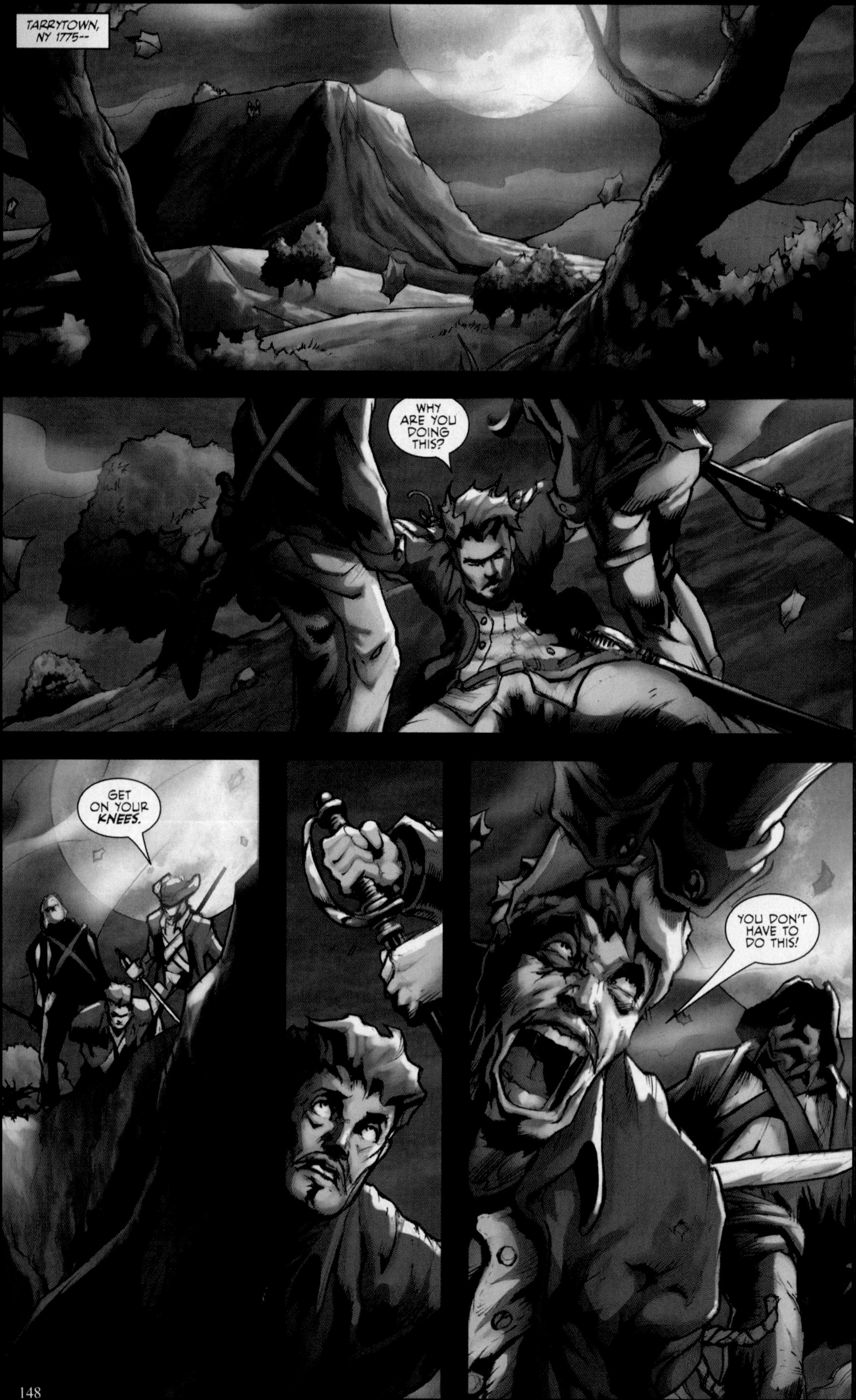
TARRYTOWN, NY 1775--
WHY ARE YOU DOING THIS?
GET ON YOUR KNEES.
YOU DON'T HAVE TO DO THIS!

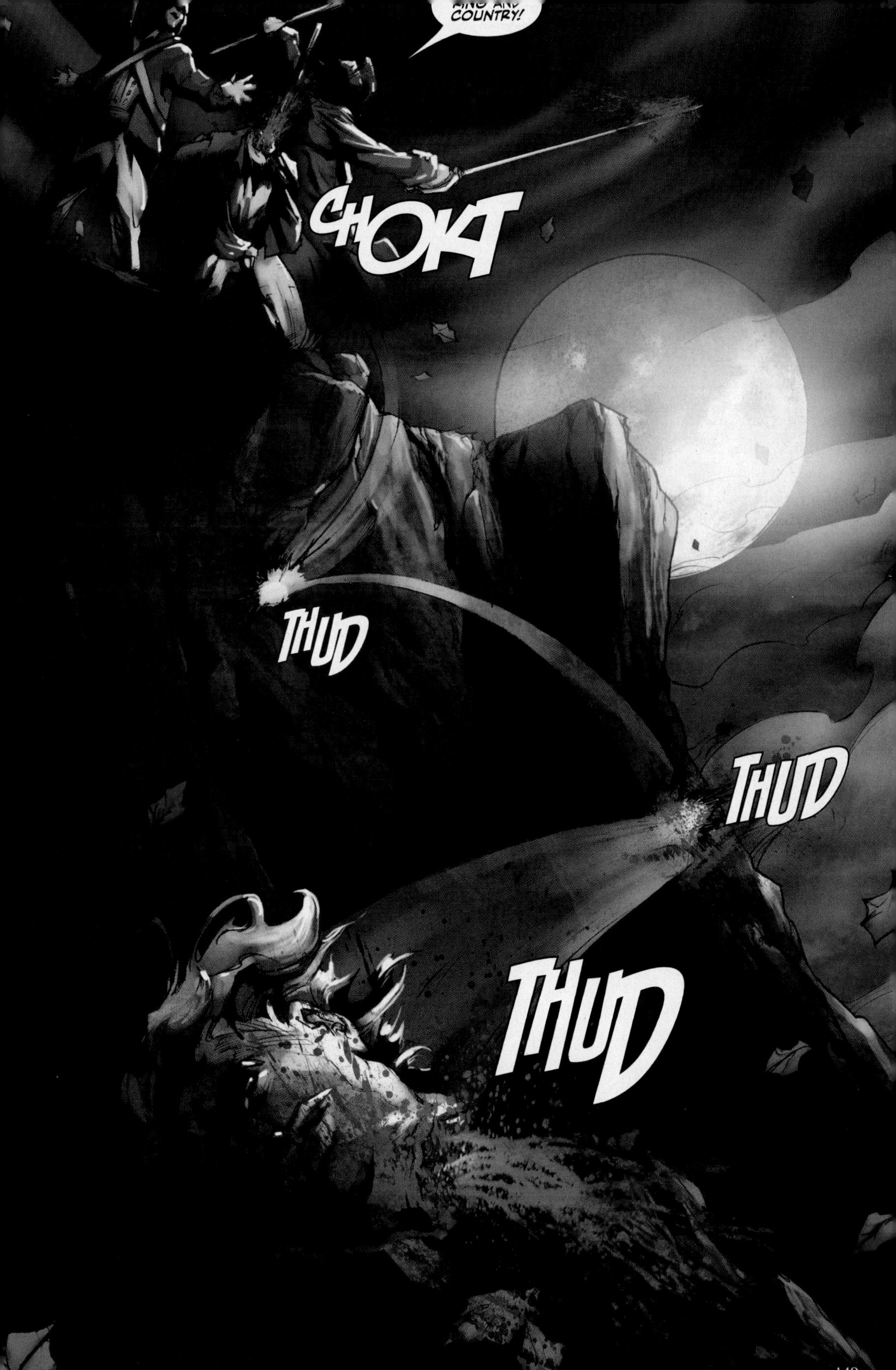
COUNTRY!
CHOKT
THUD
THUD
THUD

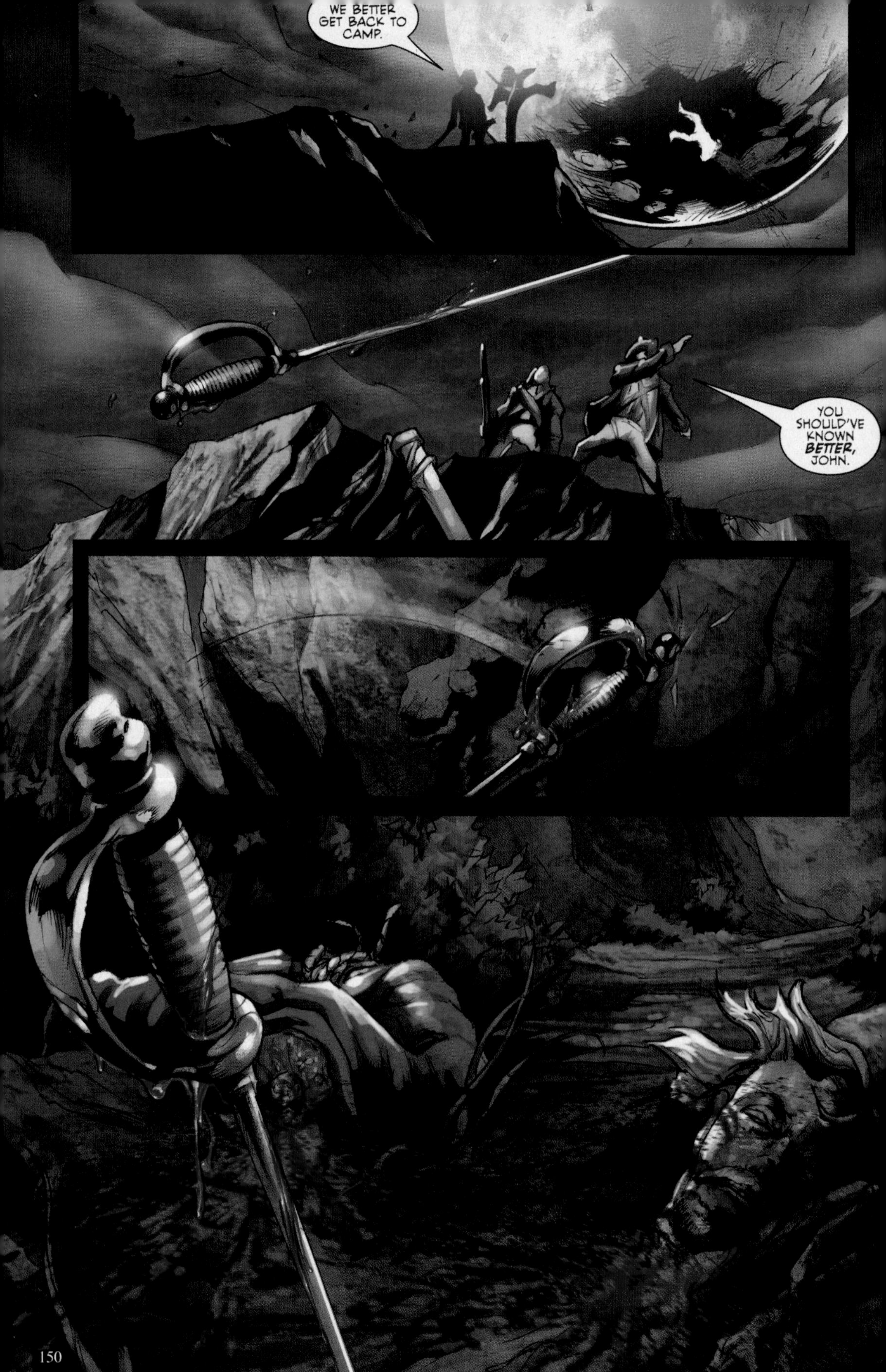
WE BETTER GET BACK TO CAMP.
YOU SHOULD'VE KNOWN BETTER, JOHN.

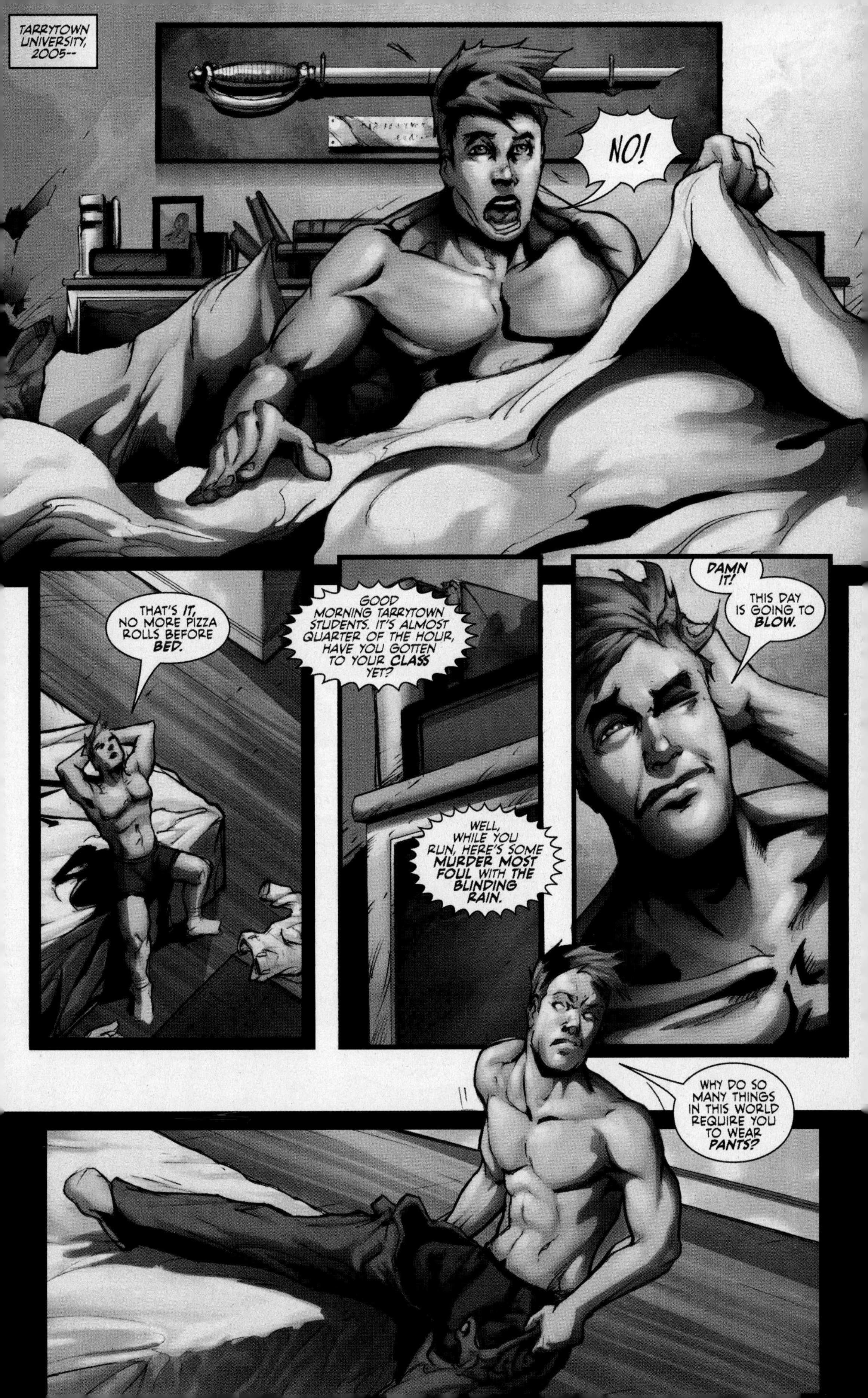
TARRYTOWN UNIVERSITY, 2005--
NO!
THAT'S IT, NO MORE PIZZA ROLLS BEFORE BED.
GOOD MORNING TARRYTOWN STUDENTS. IT'S ALMOST QUARTER OF THE HOUR, HAVE YOU GOTTEN TO YOUR CLASS YET?
WELL, WHILE YOU RUN, HERE'S SOME MURDER MOST FOUL WITH THE BLINDING RAIN.
DAMN IT!
THIS DAY IS GOING TO BLOW.
WHY DO SO MANY THINGS IN THIS WORLD REQUIRE YOU TO WEAR PANTS?

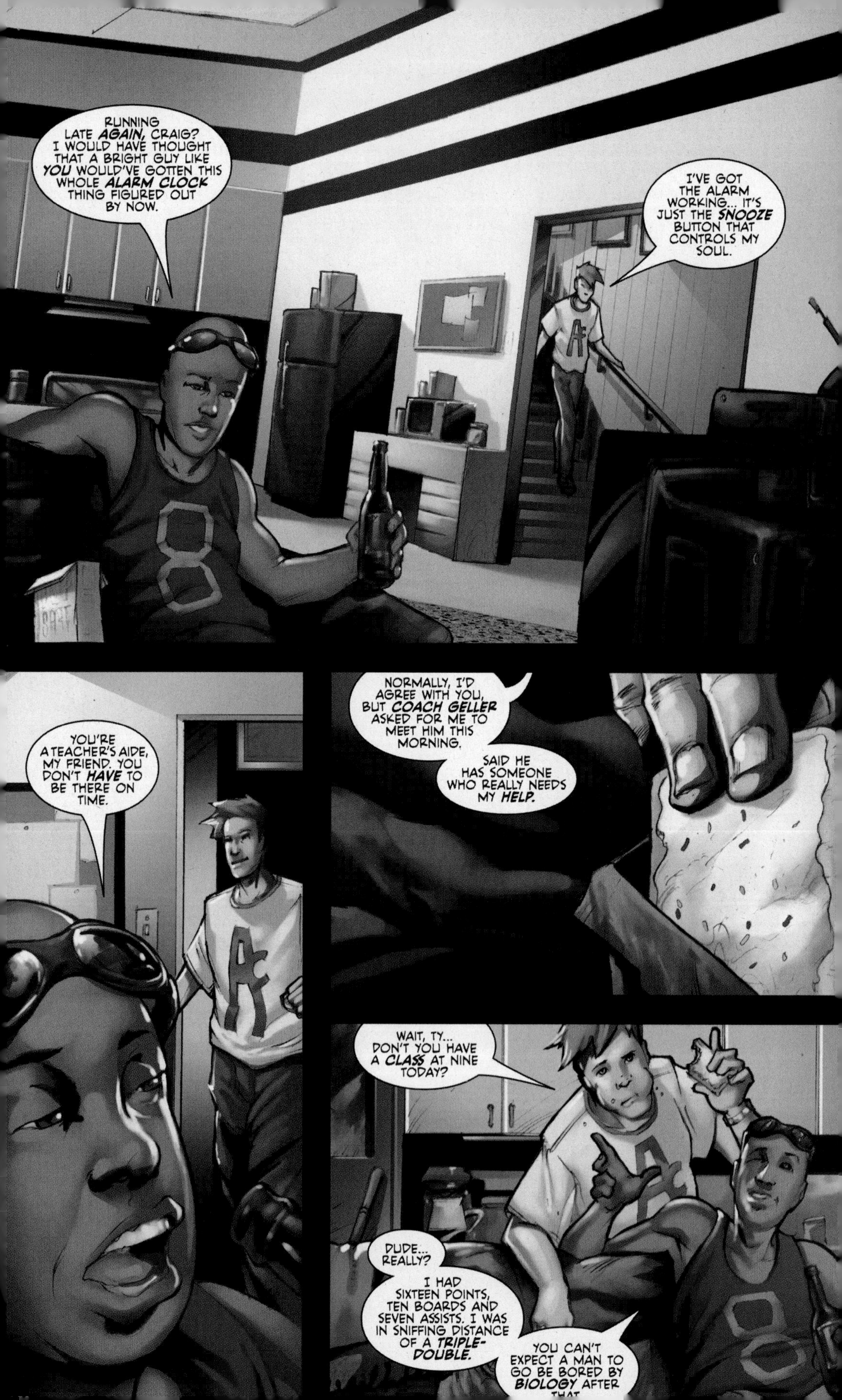
RUNNING LATE AGAIN, CRAIG? I WOULD HAVE THOUGHT THAT A BRIGHT GUY LIKE YOU WOULD'VE GOTTEN THIS WHOLE ALARM CLOCK THING FIGURED OUT BY NOW.
I'VE GOT THE ALARM WORKING... IT'S JUST THE SNOOZE BUTTON THAT CONTROLS MY SOUL.
YOU'RE A TEACHER'S AIDE, MY FRIEND. YOU DON'T HAVE TO BE THERE ON TIME.
NORMALLY, I'D AGREE WITH YOU, BUT COACH GELLER ASKED FOR ME TO MEET HIM THIS MORNING.
SAID HE HAS SOMEONE WHO REALLY NEEDS MY HELP.
WAIT, TY... DON'T YOU HAVE A CLASS AT NINE TODAY?
DUDE... REALLY?
I HAD SIXTEEN POINTS, TEN BOARDS AND SEVEN ASSISTS. I WAS IN SNIFFING DISTANCE OF A TRIPLE-DOUBLE.
YOU CAN'T EXPECT A MAN TO GO BE BORED BY BIOLOGY AFTER

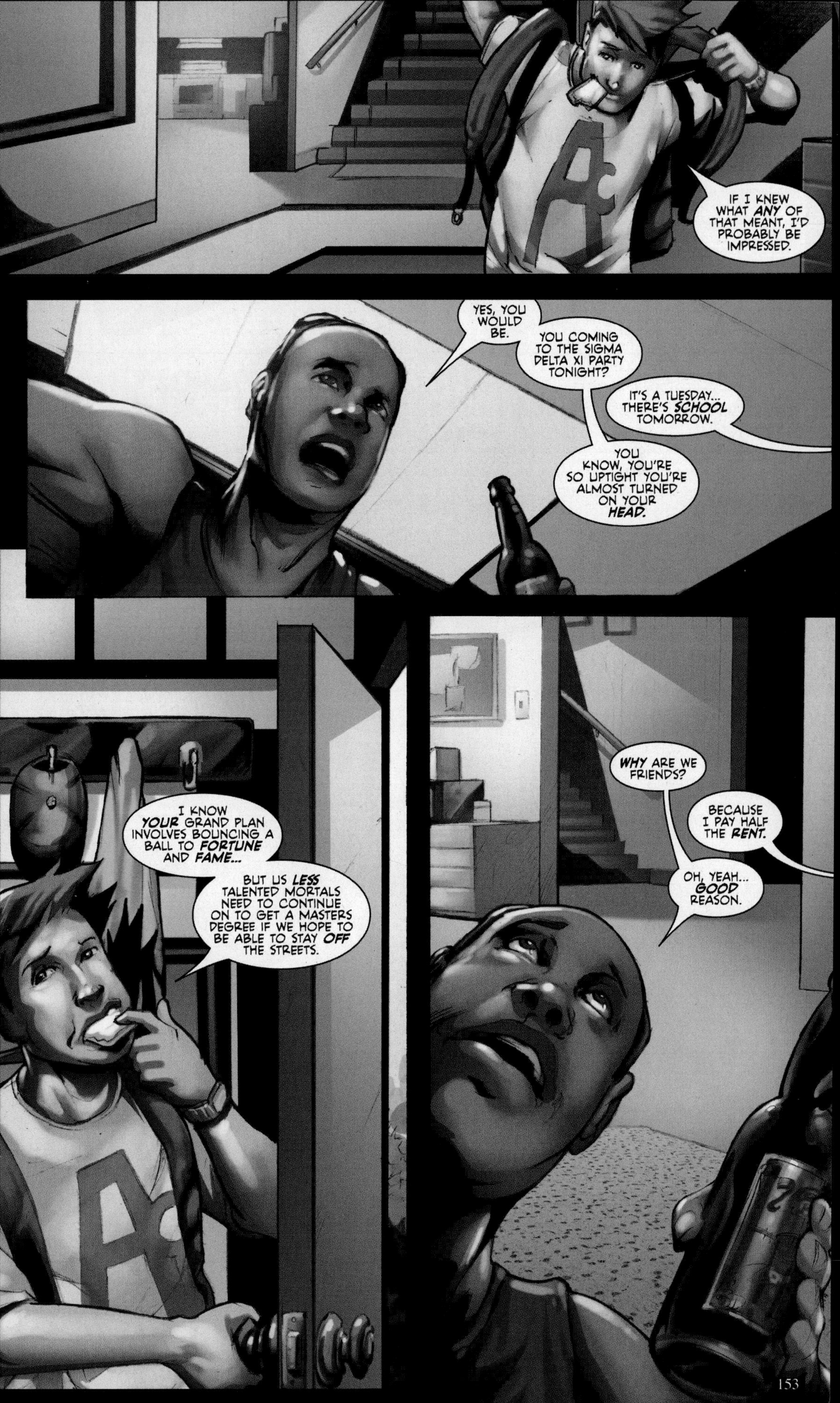
IF I KNEW WHAT ANY OF THAT MEANT, I'D PROBABLY BE IMPRESSED.
YES, YOU WOULD BE.
YOU COMING TO THE SIGMA DELTA XI PARTY TONIGHT?
IT'S A TUESDAY... THERE'S SCHOOL TOMORROW.
YOU KNOW, YOU'RE SO UPTIGHT YOU'RE ALMOST TURNED ON YOUR HEAD.
I KNOW YOUR GRAND PLAN INVOLVES BOUNCING A BALL TO FORTUNE AND FAME...
BUT US LESS TALENTED MORTALS NEED TO CONTINUE ON TO GET A MASTERS DEGREE IF WE HOPE TO BE ABLE TO STAY OFF THE STREETS.
WHY ARE WE FRIENDS?
BECAUSE I PAY HALF THE RENT.
OH, YEAH... GOOD REASON.

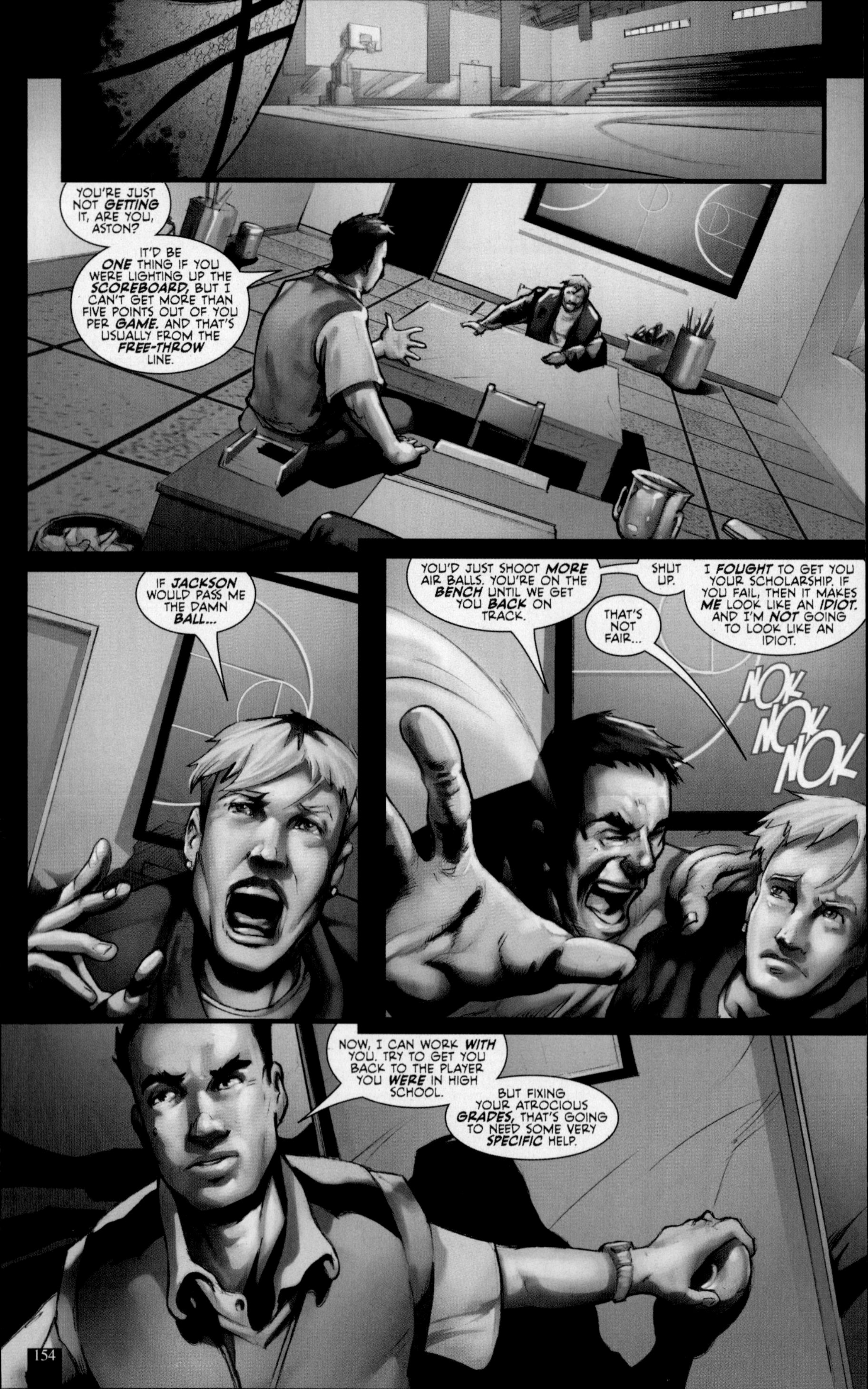
YOU'RE JUST NOT GETTING IT, ARE YOU, ASTON?
IT'D BE ONE THING IF YOU WERE LIGHTING UP THE SCOREBOARD, BUT I CAN'T GET MORE THAN FIVE POINTS OUT OF YOU PER GAME. AND THAT'S USUALLY FROM THE FREE-THROW LINE.
IF JACKSON WOULD PASS ME THE DAMN BALL...
YOU'D JUST SHOOT MORE AIR BALLS. YOU'RE ON THE BENCH UNTIL WE GET YOU BACK ON TRACK.
SHUT UP.
THAT'S NOT FAIR...
I FOUGHT TO GET YOU YOUR SCHOLARSHIP. IF YOU FAIL, THEN IT MAKES ME LOOK LIKE AN IDIOT. AND I'M NOT GOING TO LOOK LIKE AN IDIOT.
NOK NOK NOK
NOW, I CAN WORK WITH YOU. TRY TO GET YOU BACK TO THE PLAYER YOU WERE IN HIGH SCHOOL.
BUT FIXING YOUR ATROCIOUS GRADES, THAT'S GOING TO NEED SOME VERY SPECIFIC HELP.

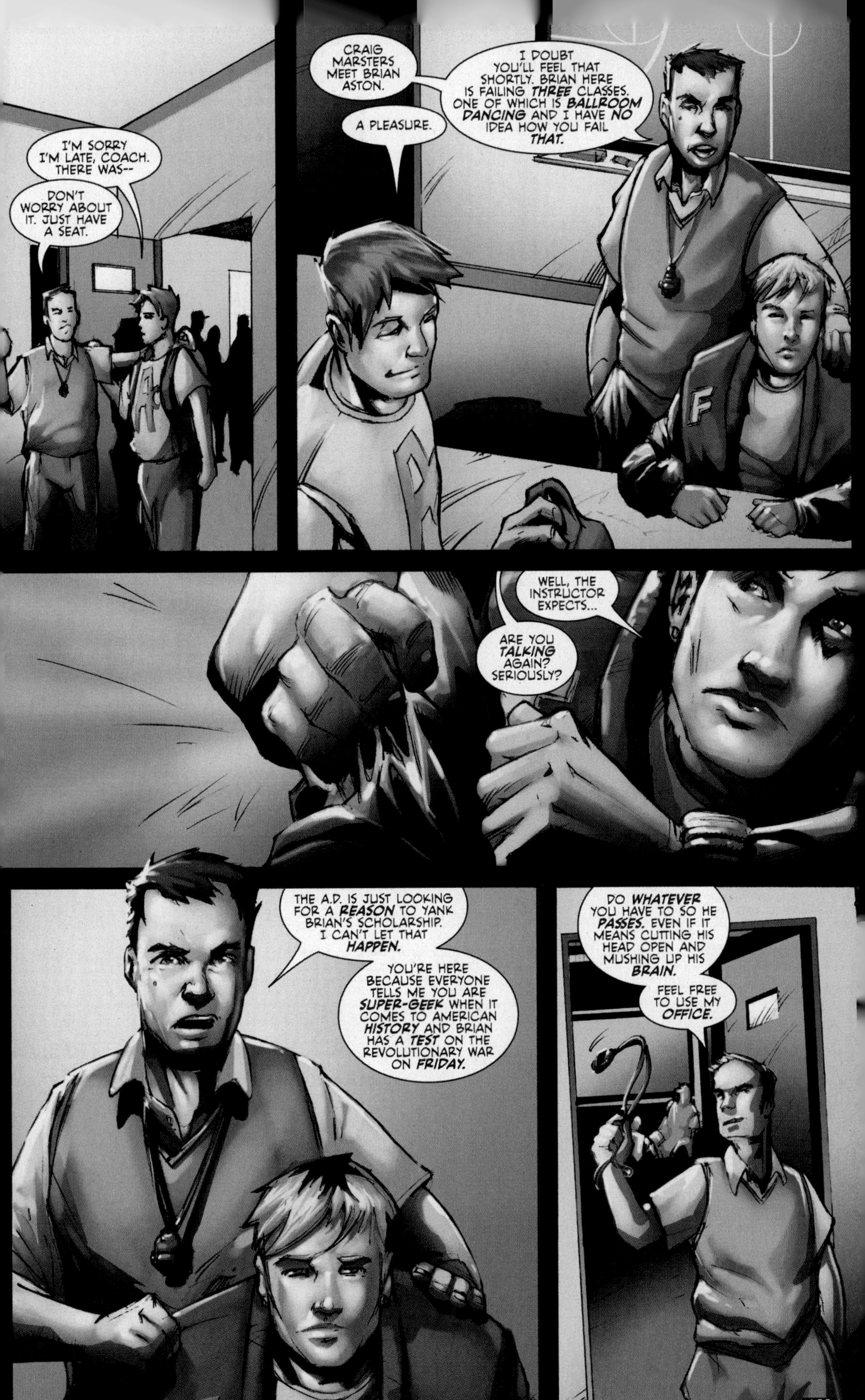
I'M SORRY I'M LATE, COACH. THERE WAS--
DON'T WORRY ABOUT IT. JUST HAVE A SEAT.
CRAIG MARSTERS MEET BRIAN ASTON.
A PLEASURE.
I DOUBT YOU'LL FEEL THAT SHORTLY. BRIAN HERE IS FAILING THREE CLASSES. ONE OF WHICH IS BALLROOM DANCING AND I HAVE NO IDEA HOW YOU FAIL THAT.
WELL, THE INSTRUCTOR EXPECTS...
ARE YOU TALKING AGAIN? SERIOUSLY?
THE A.D. IS JUST LOOKING FOR A REASON TO YANK BRIAN'S SCHOLARSHIP. I CAN'T LET THAT HAPPEN.
YOU'RE HERE BECAUSE EVERYONE TELLS ME YOU ARE SUPER-GEEK WHEN IT COMES TO AMERICAN HISTORY AND BRIAN HAS A TEST ON THE REVOLUTIONARY WAR ON FRIDAY.
DO WHATEVER YOU HAVE TO SO HE PASSES. EVEN IF IT MEANS CUTTING HIS HEAD OPEN AND MUSHING UP HIS BRAIN.
FEEL FREE TO USE MY OFFICE.

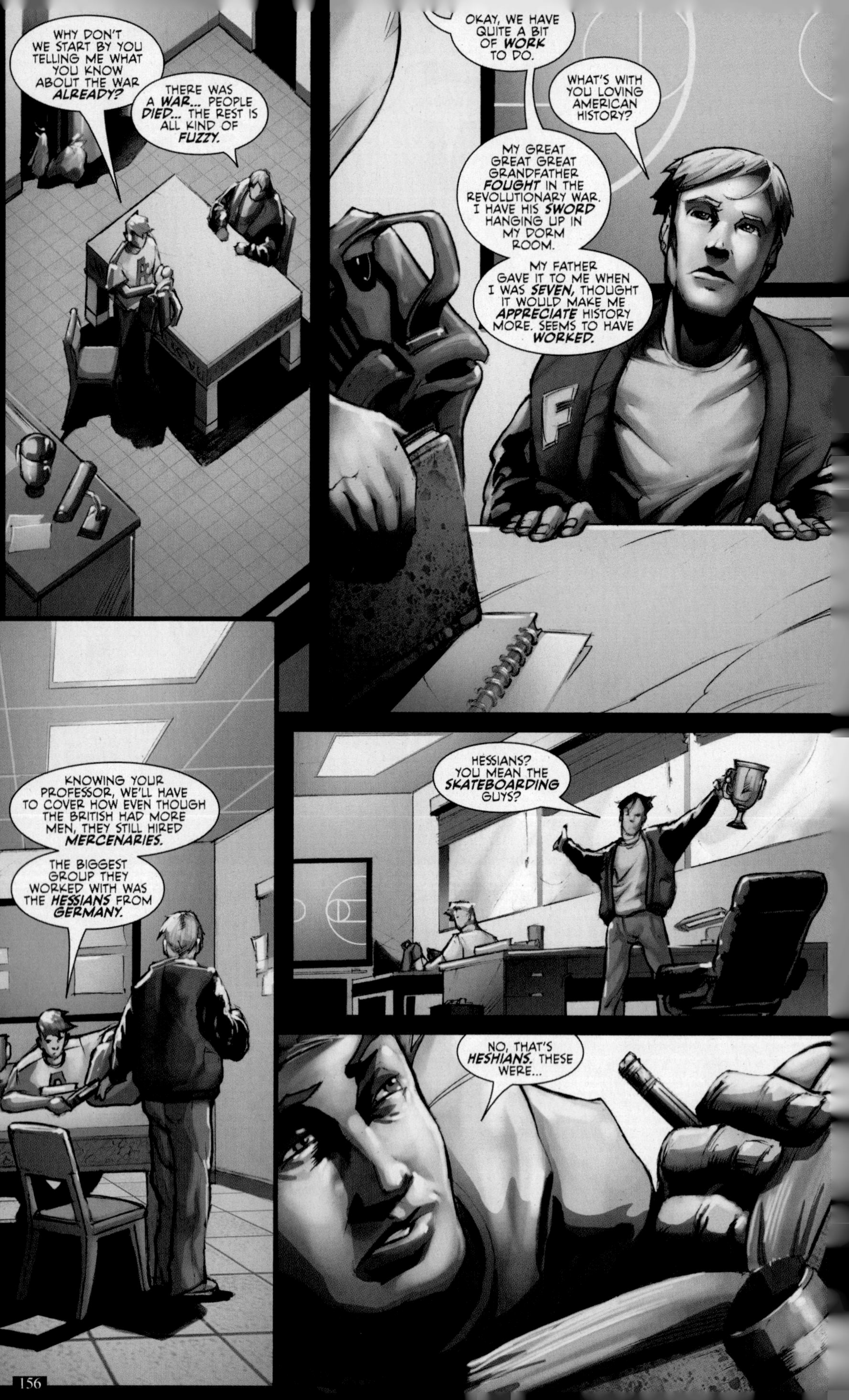
WHY DON'T WE START BY YOU TELLING ME WHAT YOU KNOW ABOUT THE WAR ALREADY?
THERE WAS A WAR... PEOPLE DIED... THE REST IS ALL KIND OF FUZZY.
OKAY, WE HAVE QUITE A BIT OF WORK TO DO.
WHAT'S WITH YOU LOVING AMERICAN HISTORY?
MY GREAT GREAT GREAT GRANDFATHER FOUGHT IN THE REVOLUTIONARY WAR. I HAVE HIS SWORD HANGING UP IN MY DORM ROOM.
MY FATHER GAVE IT TO ME WHEN I WAS SEVEN, THOUGHT IT WOULD MAKE ME APPRECIATE HISTORY MORE. SEEMS TO HAVE WORKED.
KNOWING YOUR PROFESSOR, WE'LL HAVE TO COVER HOW EVEN THOUGH THE BRITISH HAD MORE MEN, THEY STILL HIRED MERCENARIES.
THE BIGGEST GROUP THEY WORKED WITH WAS THE HESSIANS FROM GERMANY.
HESSIANS? YOU MEAN THE SKATEBOARDING GUYS?
NO, THAT'S HESHIANS. THESE WERE...

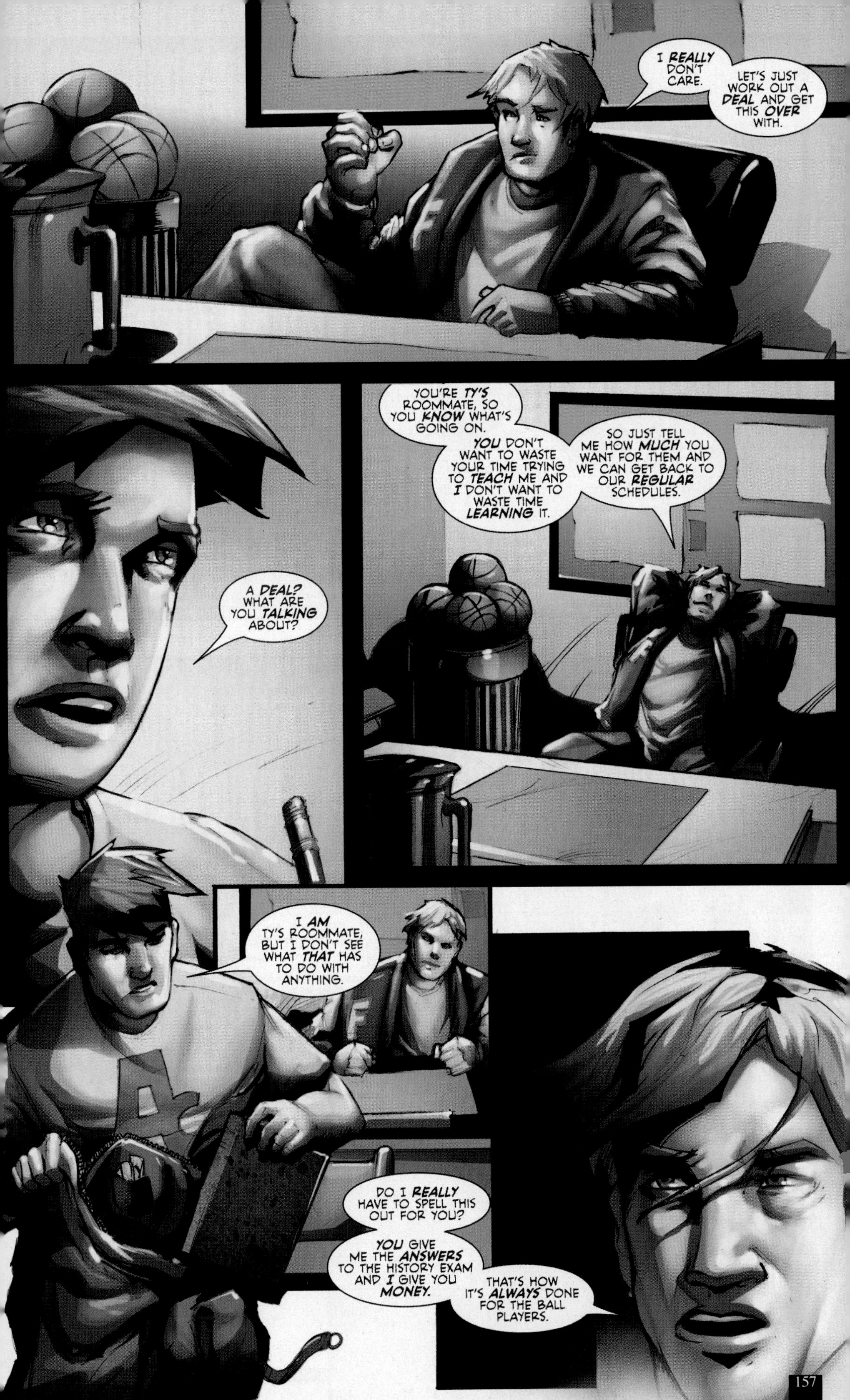

I REALLY DON'T CARE.
LET'S JUST WORK OUT A DEAL AND GET THIS OVER WITH.
A DEAL? WHAT ARE YOU TALKING ABOUT?
YOU'RE TY'S ROOMMATE, SO YOU KNOW WHAT'S GOING ON.
YOU DON'T WANT TO WASTE YOUR TIME TRYING TO TEACH ME AND I DON'T WANT TO WASTE TIME LEARNING IT.
SO JUST TELL ME HOW MUCH YOU WANT FOR THEM AND WE CAN GET BACK TO OUR REGULAR SCHEDULES.
I AM TY'S ROOMMATE, BUT I DON'T SEE WHAT THAT HAS TO DO WITH ANYTHING.
DO I REALLY HAVE TO SPELL THIS OUT FOR YOU?
YOU GIVE ME THE ANSWERS TO THE HISTORY EXAM AND I GIVE YOU MONEY.
THAT'S HOW IT'S ALWAYS DONE FOR THE BALL PLAYERS.

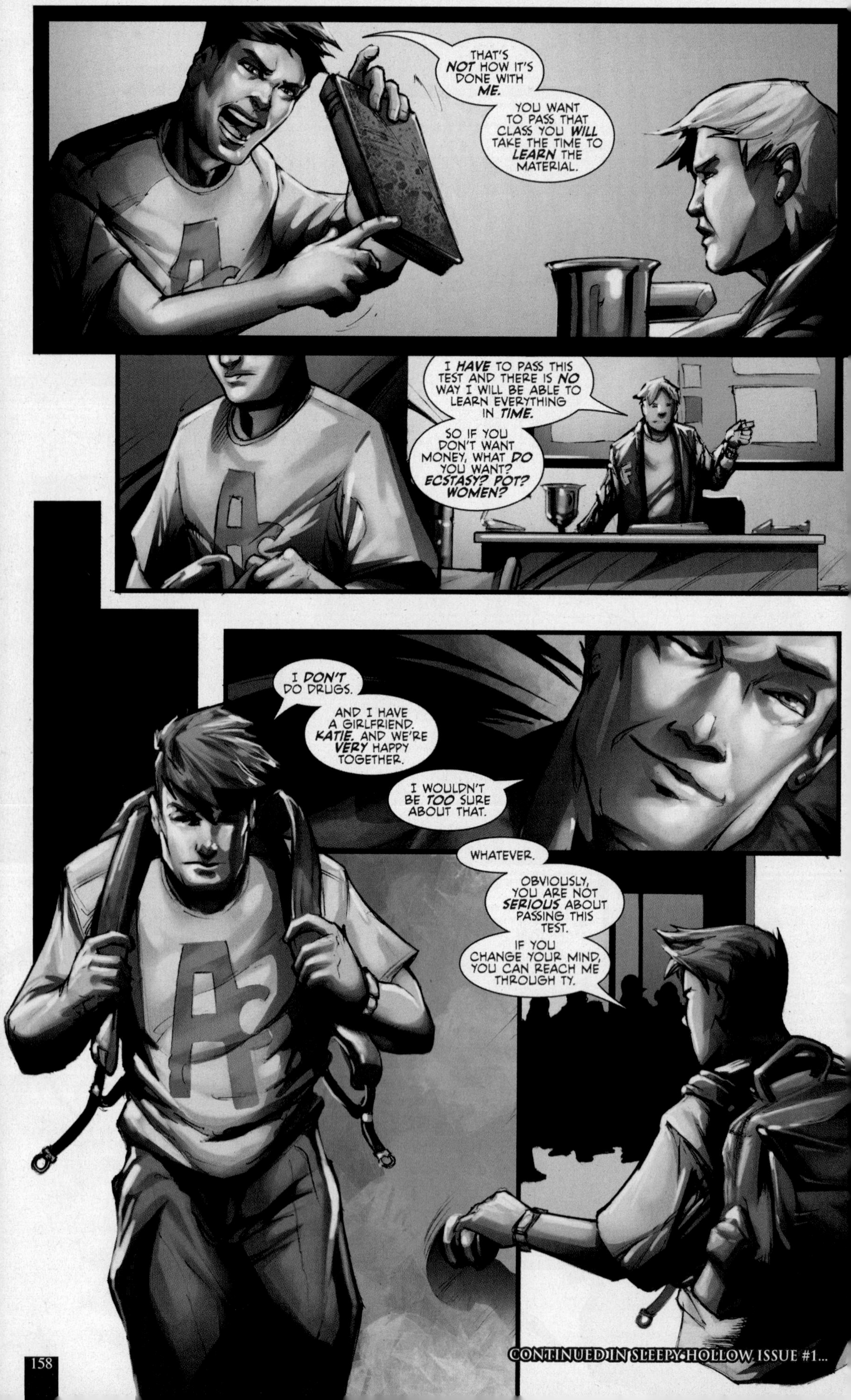
THAT'S NOT HOW IT'S DONE WITH ME.
YOU WANT TO PASS THAT CLASS YOU WILL TAKE THE TIME TO LEARN THE MATERIAL.
I HAVE TO PASS THIS TEST AND THERE IS NO WAY I WILL BE ABLE TO LEARN EVERYTHING IN TIME.
SO IF YOU DON'T WANT MONEY, WHAT DO YOU WANT? ECSTASY? POT? WOMEN?
I DON'T DO DRUGS.
AND I HAVE A GIRLFRIEND. KATIE. AND WE'RE VERY HAPPY TOGETHER.
I WOULDN'T BE TOO SURE ABOUT THAT.
WHATEVER.
OBVIOUSLY, YOU ARE NOT SERIOUS ABOUT PASSING THIS TEST.
IF YOU CHANGE YOUR MIND, YOU CAN REACH ME THROUGH TY.
CONTINUED IN SLEEPY HOLLOW ISSUE #1...

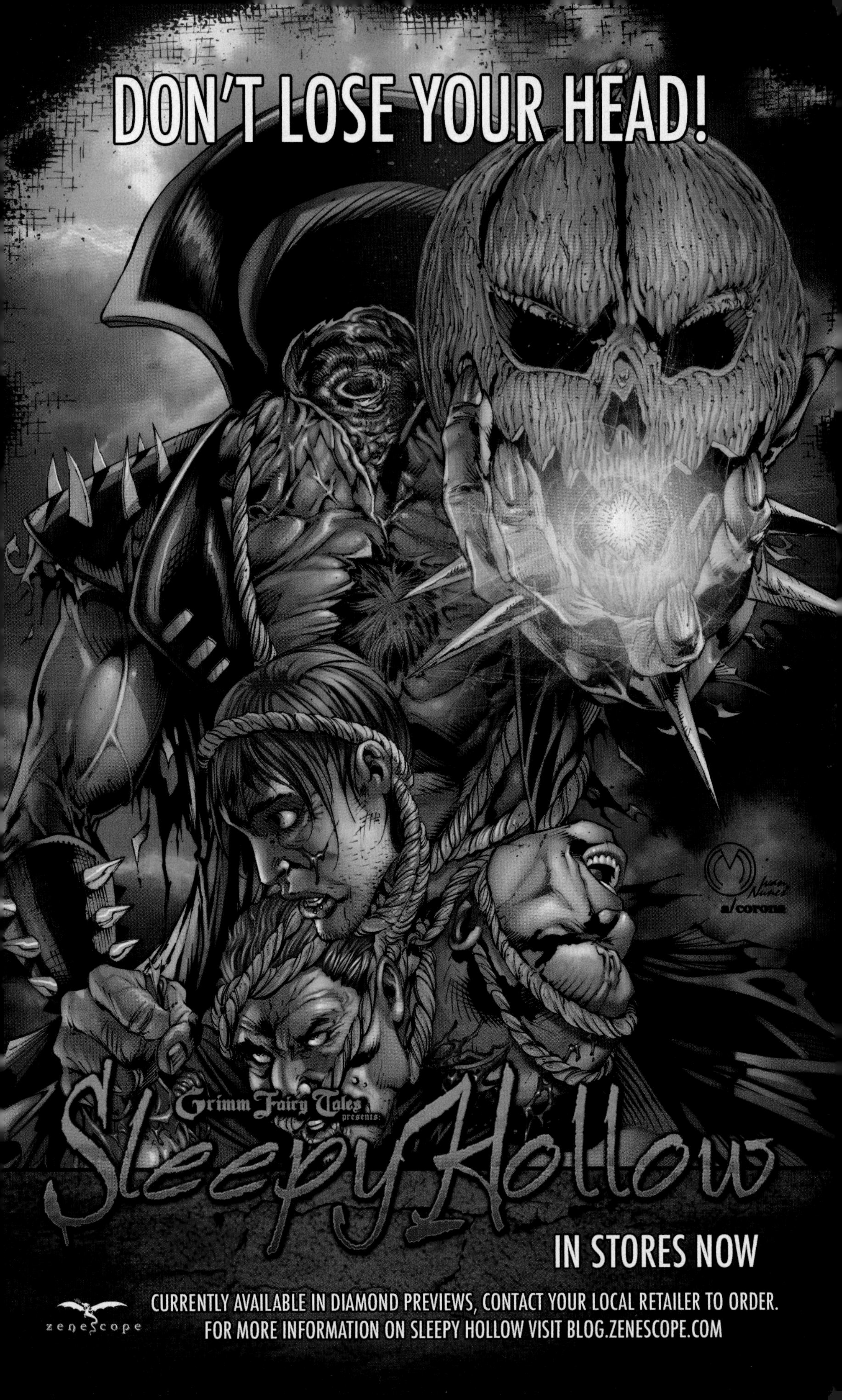

DON'T LOSE YOUR HEAD!
Grimm Fairy Tales presents:
Sleepy Hollow
IN STORES NOW
zenescope
CURRENTLY AVAILABLE IN DIAMOND PREVIEWS, CONTACT YOUR LOCAL RETAILER TO ORDER.
FOR MORE INFORMATION ON SLEEPY HOLLOW VISIT BLOG.ZENESCOPE.COM

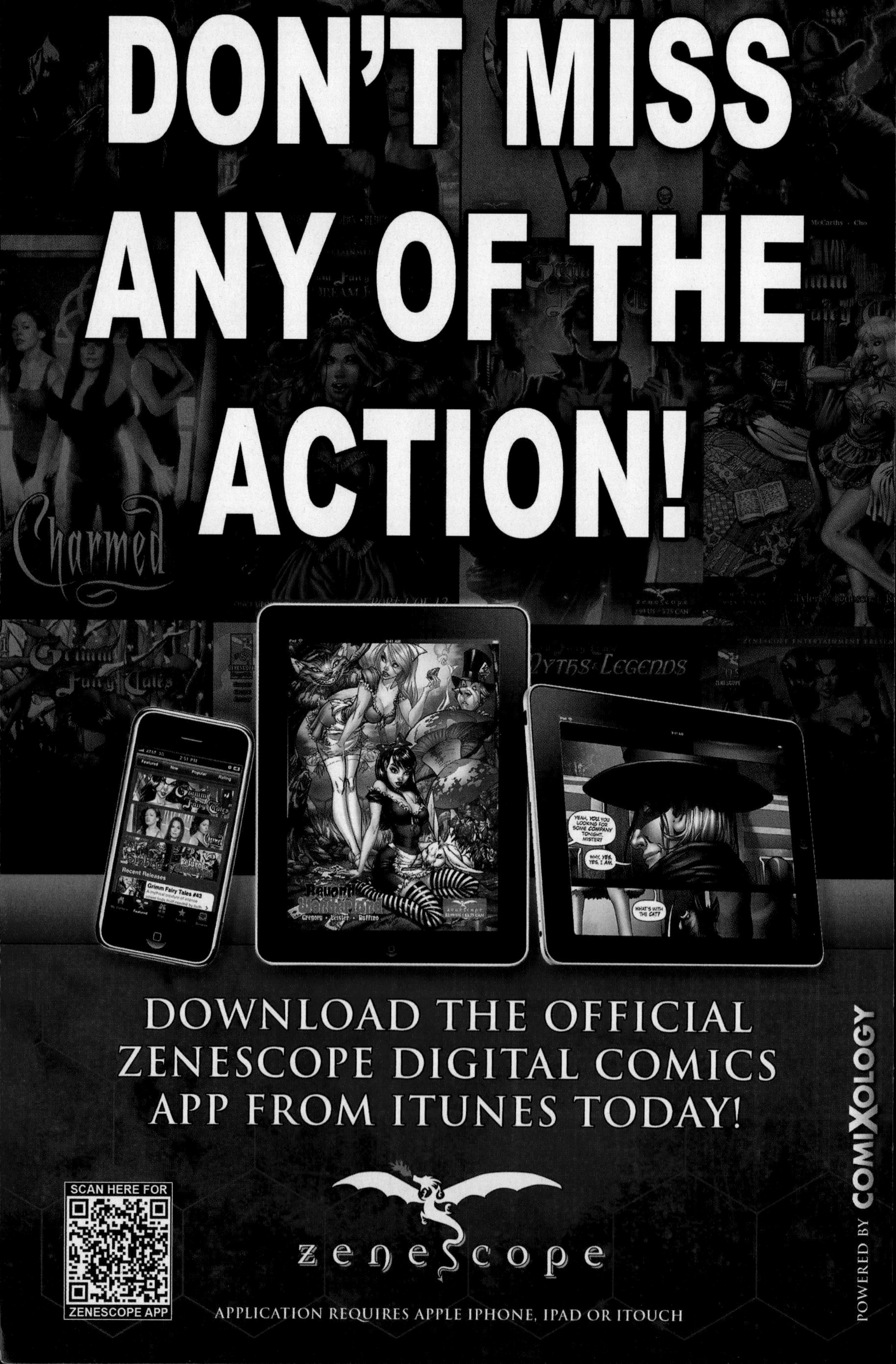

DON'T MISS ANY OF THE ACTION!

DOWNLOAD THE OFFICIAL ZENESCOPE DIGITAL COMICS APP FROM ITUNES TODAY!

POWERED BY COMIXOLOGY

SCAN HERE FOR

ZENESCOPE APP

zenescope

APPLICATION REQUIRES APPLE IPHONE, IPAD OR ITOUCH

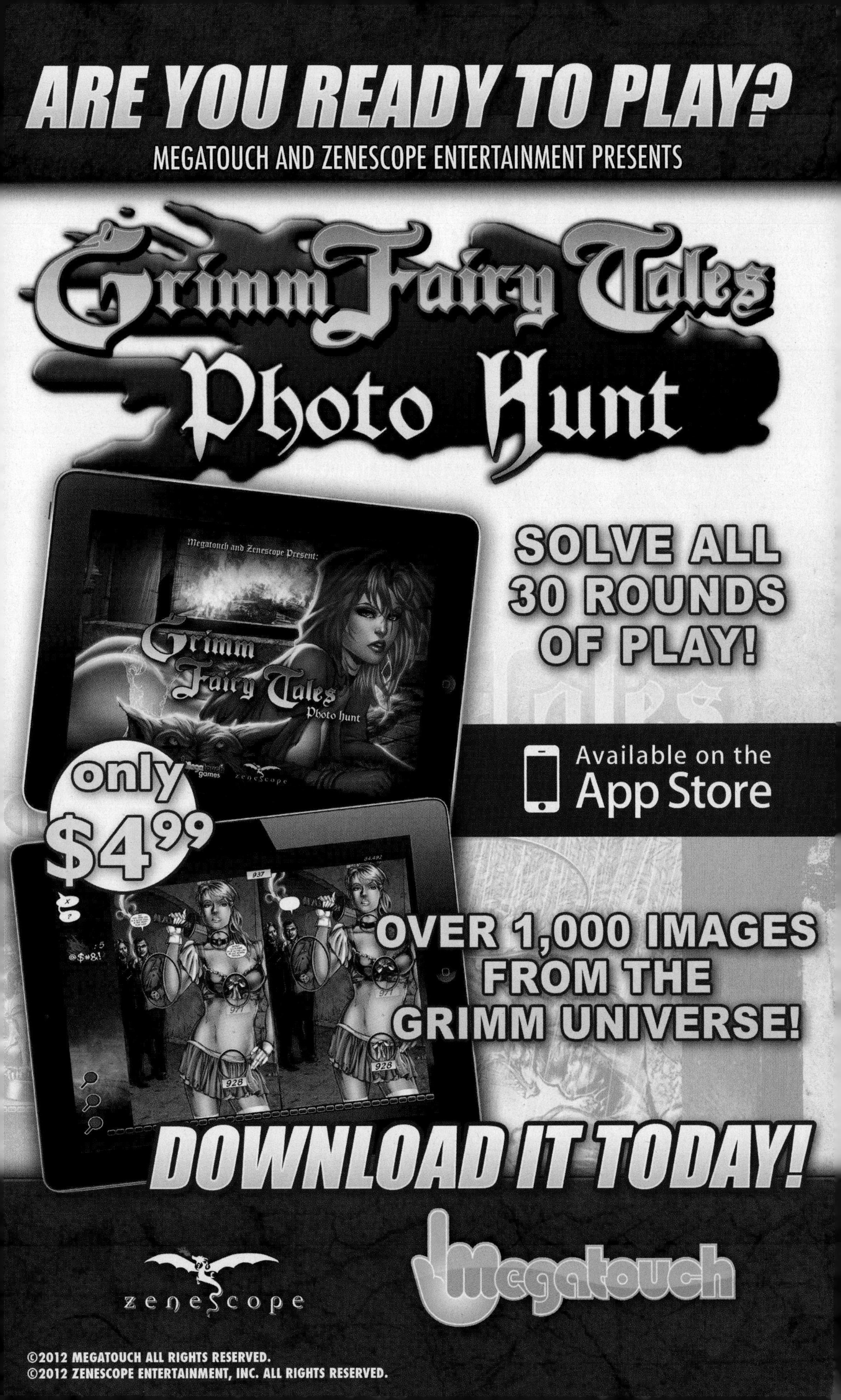
ARE YOU READY TO PLAY?
MEGATOUCH AND ZENESCOPE ENTERTAINMENT PRESENTS
Grimm Fairy Tales
Photo Hunt
Megatouch and Zenescope Present:
Grimm Fairy Tales
Photo Hunt
SOLVE ALL 30 ROUNDS OF PLAY!
Available on the App Store
only $4.99
OVER 1,000 IMAGES FROM THE GRIMM UNIVERSE!
DOWNLOAD IT TODAY!
zenescope
Megatouch
©2012 MEGATOUCH ALL RIGHTS RESERVED.
©2012 ZENESCOPE ENTERTAINMENT, INC. ALL RIGHTS RESERVED.

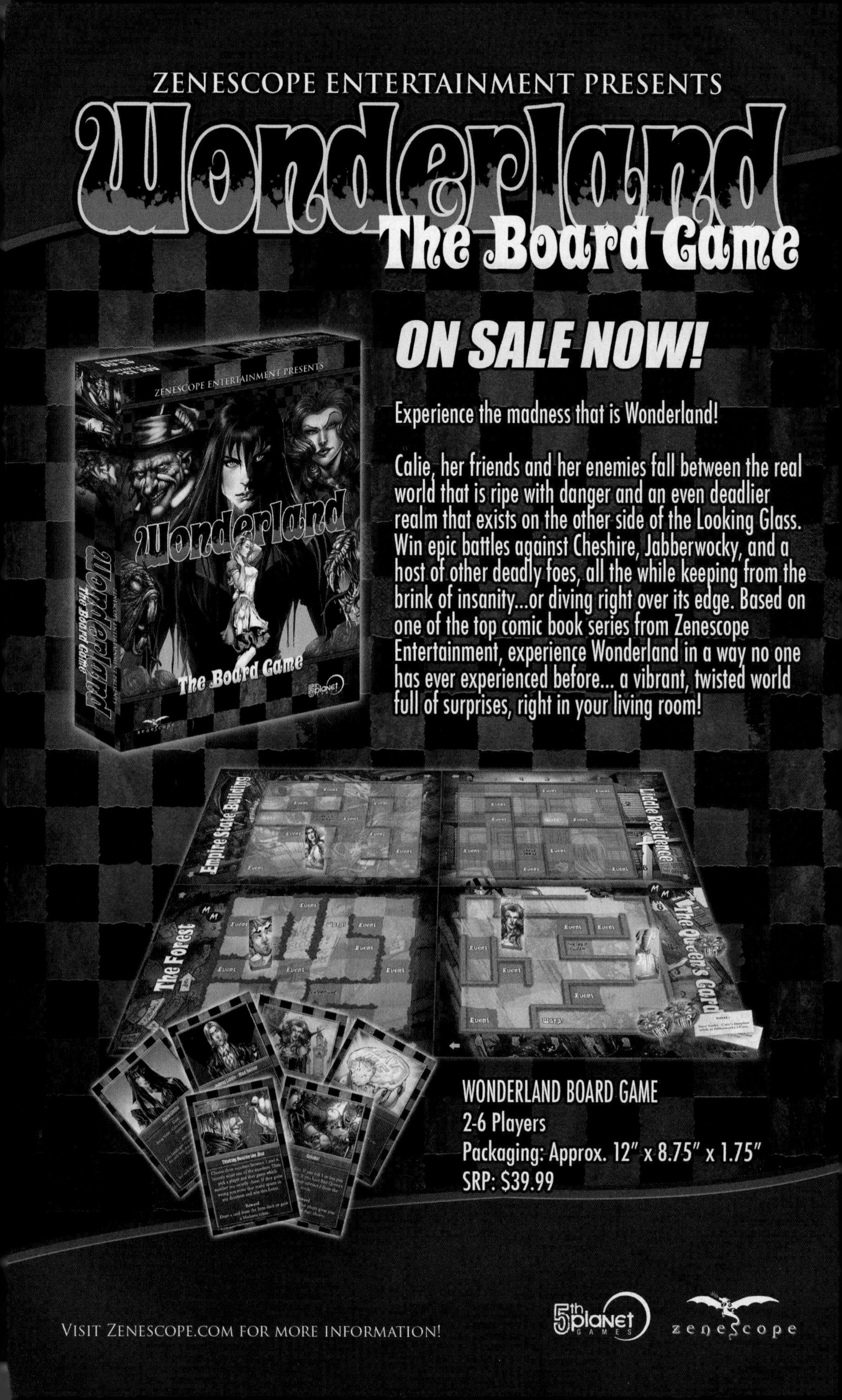
ZENESCOPE ENTERTAINMENT PRESENTS
Wonderland
The Board Game
ON SALE NOW!
Experience the madness that is Wonderland!
Calie, her friends and her enemies fall between the real world that is ripe with danger and an even deadlier realm that exists on the other side of the Looking Glass. Win epic battles against Cheshire, Jabberwocky, and a host of other deadly foes, all the while keeping from the brink of insanity...or diving right over its edge. Based on one of the top comic book series from Zenescope Entertainment, experience Wonderland in a way no one has ever experienced before... a vibrant, twisted world full of surprises, right in your living room!
Empire State Building
Liddle Residence
The Forest
WONDERLAND BOARD GAME
2-6 Players
Packaging: Approx. 12" x 8.75" x 1.75"
SRP: $39.99
VISIT ZENESCOPE.COM FOR MORE INFORMATION!
5th planet GAMES
zenescope

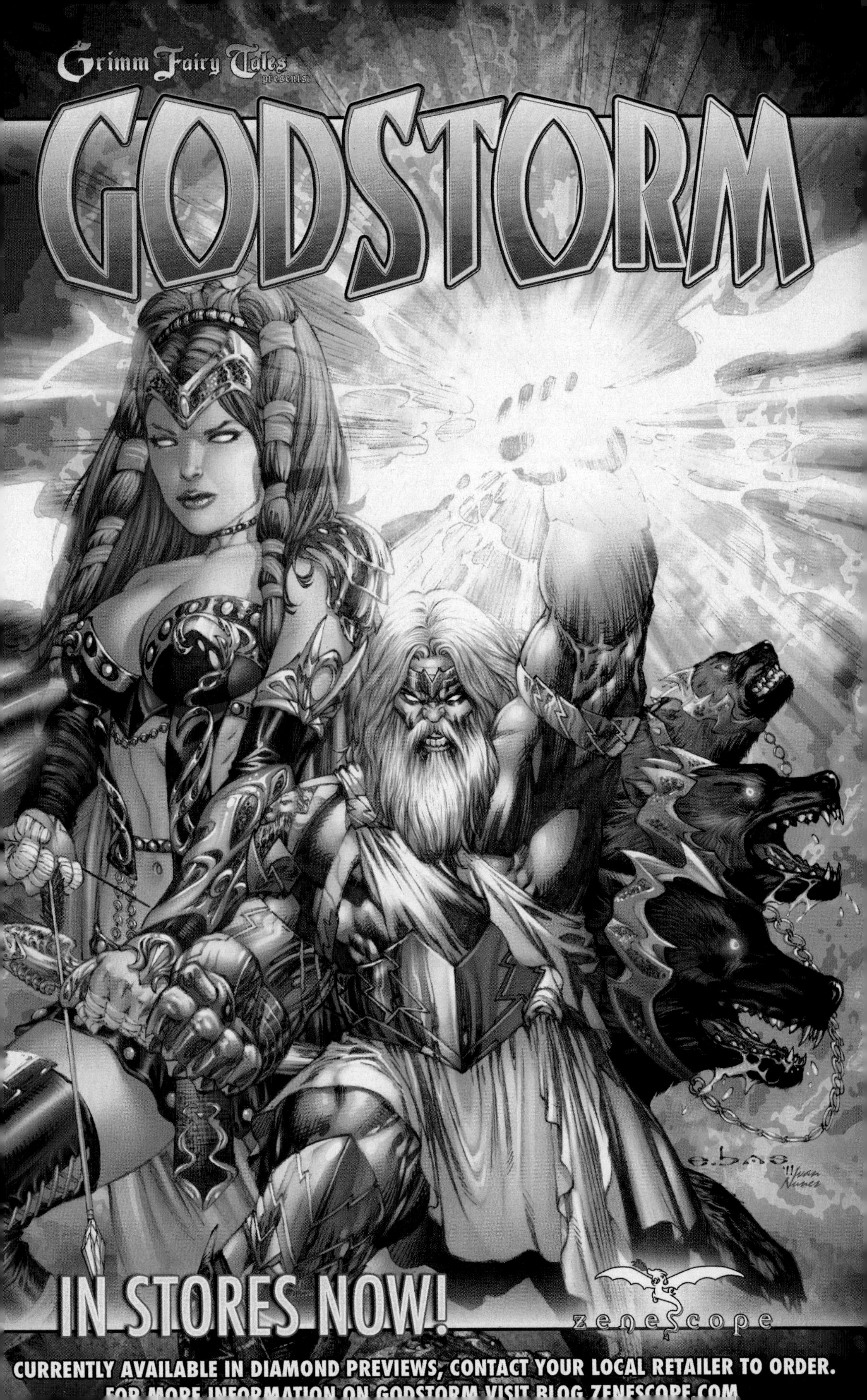
Grimm Fairy Tales presents:
GODSTORM
IN STORES NOW!
zenescope
CURRENTLY AVAILABLE IN DIAMOND PREVIEWS, CONTACT YOUR LOCAL RETAILER TO ORDER.
FOR MORE INFORMATION ON GODSTORM VISIT BLOG.ZENESCOPE.COM

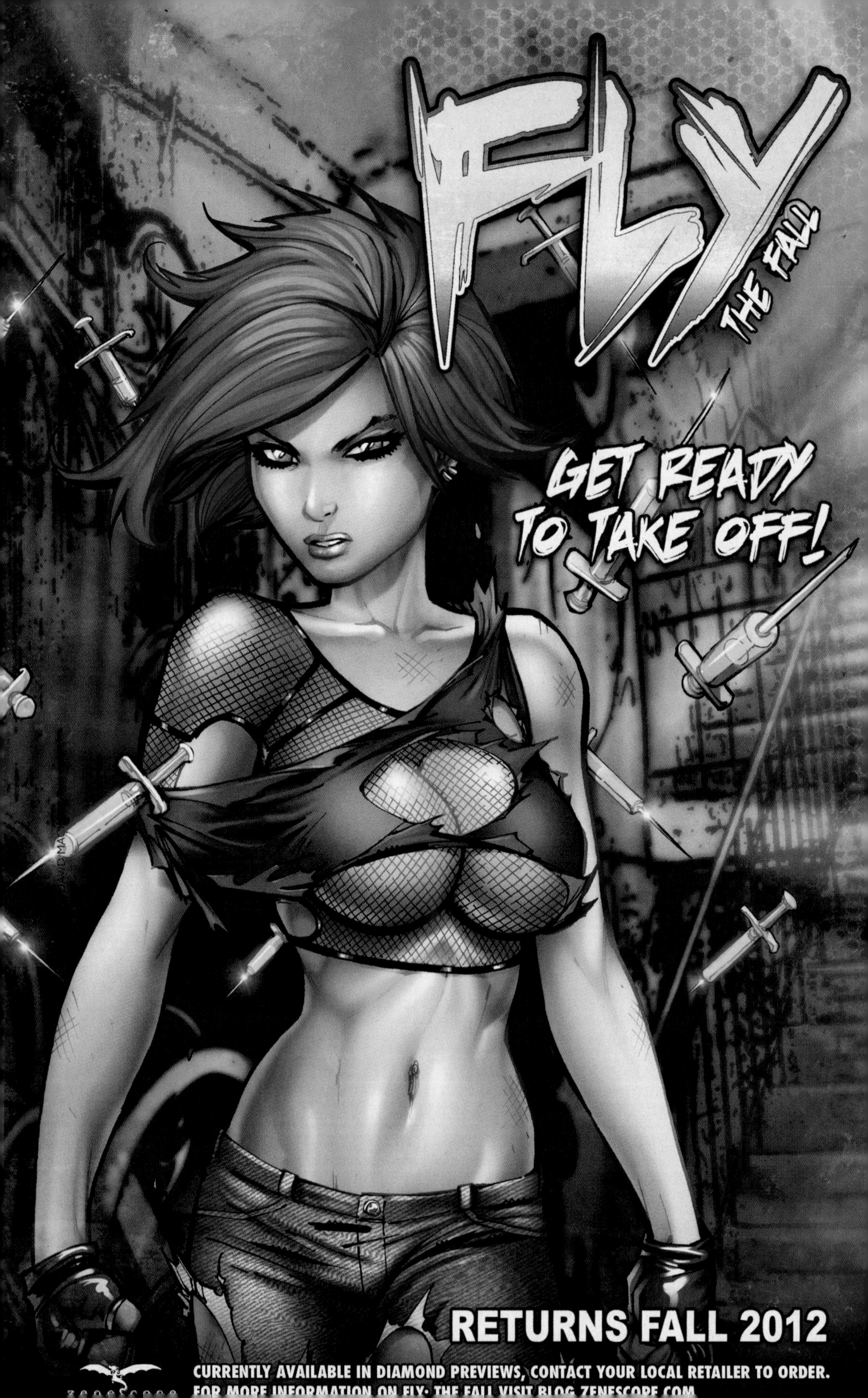

FLY
THE FALL
GET READY TO TAKE OFF!
RETURNS FALL 2012
CURRENTLY AVAILABLE IN DIAMOND PREVIEWS, CONTACT YOUR LOCAL RETAILER TO ORDER.
FOR MORE INFORMATION ON FLY: THE FALL VISIT BLOG.ZENESCOPE.COM

LET'S GET A LITTLE GRIMM ON YOUR BLACKBERRY®

DOWNLOAD ZENESCOPE'S RED RIDING HOOD THEME EXCLUSIVELY FROM THE BLACKBERRY® APP WORLD™ WEB STORE!

AVAILABLE FOR

BlackBerry 8520 / BlackBerry 8530 / BlackBerry 8900 / BlackBerry 9000 / BlackBerry 9100
BlackBerry 9105 / BlackBerry 9300 / BlackBerry 9330 / BlackBerry 9500 / BlackBerry 9520
BlackBerry 9530 / BlackBerry 9550 / BlackBerry 9630 / BlackBerry 9650
BlackBerry 9700 / BlackBerry 9800

THEME CREATED BY A3 MEDIA NETWORK

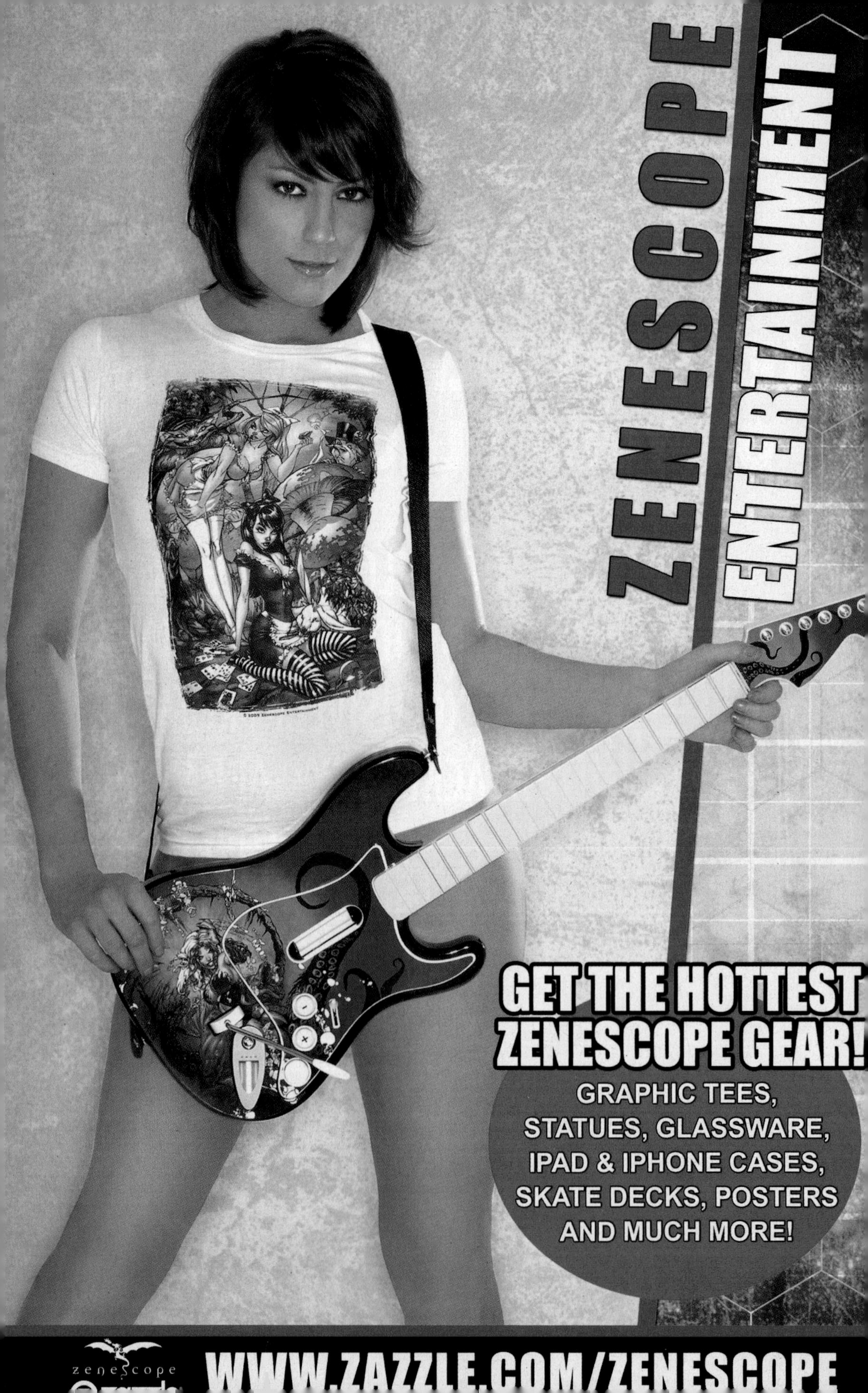

ZENESCOPE
ENTERTAINMENT
GET THE HOTTEST
ZENESCOPE GEAR!
GRAPHIC TEES,
STATUES, GLASSWARE,
IPAD & IPHONE CASES,
SKATE DECKS, POSTERS
AND MUCH MORE!
zenescope
WWW.ZAZZLE.COM/ZENESCOPE

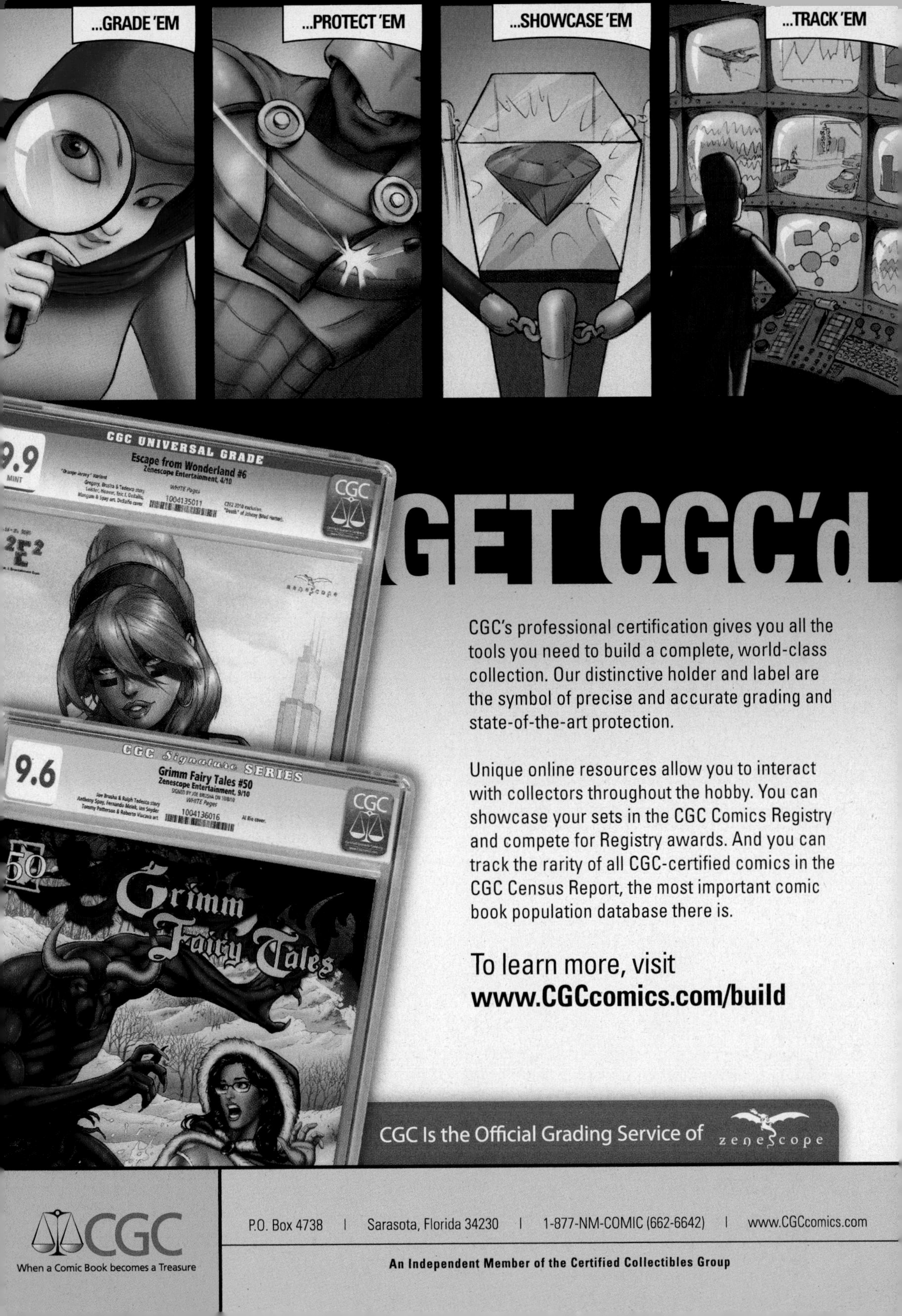
...GRADE 'EM
...PROTECT 'EM
...SHOWCASE 'EM
...TRACK 'EM
9.9
MINT
CGC UNIVERSAL GRADE
Escape from Wonderland #6
Zenescope Entertainment, 4/10
1004135011
CGC
9.6
CGC Signature SERIES
Grimm Fairy Tales #50
Zenescope Entertainment, 9/10
1004136016
CGC
Grimm Fairy Tales
GET CGC'd
CGC's professional certification gives you all the tools you need to build a complete, world-class collection. Our distinctive holder and label are the symbol of precise and accurate grading and state-of-the-art protection.
Unique online resources allow you to interact with collectors throughout the hobby. You can showcase your sets in the CGC Comics Registry and compete for Registry awards. And you can track the rarity of all CGC-certified comics in the CGC Census Report, the most important comic book population database there is.
To learn more, visit
www.CGCcomics.com/build
CGC Is the Official Grading Service of zenescope
CGC
When a Comic Book becomes a Treasure
P.O. Box 4738 | Sarasota, Florida 34230 | 1-877-NM-COMIC (662-6642) | www.CGCcomics.com
An Independent Member of the Certified Collectibles Group

Grimm Fairy Tales
MYTHS & LEGENDS